John Lennon
IMAGINED

MUSIC

[MEANINGS]

Steve Jones, Will Straw, and Joli Jensen
General Editors

Vol. 4

PETER LANG
New York • Washington, D.C./Baltimore • Bern
Frankfurt am Main • Berlin • Brussels • Vienna • Oxford

Janne Mäkelä

John Lennon IMAGINED

Cultural History of a Rock Star

PETER LANG
New York • Washington, D.C./Baltimore • Bern
Frankfurt am Main • Berlin • Brussels • Vienna • Oxford

Library of Congress Cataloging-in-Publication Data

Mäkelä, Janne.
John Lennon imagined: cultural history of a rock star / Janne Mäkelä.
p. cm. — (Music/meanings; v. 4)
Includes bibliographical references (p.   ).
1. Lennon, John, 1940–1980. 2. Rock musicians—England—Biography.
3. Beatles. 4. Fame—Social aspects. I. Title. II. Series.
ML420.L38M35   782.42166'092—dc21   2003003749
ISBN 0-8204-6788-X
ISSN 1531-6726

Bibliographic information published by **Die Deutsche Bibliothek.**
Die Deutsche Bibliothek lists this publication in the "Deutsche
Nationalbibliografie"; detailed bibliographic data is available
on the Internet at http://dnb.ddb.de/.

Cover design by Lisa Barfield
Cover photo of the "Lennon Wall" in Prague by Anna-Mari Varjonen

The paper in this book meets the guidelines for permanence and durability
of the Committee on Production Guidelines for Book Longevity
of the Council of Library Resources.

Table of Contents

Acknowledgments

Words are not enough to express my gratitude to Bruce Johnson from the University of New South Wales. He has patiently helped me to finish the manuscript, thoroughly testing my arguments, asking for clarification and refining the language. I should also thank Kari Immonen, Hannu Salmi, Henri Terho, Keijo Virtanen and, especially, Kari Kallioniemi from the University of Turku for their intellectual, emotional and material contribution. Sara Cohen, Helmi Järviluoma, Joli Jensen, Steve Jones, Antti-Ville Kärjä, Anahid Kassabian, Dave Laing, Mikko Lehtonen, Tarja Rautiainen and Will Straw deserve acknowledgments for their advice and support.

I am indebted to various people, for instance Sam Choukri, Steve Clifford and Len McCarthy, who provided me material on John Lennon and the Beatles. I also wish to express my gratitude to the TOP Foundation, the Finnish Cultural Foundation and the Ella and Georg Ehrnrooth Foundation for their financial support. For permission to use the "Lennon Wall" photograph, taken in Prague in 1997, I thank Anna-Mari Varjonen.

Finally, I am immeasurably grateful to my wife Emilia for her love and encouragement in my hours of desperation as well as moments of joy.

Turku, Finland
December 2003

1 Introduction

A Short Diversion on the Origins of Study

In 1980, three months before he was murdered, John Lennon was asked in an interview about pop historians analyzing the Beatles as a cultural phenomenon. Maybe Lennon was in the wrong mood, maybe he was not very interested in the subject, or maybe there was just some kind of misunderstanding. He found such analyses "irrelevant, absolutely irrelevant" (Sheff 1981, 76). In spite of his reputation for repartee, it was one of those rare moments when Lennon seemed to lose the edge of his famous wit. He implied that pop historians conducting cultural analyses were gratuitously digging into the graves of dead celebrities such as Glenn Miller and Elvis Presley and revealing scandalous secrets of their supposed drug use and sex life. To a pop historian like myself, this statement appears confusing, since, first, it simply seems unjustified, and, second, I feel that John Lennon himself should have known better.

From the breakup of the Beatles in 1970 until his untimely death in 1980, John Lennon gave countless interviews in which he looked back on the history of the Beatles and his own career—sometimes carefully, but usually with some heat. If Lennon's activities at given moments were mostly driven by intuition, artistic impulse, and, occasionally, commercial pressures, the way he reviewed the past was characterized by intelligent self-analysis and unflinching criticism. The past for him, especially his own, was not irrelevant. He could be serious, as indicated in his short autobiographical section in the posthumous collection of writings and drawings titled *Skywriting by Word of Mouth.* On the other hand, there was always the humorous and witty John Lennon, who as early as 1961 had written a hilarious "Beabliography," the first in a long line, called "Being a Short Diversion on the Dubious Origin of Beatles." If there was John Lennon the Beatle, the musician, the writer, the comedian, the painter, the avant-gardist, the political activist, the husband and the father, there was also John Lennon the analyst. I am not alleging that there was Lennon the historian; he is known to have read abundant history books and other scientific literature, but he certainly was apparently no expert on scholarly matters. Nevertheless, I think that it is no exaggeration to say that Lennon had a historically oriented mind in relation to the Beatles and his own career. In the same interview he described the Beatles phenomenon in interesting terms:

> Whatever wind was blowing at the time moved the Beatles too. I'm not saying we weren't flags on the top of the ship. But the whole boat was moving. Maybe the Beatles were in the crow's nest shouting "Land Ho!" or something like that, but we were all in the same damn boat. (78)

To many biographers, John Lennon appeared protean, elusive and controversial. Here the profile emerges again. At first Lennon seems to have no idea about "cultural analysis," and the next minute he is doing it himself, not in scholarly terms but by using semipoetic nautical imagery. Lennon's conflicting passions and ignorance of the cultural history of popular music become more understandable if the other side of the coin is observed. It was 1980 and with rare exceptions, academic writers were at the time not particularly attracted to John Lennon, his life, career, music and cultural meaning. Undeniably, by 1980 there was already an endless stream of biographical and journalistic writings on the Beatles and Lennon, and there had also been some scholarly essays and musicological analyses about the Beatles, who for a long time represented (along with Bob Dylan) the most legitimate field of popular music for academic scholars. The real time for the reassessment of the subject was yet to come, however, only after Lennon's death and the rise of popular music studies in the 1980s. Hence, it is not surprising if Lennon mistook pop historiography and cultural analysis for often sensationalist biographical revelations.

My study has grown out of two areas of interest: John Lennon and popular music studies. Lennon's tragic death left an indelible mark on me, and it will no doubt remain one of those memories to which I shall return as I measure my own unfolding life: "Now, what happened when I was fifteen? I spent a dull week in confirmation camp, learned to play guitar with my friend sometime afterwards and woke up to the radio news of John Lennon's murder." In the wake of tragic circumstances, John Lennon and his music appeared more present and closer to me than they ever had done, but since he was now physically separated from us, absolutely and forever, I found myself drawn to the massive flow of "secondhand" writings, stories, recollections and interpretations. In addition to the sense of loss and mourning, his death left several questions that I have attempted to answer in this study. It is perhaps pointless to ponder whether this book would have been possible if John Lennon were alive, but certainly his death has fueled my project. In this sense it is true, then, that, yes, I am digging over the grave of John Lennon and trying to discover secrets still unrevealed.

If this sounds like dirty work, there is the other area that makes my approach, I hope, more understandable and respectable. My study is a part of culturally oriented popular music studies, which, although a relatively new branch in the field of social and humanistic studies, has already built a tradition to which I may contribute. When I was younger I never thought about studying popular music, let alone John Lennon, since I mentally belonged to the school that believed that popular music can only be known, or felt, in an immediate experiential way, without explicit interventions on behalf of academic knowledge and culture. Although I gave a nod of approval to intelligent pop music, even favored it, analysis was a different matter. My skepticism was fragile, however, and one manifestation of this was my interest in the history of popular music. Ever since I started my academic studies in the late 1980s, these interests increased, and at some stage I finally realized the possibilities offered by the study of popular music and culture. It was an eye-opening moment to discover that I could investigate academically and critically a subject that had given me so much pleasure—and to do that even without compromising any of its supposedly distinctive character!

My fascination with popular music studies was mostly encouraged by the assumption that popular music is not only music but something else, too: It is history, communication, discussion, fashion, industry, attitudes and ideologies. In the end, it is arguable that the context and the culture make music matter. In music and music cultures there are always mysteries that one instinctively wishes will remain unsolved, but there are also mysteries that cry out for further investigation. This also is the line I want to draw here in my study. Academically, I am interested not in John Lennon's personal secrets, if there still are any left, but in the secret behind the *idea* of him.

The aim of this study is to shed light on John Lennon as a star. Music has inevitably been central to the writing about John Lennon, but in the context of stardom it is only one, albeit important, part of the picture. Lennon's star image was also shaped by his film roles, his work in radio and TV, his absurd books, his clothing, press conferences, interviews, performances, fans' feedback and even by conspicuously performed re-clusiveness. Certainly, as a person and creative artist John Lennon had a major impact on popular music and changed, if not the whole world, then many people's worldviews. From my point of view, the phenom-enon called "John Lennon" is, however, not only an influential maker of history but also a product of his time, a construction who was depen-dent on ideologies, institutions, practices and people framing his mass-mediation.

My approach seeks to understand Lennon's stardom as a form of dialogue: There is the man and his position in the "crow's nest," but also more general phenomena in popular music and stardom, the "moving boat." The point of departure here is the way the single star creates himself and is created, and the way the star embodies—or re-jects—common characteristics within the category of rock stardom. Thus, my "scarlet thread" is the interaction between the star and his context, and the object of my study is John Lennon both for his distinc-tiveness and his representativeness. Through critical examination of the cultural and historical background of Lennon's stardom I wish to consider the ideas and value systems of popular music in general as well as to find out why Lennon was considered important and why he remains so.

The history of John Lennon's stardom is basically a ubiquitous, glo-bal issue, but because of its multifaceted scope I have felt it necessary to confine study to Britain and the United States, the two major sites of Lennon's public activities. In what follows I shall approach his stardom by using two strategies, which occasionally overlap: thematic approach and case studies. Since Lennon is inseparable from the Beatles, the tem-poral emphasis of the study is on the 1960s. Chapters 2 and 3 mainly deal with Lennon's stardom during Beatlemania and are concerned with themes of locality, humor, masculinity and fandom. Chapters 4, 5 and 6 are about changing stardom in the late 1960s. I first examine the subjects of art and authenticity in popular music and then provide anal-yses of Lennon's "granny glasses," his Rolls-Royce and the Beatles' al-bum *Sgt. Pepper's Lonely Hearts Club Band*. Lennon's most visible years, 1968 to 1969, are first approached through two themes, the avant-garde and the messianic, which are followed by specific information about Lennon as a fool figure. Chapter 7 concerns Lennon's career in the 1970s. The emphasis is on thematic approaches but mainly because of Lennon's changing role in popular music, sections on political rock, the ethos of survival and seclusion are also as much about cases as about ideas. Chapter 8 first concentrates on one particular event, Lennon's death, and then expands to incorporate the idea of posthumous stardom in popular music. Of course, this entire study could be considered a case study about one particular area of popular music stardom.

Before proceeding to the specific dialogues between the parties involved, some contextual foundation for the study must be laid. In order to understand the reciprocal illumination between the star and his surroundings, we first need to look at the historical literature on John Lennon and the Beatles, and then to examine the idea of stardom.

The Greatest Story of Popular Music?: Challenges of Writing the History

> *There's no such thing as an ex-Beatle or former Beatle or retired Beatle because the Beatles are something else than a pop group.*
> — *The Beatles' press officer Derek Taylor, 1970*

The intertwined stories of John Lennon and the Beatles have been documented many times and in minute detail. It is thus perhaps justifiable to ask whether this well-worn terrain is not already sufficiently charted. Day-by-day accounts of the Beatles have been published; participants have frequently been interviewed and nonparticipants have been interviewed as well; written documents have been sought and found; studio sessions have been arranged in exact chronological order; radio and TV documentaries have been made, and so on. The Beatles have been rummaged around in more than any other music group, and together with Elvis Presley, John Lennon enjoys the honor of being the most written-about person in popular music. His story is so often told that anyone interested in the history of popular music knows or at least has heard its generally accepted high points: Lennon is born on October 9, 1940, he is raised by his aunt Mimi, has a reputation as enfant terrible in school, and forms a music group with Paul McCartney in 1957; George Harrison joins the group, they win fame in Liverpool, several times visit

Hamburg, meet manager Brian Epstein, move to London, replace the drummer Pete Best with Ringo Starr, generate tumultuous hysteria in 1963, conquer America and the rest of the world, release several hit songs and albums, appear in films, stop touring in 1966, produce the famous *Sgt. Pepper* album, explore hippie ideology and Eastern mysticism, begin to splinter after Brian Epstein's death, splinter further after Yoko Ono's "intervention," and break up in 1970; Lennon moves to New York, becomes involved in radical politics, releases some records of uneven quality, separates from Ono, has his drunken "lost weekend," returns home, retires for five years, has his comeback, and is finally gunned down by a disturbed fan on December 8, 1980.

While the continuous flow of information would suggest that there must come a point of exhaustion, currently it seems that there is unlikely to be a significant decline in the amount of documentation. The obsession remains. It is as if John Lennon and especially the Beatles were a fairy tale that needs to be told again and again, both for the generation that experienced the original era and by that same generation for the newcomers who have not yet been initiated into the story. The subject has fascinated journalists, biographers, rock historians, culture critics, researchers and other writers of popular music so much that it arguably has become the greatest story of popular music. As with other significant cultural narratives, this story line itself has a history.

I have elsewhere argued that the historiography of the Beatles has three distinct phases (Mäkelä 2001). The first period of Beatles histories, *contemporary histories*, is the 1960s, during the actual years of the Beatles' existence, and includes several books (e.g., Davies 1968; Epstein 1981) that move between the categories of celebration and profile. The second phase of the Beatles' histories, what I call *transitional histories*, started after the breakup of the group in 1970 and lasted until the death of Lennon in 1980. This period is most distinctively characterized by miscellaneous memoirs and recollections by the people involved in the Beatles' progress (e.g., Taylor 1974; Williams & Marshall 1976; Wenner 1980). Lennon's death put an end to the Beatles' possible comeback and marked the beginning of the third phase, that of *remembrance*, which in many ways still continues, as reactions to George Harrison's death in 2001 showed.

Because the age of remembrance has been crucial in forming current ideas about John Lennon, the Beatles and the Sixties, it is necessary to ask what kind of remembering really has occurred. One of the best-known Beatles biographies, Philip Norman's *Shout!*, appeared in 1981. Based on numerous interviews and careful study, Norman's book gives a compelling account of the Beatles but seems, in a sense, to be too complete a story. For instance, Norman sometimes goes explicitly into the minds of people (he, for example, imagines Brian Epstein's sexually oriented thoughts when first seeing the Beatles in the smoky Cavern Club), and thus moves dangerously between psychological conjecture and "truth." His narrative methods, such as occasionally using fictionalized dialogue and writing the "plot" with thrilling climaxes, provide the atmosphere of being in the core of intimate yet spectacular events. It is like reading good fiction.

The same method has often been used by other Beatles and Lennon biographers as well (e.g., DiLello 1973; Williams & Marshall 1976; Brown & Gaines 1983; Pang & Edwards 1983; Rosen 2000; Giuliano 2001). It is extremely doubtful that informants of *Shout!*, or of other accounts, really remember so well parts of discussions that took place in the past—even assuming that they attempt to tell the truth about the past and even if they can remember it. There is a famous saying to the effect that if you really lived the Sixties, you don't remember anything about it, but in the case of the Beatles the shape of memory appears for the most part as clear as daylight.

It has rarely been asked whether the stories around the Beatles are truly in the minds of the 1960s generation or whether they are stories that have become part of a mythology. This question is highly problematic since for most people, like myself, the Beatles and John Lennon are stars with whom there have been no personal contacts. They are known from various media texts, and therefore they have been experienced through mediated and recycled material. Even to most fans, the Beatles and John Lennon have mainly been sounds on records and radio, images in films and television, pictures in papers and words in print. We can thus ponder the extent to which the history of Lennon and the Beatles is "real" and in what sense it is imagined history.[1]

Considering the problems of memory and the massive body of writings already in existence, the wish to arrive at the "true" story of Lennon/the Beatles may seem a barren and unimaginative point of departure for the historian. This is not to say that these writings are useless. First of all, it is important to have different kinds of histories that provide different kinds of pleasure and imagination as well as tools for identification. I do not want to allege that the writing of Lennon's or the Beatles' history would be in some sense improved if it were primarily constituted by professional historians rather than by journalists, fans or other commentators. That would have its own twists and distortions. History is not the exclusive prerogative of the historian. History, as Raphael Samuel beautifully writes, "is the work of a thousand different hands" (1994, 18).

Irrespective of whether they are based on lies or truths, fantasy or reality, all memoirs and biographies related to Lennon and the Beatles construct stardom and are thus potentially important documents. If the historian wishes to analyze past events rather than interpretations of them, that is, to use biographies and other recollections as secondary sources rather than as primary sources, it is of course sensible to utilize the most reliable documents available. Despite the criticism that could be leveled against the dominant historiographical methods for work on Lennon and the Beatles, there are several general accounts that are serviceable if used carefully and with cross-referencing to other sources. I have found various chronicles and encyclopedias very useful, since they have set out documented events and persons involved, thus leaving broader interpretations and narration for other authors. The most useful Beatles chroniclers are Mark Lewisohn, the man behind the massive *The Complete Beatles Recording Sessions*, *The Complete Beatles Chronicle* and other writings, and Bill Harry, whose ambitiously named *The Ultimate Beatles Encyclopedia* is a major point of departure for the subject.[2] Keith Badman's *The Beatles Diary. Volume 2: After the Break-Up, 1970–2001* lists prolifically events relating to the Beatles after 1970. Besides accounts of the Beatles, Lennon's life has been investigated in great detail, as in Bill Harry's *The John Lennon Encyclopedia*, thus facilitating further research such as mine. Of all the groundworks on Lennon's artistry, John Robertson's *The Art & Music of John Lennon*, Johnny Rogan's *The Complete Guide to the Music of John Lennon* and Paul Du Noyer's *We All Shine On* are perhaps the most useful.

Numerous sound and audiovisual documentaries since the 1980s have repeated the story even more unsurprisingly than printed histories. Although rich in detail and entertaining, the much-debated (at least in Britain) *The Beatles Anthology* film series, along with its subsequent printed version, is first and foremost an authorized history, which tries to offer a canonical version of events. The same goes for Lennon documentaries, especially the biographical *Imagine: John Lennon*, which was directed under the supervision of Lennon's widow Yoko Ono.[3]

As much as the issues of memory, oral history and the "truth" concern the history of the Beatles, they apply to John Lennon as well. The 1980s marked the new beginning of a succession of publications about him and his proved to be an even more contested terrain than that of the Beatles. The biographical flow began immediately after Lennon's death, first yielding celebratory accounts filled with loss and mourning, and then, a few years later, various kiss-and-tell books. The development culminated in two major biographies: Ray Coleman's semiauthorized *John Lennon* and Albert Goldman's notorious *The Lives of John Lennon*. Although the prime examples of two strands of Lennon biography—celebrating and "myth-breaking"—they share what is basically the traditional approach, constructing a linear narrative of a life as a series of achievements, failures, desires, obsessions, fortunes and misfortunes. As Anthony Elliott (1999) notes, both authors simplistically describe Lennon's lasting cultural importance in terms of psychological factors and astounding artistic creativity.

There are some signs that general accounts of the Beatles and Lennon have partly moved from the third phase to a next phase, that of *cultural reevaluation*. What I mean by "partly" is that it seems unlikely that there will be a significant decline in the number of traditional—celebratory, profiling and revealing—accounts about persons and chronological events, but there is, however, an attempt to move from a personal to a more general level of commentary. Ian MacDonald's much vaunted *Revolution in the Head* is a compound of these phases. MacDonald, who goes through the catalogue of the Beatles' music song by song, celebrates the "higher scale of achievements" that both the group and the Sixties produced as a musical and cultural peak, followed by "a shallow decline in overall quality" (1995, 299). Although he is thus following the long line of subjective approaches among rock historians (though to my mind he tries to cloak it in the guise of objectivity), he is, nevertheless, able to make a finely argued cultural analysis by putting the songs in the context of time and society.

There have been some other attempts to undertake the fourth phase of the writing of the Beatles history (e.g., Reising 2002), but it seems that the opening of new doors is more channeled through John Lennon than the Beatles. Anthony Elliott's *The Mourning of John Lennon*, which the author describes as a "metabiography" seeking "to uncover some of the implications Lennon's assault on the ideology of celebrity carries for our personal and political lives" (1999, 7–8), is a clear reflection of the need to reevaluate the cultural heritage of Lennon. Using contemporary critical theory and a psychoanalytical approach, Elliott, who is one of the rare writers to eschew straight chronology, aims to place Lennon at the intersection of the personal and the social as well as at the interface of loss and mourning. To me, this is a welcome approach, although in the end the objective is rather unsurprisingly more an understanding of Lennon than of the culture and ideas around him.

Elliott's views are, however, not wholly new, since his point of departure is the historian Jon Wiener's political biography *Come Together: John Lennon in His Time*, first published in 1984. Wiener follows Lennon's career path from the mid-1960s in terms of the political and the personal, the community and the individual. By placing Lennon in a historical and social context and using rich material ranging from interviews and printed words to radio and television, Wiener tries to avoid the traditional trap of the ideology of artistic autonomy. To my mind, he generally succeeds despite his strong admiration for Lennon and his achievements. A further example of this "fourth phase" approach is sociologist Fred Fogo's *I Read the News Today: The Social Drama of John Lennon's Death* (1994), a catalogue of the cultural memory through which people have sought to come to terms with Lennon's murder. Fogo argues that Lennon stood as a central cultural symbol of the Sixties, the cultural ideals of which were dismantled after the tragic event in 1980. Elliott's and especially Fogo's account clearly demonstrate that remembering Lennon is a useful study in itself.

What these new histories hint, sometimes explicitly, is that the real history of the Beatles ended in 1970 only in an artistic sense. This is notwithstanding the reunion of the Beatles and John Lennon's virtual participation with his reconstructed home demos in 1995, the year of *The Beatles Anthology*. Besides the artistic narrative, there are other historical approaches to the history of the Beatles that have been largely neglected. We can find, for instance, the history of the Beatles as active discussion (for example the question of whether the Beatles will come back or not), as consumption (fan culture after the breakup), as production (creating new products, recycling old material, celebrating anniversaries of past achievements), as culture industry (organizing pop tourism) or, as already stated, as an act of remembrance (publishing biographies, broadcasting audiovisual documents, conducting research). Within all these categories there are interesting phases and forms of activities awaiting further investigation: The debate over the possible comeback of the Beatles was a major theme in 1970s popular music culture, which Lennon's death interrupted, but did not stop. Such speculation seemed to fade only after George Harrison's death. The fan culture of the Beatles did not disappear after Beatlemania or 1970; on the contrary, it had its second bloom in the forms of auctions, fanzines, cover bands, conventions, festivals and other social gatherings, and, furthermore, later entered into a new dimension of communication provided by web sites (see Einbrodt 2001) and Internet chat forums. The history of the Beatles is certainly not confined to the ideology of artistry.

In light of the foregoing account of the history of popular music, the Beatles and John Lennon, my own line of inquiry may seem anomalous. I have criticized rock historians' concentration on personalities, yet I am now about to do the same. Furthermore, I am using a chronological structure, which implies that together with countless other writers on the subject I am also a prisoner of the Beatles' and John Lennon's story. A word of explanation is thus needed. Although my focus is on a single person who is perhaps the most admired musician in the history of rock music, I am trying to avoid the trap of unreflective rock autonomy[4]. Like every rock musician, John Lennon's activities were culturally and historically constructed and incorporated attitudes of what rock is and how it should be performed, or what a rock star is and what her or his position is in society. Basically, I am not interested here in John Lennon as a psychological profile but as a star in whom is inscribed ideas relating to time and place, tradition and change. The second point, which implicitly questions the naive principle of contextless autonomy, is that besides Lennon's own actions there were other factors (which I will address in the following section), such as management, public relations (PR) activities, the media and fan comment that played important roles in the process of Lennon's stardom.

My aim is not really to find fresh factual disclosures, but to look at a familiar story by utilizing multidisciplinary approaches and methods of cultural history. Broadly, cultural history, which has grown out of social history to become a distinct field of historical investigation, refers back to Raymond Williams' idea of culture as "the study of the whole way of life." It has been defined as a study of those ideas, actions, plans, emotions or mental equipment through which the men and women of the past were in interaction with their environment. Within this scheme, cultural history seeks to explore the ways in which culture is imagined, represented and received, how it interacts with social processes, how it contributes to individual and collective ideas and worldviews, to stability and change, to social, political and economic activities and programs. In sum, cultural history defines *culture* as interaction and communication and emphasizes that history can be analyzed as living traditions (Virtanen 1993; Kallioniemi 1998; Korhonen 1999; Salmi & Suominen 2000; see also Burke 1997).

To study John Lennon as a rock star from the point of view of cultural history suggests that the star's interactions with other people, institutions, social surroundings and traditions must be taken into account. It also suggests challenging the traditional ways of writing popular music history. Finnish cultural historian Kari Immonen (1996) has asserted that these writings have been mainly either in the genre of chronicles or linear stories. In the "chronicle" approach, popular music is seen as a "closed system," a self-sufficient narrative in which the performers, styles, songs and recordings are located neither in society nor culture, but within an autonomous domain. According to this view, popular music is just popular music, an isolated island in the sea of culture. In linear histories, connections to larger contexts may be present but basically the history of popular music is seen as the history of consecutive events, each wholly determining the next, a story, in which performers and genres succeed each other in a sequence culminating in the present moment. As Dave Harker has observed, popular music, and rock in particular, has often been presented in terms of a "Darwinian progression" that involves a continual flowering of separate flora that have all grown from the rock 'n' roll seed sown in the 1950s (1994, 240–41).[5] Such approaches could also be termed neopositivistic for their empiricist confidence that the documents will reveal "the facts of the story" and that there is a wholly distinguishable generic form involved. As I have argued, these kinds of narratives have also dominated the writing of the Beatles' and John Lennon's history.

In reality, history—even a relatively brief span like the history of modern popular music—is much more complex and multilayered: If we look at the popular music charts, we can see that old styles and genres do not disappear overnight. According to sales figures, in 1967, the year known as the bloom of hippie culture, the most popular artist in Britain was the mainstream entertainer Engelbert Humperdinck. In the United States the top-selling album act was the trumpet player Herb Alpert with his Tijuana Brass. In his account of 1960s pop, Harker (1992) attacks critical histories of popular music that often ignore the fact that the most popular record in 1967 was a soundtrack, *The Sound of Music*, not the Beatles' *Sgt. Pepper*.

The history of popular music is often understood as a succession of innovations and new trends, but behind the obsession with the new, the past is always present. The continual dialogue with its own history is an essential part of popular music. Hence, besides chronological and linear stories there is the third approach, a sort of "orchestra of history," as Immonen (1996, 105), referring to the famous French annalist Fernand Braudel, beautifully calls it. This metaphor indicates overlapping synchronicities and diachronicities that are present at given times. In the "cultural polyphony" of popular music there are different traditions with different durations, traditions that live in the present moment equally, side by side (107). This suggestion resembles an argument addressed by sociologist Keith Negus in his *Popular Music in Theory*:

> New music and new cultural dialogues are made within the context of the possibilities provided by existing social relations (the industry organization, the political arrangements, the entire patterns of mediation and methods of social distribution), technological means (studio and instruments of music making, methods of storage and distribution) and aesthetic conventions (the complex of performance practices, bodily techniques and discriminations to select chords, sounds, notes, words and imagery, and then combine them in a specific way). (1996, 138)

Hence, in popular music nothing is born in an autonomous and neutral vacuum, and rock music is thus not "only rock 'n' roll," as it is often stated, but a polyphonic cultural phenomenon.

Indeed, studies have appeared that have utilized polyphonic approaches similar to cultural history. In a sense my study echoes the works of the American author Greil Marcus. Although Marcus is not a historian (perhaps he could be called a "rock-specific" version of the annalist school of historians or a rock history impressionist), his books deploy notions of a "secret history of popular music" that are familiar to the cultural historian. Marcus has proposed in several works, among them *Mystery Train* (1976), *Lipstick Traces* (1989) and *Invisible Republic* (1997), that behind the single popular cultural product or phenomenon there is a multidimensional "map," "territory," "nation," "invisible republic" or whatever metaphor he uses at a given time, and a "public secret," which is fundamentally a historical construction. For Marcus the history of rock music, and history in general, is not simply a matter of events that leave behind measurable things. History is "the mystery of spectral connections" between the people separated by time and place (1989, 4). Somehow, Marcus argues, those people seem to speak with the same language. Something deeper connects them.

For two reasons I am reluctant to adopt the term *secret history* in the study of rock stardom. First, it carries the connotation of scandal biography. This is not the kind of secret I seek. Second, although I enjoy Marcus' work, his stream-of-consciousness style is perhaps too diffuse to provide an analytical model for cultural historians of popular music. Marcus creates admirable interpretations and a rhetoric of delight, but I feel that his treatment of his source material sometimes leads to an undisciplined impressionism.

Peter Burke (1997) alleges that the essential problem for cultural historians is how to resist fragmentation without returning to the misleading assumption of the homogeneity of a given society or period. I wish to stress this too. My study is structured chronologically but I want to show that the history of John Lennon, and popular music in general, is not an unbroken linear story from one episode to another. Important issues such as authenticity and gender will cyclically reappear to emphasize spectral connections, the social and temporal fabric of Lennon's stardom. For cultural historians, there is still room to study how John Lennon was immersed in a historical process, and how the ways he was perceived formed a complex field of communication, explication and understanding. What I seek to show is that Lennon's career path is not a hermetic and finished story, an island in the sea of culture and popular music, but a "moving boat," a dynamic and open cultural construction. As such, Lennon is, of course, beyond quantification. One can, however, discuss him, present reasoned arguments, elaborate his "spectral connections" and, I hope, reveal an underlying unity without denying the diversity of the past, the polyphony of history.

Approaches provided by cultural history enable me to link John Lennon to time and place, but since the subject is unfinished in itself, it is therefore necessary to define limits to the study. I have chosen the point of view of popular music stardom, to which I now direct my attention.

Star History, Star Theories and Popular Music

> *It seemed that everyone knew me, but I knew no one.*
> —*Charlie Chaplin*

John Lennon is a very recent example of the long history of fame. In different times and civilizations there have always been people who have been more famous than others. As historian Leo Braudy (1986) shows in his account of the subject, these people have most frequently occupied positions in politics and religion. What Braudy largely overlooks is that besides political and religious "Great Men" there have been famous writers, actors, musicians, singers, comedians, jesters, and other representatives of popular culture throughout Western history as well as in non-Western cultures. These famous people did not usually enjoy political power or religious authority, but they were watched, seen, heard and sensed, and they enjoyed great respect in their times (although sometimes they were ridiculed, too). In a sense these people were stars of their times even though the word *star* itself as an expression of fame was used for the first time as recently as about 1830 (Fowles 1992).

It is agreed by historians that the rise of individualism, which was associated with the decline of the feudal system and the rise of the bourgeoisie, has been crucial to the birth of modern Western subject of fame (see, for instance, Braudy 1986; Fowles 1992). This long-term social shift also provides the ideological underpinning of the star phenomenon, but the more material catalysts are to be found in the urbanization of Western societies, the development of communication and transport technology and the growth of mass production. In the nineteenth century railway systems, telegraph and the press, as well as photography, contributed to the most important precondition for the star phenomenon: that is, that some people are recognized as special individuals by the masses (Fowles 1992; Sennett 1993). It was, however, the development of new electronic media and recording formats that finally launched the modern star system. Historians of popular culture broadly agree that the moving image was the first site for systematic promotion of stardom (see, e.g., deCordova 1990; Fowles 1992; Studlar 1996).

The particular union of popular music and modern stardom occurred in this changing social context and was consummated by the commercial breakthrough of the phonograph record and gramophone and the popularization of radio after World War I. This development enabled the ubiquitous circulation of music and increased the speed with which new musical trends, as well as star personae, were disseminated. It was, however, not only the development of recording and reception mechanisms that had major consequences in popular music stardom and fandom but also changes in the technology of reproduction (amplifiers, loudspeakers, microphones) which opened up new ways of experiencing music and performers. In the history of popular music the microphone allowed the convergence of singing, technology and sexuality in a way that was often deeply confronting. Simon Frith (1986) and, particularly, Bruce Johnson (2000; see also Whitcomb 1986; Théberge 2001) have shown how male singers such as Rudy Vallée and Bing Crosby were often criticized for emasculated moaning that led to a questioning of their masculinity. Nonetheless, this did not prevent the rise of the new style, crooning, in the 1930s. The new technology in popular music thus seriously challenged old attitudes of gender and sexuality. It also generated debates regarding authenticity. Since crooners whispered, breathed, hummed and sobbed to their microphones, it was often suggested that their performance was cheap, fake melodrama, as opposed to "real," legitimately trained singing. On the other side of the debate, pro-crooners defended the style by claiming that singing to the microphone needed careful training and that the technique, once mastered, provided intensely pleasing results.

The case of the microphone indicates that the styles of singing and, in particular, the authenticity of stars do not evolve "naturally" but through contested cultural factors. Do new technology and new styles falsify authentic popular music? Do they interrogate "basic" human characteristics such as maleness? Is the star a commodity? How is the star understood? Such questions have recurred decade after decade in popular music culture, and we also find them in the career of John Lennon.

It is indeed possible to argue that with the help of new technologies and mechanisms of reproduction and reception, the performer became a commodity, beyond the physical links between audience and star. The performer was able to become well known despite the fact that perhaps only a small percentage of her or his fans had physically seen or heard the star. It was no longer necessary for the star to travel, since star images could be circulated wherever new media technologies were available. In such circumstances the star's presence was, of course, merely a reproduction, a mechanically manufactured and distributed copy of the physical human being. Stars became known as people who were absent yet present. Interestingly, from this point of view the "earthly star" is similar to its heavenly counterpart—a comparison that curiously evokes the medieval concept of the king as having two bodies: an earthly natural body and an eternal body (see Kantorowicz 1957). Both human stars and heavenly stars seem to be within reach but are actually almost wholly unattainable. Of course, human stars can be touched, but for most of the population they remain reproduced images even if still apparently close. It is this twin nature of the star image, the mediated combination of proximity and distance, that has formed one of the most distinctive features of the star phenomenon. The star is actually one of us, but at the same time seems to evince individual characteristics that distinguish him or her from the rest of the population. What are these characteristics, then, and how is the star constituted?

Contemporary audiences of popular culture are familiar with the term *star* and can immediately suggest definitions for it, but ultimately it is difficult to form a single comprehensive definition, since the term is used very loosely and in a wide range of situations. In *Webster's Universal College Dictionary* (1997) there are two definitions of a star as a phenomenon of fame. First, the star is "a prominent actor, singer, or the like, especially one who plays the leading role in a production." Second, the star can also be "a gifted or highly celebrated person in some art, profession, or field." Adjectives such as "celebrated, prominent, or distinguished" are often used to describe stars. What definitions such as these tell us is that the phenomenon of the star is closely linked to the entertainment industry and popular culture while simultaneously being a highly dynamic category. The film researcher John Ellis sees the star as a performer who is originally produced in a particular medium but "whose image enters into subsidiary forms of circulation, and then feeds back into future performances" (1988, 91). In his groundbreaking study of film stardom, *Stars*, first published in 1979, Richard Dyer defines the star as a person who is known by people through different "media texts" (1986, 2). His interpretation complements that of the popular music researcher Roy Shuker, who asserts that "stars are individuals who, as a consequence of their public performances or appearances in the mass media, become widely recognized and acquire symbolic status" (1998, 282). What is common to all these definitions is the media: Stars are conspicuous individuals who appear and become available in the circuit of a number of mass communication modalities.

Although the star is a physical person who normally has at least some individual and creative distinctiveness, he or she is also a mediated symbol that is usually linked to the entertainment business and gains and loses value in the manner of commodities on the stock market. The word usually reminds us that boundaries are often vague and influenced by time and place. For instance, if an Olympic champion records a hit song or appears in a successful Hollywood film, is he or she then a star or still a sports hero? Or are mass-mediated sportsmen and sportswomen of contemporary culture already more "stars" than heroes? The ambiguity of the phenomenon is perhaps best seen in the confusion of the star with the celebrity, which, like *star* and *stardom*, is a historically constructed term (see Marshall 1997). The celebrity signifies a well-known person and a public figure who is not a property of specific individuals but, rather, constituted discursively by the culture industry and the audience (Turner, Bonner & Marshall 2000). The scope of the term *celebrity* seems to be significantly greater than that of *star*, and hence the star could be understood as a subcategory of the celebrity. Marshall writes that the celebrity "can be thought of as the general and encompassing term, whereas concepts of *hero*, *star*, and *leader* are more specific categories of the public individual that relate to specific functions in the public sphere" (1997, 7).

What, then, is the specific character of the star? In order to approach this it is useful to scrutinize some related key terms. A fundamental component of the star phenomenon and its vocabulary is the concept of *star image*, which is defined by film researcher Christine Gledhill as "all that is publicly known about the star" (1991, 214–17). There is, in addition, the concept of *stardom*, which could be understood as an umbrella term embracing both star and star image. In *Webster's Universal College Dictionary* stardom is defined as "the world or status of star performers or celebrities, as of the stage, motion pictures, or sports" (1997), while Dyer suggests similarly that it is an image of the way stars are living (1986, 39). It thus appears that if star and star images concern particular cases, then stardom is an expression of a larger entity referring to the cultural dimensions of the phenomenon and modes of star visibility. It is precisely because of this that I prefer to focus on John Lennon's stardom rather than his star image. The latter seems to invite a close reading of an autonomous text, rather than a contextual approach. As both a cultural historian and a Lennon researcher, I am interested in how "stardom" incorporates the contextual dimension and thus connects the individual with culture. The concept of stardom also implicitly raises questions about the ways stars function within popular music culture.

One of the main problems is that little research has been conducted on popular music stardom. Within popular music culture we can find surveys on stars and their lives, ranging from the daily music press, with its "rags-to-riches" stories of musicians, to the quasi-mythological popular rock histories. The cultural importance of stardom and musicianship is perhaps best seen in these histories, both written and audiovisual, which, as I have already argued, usually emphasize roles of key performers. The study of stardom in popular music is, with some exceptions, largely limited to personal biographies and their aim is to uncover a "hidden truth" behind the star persona (Marshall 1997, 4). For instance, in the standard John Lennon biographies we discover the kinds of repressions, the forms of anger, and the problematic relationship to his absent parents, that, according to the writers, eventually led to the behavior that forms the basis of his public performances.

Starting from Theodor W. Adorno[6], of the Frankfurt school, scholars have often paid attention to the music star phenomenon. Simon Frith (1978) has examined the role of musicianship in rock culture, Dick Bradley (1992) has referred to the relationship between singing styles and star figures in early rock 'n' roll, and Andrew Goodwin (1993) has touched upon the star narratives in music videos. Gilbert B. Rodman

(1996) has explored Elvis Presley's posthumous fame, P. David Marshall (1997) has dealt with the construction of teen pop celebrity, Keith Negus (1997) has analyzed the mediation of Sinéad O'Connor and Roy Shuker (1998; 2001) has presented an overview of the star phenomenon in popular music. Yet, so far no definitive study has been published, and it can be said that the history of star theory is explored more widely in film studies than in popular music research.[7] Since popular music and visuality have been closely linked through the modern media era, it seems likely that the star theories of film researchers can assist in the study of pop stardom. Care is needed, however. Although pop stardom and film stardom have a lot in common—notably, that they are both media creations—there are some decisive differences between them. These disparities are related to the technology of production and reception, the form of address, the industrial and commodity configuration of the musical product, and the audience's collective and individual relationship to the music and performer. The central disparity concerns the issues of reception and public performance, which are more complicated in popular music. First and foremost, as a commodity, music is very different from film. As Goodwin notes in his study of music videos, pop music is multidiscursive by nature (1993, 210; see also Frith 2001). Music can be heard on compact disk (CD), radio, television, Internet, or via phone calls, and it can be experienced on the dance floor, in clubs, during aerobics sessions, up to the last row of the stadium—in fact, almost everywhere. The reception of music is considerably more complicated than it is with film.

It can be argued that the music star's spectrum of public appearances is wider than that of the film star. For example, despite the fact that the role of the media is extremely important in the context of pop stardom, the possibility of the star's physical presence is still regarded as essential to the phenomenon. The importance of live performances in popular music is enhanced by the fact that only a few artists' careers rely exclusively on recordings or music videos. In sum, it is reasonable to suggest that star images in music are not only different from but also more complex than those of film.

In spite of these differences between star forms of film and music, Richard Dyer's (1986, 68–72) semiotic/sociological conception of "structured polysemy" of film star images seems to fit rather comfortably with the study of popular music stardom. By this conception Dyer means that the star image signifies multiple but limited meanings and effects. Sometimes various elements can strengthen each other, sometimes they can oppose each other, but by negotiations and reconciliations these differences can be organized and resolved. The complexity of the (film) star image arises from various media texts that Dyer arranges in four main divisions: (1) Promotion: material consciously constructed in order to "sell the star" (press photos, advertisements, and the like); (2) Publicity: what the press "finds out." Studios and related groups might try to control this material, for example by "leaks," but the finished version must look more "authentic" than promotional material; (3) Films: especially so-called star vehicles, which are built around the star's existing image (for example, Marilyn Monroe as a naive blonde); (4) Critics and commentary: reviews, feature stories, biographies, and so on.

Dyer's theory of media texts is of limited use for studying pop stardom. It is, however, possible to extrapolate from it a convenient set of categories, which takes account of the dimensions of popular music and includes various defining aspects of stardom. I want to call this weblike construction the *starnet* of popular music. While we can identify a range of structures and organizations, including law, music policy, authorities, tourist organizations and estates of deceased stars, which are more or less involved in creating star images and stardom, four major components can be postulated. First, there is the star, the living person, and her/his public activities. Central to these is music in its various forms (records and discs, music videos, television appearances, live performances). In addition, the star's publicity mechanisms, interviews, film roles, autobiographies and other public utterances can also define the star image to a great extent. What is fundamental here is the star's own public actions.

The second part of the starnet is constructed by promotional strategies of the music industry, especially those conducted by the particular institutions behind the star. These strategies include producing and distributing official star material such as records or discs, press photos, advertisements, and record companies' newsletters or web sites. Basically, the task is either to create new stars or to maintain preexisting modes of stardom. With already established acts the usual practice is "branding," the attempt to "structure continuities in consumer culture, where a sense of trust and security is indicated by certain symbols and

companies" (Marshall 1997, 245). The star "brand" is promoted and circulated by the music industry in various media forms. While discussing the role of star material, it is worth remembering, as Roy Shuker
(1998; see also Frith 2001) reminds us, that there is a common tendency
to equate the music industry with record companies, when the latter
are only a part of it. The music industry embraces a range of institutions
and associated markets. Besides the recording companies there are the
retail sector, the music press, music hardware, merchandising companies, and royalties and rights and their collection/licensing agencies.

The role of the music press is particularly interesting, because in addition to its position within the music industry it also belongs to the
third part of the starnet: the media and their commentary on stars.
Within this loosely organized category we can find critiques, news, columns, sketches, parodies, exposures of tabloid press and unauthorized
biographies — only a few examples that shape star images in significant ways. The division of labor between the music industry and the
media is often a line drawn in water. In the history of popular music
there are numerous examples of this symbiotic relationship starting, for
instance, from the early music press and its role as a presenter of the industry's own public view of itself and continuing with current playlists
of many radio stations. On the other hand, throughout the history of
popular music there have also been more or less serious conflicts between the music industry and the media. Nonetheless, what is fundamentally shared by these parties is their role as mediators.

The concept of mediation has attracted increasing interest in the
field of contemporary popular music research. In general terms, the
practice of mediation occurs when one party acts between two others,
bringing them into a relationship. In media discourse, which comprises
the set of all media texts, together with the practices involved in producing them, the term *mediation* refers to how messages are transmitted
between one social domain (producer) and another (consumer). What
is important in the idea of mediation in media discourse is that it links
technology, institutions and cultural forms together. Mediation must
usually be appropriate to the kind of institution in which it takes place
as well as include such an array of techniques and modes of significa-
tion that make it acceptable to those to whom it is addressed. Thus, mediation implies that the relationship between two parties is organized

according to shared social values (Thwaites, Davis & Mules 1994; Grossberg, Wartella & Whitney 1998).

In terms of popular music, Negus (1996) has identified three distinct senses of the term *mediation*. First, there is mediation as "intermediary action," which "refers to the practices of all the people who intervene as popular music is produced, distributed and consumed." This use shares some features with the much-used metaphor of the gatekeeper, but Negus stresses that there is not a one-way flow of material through various industry gates, but instead "a series of interactions and mediations as people in particular occupations connect together" (67). Second, there is the idea of "transmission," which refers to the way that various media technologies such as the printed word, sound carriers, moving image, telecommunication technologies and musical instruments have been used for the distribution of the sounds, words and images of popular music (68). Finally, there is the "mediation of social relationships," a web of unequal social relations and power struggles "that occur *between* and *across* the production and consumption of popular music" (69–70).

In the context of the study of popular music stardom, mediation is potentially very valuable. It provides a key to the ways in which the information regarding particular stars is distributed, and how different parties construct different meanings within this scheme. It also suggests that the process of constructing meaning is not concluded until the consuming of the star. The fourth and perhaps the most significant starnet group is formed by the audience, which in the end "produces" the star by "consuming" her or him—directly, by purchasing recordings, audiovisual material, T-shirts, other fan products and concert tickets, or more indirectly by attending fan club activities. Stars are for consuming. There can be no star without an audience: In popular music this fact is even more crucial than with other forms of stardom. The reason for this, according to Marshall (1997, 198), is that if the celebrity system of film is organized around auratic distance and that of television around identification with the familiar, popular music stardom is characterized by communality, the mutual commitment between artist and audience.

In studies of popular music the relationship between the star and the audience has been neglected, although public expressions of both fans' feelings and stars' reactions to them have been widely reported throughout the history of popular music. If we want to study the structure of star images as a whole ("all that is publicly known about the star"), then it must be asked in what ways the expectations, hopes and public expressions of the audience build stardom. Do audiences possess power? Apart from declarations of desperate love, fans often insist that the stars must commit themselves to their audience. This is specifically true in the teen pop genre, in which stars' relationships to their consumers are usually more sensitive and open to rapid changes than those of rock veterans with proven "staying power." From the era of Beatlemania, and even earlier, to current teen pop stars, performers have constantly been compelled to prove their loyalty to their fans.

The interactive relationship between star and audience is only one illustration of how the whole star phenomenon is based on public discourses about the star's role in society. What is obvious is that while the star image is constructed by an elaborate networking of all the participants in the starnet, it is also more than the sum of these factors. Discourses about the star overlap, compete and may also collide. Within the pattern of the starnet it is usual that "shapers" of stardom and their interests conflict—sometimes to profound effect. For instance, it is not uncommon that between the star and her/his recording company there are rifts that might concern musical and other artistic issues, and that can lead to difficult public negotiations or even court action. Meanwhile, the music press's approach may conflict with that of the artist and the recording company. Furthermore, fans dislike negative record reviews about their favorite artists and in response may publish their own reviews in fanzines or on the Internet. The last-named forum has recently been a site of debates related to the fans' use of copyrighted materials on their web sites. Further elaboration of the dynamic of the starnet would point to the same conclusion: It is because of such conflicts that stardom is not an unambiguous entity but a complex texture and a communication network.

The image of the individual star can be fluid and in tension also because of the temporal and spatial dimensions of stardom. As Dyer has pointed out (1986, 72), hierarchical relations of media texts can change at different times. As will be shown, John Lennon's career demonstrates how the emphasis of communication may move from one domain to another and how power relations between the components of the starnet are changeable. It is also useful to remember that in the age of digital and mechanical reproduction the star image can continue to survive and develop even when the star herself/himself is no longer present. The posthumous star history of Elvis Presley, with thousands of Elvis impersonators, concert reconstructions and other recyclings of his star image, has arguably been as interesting and important as his actual career. Stars die; star images do not.

Despite the dismaying fact that stardom seems open to endless interpretations, stars appear to us in particular historical frames and interact with various cultural issues. In the following chapters I have used various themes as springboards for studying the relationships between the star, the music industry, the media and the audience. Mediated sounds, styles and gestures of music stars are built upon the ideas about what popular music is and what it represents at given times. It is worth considering that stars do not merely reflect these ideas but are in the process of creating them as well. Popular music and stars are inseparable, and pop and rock stars do not shine on without the culture of popular music.

2 The Genesis of the Beatles' Breakthrough

British Pop Music Stardom before the Beatles

I wanna be a star!
—*Tommy Steele: "Hit Record"*

Concerning rock music, John Lennon was quoted as saying that before Elvis there was nothing. What his words tell us is that to him and his countless contemporaries, Elvis Presley and rock 'n' roll appeared as a sudden excitement out of nowhere, a cultural force that eclipsed and made irrelevant previous popular music. Curiously, there is a parallel to be found in Lennon's own career. Before the Beatles and the beat boom there was certainly a form of British rock music, just as there were predecessors of Elvis, but because of the overwhelming significance of the Sixties in the history of pop culture and popular music, the period 1955–1963 in Britain has frequently been more or less neglected. If Elvis has been considered the major pioneer of rock music, the same largely applies to his British counterparts, the Beatles. The period preceding them in Britain has been dismissed in general rock histories, presumably because of the writers' impression that there really is nothing worth mentioning. This view was taken by the earliest rock historians in particular. As young journalist Nik Cohn wrote in his overview of rock history, *AwopBopaLooBopALopBamBoom*, in the 1950s "nobody could sing and nobody could write and, in any case, nobody gave a damn" (1972, 61).[1]

If the period in question is examined in terms of the usual parameters of rock narratives, that is, cherishing innovative, creative and rebellious *artists*, then no doubt there is little to write about. It is the period 1959–1962 in particular, the episode of domestication between the explosion of rock 'n' roll and the beat boom, that appears, as Harker describes, the "deadest phase" in commercial terms and a *"bloody desert"* musically (1980, 73). These observations are, however, only a part of the story. First, criteria of artistic self-expression, innovation and credibility in popular music emerged only in the 1960s; in the 1950s such concepts were still mainly the preserve of classical music and jazz. Thus, the "artistic" aspect of popular music is not a very fruitful starting point for examining a period and culture in which the pop musician's primary task was not so much to break new musical ground as to build popular and durable careers. On the other hand, however, these years appear in many ways most interesting from the perspective of cultural history. In his unpublished study of Englishness in British pop music, Kari Kallioniemi argues that although the British pop scene attempted "to reproduce US sounds it constructed a star phenomenon with a subversive glamour and a domestic style that distinguished it from other contemporary scenes" (1998, 223). Thus, in Britain the interval between the invasion of rock 'n' roll and the beat boom saw the laying of the ground for the union of youth culture and popular music, and the national mechanisms for rock music stardom that paved the way for the Beatles' breakthrough.

Richard Peterson (1990) has argued in his influential article "Why 1955?" that it was not the range of individual artists or demographic changes such as the generation of baby boomers that created the opportunity for rock 'n' roll to emerge in the United States, as is often claimed. Rather, it was a consequence of systematic changes in the structure of mechanisms and assumptions of the culture industry. In Britain the shift was not as dramatic as in the United States, and it certainly did not mark the end of monopolies and the relatively homogeneous nature of the popular music industry. The British music business was in the hands of a few corporations. There were no minor recording labels and no substantial fringe radio stations, as in America, to challenge the pattern of production and distribution of musical sounds and images. The two major recording companies, EMI and Decca, dominated music production, while access to electronic media was very much controlled by the state-owned BBC.

Ruptures were appearing, however. In his study of early rock 'n' roll in Britain, Dick Bradley (1992) argues that the commodity form and the profit principle had already become pervasive by the nineteenth century, but the main economic difference between the earlier music business and the modern industry was of scale, market and technique.

The period of rock 'n' roll was also a period of great economic change (known as the "long boom") and accelerating development of the machinery of the music industry and music dissemination. As rigid and hierarchical as Britain's musical infrastructure was, it nevertheless had to face the technological and economic transition in which the music industry employed new sound media to sell a new type of product (singles, LPs and transistor radios), to a market comprising mainly the working class. In addition, and relating to changes in technology and markets, the organization of the industry was to some extent redefined by such new career paths as managers, producers and recording technology specialists. In light of these patterns, what most distinctively characterized British rock stardom before the Beatles was the convergence of established practices in the music industry and the media, economic changes and new musical activities (Frith 1987).

When rock 'n' roll came to Britain, the tension between tradition and change was best seen in the concerned reactions of adults and representatives of "official" culture (see Hewison 1986; Hebdige 1988; Bradley 1992). Yet the tension also emerged in mediations and marketing. The pattern was obvious in radio, for instance. Whereas in the United States the emergence of rock 'n' roll was in great part sustained by the boom in small independent stations, in Britain the BBC's monopoly over radio waves was unchallenged. It is a well-established fact that rock music was too much for the organization: For reasons grounded in the history and ideology of state radio, "immature" rock music did not meet the paternalistic, middlebrow standards of the BBC, which basically reflected an Establishment fear of Americanization and thus rarely broadcast rock music (see, e.g., Palmer 1976; Frith 1988a; Crisell 1994; Negus 1996).

British rock fans had few options until the brief era of pirate stations from 1964 and, finally, the beginning of the BBC's version of pop music radio, Radio 1, in 1967. But prior to the mid-1960s, there was the foreign Radio Luxembourg and its English-language service, which had gone on air as early as 1933. Radio Luxembourg was one of the most technologically mediated music institutions of the rock 'n' roll period, since, until the early 1970s, its programs consisted almost entirely of records and were heavily sponsored by record companies, which were even able to buy quarter-hour segments for their commercials.[2] By the late 1950s Radio Luxembourg was almost exclusively directed to the teenage market. With no pop music competitors on the radio waves, the station, with its prerecorded shows (which were broadcast in the evenings only), became an important source for new sounds and stars for British audiences (Frith 1978; Crisell 1994).

If the BBC and its policy toward new popular music was conventional, so, too, was the pop press of the time, but for different reasons. Beginning with the founding of *Melody Maker* in 1926, Britain has had a strong tradition of popular music press. Because there were fewer restrictions and controls over the print media than the electronic media, it is reasonable to suggest that pop papers have been the most significant medium for maintaining and restructuring the pop music scene in Great Britain (Kallioniemi 1998). This was evident already in the 1950s when new papers such as *New Musical Express* (founded in 1952), *Record Mirror* (1953) and *Disc* (1958) catered to the new explosion of music consumers, specifically teenage record buyers. What is important here in the context of popular music stardom is that the mediating role of the press was regarded as relatively unproblematic. In the print media, convention dictated that the papers basically shared uncritically the same interests as music producers and that they were straightforwardly a component of the music industry, functioning in the same way as film fans' magazines of the 1930s. Their success was dependent on their readers being interested in the stars they covered. Thus, the papers saw their concerns as identical with those of the record companies. Once this convergence of interests became of vital importance to papers, even *Melody Maker*, originally a trade journal for practicing musicians, was obliged to concern itself with new record publicity, particularly when its circulation figures began dropping and *New Musical Express* overtook it as the most popular music paper in 1958 (Leslie 1965; Cable 1977; Frith 1978).[3]

Although the role of the print media in the British pop music scene and stardom has been of great importance, there is enough evidence to indicate that it was nonetheless film and the television—along with Radio Luxembourg—that had the most crucial role in introducing and providing access to early rock music. State-run radio's resistance to rock gave films that featured rock 'n' roll a greater role in Britain than in the United States (Bradley 1992). Since, however, films with rock music were not an everyday phenomenon—the number of rock 'n' roll films, let alone British rock 'n' roll films, was rather small—it can be asserted that it was television pop shows that made rock music, and British rock music in particular, familiar and immediate to audiences.

There are at least two features that make early rock 'n' roll television important in the context of British rock music and stardom. First, many of the programs provided format models for later television pop shows. The mode of *Six-Five Special*, in particular, with both audience and performers as "stars" of the show, proved to have an influence on subsequent popular programs such as *Ready, Steady, Go!*, which became a regular arena for the Beatles and other "beat groups," as pop groups were also known. Second, early rock 'n' roll television not only followed tastes and trends, but participated in creating them as well. In his exemplary article on early British pop television, John Hill (1991) notes that partly because of low budgets and partly because American rock 'n' rollers scarcely visited Britain, shows were reliant on domestic acts. For instance, during its two-year lifetime, *Oh Boy!* presented practically all the major British rock stars and, in many cases, was actively involved in giving them their initial momentum: Cliff Richard, for example, had his television debut on the first show in 1958 and within days hit number two on the chart with his single "Move It." Basically the same had happened with Tommy Steele and his debut, "Rock with the Caveman," after being showcased on the BBC's *Off the Record* in 1956.

Television producers, especially Jack Good,[4] played an important role in the presentation of British rock 'n' rollers. Higher management often forced TV producers to censor the performances (like Marty Wilde's "belly-swinging"), but in compensation there was also an enhancement of stylish "grooming" (Cliff Richard having his hair cut, sideburns trimmed, and clothes chosen for him) and even apparent grotesquerie, like the famous scene with injured American rock 'n' roller Gene Vincent, dressed in black leather, limping theatrically down the steps while singing his hit "Be-Bop-A-Lula."

In addition to television producers there emerged a second occupational career group that would fundamentally affect the packaging of British stars: pop managers. In the mid-1950s the idea of someone personally managing music artists was unusual for the British music business, which was still a part of the larger entertainment industry rather than a division of its own. However, the need for new kinds of music stars created the need for a new kind of management, and it was further encouraged by the high profile of the most famous rock manager of the era, Elvis Presley's "Colonel" Tom Parker. The end of the 1950s in England witnessed the proliferation of pop impresarios, many of whom had already established their position in the entertainment field, particularly in theater and music hall. Besides local entrepreneurs there were managers with national reputations. Johnny Rogan, historian of British pop management, points out that the agent Tito Burns had Cliff Richard, the veteran variety manager Eve Taylor nurtured Adam Faith, and the proprietor of the famous 2 i's coffee bar, Paul Lincoln, managed several minor figures, most notably Terry Dene (1988, 24). In terms of commercial success, fame and cultural significance, they were all outpaced by Larry Parnes, "The Godfather of British Rock 'n' roll."

With his fine cigars, elegant clothes and exquisite wines, Larry Parnes was a classic caricature of the show business entrepreneur, but regarding rock 'n' roll he was at the outset completely ignorant. After working in the café business and as a theater producer, he became interested, largely encouraged by his canny business partner John Kennedy, in the new "teen craze." Eagerly looking for Britain's answer to Elvis Presley, the pair found a young man called Tommy Hicks, renamed him Tommy Steele and managed to get him a record contract. At this stage Parnes and Kennedy, who shortly gave up the music business and left the management in his partner's hands, were careful to maintain Steele's clean-cut image because of press denunciations of the violent Teddy Boy phenomenon (a proletarian youth subculture which preferred rock 'n' roll and Edwardian style of dress) and because in general, rock 'n' roll was connected with hooliganism and, curiously, venereal disease. The management's confidence was fulfilled with the immediate national success of Steele's debut single "Rock with the Caveman," which made him the first British rock 'n' roll star (Rogan 1988; Savage 1995a).

In the histories of rock music, Tommy Steele has often been called the poor British copy of Elvis. While it is true that Steele and other English rock 'n' rollers relied on sounds and ideas that American popular music provided, there is evidence to indicate that modes of rock and, above all, star images were not adopted in one fell swoop. Jon Savage writes that in attempting to replicate an American form, early British rock musicians and managers "added their own spin, a spin that has much to do with national characteristics like hyped-up aggression, obsession with image, a fear of and fascination with sex (including homosexuality), a deep strain of Gothic romanticism" (1995a, 38). Kallioniemi has noted that the manufacturing of early rock stars "grew out of the fact that most of their managers came from a theatre-business background, and sought to absorb rock 'n' roll into an existing structure of showbiz to attract audiences into the failing music halls" (1998, 216; see also Savage 1988b). In creating the packaged style of British pop stars, the emphasis on theatrical characterization and role-playing was thus a strong influence.

The exciting mix of American modes and national styles was also noted in some writings at the time. For the author Colin MacInnes, Tommy Steele appeared as a star with a fascinating paradox: He was both a softer copy of Elvis Presley, an un-English singer, and at the same time a distinct embodiment of familiar elements of English stardom, "a descendant of a long line of Cockney singers" (1993, 50). The aspect of nationality was more prosaically noted in an article in *Picture Post*, published in 1957: "Tommy Steele's greatest talent is that he is an ordinary, likeable British kid who obviously gets a kick out of life" (Philpott 1995, 67).

Tommy Steele's ascent to stardom also showed that within the triangular dynamic of music, technology and media, music stars of the period had become more crucially both the focus of public interest and the product of the convergence of a range of media. After being successfully introduced to the audience, Steele soon appeared in various television shows (he even starred in his own TV special, *The Golden Year*) and pop press cover stories, and only six months after his debut was celebrated in a biographical film and a book, both titled *The Tommy Steele Story*. Steele's life story and his star image were thus powerfully and at a rapid pace circulated in various media—in much the same way that products and images of the Beatles would be a few years later. In the film the accelerated star process is schematically illustrated in the scene where Tommy is taken to the recording studio and placed in front of a microphone; next thing we know, vinyl plates are pressed and Tommy's record sleeves are covering pop shop windows all over the country (see Bryant 1957). The overt purpose of the film and the book was to portray the rise of the rock boy wonder, but being so fully enveloped in that process, they themselves became part of it. They appeared as metastories, or strands of metastardom, both referring to Steele's career while simultaneously belonging to it as a part of the marketing and selling of the star. What the rise of Tommy Steele thus revealed was that if rock 'n' roll seemed for many like a completely new, out-of-nowhere excitement, there existed a well-oiled entertainment machine waiting to take care of business.

Tommy Steele was not Larry Parnes' only protégé. During Steele's heyday, Parnes started systematically to collect young laborers and part-time entertainers to groom them for potential teenage stardom. The training program meant purchasing new clothes from the best tailors, meeting important journalists, learning to appear relaxed and confident in social situations and adopting new, theatrically dynamic names such as Marty Wilde, Billy Fury, Vince Eager, Duffy Power and Dickie Pride. It was this range of stars, this seemingly endless succession of young men, and Parnes' promotional protocols, that evoked in the press a new concept: the "stable" of stars (Rogan 1988; Savage 1995b).

Being a manager of "personalities," Larry Parnes understood that it was not only the songs that made the performer a star, but the image as well. Parnes' discoveries came from working-class backgrounds, but as that class represented the most important market in the pop music culture of the period, their roots were by no means concealed. Parnes' method was to paint over the drabness of the working-class image with another, more exciting layer that gave an impression of "plasticity" and transformed the performer "into an electronic deity" (Savage 1995c, xxii–xxiii). What is significant here is that this kind of maneuver, in which identity boundaries are reconfigured, discloses the classic feature of star construction: the peculiar mixing of ordinariness and extraordinariness in the star image.

Parnes' career displays another pattern that seemed to fit one rule of thumb of the star phenomenon. Although Parnes' skill in packaging cannot be underestimated, he was not able to completely control dimensions of stardom. Parnes' maneuvers formed only one part—although an essential part—of the entire process. At the outset Parnes certainly managed to create stars, but the ultimate privilege of achieving national celebrity was reserved for only a few of his candidates. Furthermore, none of his protégés reached the status of international celebrity, and those who managed to succeed in Britain mostly remained so-called shooting stars, with only a brief taste of fame. Of all his young hopes, Billy Fury was the only one who was able to maintain his popularity through the years and whose talent has been generally appreciated.[5]

I have already emphasized that stardom is a complex web of components, determined by a range of factors such as the artists themselves, public relations machinery, interviews, reviews and other public comments by journalists and audiences. These factors can also impede each other, as happened with Parnes in the early 1960s. His stars and star candidates were asked with increasing frequency in the media whether they felt manipulated and exploited. Parnes, now nicknamed "Parnes, Shillings and Pence," was regarded as a ruthless businessman and a notorious Svengali, surrounded by committed but impressionable and naive teenagers (Rogan 1988). By this time his image had already become a model of parody for comedians, filmmakers and writers.[6] Suspicion of Parnes' authoritarian strategies grew gradually. Journalist Ray Coleman asked in *Melody Maker* if Parnes' "ballyhoo" and "massive brainwashing" were necessary in the current promoting of Daryl Quist, this time the singer's real name (1963, 8–9). At the time Parnes was already withdrawing from public life and the star business, and finally he went on to concentrate on organizing package tours and theater presentations.

Rogan (1988) writes that the 1950s were an age of managerial power reflecting the influence that the few major recording companies had over the fate of so many artists. In the 1960s the Parnesian paradigm of pop management, that of the "concerned parent" (11), did not entirely disappear—traces of it were still visible in the activities of the Beatles' manager Brian Epstein, for instance. However, as the idea of the Swinging Sixties and its emphasis on young creative talent gained ground, the parental paradigm appeared outdated and was replaced by "entrepreneurial expansionism in which managers and groups rivalled each other for creativity and charisma" (10). Although Parnes' old-fashioned professionalism, ideas of manufacturing and diluted copies of genuine American rock 'n' rollers could be easily criticized as tame and stagy by today's standards, the historical context of 1950s popular music culture qualifies such a judgment. Larry Parnes and television producer Jack Good represented the beginning of a British rock revolution and arguably were, in Rogan's words, "near radical visionaries" (37), whose real importance lay in their commitment to youth culture.

If Parnes was regarded during his heyday as a "spokesperson for British teenagers" (Rogan 1988, 37), there is, however, another side to the coin. This is perhaps best illustrated in a scene in the film *The Tommy Steele Story* (Bryant 1957), in which Tommy's family is informed about their son's new position as head of a variety tour. "Variety!" the mother exclaims in delight—and perhaps in relief, for now Tommy is finally moving into the *right* kind of entertainment. Indeed, the whole film is based on this presumption. In the beginning of the film Tommy is performing in a sumptuous restaurant for a privileged audience, and the route followed by this young rock 'n' roll artist to reach this peak of his career is then narrated in flashback. It was a prophetic plotline. Gradually, as the years passed, the most conspicuous elements of rock 'n' roll in Steele's songs, performances and image were replaced by the profile of "all-around entertainer." Finally, Steele established another successful career in English theater and music hall shows.

The route from rock 'n' roll stardom to family entertainment was followed not only by Tommy Steele but by other young star candidates as well. Producer George Martin (Martin & Hornsby 1979) recalls that his attempt to find EMI's answer to Decca's Tommy Steele included a young singer, Jim Dale, whose beginning seemed very promising until the manager advised his protégé to abandon pop music in favor of stage comedy. In the end it turned out to be not such a bad choice, since as an actor Dale enjoyed some success.

The trajectory to all-around entertainer at the expense of the teen audience has subsequently been regarded as an ill-judged betrayal of the possibilities of pop music. Once again, it must be borne in mind that if rock music of the 1950s took its place as a "back entrance into showbiz," it was a reasonable response to conditions at the time. British rock music was unable to develop outside the established entertainment business because there was no alternative mechanism to keep stars alive or even to create them. Due to the burden of tradition, rock 'n' roll was constrained within the prevailing orthodoxies of the entertainment industry, which attempted to control all signs of rebelliousness by either suppressing them or by softening the threat with comic elements and the foregrounding of the more amiable side of teenage high spirits. Most significantly, as many scholars (Chapple & Garofalo 1978; Chambers 1985; Hobsbawm 1989; Medhurst 1995) later emphasized, rock 'n' roll was regarded as "a passing fad" that would disappear in a few years and then be followed by other trends, like calypso, which was predicted in Britain at the beginning of 1957 as the "next big thing." In 1960, when asked by a journalist about the future of rock music, Larry Parnes made the daring prognosis "that rock will be going 10 years from today!" (quoted in Rogan 1988, 37).

If a British rock 'n' roll star wanted to maintain star status achieved through rock 'n' roll, he or she had to do it by other means. This was regarded as a necessity in America as well. Even Elvis Presley, the most popular rock 'n' roller of the era, had shown that after the initial success that rock music brought him, the next sensible career move was in light entertainment in Hollywood. The first years of rock 'n' roll were thus a search for the back door to show business. When it later transpired that rock was more than a passing craze, new strategies were needed. Since in Britain it was almost impossible for them to evolve inside the conservative music industry, they had to come, as then happened, from somewhere else.

Northern Stars: From Local Heroes to National Obsession

The island that had bravely withstood invasion from the outside for nearly 1,000 years had been conquered from within.
– Michael Braun, 1964

It can be alleged that the Beatles were the first rock group to make its local identity and cultural background a fundamental part of its fame and image. Even though the group was dependent on the culture industry, located in London, where they very soon established themselves, they still remained, first and foremost, a pop group from Liverpool. At the same time, their home city in northwest England became famous as the birthplace of the group, benefited from the beat boom, and was thus to some extent able to redefine its cultural status.

Before the Beatles, Liverpool had primarily been famous for its port and ships, waterfront prostitutes, soccer teams, stand-up comedians and its peculiar, nasal working-class accent, familiarly known as Scouse (Morris 1982; Cohen 1991). From the point of view of southern England, in cultural terms there had been nothing special in Liverpool. The pattern seemed to change in 1963–1964 when the Beatles broke through and led the way for other beat groups to conquer the national and, in some cases, international pop charts. From the beginning of the phenomenon, which soon became known as the "beat boom" (referred to in the United States as the British Invasion), Liverpool became the subject of obsessive interest. Journalists traveled from their London headquarters to Liverpool to report on the uniqueness of northern pop music, while record companies dispatched their agents to sign promising new acts—or any acts that appeared to represent the "Liverpool sound," or the "Merseybeat" scene, as it was also known.

Even though Liverpool was the first and the most significant northern city to attract national interest, other northern cities such as Manchester (the home of Herman's Hermits, Freddie and the Dreamers and the Hollies) and Newcastle (the Animals) also introduced new sounds and chart-breaking groups, making it clear that Merseybeat was not the only northern route to fame. The whole episode, during which pop stars successfully emerged from provincial regions, seemed to indicate that something new was really happening and that the character of the old cultural divide between the North and the South in England was seriously questioned.

While this chapter initially touches upon the characteristics of the Liverpool scene, it concentrates primarily on the less frequently studied relationship between popular music stardom and the South–North divide in England. Why was it that the pop group from "outside" came and conquered southern England? What sort of consequences followed? Relating to these geographical and cultural issues, I also want to examine how the idea of place-specificity, "Liverpoolness," was manifested and emphasized in the presentation of the Beatles.

There are various accounts of Liverpool's early pop music scene. Some of them provide a mythologized picture of local music-making, while others rely on the conventional approach of who did what and what happened, where and when. As an academic topic, however, the early Liverpool scene has been rather neglected, which is somewhat surprising given that since the 1990s locality and scene have emerged as key concepts in several books and articles on popular music studies. The basic emphasis of this approach has been on mapping the relationship between music-making and specific local conditions, that is, exploring the role and effectiveness of music as a means of defining locality as a part of everyday life.[7] While scholars of popular music have picked up on trends in cultural geography and ethnography and studied contemporary practices, comparatively little attention has been paid to the historical dimension of scenes and localities—perhaps largely because historians themselves have neglected the area.

One of the most distinctive differences between recent studies and earlier ones on locality has been acceptance of the complexities and diverse plurality that define local music cultures. As opposed to such terms as *subculture* and *community*, which were given rather homogeneous meanings in earlier studies, scholars have come to the conclusion that locality and scene are in many senses heterogeneous and open categories. In his influential essay on communities and scenes, Will Straw (1991) highlights that while notions of community imply music-related groups that are stable and rooted in a specific place, *scene*, by contrast, refers to a range of coexisting and interacting musical practices. Negus (1996) suggests that the characteristics of local music are in fact as varied, elusive and all-embracing as those of international pop music. Instead of trying to *define* the local (or, correspondingly, global), it might be more useful to ask how the local is given meaning in specific circumstances and how the imagined place and sense of space is produced as a cultural construction. What Negus is thus emphasizing is that in popular music *locality* may mean imaginary places as well as real places, and that many scenes, especially those that have reached legendary status in the history of popular music (Merseybeat, San Francisco psychedelia, and Seattle grunge, for example), have been observed as places of entrepreneurial activities and as highly unified, near-mythological communities.

To understand the circumstances out of which the Beatles emerged, *community* and *scene* certainly are key terms. During the beat boom, Liverpool accommodated a "real" scene of popular music, with numbers of young, semi-amateur musicians, active entrepreneurs and other pop enthusiasts practicing and interacting in the field. However, what filtered through to contemporary media and later rock histories was more like an "imagined" scene closely corresponding to the notion of "musical community." Bearing the idea of media construction in mind, the Merseybeat phenomenon could be understood as an early exemplification of place-specific music culture that initially produced itself and, in its later stages, was produced.

Rock historians, and Beatles historians in particular, have suggested a variety of explanations for the vitality of the local music culture that produced Merseybeat in the first place. Liverpool as a port city with "Cunard Yank" sailors (local seamen who worked the Cunard Line) bringing guitars and new American records to eager rock musicians, a strong tradition of oral culture, a conspicuously multicultural population, a strong sense of identity and loyalty to the city, a spirit of cooperation and a self-assertive, down-to-earth attitude are all ideas that have been discussed (see, e.g., Willett 1967; Hewison 1986; Cohen 1991; Nurmesjärvi 2000). Liverpool's cultural identity seems to incorporate a sense of disassociation from the rest of Britain, a sense of being somehow different.

Behind the mythologized picture we can, however, find some concrete factors that explain the emergence of Merseybeat. To begin with, Liverpool had a long tradition of popular music culture, with coexisting styles such as music hall, cabaret, Irish folk music, American-based jazz, and country and western, which formed a broad and solid foundation for new musicians and new styles. Among the elements of this foundation, none had a more powerful impact than skiffle, a largely amateur popular music style that hit the city in 1956 and, indeed, the whole country. Skiffle, which had its roots in American blues and folk music, was made famous largely by one performer, Lonnie Donegan, whose hit record "Rock Island Line" inspired young amateur musicians everywhere in Britain to form their own skiffle groups. It has been estimated that at the height of the boom there were more than 5,000 skiffle groups in the country and hundreds in Liverpool alone—one of them being John Lennon's Quarry Men, which later grew into the Beatles (Leigh 1984; Clayson 1996; Foster 1997; McDevitt 1997).

As a national craze, skiffle faded quickly. As exemplified in the career of Lonnie Donegan, who deserted the American South as a source of musical material and started to record old music hall numbers, skiffle accommodated previous national styles and traditions. There were, however, geographical variations. While in southern England skifflers mainly followed the same path as Donegan; in the North the popularity of the style lasted somewhat longer, providing a significant basis for a new kind of democratic musical group activity that was further developed as many of the skiffle groups evolved into rock combos. As with skiffle, when rock 'n' roll spread in Britain—only a few months after skiffle—the London-based entertainment industry and media regarded it as yet another in a succession of trends, and in order to increase and profit from its popularity, quickly tried to take control of the rock scene. In the North, however, the interventions of such mediation were less frequent, and amateur and semi-amateur musicians were freer to explore such models as Chuck Berry, Little Richard, Jerry Lee Lewis and other performers and styles of American popular music, such as black pre-soul and rhythm and blues (Laing 1969; Leigh 1984). This important cultural moment was given further momentum in the early 1960s when access to musical instruments became easier, helping to consolidate the standard lineup of drums, bass, and rhythm and lead guitars of rock groups and to modify patterns of behavior and values. Even though "Cunard Yanks" brought instruments to Liverpool, most of the Merseybeat groups bought their equipment from local stores, especially Hessy's, which perhaps was the most important gathering place for musicians (Harker 1980).

In addition to musicians' attitudes, local entrepreneurial practices and activities played a crucial role in the development of rock music in Liverpool. Jazz had been very popular, but changes in the tastes of audiences forced many local jazz clubs to close their doors or, alternatively, to open them to the new flood of rock 'n' roll groups. As a reflection of changes in music culture, the number of teenage "beat" clubs doubled between 1958 and 1965, building a web of musical places where local fame was within reach for new pop groups (Melly 1977, 64; Harry 1992, 407–8; Cohen 1991, 13). Even though national fame was an unlikely outcome for most musicians, at the local level the most popular groups attracted plenty of fans, mainly young girls. Some of the loyal followers even formed small groups and cliques, such as the Cement Mixers, Bulldog Gang and Woodentops, all of whom devoted themselves to the Beatles (Lewisohn 1996, 31).

Fans were not the only manifestations of a new kind of pop enthusiasm that began to evolve in Britain in the early 1960s. This was particularly evident in Liverpool, in the form of its own local music paper. Launched in 1961, the biweekly *Mersey Beat*, which later gave the Liverpool sound its name, played an important role in providing young musicians with a channel to local fame. Besides the interviews with visiting national stars, *Mersey Beat* introduced local musicmakers, club owners, other representatives of popular music, fans and, naturally, music groups. In the paper's columns, the local groups' camaraderie was reflected in reports of how frequently they went to see and support one another. Besides this sense of fraternity there was friendly rivalry expressed in statements by the members of the groups, and in the form of annual readers' polls and other charts. By building up a scenario of close and constant interaction between groups, followers and entrepreneurs, *Mersey Beat* thus helped to create a sense of cohesion and community in Liverpool's pop music culture.[8] This cohesion was reinforced by local managerial activity, although in the context of popular music overall, these were rather ad hoc, part-time endeavors—until Brian Epstein appeared. After taking the Beatles under his wing, Epstein successfully assembled the cream of the scene (including Gerry and the Pacemakers, Billy J. Kramer, Cilla Black, and the Fourmost) and managed to help some of them reach national star status. If any one person controlled the flow of performers from Liverpool to give it a coherent identity, it was Epstein, with his local "stable" of stars.

It is important, however, to remember that the cohesion of a popular music scene can be exaggerated. Regarding the musical side of Merseybeat, Beatles producer George Martin claimed as early as June 1963 that despite the affinity between the groups, musically there was no distinctive "Liverpool sound" but rather a varied array of styles (Johnson 1963, 3). What was more significant in the character of the Liverpool scene was its grounding on certain power relations and dynamics of exclusion, which were best seen in the way the core of the scene, musicmaking, was constructed. First, the absence of women was noteworthy, Cilla Black being the only female representative of the scene. According to Cohen (1991; 1997c) this construction might have been enforced by the fact that in Liverpool bands have often emphasized musicmaking as a business and a career, which tends to masculinize it even further. It has also been suggested that the "masculine" character of Liverpool arose from its role as a port, which encouraged the image of freeborn, free-spoken, footloose maleness. Furthermore, Mike Brocken (2000) argues that one of the consequences of the macho leanings of Liverpool's rock narratives has been that the remarkable impact of the gay community on the city's early rock has never been regarded as a significant part of the process. It should also be added that the lack of visible black and other ethnic groups in the presentation of the local music scene was notable both in the 1960s and later, especially considering that Liverpool had a rich variety of different minority cultures and musical tastes. Cohen (1991; 1994; see also Savage 1996c) suggests that one likely explanation for the poor public visibility of various musical cultures seems to be a thread of racism in Liverpool, despite the images of unity and solidarity the city has often projected, and the inherent racism of the music industry itself.

It thus seems that the unity of the Liverpool scene in the early 1960s, particularly the musicmaking part of it, was significantly compromised. Interestingly, one of the consequences of the spread of Merseybeat was that this cohesion was questioned in the city itself. As soon as the phenomenon began to gain a foothold at the national level, there arose a fear that the unity, or the image of unity, would be lost. The Beatles, who reigned in *Mersey Beat*'s columns and readers' polls from the beginning, was the biggest "star act" locally and had the greatest potential to achieve wider fame. Some of the Beatles' fans thus feared that if their favorite group were to attain national star status they would turn away from their loyal, original followers. "Eh, lads, if you have a hit record you'll go to London, then we won't see you any more. You've gorra stay in Liverpool... you're OUR'S," one fan stated in *Mersey Beat* (Smith 1977, 44). Similarly, Gerry Marsden, lead singer of Gerry and the Pacemakers, predicted in autumn 1963 that the scene would soon collapse, as the most talented groups had left the city. His group had received lots of letters from fans complaining that their favorites "don't come home" (Roberts 1963b, 5). Thus, among the supporters there was to some extent a line drawn between being one of "us" and being one of "them," the local and the national, the North and the South, reflecting Liverpool's position and identity as a city that was culturally independent and detached from the center of the music industry, London.

These fans' fears were not entirely unfounded. London's control of the entertainment production machinery and other media was self-evident, and if a promising pop musician wanted to become a star, he had to move to the capital. Liverpudlian pop singer Billy Fury had done it, and in the early 1960s there was unlikely to be a significant change in the pattern. Talent seekers frequently visited northern England and sought new artists; in 1960 Larry Parnes held auditions in Liverpool and hired the Beatles—then called the Silver Beetles—to accompany second-rate star Johnny Gentle on his Scottish tour. It was, however, out of the question for a manager to work for someone still living in Liverpool, let alone for a manager to move there. Unsurprisingly, in the leadup to the Beatles' national success, Brian Epstein was continually told that the Beatles would have to move to London (Geller 2000).[9] Even though the Beatles were first determined to stay among their original fans, who made them "feel [like] somebody" (Smith 1963a, 10), they very soon resided in the capital.

Practical considerations were not the only explanation as to why the North was not taken seriously as a site of popular music production. It was attitude as well. To illustrate, musician and author Ian Whitcomb, who briefly tasted the fruits of pop fame in the mid-1960s, recalls the attitudes on both sides of the fence, the South and the North:

> We in the comfortable South, in the Home Counties, had for years viewed all territory north of Birmingham as a foreign country. As for Scotland, it was beyond redemption, beyond the pale. Oliver Cromwell, they say, took one look over the Scottish border and decided it wasn't worth conquering. The North was cold and harsh and full of no-nonsense plain speakers who had no time for us posh, lazy exploiters in the South. (1983, 86)

The roots of the North-South divide are deep in English cultural soil, having a much longer history than that of pop music. According to historian Martin J. Wiener (1981, 41–42), the dichotomy in the images of the North and the South goes far back, to the Industrial Revolution, emerging as a historical product of established intellectual and literary streams. The two images provided metaphors of Britain. In the northern metaphor, Britain was pragmatic, empirical, calculating, Puritan, bourgeois, enterprising, adventurous, scientific, serious, and it believed in struggle. Correspondingly, in the southern metaphor it was romantic, illogical, muddled, divinely lucky, Anglican, aristocratic, traditional, frivolous, and it believed in order and tradition. Wiener claims that as a consequence of the decline of the Industrial Revolution, the southern metaphor won as a general metaphor of some kind of "essence" of England. Industrial places and characteristics, which were predominantly located in the North, finally came to mean "provincial." For Wiener, provincialism in twentieth-century Britain was not simply a matter of remoteness from the capital city, as in France. It was much more a question of remoteness from one approved style of life. Countryside life is not provincial, but the lifestyle in working-class and lower-middle-class suburbs is. In Wiener's words, provincialism is to live in or near an industrial town to which the Industrial Revolution gave its significant modern forms.

One has to be careful with this kind of classification of territories. First of all, it is not very clear who is imagining whom in these two metaphors, and, second, some of the ideas do not withstand close analysis, and are at the very least seriously contentious (particularly the notion of "Puritan" Britain in the northern metaphor). In addition to these, even though the North-South divide in a sense dates from the Industrial Revolution, it can be traced much further back, at least from the time that southern English became the nationally "approved" form of the language, with other written and spoken forms coded as remote from the "approved" way of speech. In fact, provincial stereotypes defined through speech characteristics can be found as early as the Elizabethan period.[10] Thus, it is perhaps best to consider the South-North divide in terms of the rhetoric of representations, or, as Rob Shields suggests, "imaginary geography," which is not so much linked to "institutional policies and personal practices" but instead to "spatial mythologies" and discourses of the nation (1991, 207–8). The repertoire of these "imaginaries" has produced a set of popular images that have constructed "the space-myth of 'the North'." In this process the media have played a distinct role: "The 'gloom and doom' image of the 'North' is a cultural construct which reveals more about the metropolitan mass media than any geographical or sociological truth about a locality," Steve Redhead (1990, 30) wrote about the creation of the "second wave" of the North in the 1980s, but his words could as well be applied to the "first wave."

In the context of British popular music culture prior to Beatlemania, Wiener's account of cultural winners and losers has a certain point, however, since, as I have already emphasized, the London-based industry and media played a leading role in defining the sounds and stars that were delivered to audiences. In terms of the culture industry, the North-South divide and its associated notions of provincialism were thus still a significant presence in the late 1950s and the early 1960s. "I almost asked him in reply where Liverpool was," George Martin, a Londoner and the future producer of the Beatles, recalled of his first encounter with Brian Epstein (Martin & Hornsby 1979, 122; see similar accounts in Davies 1968; Clayson & Sutcliffe 1994). Likewise, Paul McCartney told documentarian Michael Braun (1995, 31) that their "publicity man had trouble getting things in the paper because as soon as people heard Liverpool they thought we were all from the docks with sideboards." This knowledge gap raises several questions. If there was something dubious in the provincial regions, why was it then that the Beatles, so clearly identified as a northern pop group, could emerge with such power? What made Liverpool and the North acceptable?

First, when Beatlemania swept across the country it was made very clear—and unusually so—that this was not just another act launched by the London-based star machinery. The Beatles were distinctively identified with a "remote" region, Liverpool. For the members of the group this was not something to be ashamed of. In John Lennon's words, uttered in the early 1970s, the Beatles had no intention of hiding their background: "Yes, well, the first thing we did was to proclaim our Liverpoolness to the world, and say 'It's all right to come from Liverpool and talk like this'" (Blackburn & Ali 1987, 167).

Pride in Liverpoolness and northernness was often reflected in early reviews and articles about the Beatles. "Liverpool and North are fiercely proud and now the rest of England has taken them over," wrote journalist Maureen Cleave (1963a; see also Zec 1963). In a *Sunday Times* article titled "The Age of the Scouse" (April 12, 1964), it was mentioned that Liverpool has a "powerful local pride" which had led the city in the 1790s to print its own money and which had been fortified by its situation as an immigrant city. One of the most important vehicles of this local pride was, as emphasized in Lennon's words above, the Scouse accent. The provincial image of the Beatles was clearly reinforced in their vernacularity. The Beatles' accent was often ridiculed and regarded as a kind of impenetrable gobbledygook, especially by the southerners, as for example in an issue of *New Musical Express* (December 25, 1964, 3) which offered a jocular "translation" of the Beatles' talk in their Christmas record. Despite such ridicule—albeit unmalicious—the Beatles were by no means ashamed of their Scouse. The accent expressed their distance from the cultural "center" and identified them as "remote," but it also proclaimed change and the potential for renewal. Ultimately, the accent came to represent something fresh in English culture. The appeal of a marginal vernacular was not totally new, however, but rather a prolongation of the trend that had evolved sometime earlier. Historian Eric Hobsbawm points out that in the 1950s upper- and middle-class youth had begun to accept the music, the clothes and also the language of the urban lower classes, or what they took to be such, as their model (1994, 331). From a larger historical perspective, the enthusiasm for Scouse could be understood as a part of the long-standing search for the pure, the innocent and the "natural" counter-part to modern Western bourgeois society, usually taking the forms of exoticism, primitivism and idealization.[11]

In light of this, it is perhaps not so strange that the Beatles' vernac-ularity was to some extent a conscious and even exaggerated strategy. Manager Brian Epstein had cleaned up the Beatles' rough-edged per-formance and put them in new suits, but, following Larry Parnes' ex-ample, he also wanted to preserve working-class nuances in their image. In fact, Lennon's aunt was very surprised when she heard her nephew's accent on radio and television because she knew that John was able to "talk properly." Lennon's response to her was that it was a question of money and that the fans expected him to speak that way (Coleman 1988, 38).

Interestingly, in their musical performances the Beatles generally used a more "correct" English accent, and, furthermore, it was only lat-er that Lennon and McCartney evoked Liverpool in their songs, most famously in "Penny Lane" and "Strawberry Fields Forever." Lennon's decision to underline his lower-class background was one of the most crucial in his entire career. While Paul McCartney and especially George Harrison and Ringo Starr came from working-class families, Lennon was actually raised in the lower-middle-class suburbs of Liver-pool. Even though he was familiar with Scouse and working-class cul-ture, as most of his childhood friends belonged to "lower classes," he allowed it to be thought that his roots were in the working class and thus romanticized his background during his years of fame. True, Len-non did not actively hide his roots, but he was also unwilling to correct false information that was in circulation, and it was not until his last in-terviews in 1980 that he openly revised it (see, e.g., Sheff 1982).

Romanticizing marginality, be it related to class or region, is obvi-ously a key to understanding the interest awakened by the "northern-ness" of the Beatles. One of the most revealing illustrations of this was the reception accorded John Lennon's first book, *In His Own Write*, which in 1964 was an instant commercial and critical success. The praise for Lennon's book prompted the suggestion from essayist and critic Tom Wolfe that there was now a new focus for the enthusiasm of literary London for genius-savages, and that it was in part a guilty sympathy for the proles and primitives and in part a romantic awe of raw vitality (1987, 45). English literati now showed sympathy for the pop music star who had also proved to be a real talent in the field of art. This was not entirely unprecedented. In the field of literature there had already been a high level of interest in the "harsh" northern everyday life as presented in the novels of the so-called Angry Young Men, for instance, John Osborne and Colin Wilson. In the socially concerned films of the early 1960s, most notably in *Saturday Night and Sunday Morning* (1960), the urban regional setting was the central element of the story. Critics dubbed the genre as "Kitchen Sink," hailing it as a new kind of poetry of everyday life. Furthermore, "realist" dramas with regional settings were also introduced in popular television series such as *Coronation Street* and *Z Cars* (Laing 1991; Murphy 1992). It is often forgotten, however, that the new wave of film directors, scriptwriters and novelists comprised mostly Oxbridge men who were rather in awe of "romantic" northern working-class life and masculine individualism (Hewison 1981; Caughie & Rockett 1996). This characterization of the North was thus mostly the work of outsiders and, thus, "produced."

It was only when the Beatles broke through that northern England appeared to be projected on its own terms—even though their northernness was mitigated by Brian Epstein's tactics, which mirrored the prevailing practices and tastes of British entertainment industry. Epstein's position was decisive. Being both a Liverpudlian manager for the "bunch of northern lads" and a fastidious businessman with his tailored suits and elaborate manners, he straddled both sides, and it was he who played a key role as a softening mediator between northern identity and the national entertainment industry.

Popular music itself was a phenomenon of the romantic margins. It is worth noting that rock music in England developed away from the center of the music and entertainment business, as it partly did in America. According to Robert Pattison (1987, 22), rock music in America was born in "distant" southern regions, predominantly in Memphis, Tennessee, and he finds a clear parallel with Liverpool. Pattison claims that both regions were cultural watermarks, in which nineteenth-century romanticism had shifted to postindustrial processes without being interrupted by civilization. Both regions and their musicians shared the same myth of romantic sensibility and militant vulgarity.

Pattison himself is romanticizing here since, as Charlie Gillett had shown in his book *The Sound of the City* (1973), rock music had its roots in several American regions; similarly, in Britain there were other vital musical scenes besides Liverpool (see Rogan 1988; Clayson 1996). Also, Liverpool and Memphis were not necessarily such remote regions as Pattison suggests, but well within reach of modern mass media and a range of musical and cultural influences. In the case of Radio Luxembourg, for example, the concepts of "margin" and "center" appear rather relative, since in the early 1960s the station's signal was stronger in the north of England and it was more popular there than in the south (Harry 1992).

It is reasonable to propose, however, that in the history of rock music Memphis and especially Liverpool were the first examples to reflect the powerful ideology of regional marginality. In the history of rock music, "provincial" scenes have been "found" or "refound" time and time again and celebrated as an expression of authentic rock, leading to notions of authenticity and the conflicting senses of both being in and coming out of marginal spaces. Thus, discussing British popular culture, Kallioniemi writes that, while the practices and industrial resources of popular music and "Englishness" have been mainly defined from the center, a vital mythology concerning the periphery has sustained the idea that the "real" innovations and creative individuals come from the provinces, especially from the North (1998, 123).

During the Merseybeat phenomenon, regional comparisons were conducted in, for example, *Melody Maker*'s reader's column, where there was a minor debate on "London versus the 'Pool" in the summer of 1963. One reader concluded that while London was the "source of less radical music," Liverpool music's great popularity was based on its "rebellion against the tradition of sugariness in British popular music" (Peck 1963, 16). In other words, the Beatles' advantage seemed to be that they were "detached from the old hash of it all" (Morris 1966). Although the fetishization of authenticity peaked in popular music culture in the late 1960s, we can already find it strongly prefigured in the way Liverpool evolved into the capital of the beat boom.

The vitality of rock culture in Liverpool and the romanticizing of the North were no doubt crucial elements in the explosion of northern beat groups, but it is obvious that the atmosphere in Britain was in any case susceptible to such a phenomenon. Christopher Booker claims in his account of the Sixties, *Neophiliacs*, that it was no coincidence that the newly imagined "excitement" and "vitality" of provincial England, and particularly of the industrial North, played an increasing role in the restless fantasies of the London-centered, predominantly upper-middle-class "What's Wrong with Britain" press (1992, 174). It was part of the pattern that "excitement" and "dynamism" were almost invariably to be found only elsewhere. In this sense, it could be said, the Beatles and their peers in the 1960s were not the inventors but "the inheritors of the possibilities first mooted in the 1950s" (Inglis 2000b, 20), reflecting "a new wind of essentially youthful hostility to every kind of established convention and traditional authority" (Booker 1992, 33). Furthermore, the success of the northern pop group consolidated the mythologized axiom of democratic modern stardom: Fame can be obtained by anyone.

Ultimately, the rise of the Beatles and of the North strengthened the new sense of national pride. Although Britain had been one of the victors of World War II, in the early 1960s it no longer possessed the same prestige in world politics as it had enjoyed before the war. Its political status was declining, but suddenly popular music came in to help and to demonstrate that there was an incomparable national asset in the impertinent provinces. Thus, if the first kick of British rock music was felt on the local level, its final breakthrough was charged with feelings that seemed to touch the whole country. The strong sense of locality shifted to a strong sense of nationality and, with the Beatles at its center, was then exported to the rest of the world.

other category. The most famous ambassador of comic pop music was unquestionably the above-mentioned Freddie Garrity, whose star image was mainly based on visual comedy such as his swinging legs and oversized horn-rimmed glasses. In a sense, the Mancunian-born Garrity was as much in a tradition of British comedy as he was a pop star. This mixing of the traditional and the contemporary was noted by Dave Cardwell, the editor of *Teenbeat Annual*. He saw Garrity as reviving a dormant comic tradition: "He gives back to TV what the variety halls used to give. A good all round performance that has made the industry happy all round" (1965b, pages not numbered).

From 1963 to 1966, the period known as Beatlemania,[1] the Beatles seemed to meld both the cheeky and the crooner in their various star appearances. However, their music was a separate matter. In their early records, as well as in concerts, the Beatles avoided "funny numbers" and concentrated mainly on songs whose moods alternated between aggressiveness and melodrama. Even though their music during Beatlemania was "light" and characteristically up-tempo,[2] Beatles scholars have not considered it particularly humorous apart from some borderline cases, most obviously "Everybody's Trying to Be My Baby" (1964), "Act Naturally" (1965) and "Drive My Car" (1965). The first distinctively humorous song, "Yellow Submarine," did not appear until 1966. Nonetheless, since pop music stardom is built on the general circulation and recognition of the star in a range of media, it does not follow that elements absent from musical output would also be absent from the overall star package. What can be tentatively said in the case of the Beatles during 1963–66 is that although the group's main product—music—was not specifically characterized by humor, other public appearances and other aspects of the Beatles' "starnet" heavily emphasized it. They all participated to varying degrees in creating and maintaining a relationship between comedy and pop music stardom.

In studying humor and the comic in history, it is important to identify three central methodological and theoretical problems. First, there is the question of what humor and the comic disclose about the past and people living in it. Second, the comic has to be located, recognized and given meaning in its various contexts. Finally, it is important to consider the way people react to humor, and how those reactions may be interpreted (Korhonen 1999). Concerning the set of these problems and especially the question of locating the comic, one particular element that must be borne in mind here is the highly mediated nature of the Beatles; the audience encountered their humor primarily through various performances in the media. It is thus necessary to consider the particular media situations in which the Beatles used humor. Furthermore, the contextual approach also means that in studying the Beatles' humor, it is as important to examine what the construction of comic playfulness reveals about the nature of pop stardom in the early 1960s.

To begin, we need to identify the roots of the Beatles' humor. The Beatles came from a city that was nationally famous for its tradition of variety comedians. A distinctive feature of these comedians (among them Ted Ray, Tommy Handley, Arthur Askey, Robb Wilton, Ken Dodd, Norman Vaughan and Jimmy Tarbuck) was their verbal facility, usually laced with sarcasm. It can be suggested that because of this regional tradition in Britain, the Beatles' humor was more easily recognized and accepted, and indeed to an extent they were even expected to behave that way. The Beatles are "Scouse humorists as much as musicians," one commentator wrote in *The Sunday Times* (April 12, 1964).

Although the wit and the vernacular of the Beatles can be identified with Liverpool, their media presentation also drew upon a more general tradition of English humor. It is, of course, difficult to assess the extent to which the Beatles presented a sense of humor that may be regarded as typical of England. To do so is to risk an essentialism that is highly contestable and contextual. We can, however, find some concrete and commonly acknowledged connections between the Beatles and the manifestations of national humor, particularly the tradition of comedy. If we exclude here the larger music hall and variety legacy, which had some effect on practically every comedy trend in twentieth-century British culture, the terrain of the Beatles' humor makes clear reference to developments of the previous decade.

Even though live music hall and variety shows were gradually losing their cultural status in the 1950s, their traditions were not totally replaced by modern media culture nor dealt a deathblow by particular forms of Americanization. Rather, while seeking up-to-date modes of expression and communication in radio, television and film, English comedy underwent a lively transformation (Wilmut 1980). Among various examples, it was perhaps the BBC's radio program *The Goon Show* (1951–60) that exploited most effectively the possibilities provided by electronic media. Masterminded by Spike Milligan, Harry Secombe, Peter Sellers and, in the beginning, Michael Bentine, the show was grounded in verbal acrobatics and inventive sound effects as well as in musical interludes performed by a 12-piece studio orchestra, the Ray Ellington Quartet or the "Goons" themselves. *The Goon Show* presented rapid-fire, nonstop humor that sounded spontaneous and even nonsensical, but which was, as a matter of fact, based on detailed scripts written by the show's principal begetter, Spike Milligan. Presurrealistic authors Lewis Carroll and Edward Lear, the satire of Aristophanes, the anarchy of the Marx Brothers, the violence of Hollywood cartoons, comics—the name "Goon" originally came from a *Popeye* cartoon—and the broad comedy of the English music hall have been mentioned as important models for the show (Draper, Austin & Edgington 1976; Wilmut & Grafton 1976). Milligan himself stated unabashedly that the show was twenty years ahead of its time, rather than indebted to the past (1974, 13).

While *The Goon Show* achieved a fanatical following, especially among youth, it faced continual confrontations with the paternalistic BBC. According to the show's producer, the corporation made thirty attempts to stop the show until Milligan finally gave up the struggle (Lewis 1989). The BBC's disapproval was based on two considerations. First, the Goons' fascination with the limitless possibilities of sound effects and the absurdity and illogicality of their plotlines did not meet the BBC's expectations of radio "realism." Second, and more significantly, the state-owned radio company was oversensitive about *The Goon Show*'s satirical critique of various national institutions and authorities. In order to ameliorate *The Goon Show*'s satirical tone, the BBC once—when Peter Sellers parodied Winston Churchill—resorted to a measure that was very rare in the corporation's policy in the 1950s: direct censorship (Hewison 1981). Nevertheless, in some cases the Goons indirectly went so far as to satirize their own employers, as in one episode in which Sellers' lunatic character Major Bloodnok was offered an OBE (Order of the British Empire) for having successfully emptied litter bins in the thick of a battle; the show was transmitted just when two high-ranking BBC executives had been granted similar honors. Even the Royal Family, regarded in the 1950s as relatively sacrosanct, was targeted in a show that included an imitation of the queen mounting an attack on the pigeons in Trafalgar Square (Draper, Austin & Edgington 1976; Lewis 1989).

According to many critics (e.g., Nuttall 1968; Melly 1970), *The Goon Show* was of great significance to British pop culture and social protest of the 1960s. On a more personal level, during its lifetime *The Goon Show* obviously contributed to a pool of shared experience and a form of identity construction among its listeners. This was particularly true for John Lennon, for whom the show was a favorite, and who bewildered his aunt with nonstop imitation and mimicry of various Goon accents (Coleman 1988). Later he confessed his fandom and even wrote a review of Milligan's *The Goon Show Scripts*, describing the show as "a conspiracy against reality" (Lennon 1973). Between the Beatles and *The Goon Show* there also were personal links, as the Beatles' producer George Martin and the filmmaker Richard Lester, director of *A Hard Day's Night* and *Help!*, had previously worked with various Goons. In the mid-1960s the Goons and the Beatles met several times[3] (Coleman 1988; Turner 1996).

Similarities between the Beatles' public appearances and *The Goon Show* were noted on a number of occasions. Maureen Cleave's (1963c) article in the *Evening Standard* included apparently the first public reference to this connection: "Their jokes are Marx Brother and Goon and often a bit sick." The connection was repeated, for example, in comments about the Beatles' Christmas records. These flexidiscs were usually of a few minutes' duration and were posted as annual gifts to the members of the official fan club. They contained occasional music numbers, greetings to fans and sometimes absurd, Goonlike sketch dialogues. "It is all rather obscure humor and if there are any funny lines then they are obliterated by some of the noises which make up the background," sniffed a *New Musical Express* reviewer of one record in an article titled "Beatles Goon It Up Again" (Hutchins 1966b, 2; see also Smith 1963e). Furthermore, Lennon's own literary publications *In His Own Write* (originally published 1964) and *A Spaniard in the Works* (originally published 1965), both of which divided more or less equally between absurd prose, poetry and drawings, were occasionally regarded as taking inspiration from the Goons (e.g., Melly 1964).

Regarding the Beatles' songs, there were at the time no suggestions of the Goon influence.[4] They were commonly made, however, in relation to the Beatles films *A Hard Day's Night* and *Help!*. Besides being hailed as an innovative pop film, *A Hard Day's Night* was generally placed in a comic tradition referring back to the Goons and the Marx

Brothers as well as Buster Keaton and a Liverpudlian sense of humor (see, e.g., Gilliatt 1964; Gray 1964, 3; Hutton 1964; Roberts 1964b; *The Times*, July 7, 1964; Wilson 1964). The Goon connection was not explicated, but may be found in the combination of a "zany" tone set by a group of males acting comically and using a form of insider humor. It can also be suggested that the film's various jokes at the expense of the British Establishment and its pompous paternalistic attitudes evoked the Goons.

What can be said of both films is that they definitely established the image of a "great new comedy team" (Gray 1964, 3) and generally played a vital role in the Beatles' success. Of these two films, it was *A Hard Day's Night* that came closer to presenting a semifictional picture of the Beatles' life, or, as Mark Hertsgaard puts it, "a fantasy version of the Beatles' fantasy life" (1995, 82). In the film, this fantasy involved a hectic "star" lifestyle in which the heroes alternate between the demands of the entertainment industry and their pursuing fans. *Help!*, which has generally been considered their weaker film, detached the group from its Liverpudlian background and sent it into comic adventure situations around the world.

Despite their differences, which were visually embodied in the shift from grayish black-and-white shooting to lavish color, the films share several elements, such as a distinctively comic mode and music performances, as well as the Beatles representing themselves rather than fictitious characters. Furthermore, both films attempted to reinforce and maintain existing star images. While this attempt was characteristic of the pop films of the early 1960s, it also, in a larger sense, represented a particular practice of what Dyer calls the "star vehicles" of the film industry (1986, 70). According to Dyer, filmic star vehicles usually have three functions. First, the film may introduce a stereotyped version of a certain star, such as Marilyn Monroe as a naive blonde. Second, the film may present milieus, situations and other generic contexts that are associated with the star, like John Wayne and westerns. Third, the star vehicle provides an opportunity for the star to do her or his "own thing," be it a mannerism, a dance scene or a musical performance.

The Beatles' films were distinctively constructed on the happy-go-lucky image of the group. *A Hard Day's Night* emphasized a Liverpudlian brand of wisecracking and used forms of comic narrative to place the members of the group in the milieu and situations that had already been identified with their success: television studios, hotel rooms, urban districts, fan crowds and in the spotlight of the entertainment industry. *Help!* presented the image of a high-spirited group of males that was both tightly organized but nonetheless allowed individual characterizations: the witty and satirical John, the soft and sexy Paul, the reserved George and the lovable Ringo. Both films introduced several scenes in which the Beatles had opportunity to do their "own thing": perform music.

The importance of a distinctive star image was pivotal in the process of filmmaking. It was, for example, reported that the producer Walter Shenson's "exploitation of the Beatles consists in making their films as funny as possible" (cited in Giuliano & Giuliano 1995, 57). One of the paradoxes was that even though the Beatles appeared as themselves—John, Paul, George and Ringo—in these films, their characterizations were a part of filmic construction. In *A Hard Day's Night* there were some improvised scenes, as when fans break a security barrier and the stars run for their lives, but basically the scriptwriter, Alun Owen, and the director, Richard Lester, relied on "a careful build-up" which included the story line and short dialogues (Miles 1998, 160). Even though both films were regarded as "Beatles films" and they thus belonged to the catalog of Beatles products, the group itself had only limited control over the final result. This was particularly the case with *Help!*, which, according to biographical sources (e.g., Coleman 1988; Miles 1998), did not fully satisfy the Beatles.

During the actual production process, such complaints were not heard, however, partly because people involved in production are more likely to market, rather than criticize, their latest project, but also because in the context of early 1960s stardom, pop music was seen as inferior to film. There was a common feeling that stardom based on popular music is merely temporary, after which comes either a return to obscurity or a move to a career in some form of show business such as film. The likely durability of the Beatles' success was a major question constantly faced and raised by journalists, representatives of the music industry and the group itself. Opinions varied from three months to ten years, most usually settling on four or five years (see, e.g., Coleman 1964a; 1965b; Cardwell 1965a; Pugsley 1994; Braun 1995; Giuliano & Giuliano 1995; Wonfor 1996b). When the Dave Clark Five, leaders of the "Tottenham sound," shortly overtook the top position in the pop charts, the Beatles and Merseybeat were instantly dismissed as passé. Pop music was seen as the domain of ephemeral trends, keeping musicians and the music industry on their toes looking for the "back door" to show business in much the same way as in the 1950s. The musical director of the *Ed Sullivan Show* compressed the view into a few words by giving the Beatles "a year," after which they would "make a movie and make more money" (Braun 1995, 105).

British pop stars Tommy Steele and Cliff Richard had had their own star vehicle films, and there was no reason why the same could not occur with the Beatles—and other successful beat and pop groups as well. Gerry and the Pacemakers celebrated Liverpool in *Ferry Cross the Mersey* (1965), while the Dave Clark Five cruised around London in *Catch Us If You Can* (1965). The Rolling Stones reportedly planned a feature film (which did not materialize). In America Elvis Presley seemed to favor films at the expense of music, a direction that for a while appeared tempting to the Beatles. In his autobiography Brian Epstein concluded that "I see tremendous possibilities in films and this may well be the way I shall guide them" (1981, 110). The Beatles themselves did not oppose this option. In an interview for *Melody Maker*'s Ray Coleman (1964b, 9; see also 1965d; Smith 1963c; the press conference in Pugsley 1994), Lennon said that he would like to see the Beatles "making better and better films" since unlike pop music the film "allows you to grow up as a person."[5]

Films were considered an important route for pop stars to establish a durable career, but being a pop star meant also exploiting other forms of electronic media. For example, during the years of Beatlemania the group appeared on almost 90 BBC radio shows, including several special programs for public holidays. In 1963 the group even had a show of their own, the fifteen-part BBC Light Programme radio series *Pop Go the Beatles*. It followed a standardized format of the period: As resident stars, the Beatles would have a guest act each week, chosen by the BBC and usually taped in a separate session. The show also included a resident emcee jousting with the group, and listeners' requests (Howlett 1996). On radio shows, the Beatles concentrated on music. Evidence indicates that the group also performed its own versions of well-known comic songs, but this was exceptional (Lewisohn 1996, 135). Nonetheless, there was usually time for lighthearted bantering with the host, interviews and other humorous introductions, such as: "Hi, I'm John

Lennon. I play the guitar—and sometimes I play the fool" ("The Beatle Greetings" in the Beatles 1994).

To the Beatles and their pop colleagues, television provided another important media route to public notice. In the 1950s, British pop artists' attempts to gain national exposure were very much dependent on appearances on television's pop shows, which by the early 1960s had almost disappeared. After a short interval of silence, the pendulum swung back in favor of the youth audience. *Thank Your Lucky Stars*, which was produced by the ITV franchise ABC Television, was the first of the major network television pop shows in the 1960s. It was followed by *Ready, Steady, Go!* (Rediffusion Television/ITV) in 1963 and *Top of the Pops* (BBC), which arrived on New Year's Day, 1964. Of these three shows, *Ready, Steady, Go!* has generally been considered the most exciting and innovative, but the formats did not differ greatly from one another. With their mix of musical acts, hosts, active teenage participants, dancing and competitions, they all emphasized the informal party atmosphere and thus demonstrated the lasting influence of the late *Six-Five Special*.

According to Mark Lewisohn's listing (1996, 355), from October 1962 to April 1970, members of the Beatles appeared more than 120 times on British television, excluding news coverage and the screening of their promotional films. In 1963–64 alone, they made more than seventy appearances. While the contents of television shows in which the Beatles appeared during Beatlemania were mainly musical, the atmosphere was usually cheerfully high-spirited, and there were abundant opportunities for humorous chat and comic byplay. In addition to pop show broadcasts, the Beatles also appeared on various comedy shows, where they usually performed their latest hit songs and participated in sketches (see, e.g., Wonfor 1996b).

Regarding television's role, in the United States the comic element was, if anything, even more prominent than in Britain. For U.S. television the Beatles appeared on various entertainment shows (but no actual comedy shows), and caricatures of the Beatles were used in the sixty-seven-episode *The Beatles Cartoon Series*, which was first screened on ABC TV in 1965. The weekly half-hour series, which ended in 1969, featured the foursome in adventures all around the world, with such familiar imagery and characters of popular culture as vampires, mad scientists, bullfighters and pursuing fans. Whereas the animated characters visually resembled the original ones, the Beatles' Liverpudlian accent had been replaced by one more familiar to Americans, as Scouse was considered too difficult (Harry 1992).

The Beatles Cartoon Series exemplifies how the Beatles' control over their public exposure was limited. While in principle the Beatles and their manager Brian Epstein enjoyed some control over their media appearances, in practice there was no conscientious rationing, especially during the first years of Beatlemania; their strategy was simply to gain as much media exposure as possible. In addition, they had little control over existing program formats. Even though the humor and the comic antics of the Beatles may have seemed natural and spontaneous to the audience, most of the subjects and lines of discussion on television and radio shows were based on some degree of advance planning or even script. In films, established constraints were even more important. This meant, for instance, that the cruel side of the Beatles' humor was rarely expressed. What is important within the context of stardom and mediation, however, is that on the radio, as well as in television and films, the Beatles had an opportunity to appear as audible stars and to use their distinctive accent and verbal humor. Even though their output was to some extent controlled, these appearances emphasized the Beatles' image as a group of lovable jokesters.

It was not only the way the Beatles talked that was considered hilarious. Their visual appearance, most notably the relatively long and fluffy hairstyle, inspired comments and jokes in various cartoons, television sketches and other media. In America discussion of the Beatles was fixated on their hair. Some voices from the older generations demanded that the "mopheads" visit the barbershop and get a proper crewcut, which at the time was a significant indicator of male acceptability. As in the British media, such critical voices soon sank into oblivion. The Beatles' hairstyle was generally seen more as a mildly ridiculous element of youthful dynamism than an actual threat to the social order. "Americans decide the Beatles are harmless," reported *The Times* (February 11, 1964; see also Schaffner 1978; Wiener 1985).

In America the humor of the Beatles appeared most overtly in press conferences. If the Beatles' humor on radio, television and in films was constrained by prearranged controls, before the masses of journalists there was more room for spontaneity and the comedy of the absurd. On such occasions the group could be witty as well as ironically self-deprecating, humorously underscoring their supposedly poor educations:

> Beethoven figures in one of your songs. What do you think of Beethoven?
> Ringo: He's great. Especially his poetry.
> What do you believe is the reason you are the most popular singing group today?
> John: We've no idea. If we did, we'd get four long-haired boys, put them together and become their managers.
> How do you feel about teenagers imitating you with Beatle wigs?
> John: They're not imitating us because we don't wear Beatle wigs.
> (Quoted in Kelly 1994, 115, 130–31)

These question-and-answer sessions have become part of folklore of the Beatles and popular music. Apart from being prime examples of the Beatles' wit, these scenarios also embodied one of the axioms of stardom: The star is both ordinary and extraordinary, reachable and unreachable. In his short analysis on the Beatles' first American press conference, Nik Cohn notes that the Beatles "answer politely, they make jokes, they're most charming but they're never remotely involved, they're private" (1972, 132). In Cohn's conclusion, "they're anti-stars and they're superstars both."

In relation to the general practices of press conferences and other pop music interviews of the time, Cohn's notion has particular relevance. Questions were mostly not specifically related to music, but to broader entertainment culture, such as visual style, possible durability of success, the pros and cons of fame and fans, and opinions regarding the ideal woman. Because of their cultural background, rock 'n' roll enthusiasm, long experience of performing and, above all, their ability to write their own material, the Beatles' relationship to their music was crucially different from most of their pop predecessors. With few exceptions (such as *Melody Maker*), this was not fully recognized by the media. Furthermore, because critically confronting the media was out of the question at this stage of the Beatles' career, the most effective way to respond to musically peripheral questions was to joke. John Lennon remarked a few years later that the Beatles "were funny at Press conferences because it was all a joke." To Lennon, it was just "Fifth Form humour, the sort you laugh at at school. They were putrid. If there were any good questions about our music, we took them seriously" (Davies 1968, 196).

Drawing on Sigmund Freud's discussions of joking, Henry W. Sullivan (1995, 156) suggests that humor provides a socially acceptable form of aggression toward institutions, or even a form of subversion of their authority. To Sullivan, the Beatles certainly used humor in this way, especially in their early media interviews, which were full of mocking spoofs of their questioners. While there were no visible signs of "protest," aggression or subversion in the Beatles' star image, they undoubtedly used mockery in press conferences and on other occasions. The most famous ironic remark was Lennon's, at the Royal Variety Show in 1963: "Will the people in the cheaper seats clap your hands? And the rest of you, if you'll just rattle your jewellery" (see, e.g., Solt 1988). Lennon's quip was not disapproved of: "How refreshing to see these rumbustious young Beatles take a middle-aged Royal variety performance by the scruff of their necks and have them Beatling like teenagers" (*Daily Mirror*, November 5, 1963).

For a pop star living in the 1950s, it is likely that this kind of irreverent flippancy would have been unpardonable. Given that such demeanor had already been incorporated as part of the Beatles' "northern wit," this tolerance and even approval of the Beatles' iconoclastic frivolity becomes understandable. Furthermore, if *The Goon Show* had created more elbow room for socially critical humor, that space was extended by the so-called satire boom, which had established itself as one of the distinguishing features of the new British society.[6] In the early 1960s, even fun-loving and harmless pop stars were allowed to mock.

The boundaries of approved humor were equally inconstant and negotiable with the Beatles as they had been with the Goons and satirists. This did not mean that their backers did not try to stage-manage the Beatles' humor. If the Beatles themselves enjoyed joking publicly, the managerial politics of their record companies recognized that it was also crucial to the group's star image. Satire and irony were not the most approved forms of humor, however. The focus was more on a style that had already been cultivated by earlier pop stars: inoffensive fun. There are numerous examples of attempts to underline this aspect of stardom. One record company issued a memo in America advising sales and promotion staff to wear Beatle wigs during business hours, and to see how many of the retail clerks had enough of a sense of humor to start the "Beatle Hair-Do Craze" (Giuliano & Giuliano 1998, 149). The same emphasis on simple fun was evident in official Beatles press photographs in which the members of the group presented a zany image, posing in swimsuits or dressed as matadors. Tony Barrow (1985), the Beatles' press secretary, included in his very first press kit John Lennon's hilarious version of the group's origin, while manager George Martin has recalled that in the beginning the prevalent view at EMI was that the Beatles were a joke group, possibly even a pseudonym of Spike Milligan (Martin & Hornsby 1979, 127). Brian Epstein was reportedly very deliberate about the cheerful image of the Beatles and stated, "I hope everybody has a wildly, wonderfully, good time. For this—and only this—is what the Beatles are all about" (1981, 81).

The Beatles' record company EMI was eager to preserve the happy-go-lucky image of the group and therefore reluctant to publish cheerless features about them. It has subsequently been reported that the moody black-and-white photograph on the *With the Beatles* record sleeve (1963) was strongly opposed by some EMI executives, as they considered it "shockingly humourless" (Miles 1998, 157). While this cover was eventually approved, the grimly humorous record sleeve of the U.S. compilation *"Yesterday" ... And Today* was not. Its original cover introduced the group posing in butchers' aprons, holding raw joints of meat and headless dolls. Startled by the hostile reaction to preview copies from disc jockeys and the press, Capitol, the EMI subsidiary in the United States, recalled all the albums and issued a statement apologizing for what it interestingly described as an attempt at pop satire (Schaffner 1978; Wiener 1985). Referring to this and other controversies over covers, Martin Cloonan emphasizes that despite being the most popular and respected pop group in the world and enjoying a relatively high level of artistic freedom with their music, the Beatles' artistic control was far from total (2000, 130–31). What can be added to this conclusion is that the questions of artistic control and the star image were closely intertwined. Even though there was a relatively high consensus on the importance of the Beatles' humor in marketing them as stars, it was not just humor but the *type* of humor that was considered crucial by the music industry.

The importance of a cheerful and carefree image was agreed on and emphasized at almost every stage of the production process of the Beatles. The relationship between the press (especially the music press) and the music industry in the early 1960s was a close symbiosis. Later biographies and histories of the Beatles have revealed various incidents involving negative images such as drugs, sex and violence. At the time such stories were not published, even though most journalists were aware of the "darker side" of the Beatles. Chris Hutchins, then a reporter for *New Musical Express*, has recalled that his and other journalists' stories on the Beatles were designed to maintain the "clean" image that was already established and celebrated (Hutchins & Thompson 1996; see also Wenner 1980; Norman 1982). The Beatles were the nation's pop darlings, the symbol of a collective positivity that was not to be tarnished. While there were publications about British jazz musicians' bohemian and sexually adventurous lifestyles, as in George Melly's autobiographical *Owning-Up* (1977), revelations about pop stars' troubled lifestyles became more common only in the late 1960s, when the character of popular music culture had changed.

Humor and comedy were seen as a natural element of the Beatles. While there is no reason to deny that humor indeed came naturally to them, it was also emphasized in media and, to a significant extent, consciously produced. The Beatles' humor was mediated and given meanings by various people. It thus appears that the relationship between "naturalness" and production, the idea that will be advanced in the next section of this study, forms a significant key in the celebrity process of John Lennon and the Beatles.

One of the Boys: Pop Stardom and Masculinity

> It is all very well if one is married before one is a fully-grown Beatle but a fully-grown Beatle must stay single.
> —Brian Epstein

There is general agreement that rock music remains conspicuously masculine. The history of rock, ranging from individual performers to the overall structures of the music industry, provides abundant evidence of sexism, male chauvinism and the marginalization of women. However, as Cohen (1997c) argues, rock is not "naturally" male or merely a reflection of an existing male culture; it is actively "produced" as male through the practices of the music industry and everyday activities.[7] Since the popular music industry and its associated institutions, occupations and mediators have traditionally been male-centered, it can be proposed that the ways rock has been understood, mastered and circulated have worked to reinforce gender boundaries. Rock music has historically been understood as "male" because its normative systems of knowledge are themselves masculinized.

This is, of course, only one side of the coin. Popular music, and rock music as a part of it, has also on occasions challenged dominant sex and gender roles. Since the early 1990s it has been pointed out in various academic writings that popular music has incorporated various counter-discourses relating to gender. While constructing masculinity, popular music has constantly negotiated not only with a traditional masculine ethos but with homosexuality, androgyny and femininity, all of which have been regarded either as threats to or resources for popular music, depending on the context. Two lines of investigation have dominated these writings.[8] First, there have been attempts to explore the project of masculinity, which have usually meant rather unimaginative disclosures of traditional and reactionary ideas on manhood in rock music. Second, researchers have presented different cases in which hegemonic masculinity has been challenged by various political and aesthetic movements such as feminism and gay culture.

In his *Key Concepts in Popular Music* (1998), Roy Shuker reviews areas where the significance of gender in popular music is evident. While Shuker's list covers such terrain as history, genre, audiences and the music industry, stardom is not included. Yet the wide public interest in stars suggests that in the culture of popular music, stardom is among the most conspicuous fields where questions of identity and representation, including gender and masculinity, are created, maintained and discussed. In the history of popular music stardom, we can find many controversial stars who have both celebrated a "natural" division of sexes and at the same time experimented with gender expectations. Mick Jagger is a notable example of a star whose macho persona and misogyny have conflicted with his flirtation with androgyny—and raised problems for his fans as well as in academic writings (see Coates 1997; Whiteley 1997). Jagger's Janus-faced image demonstrates that the star is usually a highly flexible construction, open to different usages and meanings that are constantly negotiated. Therefore, instead of concentrating on only one form of masculine identity or one fixed character type and just discussing the star in terms of reductive, essentialist and unambiguous gender stereotypes, it may well be more interesting to approach the question of gender and stardom in popular music from the larger perspective of cultural dialogues. That is, the star ought to be situated in a continuing and shifting cultural debate about gender and sexuality. In what ways have stars like Jagger, or, as in the case of this study, John Lennon, supported or contested contemporary gender norms? How do different star and gender images relate to both established and changing cultural ideas on sexuality?

This section deals with the question of the Beatles' and John Lennon's star images from the point of view of interplay between different kinds of masculinities. In investigating this interplay I shall begin with an examination of how manager Brian Epstein's ideas on masculinity contributed to the Beatles' star image. I shall then focus on the Beatles' and particularly John Lennon's relationship to gender and, furthermore, examine the ways the pop media presented them as men, or, rather, a group of men.

Brian Epstein's strategies in managing the group have been a familiar subject in Beatles histories. To assess Epstein's role, it is useful to go back to the famous moment in 1961 when he first became interested in his future protégés:

> They were rather scruffily dressed—in the nicest possible way or, I should say, in the most attractive way: black leather jackets and jeans, long hair of course. And they had a rather untidy stage presentation, not terribly aware, and not caring very much, what they looked like. (Quoted in Lewisohn 1996, 34–35)

What Brian Epstein witnessed in 1961 was a typical Beatles Cavern Club act. During the performance, the group might smoke, eat, chew, talk, swear, laugh at private jokes, pretend to hit each other, turn their backs at the audience, shout at them and suddenly stop a song midway through. This stage demeanor had been developing in numerous performances in Liverpool and its environs and, particularly, in Hamburg, which the group visited five times between 1960 and 1962.

Brian Epstein's opinion on what constituted a good act differed significantly from the Beatles' bohemian attitude. In 1961 Epstein, then a respectable twenty-seven-year-old, was more interested in Sibelius

3 To Be a Beatle: John Lennon as a Star during Beatlemania, 1963–1966

"Great New Comedy Team": Humor and Popular Music

Let me tell you why they have had such a success in the United States—it is because they are a band of very natural, very funny young men.
—Sir Alec Douglas-Home, Prime Minister, 1964

Two distinctive and intertwining threads were woven through the media reception of the Beatles in 1963: fame and fun. During the previous decade the invasion of Britain by American popular culture, including rock 'n' roll, had been constantly debated, but now the tone had totally changed. While the potential negativity of the phenomenon was occasionally articulated, as in Paul Johnson's famous article, "The Menace of Beatlism," these sentiments were soon buried under the avalanche of positive responses. "You have to be a real sour square not to love the nutty, noisy, happy, handsome Beatles," *Daily Mirror* (November 5, 1963) stated, implying that youthful high spirits and frivolous consumption had displaced earlier suspicions of popular music. What mattered was no longer "taste" but the chart position (Chambers 1985, 52–55).

From the very beginning of their national fame, the Beatles were reputed to be a pop group with great humor. Humor and stardom had by no means been an unfamiliar combination in earlier pop music, but with the Beatles it seemed to reach a peak. Besides being a celebrated group of musicians, the Beatles were also comedians.

The Beatles were not the only pop group to make the audience laugh. The whole beat phenomenon was more or less built on the idea of fun, though to varying degrees. In Peter Everett's rough categorization, two kind of acts emerged: "the cheeky" and "the crooners" (1986, 46). Gerry (of Gerry and the Pacemakers), Freddie (of Freddie and the Dreamers) and Herman (of Herman's Hermits) had the "cheeky charm," while balladeers like Cilla Black and Billy J. Kramer fitted the than popular music. Having been in charge of the record department of the local North End Music Stores (NEMS), which his parents owned, he had some awareness of the musical tastes of young audiences, but managing a pop group was another matter altogether. Epstein had no experience when the Beatles' management contract was formally signed in January 1962. Nevertheless, he understood that in order to fulfill a key undertaking in the contract, to "arrange recording sessions," and thus convince executives of the London music industry of his group's marketability, the Beatles were obliged to change certain elements of their style and follow at least some of the norms of the contemporary entertainment business (Coleman 1989, 82).

For the Beatles to reach pop stardom, Epstein set two conditions, which eventually meant redefining them as performers as well as challenging their ideas on masculinity. First, the Beatles had to improve their professional attitude toward performance. Epstein insisted on punctuality, program planning and professional stage conduct. He even took the Beatles to see the Shadows, then the most popular British band, and pointed out to them how the Shadows bowed to their audience at the end of their act (Davies 1968; Harry 2000). Second, Epstein insisted that the group should abandon their leather jackets and wear suits, shirts and ties. Even though John Lennon and George Harrison in particular were unhappy about this, the group agreed to Epstein's conditions mainly because he promised not to interfere in the most important property of the Beatles, their music (Norman 1982; Coleman 1988). Such maneuvers indicate that Epstein's ideas on popular music stardom and appropriate pop management were based on practices that had become dominant in the late 1950s. In Rogan's analysis of pop management, Epstein followed Larry Parnes' "code of conduct" and represented the model of "The Concerned Parent" (1988, 11). Through paternalistic vigilance, Epstein sought to ensure that the Beatles' image was not compromised by immoderate rebelliousness. The Beatles had to appeal to youthful consumers but also be respectable young men in the eyes of the music industry and older audiences.[9]

What was this ideal of respectability? In the 1950s ideas about "real" manhood in British society were rather one-dimensional. Roughly sketched, the dominant model of maleness of the period was sexless, full of "common sense," decent and, above all, knew his place in social hierarchy (Savage 1991, 156). Certainly, the historical moment was characterized by what could be called hegemonic masculinity. As presented by Carrigan, Connell and Lee (1985), this concept refers to the set of taken-for-granted practices and assumptions that work, apparently "naturally," to support and reproduce the domination of men over women. In his later work Connell has advanced a more elaborate and dynamic model that goes beyond "fixed character types" to a concept of hegemonic masculinity that refers to "configurations of practices generated in particular situations in a changing structure of relationships" (1995, 81). What is thus essential to hegemonic masculinity is that it constantly seeks to defend and maintain a certain kind of patriarchy and heterosexual malehood in a society.

The dominant model of masculinity in the early 1960s did not differ very much from that of the 1950s. To consider one area, definitions of masculinity are often coded through clothes and the associated politics of style. In her study of the history of fashion, Jennifer Craik (1994, 191–92) notes that apart from various male style subcultures, such as the 1950s Edwardian look of the Teddy Boys, men were still unquestionably conservative in their choice of clothing. Thus, in fashion traditional hegemonic masculinity was still dominant. Men, especially older men, took pride in resolutely refusing to notice fashion, rejecting anything they regarded as frivolous, superficial, ephemeral and trivial. Any indication of attention to decorative dress by a man was looked on with suspicion. Craik argues that before the growing interest in design in men's clothes in the 1960s and the increasingly adventurous choices by men in the 1970s and 1980s, codes of male dress and social etiquette were conspicuously characterized by homophobic paranoia. According to Craik, one area where the sanctions momentarily broke down was sporting activities, which permitted display of the body and glorified exhibitionism and physical contact between men. Out of the sporting arena, however, men continued to eschew signs of masculine sexuality and guarded against perceived signs of homosexual and feminine codes.

In relation to the Beatles' style, Brian Epstein's strategy reflected hegemonic masculinity. As far as public image was concerned, the Beatles were to be respectable young men for public purposes. Some of his ideas, however, indicated that dominant models of masculinity were not, ultimately, fixed constructions, but were negotiable and dynamic. In addition to the demands of the entertainment industry and broader social pressures to conform to established models of masculinity, Epstein's managerial activities were to some extent also defined by a factor that has been often discussed in Beatles histories: his homosexuality.

Being homosexual and managing a pop group was by no means an unusual combination at the time. It has been widely agreed that, historically, gay culture has had a strong presence in show business and other areas of entertainment. Since British pop music and the broader traditional entertainment industry were inextricably linked, at least until the mid-1960s, the homosexual network during that period intersected the popular music scene. Rogan points out that in an era when homosexuality was a criminal activity, the music business undoubtedly provided for gays levels of tolerance, solidarity, confidence, personal power, respect and influence that had been unattainable in most areas of labor (1988, 276–77; see also Cohn 1972; Napier-Bell 1982; Frith 1988a). To Mike Brocken (2000), rock music provided gay managers and other gay entrepreneurs with an escape from their ceaseless difficulties with the "straight" society of the 1950s. While Brocken criticizes rock histories' clichéd descriptions of the gay manager attempting to entrap young musicians and generally "patrolling" the burgeoning British beat scene of the 1960s, he is convinced that the rock scene facilitated a relatively gender-free evaluation of character. This is possibly one reason why the Beatles, although they had grown up in a strongly heterosexual ethos, were agreeable to signing with Epstein, whom they recognized as gay. The Beatles, as dedicated rock aficionados, and Epstein, as a gay man, shared the sense of being "outsiders." To Brocken, as much as Epstein signed the Beatles, they, in hope of success and fame, signed him.

While setting limits for musicians, pop music stardom could also present possibilities of emancipation from contemporary mores. Craik's view of sporting activities as a terrain of alternative masculinity could be extended to pop music. In his discussion of sexual deviancy and British pop music, Savage (1991) claims that the changes associated with the Beatles were not so radical, since early English pop had already undercut dominant modes of masculinity and been suffused with suggestions of homosexual desire translated into adoration by females. To Savage, the desperation of late 1950s pop music was a first tentative step toward the imminent sexual liberation that was given formal expression in 1957 through the much debated publication of Britain's Wolfenden Report and its recommendation of the limited legalization of hitherto criminalized homosexuality. From being forced into something clandestine by the dominant culture, sexuality now emerged into the public sphere and caused heated controversy (see Simpson 1994; Spencer 1995). This is not to say that homosexuality became socially approved. In his biography of the Beatles, published in 1968, Hunter S. Davies went no further than hinting that Brian Epstein, who had died a year earlier, was a homosexual. In judicial terms, the Sexual Offences Act in 1967 ended a ten-year battle to decriminalize homosexual acts between men,[10] but the subject itself remained taboo for a long time.

There is enough evidence to sustain the assertion that after having become established in Britain, modern pop music challenged the dominant mode of masculinity. The meeting of gay aesthetics and pop music questioned constructions of male identity that had attempted to exclude characteristics considered feminine. The Beatles' success indicated that there was space for new kinds of masculinities in British culture, and even a demand for them. Even though the Beatles were not the first representatives of British pop to bring gay aesthetics into the mainstream, they did introduce new nuances. Savage writes that while their style originally drew identifiably on the show business tradition, the Beatles soon expressed a fresh sexuality that challenged previous masculine divisions between "stud" and "passive Boy Slave" in popular music (1991, 161; see also 1988b; Frith & McRobbie 1990). Instead of representing the posture of male-gang aggression or boy-next-door pathos, the Beatles were mediating a new kind of pop androgyny.

In his study of heavy metal and sexuality, Robert Walser writes that androgyny provides "male performers (and vicariously, male fans) the chance to play with color, movement, flamboyance, and artifice, which can be tremendous relief from the rigidity expected of them as men" (1993, 133). If we think of this idea in the context of pop music of the early 1960s, stars certainly worked as focal points of sexuality and sexual identities that reflected a modification of notions of respectability and authority. The French star theorist Edgar Morin was convinced that film and music stars "have helped to suppress the masculine costume inherited from British puritanism—the dark clothes of clergyman and sinner alike—in favor of bold, virile outfits (leather jackets, Italian sweaters) and brilliant colors" (1960, 169). In this situation the Beatles expressed male characteristics that had by no means been hitherto absent from popular culture, but which now seemed to attain a new level of pop visibility. As Savage (1991) notes, what had begun as a process of illustrating new ways of constructing and projecting gender and the self quickly became widespread in the public domain, even as a marketing device in the form of Beatle wigs.

As much as there has been discussion about Brian Epstein's role in shaping the relationship between the Beatles and changing ideas on gender, he was not originally involved in creating two of the Beatles' most distinctive ways of presenting a feminine style: their hairstyle and collarless jackets. These had their roots in continental influences, namely the group's interaction with bohemian art circles in Hamburg. It has been alleged that the Beatles' German friends changed the group's hairstyle, persuading them to shape it across their foreheads in a way that was then popular in France.[11] Likewise the collarless jackets, which were designed by Pierre Cardin, supposedly had their origin in a visit to Paris in 1961 when John Lennon, impressed by his German friend, bought a collarless corduroy jacket (Smith 1963d). Compared to Brian Epstein's role, continental influences of fashion and bohemian lifestyle, which generally had begun to be increasingly influential in contemporary British popular culture and music (Grossman 1976; Hebdige 1988), were thus more conspicuous in shaping the Beatles' changing attitude to masculinity. Yet, while Epstein did not invent these particular styles, he placed his imprimatur upon them by encouraging the Beatles to use them. Epstein's role was thus to allow access to different kinds of masculinities and syntheses of gender identities.

In terms of gender the Beatles thus represented something new. Yet they also represented aspects of hegemonic masculinity. In considering the relationship between "old" masculinity and "new" androgyny, it is interesting and somewhat paradoxical to note that in the beginning of their professional career the Beatles, especially John Lennon, showed resistance to symbols of both hegemonic British masculinity and androgynous elements of their visual style. In his famous comment on the "dubious origins of Beatles," Lennon had stated that the group refused to wear gray suits because "we don't like them" (1977, 17). Gray suits supposedly evoked an older generation's conservative tastes, anathema to rock enthusiasts such as Lennon and the other Beatles. After a brief debate over appropriate stage dress, Lennon accepted Brian Epstein's directives but retained signs of minor rebelliousness by having his tie at least a little askew and his top shirt button undone (Coleman 1988).

Yet Lennon was also dubious about style markers that would be considered feminine. He was not eager to adopt the fluffy hairstyle, and he refused to wear eyeglasses in public because he felt they were too effeminate. Such attitudes undoubtedly reflected Lennon's ideas on masculinity. He was reportedly the "tough guy" of the group, occasionally acting as a chauvinistic macho rocker who wanted to exclude all feminine characteristics from his image (Cott 1982b; Coleman 1988).

Even though Lennon and the other Beatles initially rejected markers of the conservative male style and also resisted markers of femininity, they soon drifted into experimentation with an interplay between these elements. One area in which the dialogue emerged was the song lyrics. While there have been studies and analyses of the lyrics of the Beatles' later period, the early stage has been largely ignored, mainly because it has been considered to represent merely a formulaic tradition of pop songs rather than authentic and original self-expression. Yet it can be suggested that the formulaic aspect does not negate pop lyrics' cultural significance. Swedish scholar Ulf Lindberg has alleged that "words *allow people to appropriate songs* for their own needs," as if somebody other than the listener had "peered into their everyday lives and given voice to their inmost feelings, only better than they could ever hope to do themselves" (1997, 19–20). Lyrics of popular songs thus play an important role in creating identities as well as mirroring them. They negotiate with attitudes, beliefs and practices that are dominant in a given society, including the presentation of ideas of masculinity and gender roles. We can find in many songs of Lennon and McCartney such expressions of emotional sensitivity and vulnerability which were incompatible with the orthodox ideal of masculinity. While in "normal" situations such confessions might have been difficult for many men to articulate, in popular music they were sanctioned and even expected. The Lennon-McCartney catalog includes conventional gender scenarios. While the song "A Hard Day's Night," for example, presents the pleasures of love and domestic intimacy in its lyrics, it also emphasizes gendered social spheres. The first person male narrator (given that the singers are male) appears as an active laborer, who works all day to maintain his family and whose woman at home is the reward for his efforts.

Missing home and the loved one who waits there was a common theme in the Beatles' early repertoire, including "P.S. I Love You," "All My Loving," "When I Get Home," and "Wait." When the scenario was inverted, as in "Don't Bother Me" (by George Harrison) and "It Won't Be Long," both of which present the (male) narrator staying at home, the feelings were of loss, loneliness and desperation. Thus, for a man, home represented a place where it is good to return to, but not to be confined in. It should, of course, be remembered that in popular music written lyrics must not be taken at face value. Recent popular music studies have argued that relying purely on words and autonomous content analysis may easily lead to misinterpretations. The way songs are performed, their tone, pitch, timbre and rhythm and the overall musical context can create contradictory meanings which, in addition, are related to audience's reception and ways of experience. In one of the key texts on rock lyrics, "Why do songs have words?" Frith (1988b) suggests that it is not necessarily *what* is said but *how* something is said, or sung, that defines the performer to the audience and constructs the feeling. Furthermore, the star status and the existing star image—Billie Holiday as a suffering artist, for example—of a given performer provides a signifying frame for these feelings and interpretations.

On the importance of how a lyric is presented, it is useful to refer to Booker, who briefly notes that the high point of hysteria in the Beatles' concerts was reserved for the moments when the singers' pitch climbed above the dominant register of male voices (1992, 65). When Lennon and McCartney, at the climax of a song, shifted into a girlish falsetto register, the audience—mainly female adolescents—broke out into hysterical screaming. At such moments it hardly mattered what lyrics the Beatles were singing.

It is important to note that while so many aspects of the Beatles' music, ranging from vocal style to romantic lyrics, opposed monolithic gender identity, this was by no means true of their other public activities. The overall image of the group during Beatlemania was marked by free masculinity and mutual brotherhood. To approach this facet of their image, it is useful to recall that the idea of "freedom" in association with popular music, especially in rock, has historically been very masculinized. Frith writes that beatnik ideology, which derived from the 1940s and was later taken on by rock musicians, equated creativity with unconventionality, and understood bourgeois convention in terms of "roots, home and family" (1984, 87; see also Stump 1997). Mothers and wives represent a mundane routine, which, according to rock myth, constrains and even saps men's creative energy. In the bohemian ideology of rock, women are physically necessary, but psychologically, socially and artistically they represent a negative influence. In the history of rock music, women have been a threat to male independence and male art.[12]

Of all the elements in rock culture, it is perhaps the model of the band that is most schematically romanticized in terms of gender politics. In her ethnographic study of the Liverpool scene, Cohen (1991) notes that male musicians rarely mentioned their girlfriends, and some of them even attempted actively to hide their "embarrassing" domestic life. On several occasions Cohen encountered the belief that basically two things split up a band: women and money. Cohen was able to conclude that marriage and fatherhood did not suit the image many groups wished to present and that women were actively excluded from the music community. Similarly, in her study of masculinity, French scholar Elisabeth Badinter (1995) argues that male groupings such as bands are not expressions of some natural instinct but of the male need to separate himself from feminine domestic space to create a new, masculine culture. While there are several other and usually more explicit reasons to form pop groups, such as a need to create music or a desire to achieve fame and money, it is evident that in the case of the Beatles there were attempts to exclude their domestic space. It is difficult to estimate the extent to which this choice was driven by the "embarrassment factor" noted by Cohen, but it certainly was encouraged by the star production machinery.

From the music industry's point of view, the myth of availability is central to the star phenomenon. In the field of teen pop stardom, this requires that the (male) star needs to be within imaginative reach of his (female) fans. In practical terms this means that the star must promote the image of a free man or at least be careful about how he might answer questions about a wife or steady girlfriend (Steward & Garratt 1984). This was a standard tactic in the early 1960s. Distancing oneself from one's home life was expected in pop stardom publicity and promotion, and the principle that "wedding bells spell death for the big names" (Roberts 1963a, 10) was constantly articulated in the pop press. As suggested in the epigraph of this section, Brian Epstein subscribed to this view, believing that the Beatles were stronger as a unit and with greater potential for stardom without visible bonds to marriage and home life.[13]

In 1963 John Lennon was the stereotype of a pop star whose links to his wife, family and home were excluded from his public image. Lennon had married his longtime girlfriend Cynthia Powell in August 1962, and their first child, Julian, had been born in April 1963, but both events were concealed from the media, fans and even Lennon's colleagues. A teenybop star of that time, Helen Shapiro, who toured Britain with the Beatles in 1963, has recalled that no one on the tour knew about Lennon's marriage (Savage 1995a, 54). When Ringo Starr replaced Pete Best as a drummer in 1962, a few weeks after Lennon's wedding, he was unaware of the situation and was informed about it only some time later. Similarly, Starr's marriage plans in 1965 were revealed to Lennon only a few days before the wedding (Hutchins 1965).

Humor was one strategy for addressing the potential embarrassment that marriage brought to Lennon's image. In a televised press conference, Ringo Starr half-whispered to a curious journalist that John's wife must not be mentioned because "it's a secret" (Solt 1988). Interestingly, Lennon himself seemed to realize the need to reduce the tension between marriage and pop stardom, and that humor was one way of achieving this: "I don't think Ringo's marriage will do the group any harm because he's accepted for what he is, as I was—a sort of comedy character" (Hutchins 1965, 3). A further strategy for appeasing the fans about his marriage was to stress, as in a *Melody Maker* article, that John Lennon was not a solo singer, or solo star, but a part of the group of stars (Roberts 1963a). In the end it was generally agreed that Beatles marriages had no effect on the group's popularity and fan base. "Fan mail does change a bit, for a start, but now they all seem to carry on as if I'm not married," Lennon responded when asked about how Ringo Starr's marriage might affect the group's popularity (Coleman 1965c, 8).

It is an anomaly that while some associations with female roles and identities are often masked or even denied in practices of popular music and stardom, others are foregrounded and valorized. The paradox emerges in two observations made in Cohen's study (1991). First, many commercially oriented groups depended upon their appeal to young women. Second, when Cohen questioned musicians about their musical experiences with regard to their childhood and family life, the hidden importance of mothers, grandmothers and aunts in their lives was often disclosed.

These paradoxes also embroidered Lennon's fame during Beatlemania. The association between the star image and women and the domestic sphere was erratic and uneven. First, it was accepted and often emphasized that the Beatles' success was very much dependent on their fans, especially young females. Furthermore, in his interviews Lennon did not try to conceal the fact that musically the most inspiring person in his childhood had been his late mother, Julia, whose eccentricity, musicality and encouragement were often mentioned (see, e.g., Coleman 1964b; Wonfor 1996a). She would also later be celebrated and mourned in his songs, for instance in "Julia" (1968), "Mother" (1970) and "Mummy's Dead" (1970).

Another interesting feature is that although domestic bonds were usually occluded in the Beatles' image, family and marriage were often used as metaphors to describe the spirit of the pop group. One area where the image of family was emphasized was the Beatles' films. They featured four inseparable young men who spent all their time together, at work as well as their free time. At the beginning of *Help!* (Lester 1965) the Beatles arrive in a normal suburb where they seem to live like ordinary Englishmen; each of them walks to his own front door as though they were neighbors in separate tract houses. Upon entering, however, it is disclosed that it is one large dwelling: They live under the same roof, and indeed even sleep in the same room. This image persisted even after the group stopped touring, as noted in a *Time* magazine article: "The Beatles keep in touch constantly, bounding in and out of each other's home like members of a single large family—which, in a sense, they are" (Birnbaum & Porterfield 1967, 57b).

Another way of modeling the group dynamic, but one that emphasized male solidarity, was the idea of brotherhood. It has been suggested that the ethics of brotherhood, loyalty and solidarity were essential imperatives in the Beatles process (Marcus 1976; Lewisohn 1988; Hertsgaard 1995). The bond between the members of the group was regarded as an important resource at the time as well. Prior to the Beatles, in British pop music stardom groups normally consisted of a leader, usually the vocalist, and a backing group. This model was rejected by the Beatles, even though record executives attempted to nominate a leader for the group. It followed that the Beatles were seen as a cohesive and egalitarian unit. One sign of this was the way they dressed and styled their hair alike. The media conspicuously underlined their similarity by prefixing their individual names with the band name. Furthermore, the press occasionally wondered if the group would remain intact under the pressure of its own celebrity. The usual answer was that because of their shared background, they were able to rely on each other. Their solidarity was part of their star image: "The four Liverpudlians virtually share a world of their own and life for any one without the other three would be all too strange," Chris Hutchins claimed (1964b, 3). The Beatles themselves preserved the image that they were a unit that was more than just a sum of four parts. "We're individuals, but we make up together The Mates which is one person," as Paul McCartney expressed in Hunter S. Davies's authorized biography (1968, 329), emphasizing the group as a male bonding.

While it is clear, even just from a consideration of John Lennon's individual star image, that there was significant space for individualization of each member, during the era of Beatlemania character differentiation took place well within the enfolding identity of the group. Together with Paul McCartney, George Harrison and Ringo Starr, Lennon was, before anything else, a member of the group, a Beatle.[14]

In the framework of gender politics, the Beatles both sustained and revised notions of masculinity. It can be suggested that it was partly this combination that made the Beatles fresh but acceptable. In many ways they seemed to challenge dominant roles of masculinity, but because they did so from within a set of culturally approved attitudes, this challenge was not perceived as a radical threat. Furthermore, the Beatles' humor softened the overall package. First, their high-spirited demeanor eclipsed to an extent some of the threatening implications of a new masculinity. Second, since the Beatles were in many ways comedians as much as musicians, the borders between sanctioned and nonsanctioned were elusive. If challenging gender expectations went too far, it was always possible to defuse it as another Beatles joke.

Playing with gender and identity was thus an essential part of the group, and more so as the 1960s proceeded. Before examining this development and associated changes in John Lennon's rock identity, it is useful to consider the role played by that heterogeneous group to which Lennon and the other Beatles were obligated for their own success: their fans.

"From You to Us": The Dialogue between Fans and Stars

Darling John,
Our plan is to be outside your hotel and when you pass we plan to break the police barricade, run up to you, and handcuff ourselves to you. Will it work?
–Judy & Joyce, Chicago, 1964

No study of stardom can be adequate without some exploration of the fans who sustain the star's celebrity. The Beatles established a strong rapport with a fan base that was international and diverse. It would undoubtedly be useful to study the unexplored heterogeneity of the Beatles' audiences in different countries, and possibly develop versions of the Beatles' reception that go beyond their youthful fan base. Nonetheless, the audiences that confirmed the band's star status appear to have been dominated by young people, and it is this group that I shall focus on. While there has been much written on the Beatles' fandom, including fans' recollections and perspectives, journalistic accounts, the phenomenon summarized as Beatlemania, and even some academic surveys, little has been written on how fandom and stardom worked together during the period 1963–66. Yet, fans played a significant role not only by conspicuously consuming Beatles products but also by attempting to influence John Lennon and the other members of the Beatles as public figures. While I shall touch on the question of fandom as a mass phenomenon, the main focus will be on fans who articulated their thoughts actively and consciously. It is also important to observe how the stars themselves responded to fans and to inquire into the forms and effects of this dialogue between the star and the fan.

In popular music culture, fans can be considered an active and distinct group of "people who avidly follow the music, and lives, of particular performers, and the histories of musical genres, with various degrees of enthusiasm and commitment" (Shuker 1998, 116). In relation to this, *fandom*, the collective term for the phenomenon of fans and their behavior, involves investing a significant part of one's own identity in an identification with some distant other—usually the celebrity—and negotiating the necessary shifts between the world of fandom and the practical contexts of everyday social life (Thompson 1995).

What, then, is the nature of the relationship between fandom and stardom? Historically, the fan has often been understood to be an outcome of celebrity, a passive response to the star system. This view has implied that the fan is brought into existence by the modern celebrity system, via the mass media (Jenson 1992). This idea was seriously challenged in the late 1980s as part of a counterreaction that sought to present fans as an exemplification of a wide range of behaviors, creative activities and discriminating practices. That the fan is not a passive consumer but a culturally active person who creates individual meanings has subsequently been a starting point for many writings, especially in the field of cultural studies. Yet, some scholars have pointed out that having agency is not the same as having power and influence. Theories about the active audience tend, as Negus writes, "to evade the issue of how the activities of consumption might be shaped by the industries involved, how musical products and visual styles are made available for 'appropriation' in the first place and how they may limit the opportunities for creative use and interpretation available at any one time" (1996, 35).

While the idea of cultural agency has dominated current fan theory, we should thus also ask more probing questions about the relationships between the stars, the music industries and the audiences. This is important also because the audience's role in popular music differs to an extent from the audience's roles in other forms of popular culture, such as film and television. To Marshall (1997), fundamental to the construction of the popular music celebrity is the communication of commitment. In this context commitment refers both to the audience's sense of its intimate relationship to the music star, as well as the way the artist communicates commitment in representing the audience. In Marshall's view, this kind of communication of solidarity and close relationship between the performer and the audience "describes the more classical construction of the popular music star to emerge in the twentieth century" (164). Although usually having no institutional power in deciding how to manufacture and distribute stars, active fans can have a crucial effect on star images and stardom, particularly if the star's fan base is large and appears relatively coherent.

A significant feature of the Beatles' fandom was that it was both a social movement and a media phenomenon. Young admirers seemed to follow the Beatles everywhere. Their visibility, extravagant behavior and desperate attempts to reach their idols were widely reported, most conspicuously in television and the popular press. Conspicuous fandom had been part of the stardom of previous male music stars, most notably Frank Sinatra, Johnnie Ray and Elvis Presley, but as Sue Wise (1990) pointedly states, the media had reported fan hysteria, yet ignored fans' own thoughts. Wise argues that no one bothered to ask, or even thought, that fans' views were worth anything. By the early 1960s, however, teenagers had taken their position as a recognizable consumer group in Western societies, and their tastes were determining styles and fashions. Teenagers' economic and cultural significance was acknowledged, and their activities were documented in popular media as well as translated into fictionalized forms of film and literature (Frith 1978; Chambers 1985; Palladino 1996).

There is a general view that the typical Beatles fan during the early 1960s was a young girl. Whenever Beatles historians discuss fandom during Beatlemania, there is rarely any mention of other types of fans. If young males are mentioned, they are not represented so much as fans but as pop and rock aficionados who "dug" the Beatles and whose associated activities were more "serious," such as collecting records and forming their own pop groups. Since such activities did not provide a mass public spectacle, the participants were not recognized so clearly as a coherent group. It was young girls who crowded the Beatles' concerts, attended fan clubs and generally made themselves heard.[15] Ehrenreich, Hess and Jacobs argue in their article on Beatlemania and fans in America that "Beatlemania struck with the force, if not the conviction, of a social movement" that was led and orchestrated by girls and young women (1992, 85; see also Muncie 2000). The most significant feature of Beatlemania was that it gave young white women, in particular, a collective identity, a space in which to lose control and to assert their own sexuality. Ehrenreich, Hess and Jacobs also allege that this development provided a germ for the subsequent feminist movement in America.

It is questionable whether the attendances of young girls at Beatles concerts could be classed as a "movement," in the sense of being an organized activity in a society. They attracted the media's attention, however. After their appearance on the popular television show *Sunday Night at the London Palladium* on October 13, 1963, the Beatles were greeted by the fans outside the building. While estimates of the number of these fans have varied implausibly from eight persons to 2,000, Fleet Street journalists seized upon the phenomenon and thus became complicit in creating the spectacle of Beatles fandom (Norman 1982; Harry 1992). From 1964 to 1966 it was common for journalists to give almost as much attention to the fan hysteria as to the Beatles themselves during the band's tours. The focus of their interest was almost wholly the female fans, who were given access to the media and an opportunity to publicly express their feelings and discuss their love of their idols. Usually, however, fans were presented as a faceless yet powerful mass. For example, it has often been argued that when the screams drowned out the music at Beatles concerts, then it was not the stars but the fans who were the pop spectacle (Coward 1987; Rollins 1998).

Besides reports of hysteria on the Beatles' tours, there were other public representations of fandom. There were two published collections of love letters that were sent to the Beatles by their American fans. Both books, *Love Letters to the Beatles* and *Dear Beatles*, were compiled by Bill Adler, who selected his material from a collection of more than 250,000 letters. Fans in pursuit of the band were portrayed in the scenes of *A Hard Day's Night* (which originally carried the title *Beatlemania*) and, particularly, in the fictitious plotlines of America's *The Beatles Cartoon Series*. The spectacle and representation of fandom were a final confirmation of the star status of the Beatles. Furthermore, these representations also provided models of how real Beatles fans should behave. Screaming, sobbing, shaking heads, pursuing idols and generally acting irrationally were soon institutionalized as appropriate conduct for the Beatles fan by the media.

This mediated image of fandom became inseparable from the Beatles' stardom also because stars and their fans were seen to have a symbiotic relationship: Fans pined for stars and stars lived on fans. What distinguished this relationship from normal relationships between two or more people was that it was rarely characterized by personal contact. Many fans actually saw the Beatles and some of them even met their idols once or more, but for the overwhelming majority of them the Beatles were physically unreachable. The Beatles were sounds on records, images on films, pictures and stories in magazines, and, with any luck, tiny figures standing on the distant stage of some large venue and performing something that, depending on circumstances, could or could not be heard. Yet, fans had their own ways of entering into the process of stardom. In the case of the Beatles' fans, besides attending concerts and physically pursuing the members of the group, strategies to attract the attention of their idols included a range of activites such as sending fan mail, participating in fan clubs and writing letters to fan magazines as well as to other papers. Reciprocally, the Beatles and their backers regarded fans as a significant factor in the fame of the group and attempted to acknowledge them in various ways. As Inglis (1995) suggests, in the early phase of their success the Beatles had to fulfill prevailing star roles and engage in traditional activities. Touring, for instance, was recognized as an important and appropriate way to maintain contact with and ensure loyalty from audiences. It was almost a contractual duty.

Tours were not enough, however. The Beatles met fans occasionally and apparently enjoyed their company in many cases, but since the group had countless supporters, the vast majority of fans remained unknown to them. Thus, fans had to be reached by the products associated with the stars rather than by the stars themselves. In this sense the Beatles fandom was a highly mediated phenomenon. Between the stars and fans there were several conduits for communication and information.

In histories of popular music, the magnitude of Beatlemania has often obscured the fact that in Britain fandom had already established itself as a part of entertainment culture and created protocols and practices that the Beatles then adopted. For example, the first burgeoning of teenage publications took place in the early 1960s, when magazines such as *Teenbeat Monthly*, *Rave* and *Petticoat* and annuals such as *Radio Luxembourg Book of Record Stars* and *Teenbeat Annual* very conspicuously participated in the construction of fandom and its relationship with the stars. Their ambiguous blending of intimacy and community was noted by sociologists Stuart Hall and Paddy Whannel (1990; see also Frith 1978; Savage 1996b), who touched on the issue of teen culture in *The Popular Arts* in 1964, and suggested that teenage magazines had manufactured and to some extent institutionalized fan club conduct. The contrived intimacy of the publications intended to signal the impression that young readers were members of a vast teenage club. To Hall and Whannel, this reflected a changing notion of stardom. They suggested that new pop idols were not remote, like Greta Garbo, "but tangible idealizations of the life of the average teenager—boys next door, of humble beginnings, almost certainly of working-class family"(35). Having been touched by success, however, the stars were different from other young people and had that "something" that was not defined so much by musical talents as by personalities.

The pop star was both a representative and yet a sharply differentiated example of "youth," and was thus often promoted as general role model. This ambiguous status was also reflected in contemporary pop biographies, which regularly balanced general advice with anecdotal specificity. Characteristic of these books was *'Twixt Twelve and Twenty* by the American pop singer Pat Boone, who epitomized the star-as-mentor role by emphasizing the importance of certain general dangers that should be avoided in order to reach mature adulthood and a happy marriage. Girls, for example, must not intrude too strongly, Boone advised (1960, 63–67). In Britain, the successes of Cliff Richard, Adam Faith and Helen Shapiro were accompanied by similar cautionary narratives.

While stars appeared as leaders of an imaginary teenage community, fans themselves also participated in creating their own communities. The American fan Carolyn Lee Mitchell wrote in her memoir that the Beatles' admirers formed a community, almost a big family, whose members must have appeared to the Beatles like "distant relatives" (Mitchell & Munn 1988, 17). Although Beatles fandom embraced a wide range of practices and attitudes, there was clearly a strong element of community coherence, as disclosed in fan club activities. The Beatles Official Fan Club, which was founded in 1962, became a center of fan activity, reaching its membership peak of 80,000 in 1965.[16] It was reported that by the end of 1963, secretaries of the club received approximately 1,000 letters every day. The most important link between the stars and their fans was the fan club's own publication, a magazine called *The Beatles Monthly Book*, which sold 350,000 copies at its peak (Smith 1963e; Harry 1984). Members of the club also enjoyed the privilege of receiving an annual gift, the Beatles' "Christmas Record." Outside the official fan organization, fans continued to pursue related activities. There were, for example, various unofficial Beatles fanzines published in the 1960s. Likewise, local, regional and national fan clubs appeared, as did small and unofficial cliques, some of them fanatically devoted to their idols.[17]

When the Beatles became famous, the apparatus of the teenage culture industry already existed. The Beatles themselves showed no great inclination to present themselves as life mentors and models, and the level of advice they provided in this area was relatively low. In interviews such questions were greeted with absurdist and sometimes irresponsible humor. Furthermore, the Beatles preferred to talk to the music press rather than to teenage magazines simply because they felt that the latter would write their own stories in any case. Teen magazines "are written by people that never leave the office—they just make it all up," John Lennon claimed at a press conference in 1965 (Beatles 1995; see also Braun 1995). However, the existence of the teenage industry meant that the construction of a relationship between the Beatles and their fans could be established relatively easily and beyond the control of the stars. According to Bill Harry's bibliographical listings (1984; 1992), in 1964 there were 17 Beatles books released, most of them hastily written booklets. Beatles-related magazines and special issues of teen magazines were published in enormous numbers all around the world.

Generally, the industry sought to bridge the gap between the star and the fan by traditional methods that were to a large extent outside the control of the stars themselves. In addition to that, the Beatles were obliged to release new records at frequent intervals, undertake international tours, appear in the media and make films. This industry-driven momentum was also evident in the ways their main product, recordings, was published and distributed globally. During Beatlemania the Beatles had no control over distribution, as in the case of the U.S. release of their albums, which differed substantially from the British equivalent.[18]

One area of extraordinary magnitude in serving fan demand was merchandising. This included a wide range of Beatles items, such as suits, shirts, shoes, guitars, miniatures, pendants, aprons, belts, coat hangers, badges, handkerchiefs, jigsaw puzzles, bags, pencil cases, trays, chocolates, bubble gum, posters, toys and other products. In America the most popular items were T-shirts, which at one point sold more than 1 million in only three days, and wigs, which reportedly became a "with it" item, especially at adults' parties. Because of the massive demand for Beatles products and the number of unlicensed enterpreneurs flooding the market, manager Brian Epstein was forced to form his own company to handle merchandising deals, especially in Britain and America (Norman 1982).

From the point of view of merchandisers, Beatles fans appeared to be one vast, ready-made target group. Marketing and selling products for fans during Beatlemania required no elaborate planning about segmented markets, since anything related to the Beatles rapidly turned over without such planning. In spite of this vastness and nonsegmentation, the relationship between stars and fans was also marked by the images of intimacy and community. Fans in particular expressed strong and visible emotions. Articulating feelings of love, friendship and desperation was by no means new in fan discourse, but with gatherings of Beatlemania fans, the public bursts of feeling were of unprecedented extravagance. This overt adoration often attracted scorn and ridicule, especially from adults.[19] Carolyn Lee Mitchell insisted that despite all mockery, fans' feeling were deep and authentic:

> The thing was, you really did love The Beatles. I mean, we *loved* them. It didn't matter if you couldn't hear the music because that became secondary. You screamed because you were excited and in some way you wanted John or Paul or whichever was your favourite to notice *you*. (Mitchell & Munn 1988, 19)

Mitchell's point, that declaring love was related to the desire to be noticed by the object of love, was shared by another American fan, Sandi Stewart, who devoted three years of her life to John Lennon: "You really do believe they can see you, just you alone, when they're up on the stage. That's why you scream, so they'll notice you" (Davies 1968, 210).

These two quotes illustrate fan theorists' current view that while fans have traditionally been regarded as "objects" of mass culture, from the fans' point of view it is the star that is the object. Certainly, Beatles fans sought special confirmation from their idols and thus in a sense appear to be objects of stars, but at the same time they were active subjects, living people who pursued stars in imaginative ways, even though most of them evidently understood that physically reaching stars was more or less a fantasy. Ehrenreich, Hess and Jacobs write that despite their expressions of love and sexual excitement, Beatles fans understood that it was highly unlikely that any of them would actually "marry a Beatle or sleep with him" or "even hold his hand" (1992, 97). Owning a piece of the star was, however, another matter altogether. In their letters to the Beatles, fans often asked for coveted objects that had been touched by the Beatles. It was not extraordinary for a fan to plead "a lock of hair, a smoked cigarette, a thread from your coat, a button from your shirt, a piece of old toast, or a bristle from your toothbrush" (Adler 1964, pages not numbered). Thus, it was not only self-effacing and passive love that marked fans' relationship to the stars but also an active desire to own a piece of the Beatles.[20]

In addition to the physical possession, there was also the question of cultural ownership. I have earlier mentioned how Beatles fans in Liverpool agonized over the possibility that if their favorite group achieved national success they would abandon their local followers. When the Beatles eventually conquered national as well as international pop charts and left Liverpool, original fans felt deserted. In front of television cameras, Cathy, an anxious fan, declared:

> The Beatles, they are the Liverpudlians, they belong to us, they belong to the Cavern. And yes, let the rest of the country have them, let them enjoy them but please let them come back at least once... just to be the same as they used to be with no change at all. It would be fantastic. (Wonfor 1996a)

The question of ownership of the Beatles was also raised in the columns of Liverpool's own rock magazine, *Mersey Beat* (see Big "Beatles" controversy, 1977). In the autumn of 1963 Liverpudlian fans felt disappointed because at that stage the Beatles performed only rarely in their hometown: "They are not our Beatles any longer," some of them complained. Following these local complaints, the paper received "hundreds of letters" from outside Liverpool taking exception to this attitude. "I, for one, am envious of the Liverpudlians, and I think they should be proud to have been able to help the Beatles climb right to the top," a fan from Manchester wrote. From Warrington came a letter that drew on a maritime metaphor: "If you launch the ship you don't expect it to stay where it was launched all the time." When asked whether they had abandoned their original followers, the Beatles justified their departure from Liverpool on the grounds that most of their television appearances had to be filmed "down in London" (Pugsley 1994).

By 1965 the Liverpool-versus-the-rest-of-England debate had dissipated, or rather shifted to another level. Now it was not only the fans from Liverpool, but British fans in general who were worried. "It's ages since they've been on TV or radio. A few appearances would be the least they could do for their loyal fans," wrote a fan from Edinburgh in "From You to Us," a readers' letters column of *New Musical Express* (November 26, 1965, 12).[21] In many readers' letters it was stated that the Beatles "do not work enough" and that they "do not care about their fans anymore" (June 4, 1965, 8). Some fans identified manager Brian Epstein as a principal scapegoat (July 30, 1965, 8). Now that the Beatles had become "global property" and were no longer as accessible as before, their loyalty to their British fans was questioned. It can be argued that when the Beatles quit performing in the following year, this was felt to be an ultimate betrayal of their fans everywhere.

Fans understood that the Beatles were busy and under great pressures, but for some of them that was no excuse for failing to appreciate and reciprocate the commitment of fans. A fan letter written in 1964 illustrates perfectly these two ideas. First, "I guess my whole purpose in writing to you was to let you know that someone else *feels* what you're going through! It's too bad that there's so much red tape, too many mobs, hotels, aeroplanes, and all the rest!" However: "After all, the Beatles—like any other phenomenal stars—belong to their fans! Remember Caruso, Valentino, Elvis, Marilyn Monroe? It's sometimes unfortunate, but true!" (cited in Braun 1995, 125–26)

The Beatles could hardly ignore this highly publicized view that, in a sense, it was the fans who had made them into stars. They were obliged to make some acknowledgment of this "contract" and to observe certain courtesies in the public comments: "Though they seem to be with us night and day now, we love the fans and wouldn't like to think we had lost a single one of them," John Lennon declared—with perhaps an ironic undertone—in an interview appropriately titled "Fans Invade Homes But Boys Love 'em" (Hutchins 1963, 8). Paul McCartney stated that "it's the fans that make it" and that "without them you're nothing" (Laszlo 1965).

Since fans demand a high level of continuity of contact with their stars, the latter often find it difficult to draw the line between proximity and distance. Publicly, John Lennon's attitude toward the real fans, whom he regarded as the most important sector of the Beatles audience

(Coleman 1964b), was sympathetic. Privately, however, he complained that it was impossible to "get away from the fans" who "treat my house like a bloody holiday camp, sitting in the grounds with flasks of tea and sandwiches" and thinking that they have come to "a Beatle National Park" (quoted in Coleman 1988, 194).

It appears that the interdependency between the Beatles and their fans was not unambiguously gratifying. Besides enthusiasm and high spirits, there were also articulations of ambivalence and burdensome anxiety. Yet, the relationship between stars and fans was to remain apparently intact until Jann Wenner's interview in 1971, when Lennon scornfully declared that when the Beatles went to America for the first time, "the chicks looked like 1940s horses" and that the Beatles shamelessly used their fans for sexual purposes (1980, 14, 84). Lennon thus cynically undermined a relationship that had previously been sentimentalized.

The empathetic balance of that relationship, however, had already been disturbed in the mid-1960s as it became increasingly evident that the Beatles had no intention of returning to the stage. By then the relationship of reciprocated courtesies and expectations between the Beatles and their audiences and fans was no longer central to the idea of the Beatles' stardom. What mattered now was not so much commitment to the fans but commitment to the self. In what follows I shall examine this shift, the birth of a new "rock ideology" in popular music culture, and how it sprang from the Anglo-American context and, furthermore, was implicated in the idea of artistry, the role of tradition, and social changes. Popular music stardom was for the first time seriously problematized from within the same culture that created and maintained it. This reconfiguration did not apply only to the Beatles, but to popular music in general; however, it was crystallized most clearly in the development of the Beatles, and particularly in John Lennon's changing status.

4 Changing Popular Music Stardom of the 1960s

From Art School Experience to Swinging London

Being a modern pop star is a sort of way of being intellectual without being intellectual.
—Pete Townshend of the Who, 1967

In the spring 1966 John Lennon was interviewed by the journalist Maureen Cleave for the *Evening Standard*, one of London's two evening papers at the time. This interview has become notorious for Lennon's comments on vanishing Christianity and his assertion that the Beatles were "more popular than Jesus now." When excerpts from the interview were published in the United States later, in July, it was this particular section that sparked a storm of protest, with public burning of Beatles records. The main point of the original interview, however, was not the state of Christianity but John Lennon's way of life. Cleave, who was one of the Beatles' "court journalists," presented Lennon as a pop millionaire surrounded by his wealth, including Tudor house, swimming pool, three cars, five television sets, large collection of books and novelties such as large quantities of model racing cars, strange little winking boxes, a huge altar crucifix and a gorilla suit. In the interview Lennon appeared as a celebrity whose position was thus demonstrated with standard signs of success, but with an eccentric flavor. The essential point is that Lennon seemed to be bored and even unsatisfied with his achievements: "You see, there's something else I'm going to do, something I must do—only I don't know what it is."

To me, the interview, subtitled aptly "A Young Man, Famous, Loaded, and Waiting for Something," is one of the most fascinating primary sources on Lennon of the time, illustrating the beginning of his shift from high-spirited pop stardom to serious pop artistry. In fact, in the career of Lennon and the Beatles, the year 1966 has often been mentioned as a significant watershed that, most notably, meant a growing interest in more ambitious and complex music-making. Moreover, the Beatles' visual image changed to a more individual style, they became interested in the arts, philosophy and drugs, and they managed to reassess their position in relation to the media, the music industry and their audience.

Instead of recounting these changes in this chapter, my intention is to examine the cultural and social background of the change, the context that enabled Lennon and the Beatles to do, as Lennon urged, "something else." While I shall investigate Lennon's changing identity as a star and artist in more detail in the next chapter, here I want to emphasize two sociocultural factors, the so-called art school experience and the idea of authenticity in folk music culture, that had a powerful effect on Lennon's career as well as contributed to the general development of Anglo-American pop music culture in the 1960s. Both of these have been examined in more general terms in popular music studies (see Frith 1981; Frith & Horne 1987; Walker 1987). Nonetheless, I want to discuss them because they form an underpinning for the changing idea of rock musicianship in the 1960s and, more important, because their effects on Lennon's stardom warrant closer investigation than has been conducted by previous studies.

Regarding popular music, and rock music in particular, the most conspicuous change in the 1960s was that the form of culture previously associated with working-class teenagers found a new audience in middle-class youth. The middle-class adoption of the trappings of working-class teenage life had already started in the 1950s—in fact, long before that, if it is understood as a continuation of Western bourgeois society's long-standing idealization and romanticization of "lower" social groups. Yet, it was only in the 1960s that educated middle-class youth finally discovered and then claimed rock music on their own terms (Chambers 1985). In this process of changing class dynamics, middle-class youth sought originality and authenticity from lower classes but articulated the process in terms of an aesthetic vocabulary derived from "high" culture. An important consequence of this development was that musicians, journalists and fans reacted against the discourses of the music industry and attempted to legitimate popular music, or, more specifically, "rock" music (Vulliamy 1977). Within this process of legitimization, the well-educated middle-class rock audience, "and performers from a similar background who were making reference to poetic and literary themes," interpreted their music as more significant than that of a predominantly working-class youth that was stereotyped as being more concerned with sex, love, romance and everyday issues (Negus 1996, 155).

If we focus on the relationship between popular music and education in Britain, it is evident that the 1960s as a social revolution were to an extent a continuation of the process whose seeds had largely been sown in the previous decade and even earlier. The educational hierarchy, which for a long time had reflected relatively inflexible traditions of class-consciousness in Britain, began to change after World War II, when demands for a democratic, egalitarian and competitive society resulted in a more liberal system. The entry-by-merit scheme established in the 11+ exam for the traditional grammar schools opened up the mainstream of higher education in large numbers to working-class and lower-middle-class children. Old barriers to the institutions of further education were not totally demolished, however, since universities and teacher-training colleges usually had their own high academic criteria for entry that distinguished them from the art schools, which had a more informal entry system. It was possible to join the basic intermediate course at a local art school without any official qualifications and on the merits of artwork alone (Evans 1987; Frith & Horne 1987).

One consequence of this development arguably was that art schools attracted young people who were not interested in traditional working careers. In George Melly's words: "The art schools were the refuge of the bright but unacademic, the talented, the non-conformist, the lazy, the inventive and the indecisive" (1970, 131). Whether this is an over-romanticized interpretation or not is difficult to measure. Nonetheless, this was exactly the case with John Lennon, who has come to stand as an emblem of British art school experience. He was artistically talented but also a troublemaker who had difficulties adjusting to the regimentation of the school system. After his poor showing in local grammar school, Lennon had two choices: He could start working or apply for art school. It illustrates Melly's point that, despite failing all his O-levels in grammar school, Lennon was accepted into the Liverpool College of Art on grounds of his portfolio of cartoons and the generous recommendations of his former headmaster. Lennon exemplified the nonacademic-minded student who happened to show some artistic ability and was thus able to enjoy higher education (Walker 1987; Coleman 1988).

While art college was not crucial to Lennon as a place to learn visual arts and design, it provided other abundant benefits. Art schools supplied time and space for young amateur musicians to rehearse and practice, and often also provided their first audiences from other students at the college. Lennon had opportunities to meet other amateur musicians as well as being allowed to use college premises for lunchtime sessions. His group also performed at the school. More important, it was the experience of the community, the free atmosphere, that attracted him. Although the other members of the Beatles did not attend art school, they, too, were fascinated by this atmosphere and were regularly seen at students' parties.[1]

In their notable study of the interconnections between art schools and popular music in postwar Britain, Simon Frith and Howard Horne argue that the "art school experience is about freedom and experimentation, doing what you like and not really caring whether anyone else likes it" (1987, 36). While Frith and Horne identify the changing structure of art schools in the postwar British education system, they also show how certain notions of the artist have dominated this "art school experience," entailing ideas that were to a considerable extent based on bohemian dreams and the romantic ethic: individual creativity, freedom and artistic expression. Art schools were undoubtedly a sort of test laboratory where modern youth culture—musical styles and tastes being one of its most significant determinators—and romanticism met.[2] This interplay appeared first as a bohemian taste for jazz and then shifted to the styles of skiffle, blues, rhythm and blues and, finally, rock 'n' roll. The notable shift was that whereas the jazz phase in the 1940s and the 1950s had provided mostly fans, in the later phase art schools produced also musicians, including such familiar names of the 1960s British rock music as John Lennon, Eric Clapton, Keith Richards, Pete Townshend, Ray Davies, Syd Barrett, Eric Burdon and Jimmy Page (Frith & Horne 1987; Walker 1987).

It has been suggested that without art schools the history of British pop in the 1960s would have been somewhat different, since art students who became rock musicians inflected popular music with romantic fancies.[3] Not all significant British musicians at the time had gone through art school, but those who had arguably "brought into music-making attitudes that could never have been fostered under the pressures of professional entertainment" (Frith & Horne 1987, 86). It may appear strange that "raw" and "primitive" rock music on the one hand and "European" and "high art" ideology on the other hand had such a successful interconnection. One reason for this convergence was that the parties involved shared to a certain extent the same aesthetic principles. Rock may be more vulgar than romanticism, as Pattison argues, but it "adopts the Romantic notion of the primitive as the cornerstone of its mythology and takes over the Romantic conventions associated with it" (1987, 38). To Pattison, rock is thus "another stage in the progress of Romanticism." Pattison's view itself is very much colored by "rock romanticism" and is something of an anachronism, as well as being more applicable to the American rock tradition than the one in Britain. Nonetheless, it has a certain relevance to English pop, at least in the case of John Lennon.

When Lennon entered the Liverpool College of Art in 1957, he appeared as a typical rocker with his greased-back hair, drainpipe trousers, leather jacket and "slim-jim" tie. He adopted a vulgar attitude and confused his fellow students, who generally assumed a more bohemian style of casual jackets with leather elbow pads or duffel coats. Influenced by his closest colleagues, his girlfriend Cynthia Powell and Stuart Sutcliffe, a talented art student and musical colleague whose appearance suggested a combination of bohemian manners, James Dean image and Teddy Boy styles, Lennon began to take on a more "arty" look as well as to adopt a romantic aesthetic. On one occasion, he and his mates were portrayed by *The People* magazine as typical examples of art students living in "the Beatnik horror." Nevertheless, Lennon did not disown his rocker background. By 1960, when he finally abandoned his unsuccessful studies, his idols ranged from Vincent van Gogh to Elvis Presley (Lennon, C. 1980; Coleman 1988; Goldman 1988).

It is, however, important to add that in the early 1960s Lennon's musical expressions and mainstream pop music were not yet inflated by an art school sensibility. Pop music was still considered teen-oriented entertainment. Because of the imperatives of the star machinery, John Lennon and the Beatles attempted to fulfill traditional star roles through conventional star practices, including world tours, media appearances and regular output of recordings. Inglis writes that, as newcomers, the Beatles would have been scarcely able to dislodge the foundations upon which the structure of the popular music industry had been built. By 1966 their status and influence, however, "had provided them with a massive deposit of idiosyncrasy credits, against which they were now able to make repeated and substantial withdrawals," and they began to introduce a range of innovative features into their activities (1995, 60, 67). It was during this period that Lennon articulated in nebulous terms to Maureen Cleave his disillusionment with the traditional role of pop star.

Later writings (Wiener 1985; Evans 1987) have noted how art school provided John Lennon with psychological resources he would need to reinvent his career in the mid-1960s. At the time the significance of this background, however, was not widely recognized: He was considered more a working-class lad transformed into an intellectual rock artist than an art school student making a career in pop music. In the early 1960s Lennon's own thoughts on the subject were sparse, mainly represented in short reminiscences of how life at the art school was so free that he "went potty" (Cleave 1963b) or how he "met some great people and had a laugh and played rock 'n' roll" (quoted in Roylance et al. 2000, 13). In his later interviews (e.g., Sheff 1981) he acknowledged his studies and art school experience more explicitly but without entering into detail. Thus, it is difficult to locate the precise point at which John Lennon began consciously to realize the connections and to articulate and exploit them as part of his artistic image. This question resonates in the area of pop music in general. The first art school graduates to enter the commercial world and to project that art school background into the image and discourse of mass pop culture were not pop musicians but fashion designers, most famously Mary Quant, known as "the mother of the miniskirt," who opened her clothes shop in 1955 and established the boutique as a tool of mass marketing (Frith & Horne 1987). It is reasonable to suggest that in mainstream popular music, attempts to redefine the conception of what it means to be a "pop artist" emerged only after the Beatles had made pop music more respectable for older audiences and the art world. Furthermore, in British pop music, the first cultural moment that conspicuously marked the integration of art and commerce, a social commingling of high and low pop worlds, was the so-called Swinging London scene in the mid-1960s. It can also be suggested that Swinging London was the first concrete embodiment of how the aesthetic training of art school graduates influenced the music they made, and, furthermore, how they attempted to redefine modes of pop stardom.

From 1965, British magazines and papers presented several colorful articles on London as a center of new excitement, but it was a ten-page cover story in the April 15, 1966, edition of *Time* magazine that established the city as a pop capital of the world. Because of the overt media coverage, Swinging London—with its references to eccentric bohemianism, modernity, hedonistic lifestyles, fashion and a classless vitality—has often been criticized as media mythologization (e.g., Hewison 1986, 76–78). Nevertheless, it introduced a new meritocracy that included such young media figures as pop singers, models, actors, fashion designers, photographers, artists and gallery owners. In his otherwise sardonic overview of the phenomenon, Booker writes that these media figures associated with Swinging London "were, in different ways, concerned with the creation of 'images'" and that these "New Aristocrats" subsequently participated in creating images of youth, vitality, creativity, originality and excitement, as well as the myth of a classless society (1992, 19–20). Jonathan Aitken explained in his *The Young Meteors*—at the time the most comprehensive map of the activities of Swinging London—that an integral part of the phenomenon was the attempt to replace the old criterion of taste with the new criterion of talent. Basing his survey on more than two hundred interviews and presenting segments on fashion designers, photographers, art dealers, actors and pop musicians, Aitken concluded that "young people in London with ability and ambition, today more than at any other time are finding it comparatively easy in most fields to achieve success, recognition and good financial rewards at a moderately early age" (1967, 276).

If this definition is placed in the context of celebrity and stardom, the young meritocracy of Swinging London appears as a classic example of what Alberoni calls "the powerless elite." Alberoni suggests that in modern societies there are persons and groups "whose institutional power is very limited or non-existent, but whose doings and way of life arouse a considerable and sometimes even a maximum degree of interest" (1972, 75). From this point of view, it is not essential to decide whether or not there existed a real meritocracy with a real socioeconomic cohesion or whether Swinging London's young aristocracy was merely a loosely affiliated group. What is fundamental is that Swinging London aroused considerable interest, was conceptualized as a cultural phenomenon and introduced the idea of a new class, "the talent class," as Aitken named it. This entailed a significant reevaluation of pop music and stardom. Although frustrated at the promise of social change apparently degenerating into cultural decay, Aitken concluded that "on the highest level the quality of British pop music and pop singers is the best in the world" and that the "pop scene does have a few genuine prophets, poets and artists" (261).

The Beatles, with their changing music as well as their public enthusiasm for the London galleries and various other happenings and fashionable boutiques, symbolized a crossover dynamic in Swinging London. In a sense, for the Beatles, who had already learned to traverse a range of media forms, this new social mobility was just a more elaborate version of their previous practices. But whereas the earlier phase had been contextualized by an idea of the teen idol as an ephemeral commodity confined to a commercial pop industry, there now emerged a compulsion for John Lennon and other pop stars to articulate commitment also to romantic ideas of self-expression and creativity.

This brief ferment in the mid-1960s, the shift from the music industry's established mode of innocence and escapism to the need for music to symbolize and express the feeling of a new generation, provided new criteria for popular music stardom. Musicians redefined their practices. They mixed aesthetic and commercial judgments and reevaluated their identities as stars. Art school experience played an important role in this development, which was given a further impetus by the ethos of Swinging London, but there was also another crucial element involved. Whereas art school experience tended to be associated with a British profile, American folk music culture, with its imperatives of authenticity, would also exert a significant influence on John Lennon as well as other music stars.

Authenticity, Folk Ideology and Cultural Interaction

> *There is something authentic about any person's way of giving a song which has been known, lived with and loved, for many years, by the singer.*
> —Carl Sandburg, poet and amateur collector of folk songs, 1927

Authenticity has indisputably been a central concept in the discourses surrounding popular music. Since the 1980s, when the term conspicuously surfaced in popular music studies, scholars have attempted in various ways to identify authenticity, or, rather, the multiplicity of authenticities in music cultures.[4] Frith (1981; 1986) has been prolific in analyzing the discourses of subcultural and technological authenticities crucial to popular music, while Grossberg (1992a; 1992b) has studied rock fandom and the ideology of authenticity in the postmodern condition. There have been explorations of particular phenomena and styles, as in Marshall's examination of the connection between "boy bands," subculture and authenticity (1997) and Moore's analysis of progressive rock (1993). Peterson (1997) has traced images of authenticity in country music, Taylor (1997) has scrutinized world music markets and Thornton (1995) has studied artistic and subcultural authenticities in dance club cultures.

For the time being, authenticity as a value has firmly established itself in popular music. Thornton writes that "authenticity is to music what happy endings are to Hollywood cinema—the reassuring reward for suspending disbelief" (26). In an age of endless representations and global mediation, the experience of musical authenticity is valued as a counter to alienation and dissimulation. It works, especially in the field of popular music, "as a balm for media fatigue and as an antidote to commercial hype" (26). Thornton suggests that authenticity has remained the most important value ascribed to popular music: It continues to provide a powerful tool for musicians, critics and audiences to frame and evaluate music, and, as such, serves an important ideological function.

Although notions of authenticity thus seem to pervade popular music culture as a whole, there are areas where it is of particular significance. The most common locus has remained the production of music: It has been regarded as pivotal that there is an element of auteurship and self-expression present in the musician's activity (Shuker 1998, 20). Generally, how the "authenticity" of the individual performer is determined has been dependent on "how he or she expresses the emotionality of the music and his or her own inner emotions, feelings, and personality and how faithful the performer is to the intentions of the musical score" (Marshall 1997, 150).

With respect to this view, the idea of authenticity has been one of the central criteria of popular music stardom. While stars have often been regarded as the result of fabrication, there have also been esteemed figures, like John Lennon, who can be considered both stars and auteurs, "combining a high level of creativity and innovation in their work with broader media interest and public visibility" (Shuker 2001, 116). It seems that in order to understand the particular kind of authenticity and rock stardom that has been applied to Lennon, *rock auteur* is the key term. Shuker (2001, 118–19) has listed several interlocking criteria that critics and fans generally invoke to identify the rock auteur. These are: the ability of the auteurs to break new ground, innovate and cross or blur genre boundaries; the ability to perform their own original material, especially by writing their own songs; the exercising of a measure of control over various facets of the production process; and some sense of personal overarching vision of the music and its relation to the canon. Auteurs also usually maintain a high profile over a period of time.[5] Although these criteria converge to accord the auteur figure an iconic, near-mythic status in rock, it should be remembered that different rock genres understand and express the idea of the auteur in nonidentical fashions. This is so because rock culture incorporates different kinds and competing definitions of authenticities. According to Keightley (2001, 136–39), within these factions of rock authenticity we can identify two major tendencies, romantic authenticity and modernist authenticity, both of which seek to contest the mass pop mainstream and to create and organize internal differences within rock culture. While romantic authenticity draws upon tradition and continuity with the past, a sense of community, sincerity, direct expression and "natural" sounds, modernist authenticity emphasizes experimentation and progress, the status of the artist, obliqueness and "shocking" sounds. The problem with this categorization is that, especially in the field of stardom, it is difficult to find performers who could exclusively be labeled either "romantic" or "modernist." Keightley admits that these two modes are tendencies rather than absolutes and often overlap in a single genre or performer. In fact, it is those performers who deploy romantic and modernist authenticity more or less equally who are often regarded as auteurs in rock culture.

Before we enter more closely into this relationship between rock auteurship and stardom, it should be noted that understanding authenticity merely as a property of music, musicians and audiences does not do justice to the overall picture. To Stokes, because of various ways in which authenticity is structured, defined and employed, it is important to see authenticity as "a discursive trope of great persuasive power"

(1994, 7). It focuses a way of talking about music, a way of saying to people what is really significant about music. Viewing stardom and authenticity as discursive constructs, it is necessary at any given time to identify the subject producing statements of authenticity and recognize different categories through which such views are mediated. For example, authenticity may work as a powerful marketing tool. As illustrated in Peterson's *Creating Country Music: Fabricating Authenticities* (1997) and Taylor's *Global Pop: World Music, World Markets* (1997), the idea of originality clearly appears central to the production and circulation of particular musical genres and stars.

Scholars of popular music seem to agree that even though there exist assumptions about an untainted, original and actual essence in popular music, authenticity is not "natural" but a cultural construction that is deployed with considerable symbolic force and is constantly used as an argument to justify and legitimate certain forms of music. I mentioned in chapter 1, section 3, "Star History, Star Theories and Popular Music," that debates on what is "real" and acceptable in popular music were already active in the late 1920s and early 1930s, when new technologies changed the ways music was produced, distributed and experienced. Having its roots in the technological and social changes of the late nineteenth century, the dilemma of authenticity in popular music considerably predates the 1960s. For example, Peterson (1997) argues that in the United States country music authenticity and originality had been fully fabricated as early as 1953. Nevertheless, it was in the 1960s that authenticity shifted from being part of a more or less latent cultural agenda in Western popular culture to become a serious, audible debate (although not always explicitly in those terms), generating a distinctively Sixties rock formation.

How, then, was the Sixties version of rock authenticity developed and how was it related to stardom and John Lennon? First, it can be suggested that the Sixties rock formation predominantly has its roots in American popular music culture, particularly in the shifting arguments about the musician and the community. Second, the influence these arguments had on John Lennon's identity as a musician, artist and star was the result of the dynamics of cultural interaction between Britain and America in the mid-1960s.

It has been argued that in the 1960s American art schools did not seem to have produced students with music-making interest to the

same extent as in Britain (Frith & Horne 1987; Walker 1987). Nevertheless, popular music was the subject of reevaluation also in America.
Since music was needed to express the spirit of a new rock generation
and symbolize cultural and political changes, the role of the musician
had to be redefined. Whereas in Britain art schools provided tools for
solving the problem through ideas regarding personal creativity and
commercialism, in the United States the key was folk music and its
ideological rhetoric.

Frith (1981) has asserted that the American folk music movement
and the ideology of folk were the main components in developing authenticity as a basis of rock musicianship and rock stardom in the late
1960s. The so-called folk argument entered rock music via the American "folk revival" of the 1940s and 1950s. Central to the folk argument
was that there was no distinction between folk artist and folk audience:
Authenticity in folk music meant that music was made directly and that
the artist was the spokesperson of her or his community.[6] Frith suggests that during the 1960s these ideas were centralized in mainstream
popular music, as the folk emphasis on songs and lyrics, on the performers' honesty and insight, was adapted to the commercial needs of
rock. At the same time, however, the original folk argument was subtly
transformed. The democratic aspect of folk, that anyone could play folk
music, was welded to the idea of individuality, that not anyone could
play it with *originality*. Although folk rockers thus individualized folk's
view of authenticity, they still wanted to provide the feeling of the special relationship between the artist and the audience. This view of community was responded to by the new rock culture, which was largely
composed of middle-class youth. Thus, rock music was not made by a
community, but provided a particular sort of communal experience, a
fantasy of rock's own identity and, furthermore, a myth of the particular "Sixties rock generation," which found its voice in Woodstock and
other massive rock festivals.

One important consequence of this development was that "rock"
and "pop" became differentiated. From the contemporary point of
view, to define rock music comprehensively and exclusively as a particular genre or a particular form of popular music has proved to be too
difficult a task for scholars. Rock is an open category, which means that
discussions of rock may be engaged with in different ways and the music can take on different characteristics simultaneously (Moore 1993;

Fornäs 1995; Negus 1996; Keightley 2001). While contemporary rock appears as too complex a hybrid to categorize in scholarly terms, there was greater unanimity on the definition of rock in the late 1960s. At the time, "rock" was widely perceived in relation to its "other": "pop." While "rock" became synonymous with real, original and true music, negative epithets such as *inauthentic, commercial* and *fake* were assigned to "pop." The usual claim in the 1960s was that despite being popular music, "rock" music was not controlled by the entertainment industry to the same extent as "pop" music. Rather, it was an authentic expression of a new generation. Rock, which thus was as much an ideological formation as a musical category, was attached to "the people," but since rock also carried connotations of self-expression and creativity, art, and the romantic view on art in particular, became the other key determinant (Frith 1981). Rock was part of a "long tradition of folk art," wrote Carl Belz (1969, 3), one of the first rock historians to articulate this dualism.

When "rock" distanced itself from "pop," it also meant redefining stardom. Since the *star* had been used as a marketing term in "pop," for rock fans it carried questionable associations with superficiality, artificiality, corruption, calculation and production. In a sense it would perhaps be more appropriate to speak of the celebrated rock auteurs of the 1960s as opinion leaders or heroes rather than stars, but the fact remains that as visible public figures they still formed part of the phenomenon of stardom. The other important feature in this development was that while at the time "rock" was perceived as more radical than "pop," later studies have noted the more reactionary aspects of the former. For example, "rock" was to a considerable extent a gendered conception. "Pop" was primarily aimed at creating "affective sensations" that were identified with a female audience, while "rock" formation grounded itself "through an emotional connection to performance that was inherently narcissistic, in that its male performers appealed predominantly to young, male audiences" (Marshall 2000, 167).

In this binary scheme, in which rock was metonymic for authenticity and pop for artifice, authentic rock became masculine and artificial pop became feminine. In the gender hierarchy of rock culture, the masculine represented higher status and values and thus reinforced traditional gender hegemony (Coates 1997; Whiteley 2000). While American folk music culture introduced a considerable array of celebrated female artists, such as Joan Baez, Judy Collins, Buffy Sainte-Marie and Mary Travers (of Peter, Paul and Mary), this gendered model was complicit in preventing them from becoming eminent rock figures. Such a role was reserved for men, especially Bob Dylan, who indisputably came to embody the coupling of the folk argument to the rock argument.

In the early 1960s Bob Dylan had appeared as a contemporary equivalent of the 1930s folk hero Woody Guthrie, a hobo-like bard who was devoted to romantic folk stories. In 1963–1964, however, he became a leading singer, poet and visionary of the protest movement in America. Dylan was regarded as a social critic who could penetrate behind the masks of those in power (as in "Masters of War") and an apocalyptic allegorist committed to prophecies of nuclear disaster ("A Hard Rain's A-Gonna Fall"). Primarily because Dylan himself was unwilling to wear the mantle of a folk leader, his lyrics changed from social statements to a more mystical and personal direction. Influenced by British beat groups and their American equivalents, especially the Byrds, he also espoused an electric sound. In the history of 1960s popular music, Dylan's change from a solo acoustic balladeer to a rock band leader has remained a crucial moment. It was also a catalyst for the heated debate on stardom and the cult of originality, materializing especially in the American protest magazines *Sing Out!* and *Broadside* in 1964–1965. Following the release of his fifth album, *Bringing It All Back Home* (1965), which introduced electric backup in seven songs, Dylan was vigorously accused of trying to pursue a false kind of celebrity[7] (Anderson 1981; Shelton 1986).

Although the mythologizing of Joe Hill, Woody Guthrie and other folk legends had demonstrated that folk culture itself centered on forms of hero worship (Hampton 1986), it was now mass culture and the interventions of the music industry that were seen to violate the purity of folk practice and discourse. For the patrons of folk originality, Dylan's performance with a rock group at the Newport Folk Festival in 1965 was the final proof that their former hero had indeed been corrupted. This concert has remained the symbol of the beginning of the new rock music and the end of the folk revival.

Dylan's main contribution to the development of rock auteurship was not in his decision to make folk electric—in fact, the Byrds had already done it with their chart-topping version of Dylan's "Mr. Tambourine Man"—but in bringing a new kind of lyrics into pop music and hence transferring folk's authenticity and the ideal of self-expression to rock ideology. Dylan's ambiguous lyrics guaranteed that he was soon understood more as a rock poet than a pop star. As Laing noted in 1969, rather "than any formal or technical innovation, Bob Dylan gave pop music a new idea of itself and gave its musicians a new sense of the possibilities of the pop song" (167). Mainly because of Dylan, "free," "change" and "progressive" were carried into the vocabulary of rock musicians.

Frith notes that the main paradox of rock ideology in the 1960s was that "performers' claims to represent community (unlike the usual 'plastic' pop singers) were supported by the marks of their individuality" (1981, 164). Like their romantic predecessors, rock artists on one hand represented folk and on the other hand were allowed — if not obliged — to stand as modern equivalents of poets and artists of genius. It was not unusual, for example, for the representatives of the new rock press and counterculture journals to treat highly regarded rock artists (Dylan, the Beatles, the Rolling Stones) as geniuses who in some mystical way were at the center of what was happening or, even more, ahead of their time. Dylan, for example, was elevated above other folk artists.

Plaudits of Bob Dylan as a major cultural figure who is always "one step ahead of the game" (Landau 1969, 217) were characteristic of American rock journalism, but the new folk rock with its aura of authenticity was also greeted similarly in Britain. Because of his electric backup, Dylan's 1966 tour in Britain was first received with uncomplimentary reviews, but it was not long before the tone changed, as British pop stars began to defend him and praise his innovativeness (Shelton 1986; Marcus 1997). Dylan had already enjoyed respect among British pop musicians, as exemplified in *Don't Look Back*, D. A. Pennebaker's famous documentary film of his 1965 tour. It may appear strange that rather than studying their own national folk scene, which at the time was in a vigorous phase, the white rhythm and blues artists and pop "talents" of Swinging London were inclined to be more impressed by the American folk rock hero. The main reason for the Dylan cult among British musicians was that Dylan's star image, which reconciled various cultural binarities such as high/low and authentic/commercial, provided a solution for dilemmas in pop culture. He wrote his own songs and seemed to enjoy considerable artistic freedom, despite being signed to a major recording label, Columbia. Moreover, he was fun!

Pennebaker's film documents how Dylan's press conferences at the time were marked by jokes and an absurdist sense of humor, suggesting that he was willing to toy flippantly with his star role and to question the seriousness associated with his music. If British pop stardom at the time was developing toward interplay between style and difference, humor and seriousness, romantic visions and modernist artistry, Dylan's attitude demonstrated that pop stars were on the right track. His metamorphosis from a folk hero to a folk rock idol signaled that the musician could indeed be the auteur and the star simultaneously.

It can be suggested that American folk ideology and British art school experience were the two most powerful forces underpinning the rock auteur in the 1960s. Their combined impact on the rock auteur seems to be reflected also in the fact that the United States and England were the most influental nations to produce pop music and define musical styles and fashions in the 1960s. Furthermore, after the British Invasion in America, musical innovations seemed to flow freely back and forth between America and Britain. Initially, American rock music had been the most significant source of inspiration for British beat groups, but in the wake of the British Invasion new American pop groups started to adopt various imageries of Englishness and musical ideas from their beat colleagues. In spite of different national traditions, new rock music was considered a phenomenon able to cross geographical boundaries and, in a sense, to form an international community.

Yet, the free musical interchange between America and Britain is partly a mythologized picture cherished by rock histories, star biographies and other memoirs. While musicians, the media and audiences in the United States welcomed the British Invasion, the American music industry was concerned to see domestic teen idols slipping down the charts. What followed was that in spring 1965, several British artists and groups faced problems with obtaining permission to work in the United States. Sandie Shaw and Twinkle were banned outright from appearing in the country (Shaw would have been accepted if she had had an American band to accompany her) while for the Hollies, the Animals, the Zombies, Freddie and the Dreamers, the Nashville Teens and Wayne Fontana and the Mindbenders, entry would have been approved subject to various bureaucratic restrictions. As reported by Derek Johnson (1965, 5; see also Dawbarn 1965a; Whitcomb 1983), a columnist for *New Musical Express*, the United States justified the constraints on the grounds that British performers were "insufficiently well-known in America to warrant them working there" or that they had "nothing original to add to the American show business scene." Johnson commented that the obvious reason for the policy was not based on performers' insufficient popularity but on "sour grapes," the fear that the British Invasion would do serious damage to the American music industry. The initial decision to regulate the flow of foreign pop performers rested with American labor groups, especially the American Federation of Musicians and the American Federation of Radio Artists, which advised the immigration authorities about British musicians' working permits. For a short time there were speculations as to whether American pop groups should, in turn, be banned from Britain, but as soon as the British Invasion started to show signs of subsiding, the controversy decelerated.[8]

While in the overall picture of 1960s popular music this incident may be regarded as a minor episode, it signaled two important things. First, even though a tendency was emerging to understand new rock music as an autonomous realm of musicians and their community, institutionalized music policy still played an important role in the daily praxis of musicians and in the interconnection between music cultures. The second point is that this episode strengthened hierarchical relationships between performers. While the major ports of entry attempted to shut their gates to British pop performers, the episode had no apparent effect at the highest level of star hierarchy and did not prevent stimulating cultural interaction at that level. The Byrds and the Beatles, for example, were "exchanging tricks and innovations" and discussed the pros and cons of stardom (Taylor 1987, 20).

This international rock meritocracy resembled the pattern of Swinging London: Both were based on the paradoxical convergence of pop hierarchy and classless vigor, elitism and democracy. In rock culture this meant an international yet — since it was to an extent created by the media — imaginary star community that was predominantly reserved for talented and established male musicians. John Lennon would later recall his days of fame in Swinging London as "a great period," during which the Beatles "were like kings of the jungle" and the whole scene "was like a men's smoking club" (Wenner 1980, 88, 90). Such a description could as well be applied to the international rock hierarchy of the 1960s.

The Beatles and Bob Dylan were indisputably among the most eminent figures inhabiting the masculinized community of rock musicians. During the period from 1964 to 1966, they also influenced each other. This is suggested in Inglis' detailed analysis of the dynamics of musical and professional interaction between the Beatles and Dylan. Inglis argues that by fulfilling four important conditions, "common goal, voluntary action, active cooperation, and self-control," the Beatles and Dylan created a synergy that transformed the contours of popular music in the 1960s and has done so since (1996, 75–76). The common goal was commercial success and musical development, meaning that the artistic environment in which the Beatles and Dylan found themselves could be dismantled and restructured. By "voluntary action," Inglis emphasizes that there was no legal, contractual, or managerial compulsion for them to act in pursuit of these goals. Relating to this, active and productive cooperation in pursuing goals was likewise satisfied by both sets of performers, especially during 1964–1966. Finally, the Beatles and Bob Dylan enjoyed and used their status in ways that emphatically realized and celebrated artistic self-determination.[9]

Inglis also examines the particular relationship between Lennon and Dylan, suggesting that they appeared to be a mutual source of influence, even though their contacts were limited to irregular meetings and they did not appear to have contributed to each other's recordings or concretely produced any joint compositions. The most important characteristic of their artistic relationship was that it was founded on the mutual recognition of each other's significance (72–74).

What needs to be added to Inglis' analysis when studying the significance of Dylan's influence on Lennon's stardom are the more specific questions of self-expression and self-identification. Dylan clearly inspired Lennon and encouraged him to reconfigure his status and identity as a pop star. Regarding the Beatles' music, the first obvious example of Dylan's influence was heard in "I'm a Loser" in 1964. The song, originally penned by Lennon, was musically closer to country and western than folk music, but its introspective and despondent lyrics contained familiar, Dylanesque metaphors about "a clown" who is beneath the mask "wearing a frown." At the time Lennon made no secret of the fact that the song was inspired by Dylan. He even clarified that "I could have made 'I'm A Loser' even more Dylanish if I tried" (Coleman 1965a, 3). Analysts of Beatles songs have proposed that Dylan's influence culminated in the following year in "You've Got to Hide Your Love Away" (Robertson 1990; Hertsgaard 1995; MacDonald 1995; Turner 1996).

These musical influences are relatively easy to trace, and, as noted above, they were occasionally disclosed at the time. Regarding the ideological side of Dylan's influence, finding the exact moment when Lennon started to present himself more as a rock auteur than a pop entertainer is more difficult. Nevertheless, there have been attempts to define this moment in the Beatles and Lennon historiography. Regarding Lennon's music, was self-reflection already evident in the lyrics of "Misery" and "There's a Place," on the Beatles' debut album, as some critics (e.g., Robertson 1990; Turner 1996; Harry 2000) have argued? Or was the starting point the "emotional authenticity" of "Help!" (Wiener 1985, 144; see also Riley 1988; MacDonald 1995)? Even though "Help!" might originally have been about Lennon's identity crisis and the true cry for help, such interpretation seems to have emerged largely as a result of later reflection. If Lennon himself "didn't realize it at the time" but wrote the song because he was "commissioned to write it for the movie" (Sheff 1981, 110), it is reasonable to suppose that hardly anyone else did either. Certainly such an interpretation was not sanctioned by the Beatles' management or the media. Furthermore, while audiences might have perceived "Help!" or the set of other Beatles songs as self-expressive, at the time such assumptions did not enter into public discussion.

There were several reasons why questions of rock auteurship were not posed within the pattern of John Lennon's starnet. First, pop songs were not explicitly presented as autobiographical. More concretely, "Help!," or whatever song originally written by Lennon, was not credited as Lennon's composition but as a Beatles song, another celebrated piece in the output of Lennon and McCartney's songwriting. The third point is that the Beatles' musical arrangements, such as the mellow band sound and relatively fast tempos, made even the most dramatic songs like "Help!" (which, it must be added, was the title song of the Beatles' comedy film) sound like an expression of optimism. Finally, the most significant barrier to the projection of conspicuous subjectivity in Lennon's songs was his star image. Several biographers (Christgau & Piccarella 1982; Koski 1986; Robertson 1990) have noted how the collective positiveness of the group, sustained by mediated star material, occluded frictions. Since the Beatles' first steps into the limelight were accompanied by humorous effects and an explicit desire for success, it would have been difficult to recognize sentiments of loss, pain and anguish, whether they had been consciously written into the songs or not. "Authenticity" during Beatlemania meant commitment to the teenage audience and celebration of success rather than to the ideal of individual artistry. It is, in fact, significant that Lennon's original proposal for the title of the Beatles' first film, before Ringo Starr's phrase "a hard day's night" replaced it, was "Authenticity" (Hutchins 1964a, 14).

Even though Lennon himself initiated the tendency to reinterpret his past in the late 1960s, it should be borne in mind that the question of authenticity and auteurism is not only the property of the musician. Later interpretations of Lennon's songs, as documented above, have played an important role in our understandings of the "real" John Lennon and his intentions. Yet, it could be alleged that with their attempts to trace Lennon as an artist, critics and rock historians have in some cases fallen into overpsychologized conclusions and thus emphasized and constructed the profile of the autonomous artist. This is to say that the rock authenticity of Lennon has to a considerable extent been a matter of retrospective mediation.

During Lennon's career, the idea of authentic rock artistry was not explicitly articulated and mediated until about 1967. I have maintained that his development as a rock auteur and the establishment of a canonical rock hierarchy were sustained by the ideas, principles and functional modes that British art school experience and American folk ideology provided as they started to permeate popular music in the mid-1960s. These propositions will be examined in more detail in the following chapter. I have thus far approached Lennon's career thematically, but now I shall modify my approach and examine certain events and changes in Lennon's life. First, Lennon's adoption of granny glasses and his colorfully painted luxury car provide particular platforms from which to explore Lennon's public self-construction as a star. Following this, I shall once more revert to the relationship between John Lennon and the Beatles, focus upon their album *Sgt. Pepper's Lonely Hearts Club Band*, and examine questions of mediation and technology in 1960s popular music.

5 Signs of John Lennon's Rock Stardom

The Case of the Granny Glasses

If you're going to wear glasses, then really make it obvious you're wearing glasses.
— *The drummer Jerry Allison to Buddy Holly*

On September 5, 1966, John Lennon flew to Hannover, Germany, to join the filming of Richard Lester's *How I Won the War,* in which he would take the supporting role of Private Gripweed. The next day he was given a regulation army haircut and handed a pair of spectacles to wear for the part. While the world premiere of the film would be delayed until October 1967, the change in Lennon's style, especially his hairstyle, immediately made news. The adoption of round, wire-framed "granny glasses," however, had the more far-reaching effects on his star image simply because while his hairstyle would frequently change, the glasses remained a permanent part of his image until about 1973.[1] These glasses came to symbolize the "new" John Lennon, and eventually became known as "Lennon glasses." They also influenced musicians, artists, bohemians, counterculture activists and young people to wear similar glasses (Wiener 1985; Coleman 1988).

The change in Lennon's image clearly expressed the Beatles' transition from a collective identity to a focus on the individual. Lennon's choice to adopt glasses was, of course, only one episode in this development, which in a broader sense reflected a rupture in popular culture and the reevaluation of pop stardom. While analysts have paid close attention to Lennon's music in order to trace his artistic transformation and, in some cases, have elaborately contextualized it, his other "signs" have often been disregarded. Yet, they formed an elementary part of Lennon's stardom at the time. My argument is that in addition to musical achievements, Lennon's "new look," embodied in the adoption of round-rimmed glasses, deeply affected such issues as reinvention of identities, fashion and the search for authenticity in popular music.

John Lennon clearly contributed to the emergence of eyeglasses in the iconography of popular music. Prior to him, standard horn-rimmed spectacles played an important role in Buddy Holly's "soft" pop image, while similar glasses on British pop stars, for example Hank Marvin (of the Shadows), Brian Poole (Brian Poole and the Tremeloes) and particularly Freddie Garrity (Freddie and the Dreamers), emphasized stars' comic attributes. Sunglasses were occasionally used to achieve a certain effect, as exemplified in Roy Orbison's "mystery image," although on Ray Charles and Stevie Wonder they were more an emblem of their blindness than a particular "soul style" (which, in this sense, was reinforced by the *Blues Brothers* film in 1980). While bespectacled stars were unusual in pop music, in various youth and urban subcultures glasses, particularly dark glasses, had been used as a sign of differentiation. Since the 1930s sunglasses had been associated with sport and other leisure activities and Hollywood stars' lifestyles, but after the war they became popular also among bohemian youth (Corson 1967). A few years later, within the British mod culture there existed a fascination with tinted glasses, presumably originating from the Jamaican "rude boy" style (Chambers 1985). At the same time, among the West Coast youth culture in the United States, exotic glasses began to signify fashionable attitudes. Roger McGuinn, the leader of the Byrds, was one of the first pop stars who consciously attempted to create a new kind of pop intellectual image with his rimless, rectangular glasses, originally purchased from a novelty shop (Rogan 1991).

There appears to be no documentation of Lennon's motives in adopting round-rimmed glasses as a permanent part of his image. It might be that the decision merely reflected subcultural enthusiasms and styles of the time, or an increasing interest in glasses in general, or that Roger McGuinn, personally known to Lennon, might have influenced him. Whether or not just a fashion whim, what is evident is that Lennon indeed needed glasses. According to biographical writings, he was seriously nearsighted and was dependent on optical assistance just to negotiate everyday life. Before the adoption of round glasses, Lennon had had a pair of black horn-rimmed spectacles, but he was clearly dissatisfied with them. He may have worn them in the recording studio, surrounded by his closest friends and colleagues, but he would remove them immediately in most of the other social situations and thus prefer to be half-blind rather than to be seen with glasses on.[2] During

Beatlemania, Lennon experimented with contact lenses despite the fact that at the time such devices were technically undeveloped and inconvenient to use. They regularly proved to be an occupational hazard and Lennon would repeatedly have to hunt for lost lenses (Lennon, C. 1980). In this connection, it is obvious that John Lennon's image as a "witty" Beatle who "peers down his nose, arrogant as an eagle" (Cleave 1966) was partly a result of his nearsightedness and reluctance to wear glasses.

It was, however, no secret that Lennon had glasses. The subject was treated, for example, in a *New Musical Express* interview (Smith 1963a, 10) in which it was explained that Lennon does not use glasses on stage because he "doesn't want the group to be accused of any imitation" of the Shadows (from whom, however, the Beatles had adopted stylish clothes and elaborate stage mannerisms) and their solo guitarist Hank Marvin, who had similar, heavy-rimmed glasses. Lennon evidently felt called upon to justify his choice not to wear glasses. Michael Braun's *Love Me Do!* includes an illustrative episode in which the Beatles are preparing for a performance, reporting that "John is ostentiously removing the glasses he constantly wears off-stage. 'Mustn't spoil the image', he says" (1995, 44).

Although it remained unclear whether Lennon was thinking of his own star image or the collective image of the Beatles, the public presentation of the glasses seemed to matter to him. But did they really matter in terms of "image"? To answer this, Braun's report includes another and perhaps more telling episode. Lodging in a Paris hotel suite and waiting for the evening's performance, the Beatles received a petition delivered by a special messenger and signed by two hundred girls. It contained a list of demands for the group, including for "John Lennon to wear his glasses on stage" (79). If this most important segment of the Beatles' audience, female teens, did not object to Lennon's glasses, then the suggestion that the glasses spoiled the image seems inadequate. In fact, there appears to be no evidence that manager Brian Epstein or other promotional forces actively opposed Lennon's glasses and directed him to remove them. It seems that the avoidance of glasses was Lennon's own decision about his identity as a pop star and, more generally, as a man. By his own recollection he was very concerned about his manhood: "I spent the whole of my childhood with shoulders up around the top of me head and me glasses off because glasses were sissy, and walking in complete fear, but with the toughest-looking little face you've ever seen" (Cott 1982b, 189).

To Lennon's mind, wearing glasses had been an effeminacy that for a man suggested weakness. In the aspiration to stardom, Lennon had abandoned his jeans and leather outfit and accepted new looks, such as a fluffy hairstyle and collarless jackets, but wearing glasses would have been too much for him. It could be speculated that heavy-rimmed glasses might have complemented the Beatles' image as a comic male group, but evidently Lennon was reluctant to emphasize that kind of humor and risk compromising his masculinity. Why, then, did he suddenly begin to wear round-rimmed glasses that, even more than his previous black horn-rimmed glasses, suggested femininity, and even senile infirmity in the term "granny glasses"?

It is significant that Lennon adopted his new glasses originally for a film role that, for the first time, was not himself, his "real" personality. Any associations between eyeglasses and femininity in the film reflected on the character he was playing rather than on John Lennon. In any event, however, such associations were implicit. As a story about men in war, Richard Lester's *How I Won the War* represented a film genre that characteristically emphasizes elements of defeat, combat and triumph, specifically in a context of male comradeship that commonly excludes the traditional social spheres associated with women. Yet, war films' emphasis on the masculine does not mean that questions of gender identity and femininity are excluded. Anthony Easthope writes in his study on masculine myths in popular culture that in "the dominant versions of men at war, men are permitted to behave towards each other in ways that would not be allowed elsewhere, caressing and holding each other, comforting and weeping together, admitting their love" (1992, 66). In Easthope's argument, war releases homosexual desires or at least allows men to express their otherwise forbidden "feminine" sides. Martial regimes admit "deviant" behavior.

How I Won the War is indeed very much about deviance. The film has been described as a black farce and satire exposing the lunacy of war and the obscenity of war movies (Sinyard 1987). It tells an absurd story about a British platoon that is sent to establish a cricket pitch behind enemy lines somewhere in North Africa during World War II. Being a surreal satire, the film exaggerates the characters and allows them to cross the limits of normality in a way that would not have been pos-

sible in conventional war films. *How I Won the War* is crowded with caricatures of familiar soldier stereotypes of the genre. Among this
repertoire, John Lennon was cast in the role of Private Gripweed, a ste-
reotypical good-for-nothing soldier, a schoolboyish and reticent wimp
nerdishly obsessed with collecting medals and insignia. Absurd, Goonlike one-liners highlighted his eccentricity. Asked if he is married, Gripweed replies: "No, I play harmonica." In the plotline Gripweed appears
uncertain about his identity as a man and soldier, a sharp contrast to the
heroic and resourceful male in control of his emotions and actions. Arguably, round-rimmed glasses were given to Lennon in order to emphasize the character's comicality, vulnerability, innocence and hints of
sexual ambivalence.

There are three obvious explanations as to why Lennon did not
abandon his glasses when shooting concluded in November 1966. First,
the comic element clearly softened the impact. It should be noted that
Lennon appeared publicly wearing granny glasses for the first time on
Boxing Day 1966, playing a cheeky nightclub attendant in the British
television comedy series *Not Only ... But Also*, establishing some linkage
between the spectacles and the Beatles' comic image. Second, while
crossing gender barriers had already been present in popular music
and its star images, the mid-1960s saw more conscious and visible attempts to play with sexual identities. Distinguishing themselves from
older generations, some male rock stars challenged hegemonic masculinity through gestures of allegiance to femininity. Longer hair was one
indicator, but there were also more provocative gestures, such as the
Rolling Stones' grotesque promotional film for their single "Have You
Seen Your Mother, Baby, Standing in the Shadow," released in 1966, in
which the members of the group appeared as caricatured female stereotypes but without apparent concessions to cross-dressing of the vari-
ety-show tradition. It could be argued that such strategies did not
represent real investments in the feminine as a new terrain of consciousness, but were a form of "gender tourism," allowing bands to
venture into alternative identities and then safely return "home" to
their dominant roles of masculinity (Reynolds & Press 1996, 385–86).
The provocative play with gender expectations did not prevent the
Rolling Stones from presenting a misogynistic image and chauvinistic
song lyrics. Thus, the terrain of femininity could be converted to a play-
ground of sexuality that represented no real threat to male rock musi-

cians and their position as guardians of hegemonic masculinity in rock culture. Similarly, Lennon's glasses might have initially carried associations of femininity, but as part of this gender tourism and playfulness, they did not seriously compromise his masculinity.

A third reason for Lennon's enthusiasm for his spectacles is that they had recently changed from being regarded as a necessary supplement to poor vision, to being a sign of personality and more generally a fashion marker. The image of glasses as a sign of weakness or "femininity" in men faded in the 1960s. According to Corson's (1967) study of the history of optical devices, it was not until the 1940s that glasses changed from being merely acceptable or utilitarian instruments to being regarded as part of fashion culture. In the 1950s, when frame design became an industry of its own, manufacturers systematically began to market glasses as attractive accessories by designing exciting styles. In 1964 the idea was given particular impetus with the formation of the Fashion Eyewear Group of America. In 1966 eyeglasses flooded the market in a variety of new designs: large squares, rectangles, octagons, ovals, all of which were available in stripes, checks and solid colors. Besides mass-produced models, unique custom-designed products were crafted. For women there were, for example, frames hand-covered in lizard skin to match handbags.

Noting the sudden fashionability of eyeglasses, Corson wrote: "For the moment, at least, eyeglasses seemed to be not so much for seeing as for being seen" (240). Wearing glasses was no longer a sign of weakness but reflected the ethos of fashion and a dynamic new generation. Since pop music and fashion trends were now closely related—as epitomized in the phenomenon of Swinging London—there was no impediment to eyeglasses finding their way into the iconography of popular music. In 1965 sunglasses had already been advertised in the pages of *New Musical Express*, and between May and August 1967 "grannies" were offered for sale in almost every issue of the paper. It became virtually de rigueur for fashion-conscious musicians to adopt glasses of one sort or another.

In addition to the reevaluation of masculinity, the union of fashion and pop culture contributed to another important issue: interest in the past. Elizabeth Wilson (1985) points out in her cultural history of fashion and modernity that 1960s culture was characterized by an obsession with pastiche and nostalgia, particularly in relation to changes in the fashion world. Fashion was no longer dominated by Parisian haute couture but was continuously in motion and quick to utilize popular culture, the cult of youth and the magic of the past. As with other markers of fashion, eyeglasses became the subject of nostalgic designs. According to Corson, one reason for reviving old styles in new materials lay in the need to supply an endless stream of new designs as rapidly as possible. This demand converged with what he describes as a "fad, probably started by young people and encouraged by the designers and optical shops, for wearing aggressively old-fashioned spectacles" (1967, 236–37). In addition to granny glasses, most with tinted lenses and available in other shapes than round, old styles meant heavy horn-rims, small gold or steel oval frames, octagonal frames in white gold or silver, small rectangular frames in imitation of eighteenth-century styles, half-moon "pulpit" spectacles and even lorgnettes. Through glasses, the past became present. In England, old styles in eyeglasses were associated with the Victorian and Edwardian eras. John Lennon, for example, was compared to a Victorian watchmaker in a *Melody Maker* article (Hutton 1967, 5).

For Lennon as well as his band colleagues, old-fashioned glasses were not the only way of articulating interest in the past. On the cover of their *Sgt. Pepper's Lonely Hearts Club Band*, the Beatles posed in lurid Edwardian military-band uniforms, marking the emergence of anachronistic dress styles into mainstream pop and fashion (McRobbie 1988). Elements of the past were also heard in the songs of the album, including "Being for the Benefit of Mr. Kite!," which took its lyrics from a Victorian circus poster, and the music-hall pastiche "When I'm Sixty-four." Such revivals of old sounds were not unusual in British pop music at the time. Among those groups who used heritage imagery were, for example, Herman's Hermits, with their top-ten ditty "I'm Henry the Eighth, I Am," which was originally written in 1911 and jovially dealt with working-class identity; the Kinks, who distinctively modulated their style from rhythm and blues guitar rock to a form of imperial nostalgia and gradually became to epitomize 1960s "pop Englishness"; or the New Vaudeville Band, whose exploration of prewar music culminated in their hit single "Winchester Cathedral." The most famous example of the "vaudevillian'" sound was Sandie Shaw's "Puppet on a String," which not only won the 1967 Eurovision Song Contest but hit number one and spent eighteen weeks on the U.K. charts.

Rock histories have often presented the late 1960s as an era of musical progression and the Beatles as its embodiment, ignoring the enthusiasm for past styles and fashions. It should be noted that while the 1960s later became a focal point for the tremendous revival in popular music, a strong linkage between heritage and pop existed already at the time. It was particularly during 1966–67 that British pop was pervaded by nostalgia (Kallioniemi 1998). At least two reasons present themselves. While nostalgic elements of British pop music in the mid-1960s could be understood as an extension of the long English tradition of pastoral mythology and the dream of the "Arcadia in Albion," they were at the same time part of pop music's own views of itself. In the search for their own voice, the idea of originality had become important both for the musicians and their devoted audiences, taking forms that were in relation to "otherness," "folk" and art. In such a situation the past, especially the kind of past that could be associated with purity, innocence and originality, emerged as a significant resource working to construct ideas of what popular music would mean.

One area where the connection between nostalgia[3] and search for authenticity was articulated in the 1960s was the musicians' interest in the images of childhood. The second half of the 1960s produced a proliferation of pop songs that venerated childhood and the innocence associated with it. In England the subject was projected by the Alan Price Set ("Simon Smith and His Dancing Bear"), Manfred Mann ("Haha Said the Clown"), the Hollies ("Lullaby for Tim") and Tomorrow ("My White Bicycle"). For early Pink Floyd, led at the time by Syd Barrett, naive psychedelia was an important musical trademark. Of all the genres of adolescent and adult popular music in the 1960s, it was psychedelic rock music, and British psychedelia in particular, in which the childlike worldview became most prominent. Historians of popular music have suggested that unlike their American counterparts and their connections to countercultural politics, the English pop groups were too inner-directed and childlike for such conditions. MacDonald, for example, writes that the "true subject of English psychedelia was neither love nor drugs, but nostalgia for the innocent vision of the child" (1995, 173; see also Reynolds & Press 1996; Savage 1996a; Kallioniemi 1998).

These sentiments resonated with romantic ideology. Campbell writes that it is the "complete ethos of childhood" that embodies romanticism, and hence stands opposed to that "ethos of bureaucracy" that represents adulthood (1987, 224). If rock music of the late 1960s to some extent worked to revitalize romantic ideology, as has often been discussed (e.g., Pattison 1987; Meisel 1999), the emergence of childhood as a central theme in rock is hardly surprising. The idealization of childhood converged so comfortably with 1960s rock music and its pining for authenticity because both were seen to represent principles that opposed the adult world and its conventions.

This theme emerged also in John Lennon's work and image, his glasses being a conspicuous example of the development. Biographers (Coleman 1988; Goldman 1988) recall that Lennon had long had defective eyesight, yet it was not diagnosed until he was eleven. As a result young Lennon was offered a pair of glasses, granny glasses as it happened, but since he refused to accept them he was then given a new pair of horn-rimmed glasses. It is tempting to interpret the recurrence of round-rimmed glasses fifteen years later as some form of deeply rooted atavism, but this remains speculative, and has no verification from Lennon himself. Nonetheless, Lennon's musical activities with the Beatles from the mid-1960s onward increasingly referred back to childhood. Lennon himself had already admitted the influence of children's writer Lewis Carroll on Lennon's books *In His Own Write* and *A Spaniard in the Works* (Harry 2000). Carroll's surrealistic visions were introduced in his song lyrics as well, most notably in "I Am the Walrus" and "Lucy in the Sky with Diamonds" (Roos 1984). Other childhood references in Lennon's music included the idealization of boyhood in the lyrics of "She Said She Said," fantasy/fairy tale imagery in "The Continuing Story of Bungalow Bill," and circus narrative and carousel sounds in "Being for the Benefit of Mr. Kite!" Childhood in Liverpool was evident in "Strawberry Fields Forever" and in the reminiscences of "Penny Lane" (originally written by Paul McCartney), both of which were released as a double A-side single in February 1967.[4]

Although Lennon would deal with his childhood experiences more explicitly (and less nostalgically) in his first solo album, *John Lennon/ Plastic Ono Band*, released in 1970, childhood and memories of the past as sources of inspiration became evident in the mid-1960s.[5] This is not merely apparent with the benefit of hindsight; the "golden age" of childhood and its influence on popular music in general and the Beatles specifically also attracted the notice of some contemporary critics. Michael Wood, for example, wrote in 1968 about how the Beatles' songs and Lennon's books incorporate nostalgic elements, expressing "the *good child's* hostility to grown-ups" (1987, 149).

Goodwin notes that the return to "roots" has been one of the most significant myths of popular music and an important theme in constructing star images (1993, 116–17). It is an element in popular music that was of particular significance for John Lennon as well as other musicians writing music at the time, expressed through this fascination with the past and particularly images of childhood. For Lennon, reconstruction of his identity as a star and through his own past constituted a watershed in his career. The imaginative return to a time before the Beatles suggested a return to a state of innocence and provided an opportunity for Lennon to purify and authenticate his status as an artist, and thus refine his star image.

Lennon's granny glasses did not explicitly articulate this childhood nostalgia but complemented the theme. There was, however, another nostalgic element involved, an element that more visibly pervaded not only Lennon's star image but the connection between 1960s fashion and pop music. In addition to being a way of confronting and refusing the bureaucratic ethos of adulthood in favor of childhood innocence, Lennon's spectacles also carried other associations, because the old-fashioned granny glasses had acquired different connotations for different generations in Britain. Angela McRobbie, one of the few writers to touch the subject of "grannies" in 1960s fashion and popular culture, writes that because granny glasses like Lennon's had previously been free of charge at the National Health Service and usually prescribed for indigent citizens, for the older generation they carried "the stigma of poverty and the mark of parental will imposed on unwilling children" (1988, 26). Placing granny glasses in the context of a general interest in old styles at the time, McRobbie continues that for the older generation "markets for old clothes and jumble sales in the 1960s remained a terrifying reminder of the stigma of poverty, the shame of ill-fitting clothing, and the fear of disease through infestation, rather like buying a second-hand bed" (34).

Hence, in addition to the reevaluation of masculinity and the compulsion of nostalgia, Lennon's glasses may be connected to a third theme that marked 1960s pop culture: the aestheticization of poverty. McRobbie writes that while secondhand style has a long history in British culture, it was during the hippie subculture in the late 1960s and its antimaterialistic posture that the interest in the old, the used, the overtly cheap and apparently unstylish entered mainstream fashion in disavowal of conventional middle-class smartness. As a part of this development, Lennon's cheap, shoddy spectacles not only became one of his trademarks but also came to represent a casual disregard for obvious signs of wealth, and a disdain for "the colour of money" (26).

According to Wilson (1985, 194), the essence of hippie style was a belief in the natural that was manifested in the cult of the authentic, the imaginary return to the past and the rejection of the fashions imposed by the fashion industry. This meant an identification with poverty in the name of style. Cheap clothes were worn as a distinctive style, designed to define a distance both from "straight," conventional dress and from the shabby grayness of genuine poverty (McRobbie 1988, 26). Since this involved an element of flirtation with the outrageous violation of "good taste," countercultural fashion also emphasized provocative self-presentation. The chief caricaturists of this playfulness were pop stars who in London traveled in their luxury cars to rummage for clothes in fashionable, curiously named secondhand shops such as The Charge of the Light Brigade, I Was Lord Kitchener's Valet or Granny Takes a Trip. The trend was noted also in the pop press. Selecting the pop group Dave Dee, Dozy, Beaky, Mick & Tich, then at the pinnacle of their fame, *New Musical Express* (November 11, 1966, 14–15) reported how these young popsters "go mad at 'I was Lord Kitchener's Valet'." Reflecting the new union of pop and fashion, advertisements for fashionable clothes—at first for swinging and mod clothes and then for psychedelic retro clothing and related secondhand shops—flooded the pages of British pop magazines (Moore 1998).

Mixing images of poverty and aristocracy was a form of pop-elitist play in which Lennon and the other Beatles also participated by dressing in old but fashionable clothes and regularly appearing in secondhand shops—or even by opening a clothes shop of their own.[6] Within this framework, the aestheticization of poverty in fashion and pop music stardom thus followed a familiar line of the idealization of "low cultures," of *nostalgie de la boue*, in Western societies. However, on this occasion such aestheticization did not appear merely as one among many other subcultural style markers, as it had been, for example, with the middle-class adoption of the trappings of working-class teenage life in the 1950s. For the first time it became a worldwide fashion. Moreover, the visibility and significance of the phenomenon also indicated that pop music had started to enjoy broader cultural legitimation and that as visible public figures, pop stars played an important role in the development.

In relation to Lennon's stardom, what has arguably remained the most significant aspect of his granny glasses is not so much related to aestheticization of poverty nor sentiments of gender emancipation and nostalgia. Writing on retro-chic style, the late historian Raphael Samuel (1994, 97) noted that John Lennon's granny glasses, along with his astrakhan coat, "had become Trotskyist wear by the early 1970s and later still—the position they have retained—the standard spectacles for the studious and the owlish." Since round-rimmed glasses have often been associated with literary interests, the "thinking" professions and intellectualism, this image also applies to the "star semiotics" of John Lennon's granny glasses.[7]

Inglis (2000b) has argued in his article on the Beatles and intellectualism that the nature of the Beatles' appearances in the 1960s gradually changed, from singing their hit songs to participating in interviews and discussion in which the stars offered opinions and interpretations on events and issues often unrelated to the traditional concerns of the pop star—the war in Vietnam, drugs, social problems, the music business and religion, for example. What replaced the musical emphasis was an emphasis on the Beatles as men of ideas. This scheme somewhat simplifies the development since, as I have argued, the Beatles were celebrated from the onset of their fame in relation not only to musical but also to other star forms. However, the Beatles were clearly increasingly assigned new roles as "pop intellectuals." According to Inglis, "the Beatles (and some of their peers) were elected to act as a spokespersons for a generation, to define and guide a global counterculture, to distinguish the valuable from the worthless, to offer new insights and philosophies, to transform the world—to assume the mantle of (surrogate) intellectuals" (13).

Photography and film archives on pop musicians prior to 1966 show a dearth of spectacled pop performers, especially male stars. While this may reflect the stars' own ideas about their masculinity, as with Lennon, it is also likely that managers and promotional executives advised pop stars not to appear in public wearing glasses. While "respectability" undoubtedly played an important role in the construction of pop stardom, eyeglasses meant the wrong kind of respectability: conformity to adult standards of studiousness, mild-mannered intelligence and mundane bureaucracy. These would not have fitted leisure-oriented teenybop star images. For some stars, glasses might have been useful to establish comic status, but for pop stars who were seriously committed to youth culture, they represented an irrelevance or even a handicap.[8] During the reconfigurations of popular culture in the 1960s and its new equivocation of tone and identity, this coding was reevaluated. Glasses became, along with other meanings, the emblem of "men of ideas."

For John Lennon's star image, his appearance without the other Beatles, with a new image and in a film that critiqued military mythology, was a significant event. It helped to remake his star identity, from that of a member of the pop group, to a self-determinative individual with a somewhat intellectual aura. Some of these qualities were proclaimed through the granny glasses, which were a clear metaphor of his maturing as an artist and star. This transition from entertainer to artist and public intellectual has been noted, but scarcely analyzed, by most Beatles and Lennon biographers. What I have argued here is that as cultural history and in terms of fashion, the development toward pop intellectualism was also accompanied by the reevaluation of masculinity, a pining nostalgia and the aestheticization of poverty.

This transition did not happen overnight, however, and the "old" mode of stardom could not be abandoned at a stroke. Lennon's new status as a serious yet playful pop intellectual carried with it a range of problems and tensions, particularly regarding success and its symbols.

Psychedelic Rolls-Royce

It altered our ideas of what luxury should be.
—H. Nockolds, the writer of *Rolls-Royce: The Magic of a Name*, 1949

On May 25, 1967, John Lennon "published" an extraordinary "work of art," a new, colorful design for his Rolls-Royce Phantom V, which he had originally purchased two years earlier. In the historiography of the Beatles and Lennon, this event has been disregarded as little more than a curiosity, eclipsed by the Beatles album *Sgt. Pepper's Lonely Hearts*

Club Band, which was released a week later and soon came to be considered a peak in the group's career as well as a cultural benchmark. Even though music remained central to the Beatles' and to Lennon's stardom, his celebrity continued to incorporate gestures that seemed to have only little relevance to music. Yet, they clearly were connected to the ideas of musical culture, fashion and the ways stars were supposed to act. In this connection, the transformation of Lennon's car is a reference point from which to explore the connections between music stardom and fashion as well as to analyze changing expectations that were imposed upon Lennon and other music stars in the 1960s.

As with the granny glasses, there is little documentation of Lennon's motive in redesigning his Rolls-Royce. According to various sources, Lennon had decided that the car would accompany him while filming *How I Won the War* abroad in 1966. In Spain, where the film production moved after shooting in West Germany, the Rolls-Royce was scratched by sand and road grit. When the filming was over, the car was transferred back to England where the damage was assessed. The task of repair was then undertaken by J. P. Fallon Ltd., a coachworks company in Surrey. The renovation took several months, and when the formerly dark limousine finally emerged from the garage, it was not only repaired but covered in brilliant yellow primer and extravagantly colorful designs.[9]

Public reaction to the car was mixed. Lennon's Rolls-Royce was called a "yellow peril" that looks "like a four-wheeled flower show" and a "gipsy caravan" (Boring 1967). Amused by the unveiling of the Rolls-Royce, some journalists wrote about a "shrieking yellow" and a "cross between a psychedelic nightmare and an autumn garden on wheels" (see Schaffner 1978, 94; Taylor 1987, 149; Clifford 1999, 11). It was also suggested that the startling appearance of the car posed a hazard to unsuspecting drivers. When the car participated in a concours d'elegance in London, it was ruled out of the competition because, according to the chairman of judges, it "was in extremely bad taste" (*Liverpool Echo*, June 26, 1967). A representative at Rolls-Royce's Mayfair headquarters was only a little more diplomatic, stating that the company did not want to comment on "our customers' foibles" (Boring 1967). The firm was more concerned about the rumors that a merchandising concern was planning to flood the toy shops with models of Lennon's car.

Lennon's Rolls-Royce was immediately placed in the context of contemporary fashion and styles. In its brightness, the car signified attitudes that, depending on commentators, were either exciting or tasteless but in any case fashionable. Dark suits, which had previously been intrinsic to the conventional male "uniform" as well as characteristic of the Beatles during Beatlemania, were to an extent replaced by more lurid costumes. Exotic shirts, scarves and bright trousers were appreciated not only by youth but also by all those who aspired to be "with it" in popular culture. Even the manager Brian Epstein, the archetype of an old-time show business tycoon and gentleman, changed his style and started to pose with floral-patterned shirts. The powerful connection between fashion and the media images of youthful, urban lifestyles in the midst of the Swinging London phenomenon eclipsed the fact that outside the "center" the enthusiasm might be less extravagant. Derek Taylor, who would return from America and rejoin the Beatles as their press officer in 1968, visited Liverpool during his winter holiday at the end of 1967 and, dressed up as a "flower man," faced a reception that was "even frostier than the weather" (1987, 151–52).[10]

Nevertheless, this metropolitan change introduced a new vividness to fashion and to the whole spectrum of popular culture. In England, art school graduates interested in visual design and poster art often emphasized in their works a paradisal realm of pop culture and were influenced, for example, by art deco, folktale imagery and mysticism. Colorfulness was also manifested at various musical and/or visual events of London underground culture, as for example the 14 Hour Technicolor Dream, which was organized in the summer of 1967 as a benefit for the underground paper *International Times*. Examples of a new visual extravagance entering the media and visual arts in Britain are abundant. Lavish Sunday issues of newspapers, which had been introduced in the early 1960s, became more common. BBC 2 was the first television channel in Europe to start color transmissions, in July 1967; black-and-white feature films were almost wholly replaced by color films, as had already happened in the transition from the Beatles' *A Hard Day's Night* to *Help!*.

In this colorful context Lennon's Rolls-Royce was immediately labeled *psychedelic*, a term popularized by Timothy Leary, Ralph Metzner and Richard Alpert in their book *The Psychedelic Experience*, published in 1964. *Psychedelic* connected the interest in bright colors with drugs, especially the new drug LSD, and soon came to refer to particular fashions and more general areas of experience. As such, it had its roots in Aldous Huxley's mescaline-inspired essay, "The Doors of Perception," a main source of inspiration also for Leary, Metzner and Alpert. Partly because mescaline and LSD, known also as "acid," had similar effects, Huxley's (1973, 27) semimystical descriptions of the visionary quality of a glass vase of flowers, folds in the trousers ("what a labyrinth of endlessly significant complexity!"), the texture of gray flannel ("how rich, how deeply, mysteriously sumptuous!") and other mental landscapes became cult phrases in the 1960s and underpinned descriptions of the "psychedelic experience."

Such interests soon entered popular culture, leading to an emphasis on mosaic-like ornaments, floral patterns, surrealistic spirals and bright colors in various cultural artifacts. In popular music, rock groups imitated the psychedelic experience through florid and meandering arrangements, improvisation, sound experiments and stream-of-consciousness lyrics. Part of the psychedelic enthusiasm was the emphasis on innocence. In fact, Huxley had observed in the 1950s that using mescaline leads to the intensification of visual impressions and that the eye recovers "some of the perceptual innocence of childhood" (1973, 23). Such experience was later amusingly confirmed by Derek Taylor: "My boyhood innocence seemed to have been returned to me by LSD. Some found only God. I also found Piglet and Pooh and Mr. Toad" (1987, 74).

Because of its kaleidoscope of colorful designs, John Lennon's Rolls-Royce seemed to reflect this psychedelic style. The bottom layer of the car was painted bright yellow, while the accompanying colors included blue, red, green, turquoise and gold. The car was decorated with autumnal dahlias, chrysanthemums and delphiniums on the doors and the zodiacal sign for Libra (Lennon's star sign) on the roof. Such elements of flora and astrology, as well as the spiral patterns in wheels, clearly referred to the interests of psychedelic and hippie cultures. The extensive scrollwork, semicircular arches and festooning ornaments, however, in my view reflect more art deco and Romany art than the usual iconography of hippie culture, giving the car an antiquarian and exotic reference.

As indicated in earlier sections of this study, an identification with various "others," such as working class, black culture, poverty, and, to some extent, femininity, was characteristic of popular music culture in the 1960s. Exoticism gave an extra dimension to this romanticism, which hinted at emancipation from Western conventions. The association between Romany and rock cultures instilled the image of the gypsy as a rootless bohemian and traveler free from social responsibilities with rock music and its male ethos (Street 1986, 139). The most notable personification of this association was Jimi Hendrix, who used gypsy imagery in his songs and his visual style, and in 1969 even formed a short-lived group called the Band of Gypsys.

Whereas initially Lennon's new paint job for his Rolls-Royce reflected changes in visual fashion and the emergence of psychedelia, it thus also played with otherness. During Beatlemania Lennon had epitomized the star who successfully represented the margin or other in popular culture, a regional musician conquering the center of entertainment and "culture." Now, through his new car, this model was replaced by the idea of the pop celebrity who had established himself as a part of that center, playing with the image of the other. His Rolls-Royce represented the pride and quality of British car design, but at the same time it fixed on the interest in Romany art.

Given the simple fact that the Rolls-Royce was not just any automobile, but one that enjoyed special status and cultural meaning, Lennon's transformation of his Rolls may also be read as an attempt to redefine himself in response to a tension between the traditional star role and new, contemporary expectations projected upon him. Prior to Lennon, the combination of celebrity and the car had developed a variety of forms. Although the proclamation of celebrity through modes of transport is as old as celebrity itself, the development of the automobile, and then its mass production, provided new dynamics within which this connection could be articulated. By the 1950s the car embodied modernity and was often associated with youth, sex, freedom and democracy. Especially in the United States, cars also came to signify social status and differentiation. In his best-selling investigation of class structure in America, *The Status Seekers*, first published in 1959, Vance Packard claimed that the car was the most important socio-hierarchical indicator, "a status symbol." The car at the apex of this hierarchy, or in Packard's words, at "the end of the rainbow," was the Cadillac, which became the embodiment in chrome of the American dream, representing the aspirations of ordinary Americans and developing vivid meaning as a success symbol for many self-made men (1970, 280–84).

Besides self-made businessmen, the nouveaux riches of the entertainment world increasingly resorted to cars in order to show their status. One of the first things Elvis Presley did after his first chart-topping record, "Heartbreak Hotel," was to buy four Cadillacs and then pose with them for the media. In Britain, the pattern of the celebrity and the car was somewhat more complex, balancing among the issues of mass production, leisure and class. Whereas the mid-century American car industry produced large and extravagant models, which were generally considered vulgar by the European literati, in Britain the main emphasis was rather on cheap mass production. Out of gasoline rationing following the Suez crisis, and the need to save road space, there emerged an obsession with compactness. The answer to this in 1959 was the Mini Cooper, which epitomized an affordable and functional car and contributed to the independent and leisure-filled Swinging Sixties lifestyle, of which another motored symbol was the Vespa scooter (Lewis 1989; Holden 1998). Yet, there also emerged a growing fascination with the excess associated with "new money" and celebrities. The car as an extravagant, even vulgar demonstration of the rags-to-riches story was epitomized by the gold-plated and zebra-skin-upholstered Daimler owned by Sir Bernard Docker and his wife Lady Norah Docker. It evidently was the most famous single car in 1950s Britain (Lewis 1989).

In light of this ethos of self-made success, it is hardly surprising that when the Beatles were asked what they would like to be, "rich and famous" was the usual reply (see, e.g., *New Musical Express*, February 15, 1963, 9). After their first taste of success, the reply to the question became, "Make more money" (see, e.g., Kelly 1994, 123). Even though such sentiments might have been laced with irony, the received logic of pop stardom at that time provided no alternative. Success in popular music was measured in commercial rather than in artistic terms, and in the early years of his celebrity, Lennon simply acted the way pop stars were supposed to—as an ostentatious consumer. In 1964, advised by Brian Epstein, Lennon bought a twenty-seven-room Tudor mansion in Weybridge, which, in producer George Martin's words, was "one of the poshest parts of the London commuter belt" and a place to be "if you were big in the British media" (Martin & Pearson 1995, 71–73). By 1965

Lennon had purchased three cars, a Mini Cooper "for pottering about in," a Rolls-Royce "for relaxing" and a Ferrari "for zoom" (Coleman 1988, 191). In June 1965 Lennon bought his second Rolls-Royce, the Phantom V model that he would later have repainted. It was reported that the car included such comforts as a portable television, a cocktail cabinet, a writing table, a refrigerator and stereo and radio equipment (Hutchins 1966a). Furthermore, Lennon's Rolls-Royce was one of the first automobiles to be fitted with one-way glass, a feature that was, according to Clifford (1999, 7), highlighted in many of the contemporary news and magazine reports. It was not long before tinted rear windows became a trademark of celebrity.

Rolls-Royces, which had been on the market since 1904, were originally not very popular among British pop celebrities. Young stars usually preferred fast and youthful sports cars rather than smooth, silent and solemn Rolls models that carried modestly allusive names such as the Silver Ghost, Silver Cloud, and Phantom. When the new "pop aristocracy" of Swinging London started to flirt with the lifestyles of the old regime, heavily coded artifacts such as the Rolls-Royce were deployed in nontraditional ways. Before long even fashion photographers were replacing their E-Type Jaguars with Rolls-Royces. Rolls-Royce reacted to this changing demand by manufacturing a new design in the mid-1960s, the Silver Shadow, which eventually became the company's most popular product. The British press named it a "mod model" (Morgan 1996).[11]

By having his Rolls-Royce painted, Lennon added an extra element to this play. Lennon ridiculed signs of stardom and made irony of his position—much in the same way as the extraordinary disc jockey Jimmy Savile did, who was famous for his blood-red Rolls-Royce, big cigars and platinum blond hair. The episode could be regarded as an eccentric extension of the humor that had been characteristic of Lennon's and other Beatles' stardom. Since a Rolls-Royce, however, was an ultimate index of wealth, the joke was more overtly ideological. The new generation of rock stars aspired to a new form of authenticity that involved social dissent and revolution. In cultivating such a profile, the simple accumulation of the traditional trappings of wealth was problematic. Thus, around 1966, money started to cause problems for Lennon, forcing him to interrogate his own star status: "I often think that it's all a big conspiracy, that the winners are the Government and people like us who've got the money. That joke about keeping the workers ignorant is still true" (Cleave 1966).

It is evident that when old modes of "pop" stardom and new demands of "rock" clashed in the mid-1960s, money became a problematic issue in popular music. Street has suggested that "while private wealth may in fact make no difference to the music itself, the idea that it does is crucial to how the role of the rock star is constructed" (1986, 135). Street writes that whereas "pop" stars are supposed to be wealthy and extravagant and there is thus no need for them to feel guilty, the "rock" ideology stresses suspicion of wealth and its effects. In "pop" wealth is fun, or at least an accepted part of the business; in "rock" money brings both practical and ethical problems (137). In a subsequent era when categorizations of "pop" and "rock" have been blurred, it is easy to forget how sharp the distinction was in the 1960s and the 1970s, and the important role the question of money and "selling out" played in discussions about popular music stardom. The Beatles might complain about high taxes as late as 1966 in their song "Taxman" (written by George Harrison), but soon money became taboo.[12] If money was discussed in interviews, Lennon stifled the matter by answering that such things were too complex for artists and were better left to professional accountants (Hutchins 1966a, 3; Davies 1968, 304). Money was something extra, a by-product of musical talent, to which one paid no attention.

Humor was another strategy, and obviously the painted Rolls-Royce was originally meant to be a sort of joke on wealth. Such humor, however, had a serious side. Possessing a limousine like a Rolls-Royce usually indicates that the owner is a wealthy person, but in 1960s England, a Rolls was also a symbol of its owner's social status and power.[13] Even though self-made celebrities began to flirt with such luxury, a Rolls-Royce nonetheless remained a flagship of the Establishment and the aristocracy. Some writers (Lydon 1970; Clifford 1999) have therefore alleged that by painting his limousine so colorfully, Lennon not only ridiculed this order but showed a disdain for conventional taste and introduced a countercultural element. Lennon's car was significant as a class status symbol, but was then placed within a different ensemble, that of changing popular music stardom. His Rolls-Royce still represented a limousine reserved for the privileged few, but now it was also, at least to some extent, associated with countercultural activities.[14]

The metamorphosis of Lennon's Rolls-Royce was thus an ambiguous episode, reflecting a confusing rupture in popular music culture. On the one hand rock music sought its voice from the streets, youth culture, nostalgia and exoticism; on the other hand it flirted with signs of aristocracy and traditional pop stardom. Lennon and the Beatles had somehow to reconcile their spectacular fortune with the austere rejection of worldly affluence demanded of rock authenticity. The shift from the vulgar affluence of the traditional pop star to the new rock authenticity involved a transitional stage during which competing sign systems had to be reconciled. Instead of renouncing his Rolls, Lennon reconfigured it as a symbol in which pop affluence converged with countercultural rock. To illustrate this star equilibrium and its response, Ian Whitcomb's account of his own short career as a mid-1960s pop star includes an intriguing episode in which the author is sitting in the backseat of his limousine and gliding through the heart of hippie culture, the Haight Ashbury district in San Francisco. Suddenly a passerby yells at him: "Hey, man. If you ain't a Beatle, then get the fuck outta here. We don't dig tourists from straight society!" (1983, 247) The Beatles were accepted as being a part of the rock community—or, rather, its spokespersons—and even though the Beatles did not actively participate in this community after their cessation of live performances in 1966, they evidently were keen to preserve the image of such membership. Lennon's Rolls-Royce was a gesture toward this image which, perhaps, was more tellingly produced by another painting-the-car project, the Beatles' television film *Magical Mystery Tour* (1967).[15]

Lennon's Rolls-Royce and *Magical Mystery Tour* represented a means of re-creating a connection between the stars and their audiences. Even though the balance of rock stardom, at least in the case of the Beatles, was clearly shifting from the responsibility to the audience toward the responsibility to the self, there was still a need for John Lennon to take notice of fans, who, according to him, "bought the car" and had the "right to smash it up" if they wished (Coleman 1965d, 11). By painting his Rolls so outlandishly, Lennon made an imaginary junction between millionaire stardom and the fan. The metamorphosis was, of course, not complete: The Rolls-Royce had been transformed to a colorful and more visible vehicle but it still was a special car and, with its tinted windows, a mobile bastion of privacy.

Apart from suggestions of fashion, eccentric humor and counterculture, Lennon's Rolls-Royce also stands as a metaphor of the play between hiding and showing, the private and the public, in late 1960s pop stardom. This draws attention to a more deeply embedded problem in Lennon's way of articulating his own stardom. The psychedelic Rolls on one level appears to be a resolution of the paradox of commercial success and rock authenticity. But it was still a Rolls, its tinted windows providing a vantage point for an unseen "insider" looking out. I shall examine this problem further in the next section, which deals with the Beatles' decision to leave the concert stage and focus on recordings, especially *Sgt. Pepper's Lonely Hearts Club Band*.

The Spirit of *Sgt. Pepper*

Men need machines but machines need men and ideas to produce meaningful experience.
–Arnold Shaw on the rock group Soft Machine

The Beatles' stardom from the mid-1960s onward was characterized largely by their abandonment of live concerts. After nine years and more than 1,400 live performances, the Beatles appeared before a live audience for the last time on August 29, 1966, in San Francisco (Lewisohn 1996).[16] From that time on, they mainly concentrated on recording, becoming more distinctively musicians whose main concern was to exploit the studio for their artistic purposes. By taking this major change as a point of departure for this section, my argument is that the Beatles, with their album *Sgt. Pepper's Lonely Hearts Club Band*, were key mediators in the changing relationship between technology, aesthetics and popular music stardom. Since the album (hereafter referred to as *Sgt. Pepper*), which among other consequences came to signify the music industry's shift from the single format to long-playing (LP) records with extravagant cover art and printed lyrics, has been the subject of frequent discussion, I shall not give a descriptive analysis of its contents here.[17] My contribution to the continuing reassessments of the album is to explore how it defined the changing star roles of John Lennon and other members of the Beatles.

Beatles historians have had a tendency to regard the group's studio years, from 1966 onward, as a creative and even a revolutionary period that profoundly changed the ways of making popular music. Because of this emphasis, before I reassess the argument regarding the "studio years," it should be noted that the group indirectly had an effect on pop performance practices as well. Even though the Beatles were not the first group to bring pop music to stadiums and other large arenas, they were the first fully electric group to establish such performances as a standard practice in popular music culture. Furthermore, although the Beatles certainly were not the first ensemble to face the problems of inadequate pop concert facilities,[18] they have remained the major example of a poorly equipped music group.

The physical and technological infrastructures of the Beatles' performances were far from the massive multimedia mise en scène that in subsequent decades gradually became essential to popular music performances and stardom. In their first American concert at the Coliseum in Washington, D.C., the Beatles appeared before 8,000 fans who had gathered to watch the new British sensation. "Before" is a somewhat misleading expression in this instance, since after rushing through the crowd the Beatles reached the stage, which was set in the middle of the arena. Having made their entrance, Ringo Starr attempted to reposition his drum kit and George Harrison had to change his microphone, only to discover that the replacement was faulty. During the performance the Beatles repositioned themselves and their equipment three times in order to face the audiences behind and on the sides (Lewisohn 1996, 146; Wonfor 1996c). The famous 1965 Shea Stadium concert film clip, in which the Beatles are carrying their instruments and running through the vast field, provides a similar account of the undeveloped performance practices. Another example of the primitive conditions appeared during the Beatles' final tour in Cincinnati, where the rainy weather became a problem. The concert had to be canceled because the organizers had not built the shelter over the stage (Norman 1982, 334). Audience interaction was a problem as well. According to the Beatles' recollections (see Wonfor 1996d), constant waving and screaming of fans drowned out their playing and, in some cases, forced them to speed up the tempo to finish their songs as soon as possible. In the end, such frustrations, aggravated by technological inadequacies, fueled the Beatles' decision to abandon live performances.

It is evident that in the early 1960s pop concert sound systems were becoming inadequate for the requirements of modern pop stardom. Although Brian Epstein directed concert organizers to provide the Beatles with the latest hi-fi technology, it appeared that amplifiers, loudspeakers and other stage equipment, which were predominantly built to meet the modest demands of club venues, were not adequate in larger venues. For example, at Shea Stadium in 1965 there were no elaborate sets or lights, only a standard house Tannoy system, which was used to announce baseball scores to Shea's regular patrons (Cunningham 1999).

That serious attempts to introduce better sound systems would begin only after the Beatles had secluded themselves behind the doors of Abbey Road Studios is one of the ironies of 1960s popular music. It was mainly the launching of the stadium concerts by the Beatles, and the advent of rock festivals a few years later, that intensified the cooperation between sound system manufacturers, musicians and concert organizers. In 1967 Watkins Electric Music introduced a 1,000-watt public address (PA) power amplification system, which meant that now the signals from an act's "backline" (the musicians' amplifiers, speakers and instruments) were mixed and processed to the main banks of loudspeakers. At the same time there appeared significant progress toward better microphones with greater dynamic range, and in 1969 onstage monitoring was developed as an independent sound unit (Bacon 1981). During the psychedelic period a new set of technological demands emerged, and some bands, like the Grateful Dead and Pink Floyd, invested in better light systems, pioneering the development of music performances as mixed-media events. However, the development was relatively slow, and it was only during the 1970s that the technological spectacle was advanced, particularly by progressive rock groups (Cunningham 1999).

In the history of popular music, technical innovations have often accelerated the development of new styles, trends and practices. In the case of the Beatles the pattern was reversed: Conditions were not adequate to convey their musical ideas in live performance. The result was that instead of live performances the Beatles devoted themselves to the aesthetics of recording. This shift also had an effect on the aesthetics of popular music stardom.

What is important to note in terms of stardom is that from September 1966 to June 1967, the Beatles excluded themselves from the media. On the basis of the issues of *New Musical Express* published during that period, it could be concluded that the most important band was not the Beatles but the Monkees or Dave Dee, Dozy, Beaky, Mick & Tich. In quantitative terms purely, one single ("Penny Lane" / "Strawberry Fields Forever") and terse and sporadic comments made by the members of the group were a radical change from the Beatlemania period when the group was almost constantly "within reach" of the media and the fans. As illustrated by Curtis (1987, 188), the Beatles had achieved their celebrity by performing "outside," in public places such as the Cavern Club in Liverpool and later literally outside in stadiums and other outdoor arenas. Now, however, they had gone inside, to Abbey Road Studios, where only the privileged few were allowed.

What distinguished the Beatles' retirement from other famous musical seclusions of the time (such as those of Glenn Gould, Bob Dylan, Phil Spector, and Elvis Presley) was the fact that rather than being a maneuver conducted by an individual celebrity, four people acted in concert over the matter.[19] The foursome being almost incommunicado for months, the logical conclusion for journalists was to speculate that the group was about to disintegrate (see, e.g., Dawbarn 1966). The Beatles' silence—their retirement from touring was not formally announced until December 1966—stirred up much uncertainty and prompted journalists to harass the members of the group arriving at Abbey Road Studios.

One consequence of this shift was that the role of star mediation became more significant. The silence of the Beatles persuaded their recording company EMI to rethink the relationship between the artist and the audience. One response by EMI was the release of a compilation album, *A Collection of Beatles Oldies*, in December 1966 in an attempt to maintain a merchandising presence (Inglis 1996). Even though the Beatles were "inside" and thus not physically available for the concert-goers, as a mediated production they continued to be "outside." What followed was an abundance of nonspatial elements permeating their image. The idea of the ethereal had previously to some extent characterized the Beatles' stardom, inscribed in their films and in the form of the American cartoon series, and in a way, in the star phenomenon itself, which often constructs stars as mediated, unreachable and supernatural objects. It should also be noted that before abandoning the concert stage the Beatles had already minimized their appearances on television shows and, instead, produced promotional films of their songs that were distributed to the TV stations around the world to fulfill the obligations. This practice, which could be seen as a precursor to the music video boom of the 1980s, exemplified the point that instead of sending physical human beings to promote their products on television, it was much more effective to circulate a "copy" of the star, an ethereal audiovisual image. After the Beatles' withdrawal, this element took more fictionalized forms. During the *Sgt. Pepper* sessions, journalists and fans swarmed in front of Abbey Road Studios seeking comments from the musicians, who, after a few quick words, slipped into the studio sanctuary, virtually another world, hidden from the public eye. The element of fiction and fantasy was enhanced by the Beatles' appearance as four magicians in the television film *Magical Mystery Tour* and as good-natured heroes resisting the evil Blue Meanies in the animated feature film *Yellow Submarine* (1968). A further example of the Beatles themselves consciously deploying fictionality was the creation of Sgt. Pepper's Lonely Hearts Club Band as a quasi-music-hall alter ego band. Inspired by the exotic names then popular among the Californian psychedelic groups, Paul McCartney, the originator of the idea, later explained that the aim was "to lose our identities, to submerge ourselves in the persona of a fake group" (quoted in MacDonald 1995, 184).[20] In terms of public relations, really expunging the Beatles as an identity was completely out of the question. The advertisement for the album left no room for doubt: "Remember Sgt. Pepper's Lonely Hearts Club Band is the Beatles" (*Melody Maker*, June 3, 1967 & *New Musical Express*, June 3, 1967).

Although *Sgt. Pepper* at the time enhanced the Beatles' fictionality, later recollections and histories have accentuated the more concrete side of the process. It is evident that *Sgt. Pepper* has considerable weight in Beatles history. In fact, the album has thus far been the most thoroughly analyzed in the history of popular music. Telling stories behind the songs, the compositional processes, the sources and the technological strategies of the album has become a minor industry in itself. Who was the meter maid in "Lovely Rita"? How was the carousel effect in "Being for the Benefit of Mr. Kite!" created? In attempts to solve such mysteries, Beatles enthusiasts have had an endless pop archaeological field day, in which a "Splendid time is guaranteed for all" (Beatles 1967, back cover printing).

One particular area of interest has been the ways in which the Beatles exploited the facilities of Abbey Road recording studios. Beatles historians have repeatedly emphasized that the technical conditions required to create such a masterpiece in 1967 were relatively undeveloped, compared with technology that emerged over the few years following *Sgt. Pepper*. For example, multitracking was still in a primitive state (during the sessions the Beatles had no more than two four-track recorders), there were few effect boxes, and tape synchronization needed careful crafting. Geoff Emerick, then a sound engineer at Abbey Road, has later recalled that "we never had the luxury of 1980s gimmick boxes then, just ordinary tape machines" (Lewisohn 1988, 114). George Martin, whose central role during the sessions has been frequently acknowledged, has said that whenever he describes the primitive state of recording technology in the mid-1960s, he feels like "Baron von Richthofen describing the Fokker Triplane to a group of Concorde pilots" (Martin & Pearson 1995, 22).

Another problem was a range of restrictions in terms of regulation and protocols. Until about 1972, the Musicians' Union in Britain attempted to control—if rather unsuccessfully—the activities of its members in recording studios, to ensure, for example, that each session started and finished at fixed times. The union also exercised its power in the matter of overdubbing, which was at one stage strictly forbidden, mainly because its rules directed that the recording procedure should as far as possible replicate the live performance. New electric instruments such as the mellotron, a predecessor of the synthesizer, were also often regarded as a threat to live music (Thornton 1995). Apart from the union's activities, recording studios had their own, often very rigid technical guidelines. For example, there was a rule at Abbey Road that microphones were not to be placed closer than 18 inches from the bass drum. It has also been confirmed that the studio was reluctant to commit itself fully to the technical advances of the day (Southall, Vince & Rouse 1997; Miles 1998).

During the *Sgt. Pepper* sessions the Beatles and their assistants continually flouted technical and musical regulations imposed both by the Musicians' Union and the Abbey Road studio executives. Recording sessions lasted sometimes through the night, microphones were set wherever they collected the sounds best and guitars or bass were recorded straight through the mixing console. New machines were invented, like the washing machine look-alike "frequency changer" that would explode in a shower of sparks if it was overextended. When these unorthodox methods became public knowledge, it soon followed that in order to record new, ambitious groups and to achieve up-to-date recording standards, studios were forced to change their arrangements, recruit younger staff and update the equipment (Lewisohn 1988).

Considering how innovation and boldness have been at the foreground in discussion of the creation of *Sgt. Pepper*, it could be suggested that material conditions in the recording studio were informed by a certain kind of rock auteurship. The idea that the recording studio could work as an autonomous creative center for popular music precedes this particular project. Talented producers like Sam Phillips (the "discoverer" of Elvis Presley and owner of Sun Records), Norman Petty (the producer for Buddy Holly), Robert "Bumps" Blackwell (the pioneer of multimike recordings and mixing, producer for Little Richard and Sam Cooke) and Joe Meek (best remembered for the Tornados' million-seller "Telstar") were interested in developing recording technology and to some extent understood its meaning as a vehicle for pop stardom. It should, however, be remembered that experimentation with the creative possibilities of recording technology predates modern pop and rock music and can be traced at least back to the 1920s. Duke Ellington, for example, was interested in extending the use of electronics and applying it to the acoustic content. Furthermore, in 1930s and 1940s cartoons and radio jingles, such American composers as Carl Stalling and Raymond Scott explored electronic music, enlarging the possibilities of recording technology. Although new sound technologies thus were dynamically engaged with popular culture, it is difficult to discover any *stars* between the 1920s and 1950s whose images would have been characterized by the presence of recording technology. It was arguably Phil Spector, the creator of the "Wall of Sound" and the master behind various American "girl groups" in the early 1960s, who headed the emergence of the combination of "sound genius" and the star in popular culture. Spector was not only recognized as a self-conscious, creative, business-wise and independent producer-artist but lived a highly visible star lifestyle, thus combining the requirements of an auteur and the excessiveness of traditional pop stardom (Shuker 2001).

As the studio rather than the stage became the crucial site for the in-cubation of music, certain recording genres began to acquire an aura that contributed to the mythos of auteurship. Inspired by the Beatles, the Beach Boys, Frank Zappa, Pink Floyd and others, musicians' ability to create, build and manipulate sounds in the studio gradually formed the basis of an important aesthetic. This studio imagination meant, to use Peter Copeland's (1991) distinction, that "natural" outcomes were enhanced and interest in "unnatural" possibilities grew. Instead of re-producing the original sounds with as high a degree of fidelity as pos-sible, producers and musicians increasingly tended to add electronic technologies to them. Making a comparison with the traditional aim of reproducing sounds as realistically as possible, George Martin defined the new situation: "Now we are working with pure sound. We are building sound pictures" (Birnbaum & Porterfield 1967, 58).[21]

It could be argued that *Sgt. Pepper* contributed to the way in which exploitation of recording technology as a creative component of music-making gradually became part of the rock auteurship and star image in popular music. *Sgt. Pepper* remains an early exemplification of how the relationship between the musician and technology has become central in the construction of pop music stardom and authenticities, in partic-ular how far and in what ways the musician actively establishes cre-ative sovereignty over the technology.[22] In the mythologization of the Beatles, their relationship with technology is exemplified by *Sgt. Pepper*, which is widely regarded as the ne plus ultra of 1960s popular music and technology, the apotheosis of the musician's creative mastery over, and through, the machine.

It is, however, worth asking whether *Sgt. Pepper* really revolution-ized the making of popular music. Journalists and pop historians have often regarded the meeting of new technologies and popular music as a democratizing development. In cases such as the cheapening of syn-thesizers in the early 1980s or the breakthrough of computer-based home studios in the late 1990s, this certainly is so. It is also reasonable to suggest, as Moore does (1993, 57), that in the late 1960s far-reaching technological developments in the studio together with the economic growth of the record companies enabled new experiments. However, when examining the question of musical creation alongside the matter of popular music stardom, especially with the case of the Beatles and *Sgt. Pepper*, the pattern looks more ambiguous.

In the early 1960s bands did not spend much time and money in the recording studio. The Beatles' debut album, *Please Please Me* (1963), was basically made in one day during which the group recorded ten songs. Later in the decade it became a trend for some groups and artists to exploit existing studio technology more elaborately, at least for those for whom the resources were available. Since the Beatles had proved to be a commercial gold mine and also because EMI owned both Abbey Road Studios and the Beatles recordings, the band was relatively free to set its own budget for *Sgt. Pepper*. The sky was not the limit, of course, and there was some management criticism of the fact that the album cost £25,000, which in 1967 was as much as it would have cost to record five albums for London's New Philharmonia Orchestra (Birnbaum & Porterfield 1967, 58). Nonetheless, this fact itself indicates that evidently money was not a major constraint during the project.

In comparison with other artists, the Beatles were privileged. In his subsequent analysis of *Sgt. Pepper*, Moore modifies his earlier position, claiming that the attempt to create challenging sound pictures in the late 1960s "moved the music to regions out of the reach of amateur and semi-professional performers, who had neither access to the studio technology involved nor the finances to afford the live equipment required for successful performance" (1998, 78). The technology that the Beatles exploited in the studio may have been primitive compared to later conditions in popular music, but it was close to the most advanced technology available and they had all the time to take the best out of it. Furthermore, musicians who could afford it, like John Lennon, even built their own home studios. Thus, from the technological perspective, *Sgt. Pepper* did not signal the democratization of pop music but the reassessment of aesthetic criteria in popular music stardom and the formation of a new kind of hierarchy, a "pecking order" of rock, which would later evolve into a canonical discourse.

Shuker (2001) argues that the status hierarchy among performers of popular music ranges from those musicians starting out, largely reliant on "covers," to session musicians and to performers who attempt, with varying levels of critical and commercial success, to make a living from music. This last group has its own differentiations and hierarchies of journeymen players, artists and stars. At the apex of the pyramid there are stars, and especially those stars who also enjoy auteur status. During the *Sgt. Pepper* process the Beatles may have become a group of aesthetes detached from the usual pop practices and even everyday life, but at the same time they began to represent pop celebrities who were independent, innovative, visionary, willing and able to develop new areas and to control the final result—all features that, according to Shuker, are characteristic of rock auteurism[23] (112–19; see also the traditional model of the rock career in Frith 1988c).

Although Shuker stresses the point that the hierarchies of popular music have become contentious and vague, it could be suggested that the pattern was relatively clear in the late 1960s. It was the rock press in particular that participated in the formation of this hierarchy. The new generation of critics emerged as central to the terms of rock/pop canonicity and decreed that the crucial strategy for the musician was perhaps no longer simply to release two albums and three singles yearly, but to cultivate their artistic identities and create works of enduring aesthetic worth (Chapple & Garofalo 1978; Frith 1978). While *Sgt. Pepper's* release was accompanied by some speculations that the Beatles had gone "too far" for their fans (see the reception of the album in Moore 1998), such reservations were not supported by the rock press, which was codifying the ideology of rock and legitimating "its" music as opposed to the older generation's tastes. Even though many critics (e.g., Peyser 1969; Poirier 1969) immediately recognized how the concept of *Sgt. Pepper* was pervaded by the presence of history and temporal displacements, as exemplified in the range of historical personages in the cover art and in the English music hall heritage in the songs, it was more typical to embrace the album as a harbinger of a new type of pop art and rock culture. The Beatles represented the "best rock," which is "moving with unprecedented speed into unexpected, more artistically interesting areas" (Peyser 1969, 136). To Birnbaum and Porterfield, they were "leading an evolution in which the best of current post-rock sounds are becoming something that pop music has never been before: an art form" (1967, 56).

Attempts clearly have emerged to understand and legitimize *Sgt. Pepper* as a sign of the times, a "cinematic dissolve from one Zeitgeist to another" (MacDonald 1995, 198). This has led to debate over which zeitgeist. Sheila Whiteley argues that *Sgt. Pepper* represented "the juxtaposition of the inhumanity of the dominant culture with that of the counter-culture, the need to know oneself, to open up to alternative experience" (1992, 60). Such a view is put into question by Negus (1996,

156–58), who finds the album important primarily due to its musical dialogues and for the way it crosses boundaries of historical eras and genres. *Sgt. Pepper* was in many ways an extraordinary recording because of its synthesis of different music genres. In terms of production and the musical elements employed, the Beatles used Indian instrumentation, brass bands, orchestras, circus sound effects, music hall devices, romantic ballads and surrealistic sound collages and drew on a range of identifiable musical genres that in the tradition of popular music could not unambiguously be referred to as rock music. Negus' main intention is to emphasize that *Sgt. Pepper* has been heard simply as an album representing countercultural sentiments and "rock." Not only was the album not produced as a "rock" album, it was not listened to just by "rock" fans but by numerous people, from children to older adults, around the world. Negus argues that the "history of the 'rock era' often presents the meaning of the Beatles' music only from the perspective of British or US 'rockology'" and that this history fallaciously refers to "*Sergeant Pepper* as the peak of the rock era or the quintessential rock album" (159). Given the fact that at least in contemporary journalistic writings *Sgt. Pepper* is usually treated as a pop record rather than a "rock" LP, Negus' conclusion is slightly misleading. Following the reevaluation of "pop" in popular music discussion in the 1980s, the aesthetics and the music of *Sgt. Pepper* have been understood as much as a Sixties pinnacle of pop modernism as a peak of the "rock era."

While it is now difficult if not impossible to locate the exact place of *Sgt. Pepper* in the pop/rock canon, in 1967 there were arguably two dominant factors situating it in the discourse and imagination. First, the role of the professional rock journalist was crucial to the mediation of "rock" and *Sgt. Pepper* as a harbinger of a new type of "rock art." That this new occupational group and its attempt to promulgate a new rock ideology emerged around the same time as *Sgt. Pepper* is a significant synchronicity. If rock culture took possession of the cultural capital of *Sgt. Pepper* without visible struggle, it was mainly because the evolution of "rock" in the late 1960s was a dynamic process that managed to appropriate various forms of culture. Within this development, the Beatles were placed at the center of "rock" and were seen to represent the "revolutionary" tumults of the counterculture. It thus followed that if the Beatles had earlier been dependent on teenybop fan culture and its demands, their new position was to an extent determined by the ideals of rock culture and rock journalists.

The other and perhaps more important determinant of the meaning of *Sgt. Pepper* was the image of the Beatles themselves. Even though some critics were surprised and even confused by *Sgt. Pepper*, it was certainly not because the album was an obscure work: The LP was made by the most famous pop group in the world. Thus, as much as *Sgt. Pepper* redefined the Beatles as the "most effective avatars" (Leary 1998, 69), the stardom of the Beatles defined *Sgt. Pepper*. Their star image was shifting toward a new kind of pop intellectualism, demonstrated by their interest in social issues such as drugs, religion, the war in Vietnam, and, increasingly, the function of art and music in society. This made it easier to situate the LP in the categories of counterculture and "rock." Even though the Beatles would articulate their social concerns more seriously and elaborately during subsequent years, their early interest in such issues in the mid-1960s was generally noted because it had not traditionally been a part of pop stardom. Apart from such utterances, other Beatles gestures and styles had already been, at least to some extent, attached to the counterculture, as disclosed in the cases of John Lennon's granny glasses and his Rolls-Royce. Hence, there was a developing framework of stardom that provided a particular discourse that listeners could bring to the album.

It is a matter of debate as to whether or not *Sgt. Pepper* really was the peak of the Beatles' career and a quintessential musical work in Western music history. What is clear, however, is that it was an LP that marked a new kind of union between technology, aestheticism and stardom. The Beatles' music was no longer identified and evaluated in terms of the standards of live performance; rather, it was considered through its creative incorporation of studio technology. *Sgt. Pepper* reinforced the Beatles' stars-as-auteurs position and contributed to the formation of a new kind of hierarchy of musicianship in rock culture. Inversely, through *Sgt. Pepper* rock culture appropriated the Beatles as its spokesmen.

In more concrete terms, *Sgt. Pepper's Lonely Hearts Club Band* has remained the swan song of the Beatles as a harmonious entity. Even though their abandonment of live performances was accompanied by rumors about the disintegration of the group, the release of a new recording silenced such suggestions. It is also arguable that since the

Beatles had undertaken their extraordinary retirement as a group, the feeling of cohesion actually increased during the period. This, however, was short-lived. The Beatles were still to release three more albums (*The Beatles*, *Abbey Road* and *Let It Be*), none of which has been regarded as the embodiment of the same level of cooperation.

The group cohesion in *Sgt. Pepper* is also the reason why I have in this section largely ignored John Lennon. Yet, as I have argued in the previous two sections, Lennon's stardom clearly was in a transitional stage, moving away both from the boundaries of traditional pop stardom and the Beatles. Even though being a Beatle was the most important single determinant of John Lennon's stardom until the dissolution of the group in 1970 and even beyond, I shall now shift my focus from his association with the group to examine specific relationships and conflicts between the various components of his starnet.

6 John Lennon, Rock Culture and the Imperative of Activism in the Late 1960s

Unfinished Participation: Avant-garde and Rock Music

> *Please burn this book after you've read it.*
> — *Yoko Ono: Grapefruit. A Book of Instructions*

The late 1960s was a very intense period for John Lennon. Together with his new wife, Yoko Ono, Lennon sought to work within the mass media, committing himself to peace campaigns and exploiting his own status as a highly recognizable star. The years 1968 through 1970 remained Lennon and Ono's most visible, marking the beginning of a relationship that would become one of the most publicized love stories and artistic collaborations in the twentieth century. Political leaders aside, there is probably more media documentation of their activities during that time than exists for any other public figure: Lennon and Ono made their honeymoon a much-publicized "bed-in," planted acorns as a message of hope, launched the "War Is Over (If You Want It)" poster campaign, supported various other peace campaigns, wrote open letters to editors, appeared in public enveloped in bags, arranged art exhibitions, published drawings and gave concerts. They also released several experimental records and produced films. Recording with the Beatles became almost a sideline for Lennon at the time. It is evident that as a visible media figure with an increasing spectrum of activities, Lennon was no longer "just" a pop musician but an all-around celebrity armed with a social mission. Nevertheless, in public Lennon was still mainly referred to as a Beatle and being a rock star still formed the core of his celebrity.

The aim of this chapter is to examine Lennon's star career from 1968 to 1970 in Anglo-American culture through the idea of the "avant-garde peacenik," a character type that Wiener used in his political biog-

raphy *Come Together* to describe late 1960s Lennon. What Wiener is referring to by this figure is that Lennon's career in the late 1960s was
characterized by interests in experimental art, New Left media politics
and the ideal of world peace. Wiener suggests that in order to transform
himself as an artist and star, Lennon needed to join in transforming the
world and to take on "the project of sixties radicalism as his own: a si-
multaneous struggle for personal and political liberation" (1985, xvii).
Within this framework, Lennon intuitively blended various ideas then
current in culture: politics and art, private and public, individuality and
community, "low" and "high."

To contextualize Lennon's avant-gardism, it should be noted that
the late 1960s has generally been labeled as a period of radicalism in
Western societies. There were heated debates, even conflicts, not only
between political opponents but also across generations, as reflected in
the "student revolution," the hippie movement and other countercultural forms. There was abundant discussion of political revolution.
Even though fundamental power structures largely remained intact,
nonetheless, there seems to be agreement that significant changes of attitudes occurred.

For the historian Eric Hobsbawm (1994), the challenging of conventions in the 1960s reflected the cultural revolution that overtook Western societies in the later twentieth century. Hobsbawm writes that
postwar developments can best be understood as "the triumph of the
individual over society, or rather, the breaking of the threads which in
the past had woven human beings into social textures" (334). This overturning of older conventions produced traumatic insecurity. Hobsbawm goes on to argue that the drama of collapsed traditions and
values of the late 1960s was reflected in the rise of what came to be
called identity politics: the demands of ethnic, national, sexual and religious minorities and the nostalgic search for a hypothetical past era of
unproblematic order and security (341–42). This drama was visible in
the counterculture, incorporating a range of "movements" organized
around the nominal objective of social liberation, in opposition to those
who represented, in countercultural phraseology, the "Establishment"
or the "System."

In this instance, it is not necessary to trace the more general political
and artistic movements or the detail of the revolution of everyday life.
What is important to remember, however, is that when we generalize

about an era, referring to it as, say, the "swinging" or "revolutionary" Sixties, we invoke images that have been felt and experienced in different ways by different people. The feminist author Sara Maitland emphasizes in her recollection of the 1960s that wherever she was and whatever she did, the real Sixties always seemed to be "somewhere else" (1988, 11). Relatively few people were directly involved in revolutionary events, which most people heard and saw through the media. This view is supported by the historian Robert Hewison (1986, 276), who argues that even though 1968, the culminating year of demonstrations and student revolts in Western societies, called attention to significant changes in society, they were most acutely felt among the intelligentsia. The year 1968 did not mean the revolt of the oppressed but the revolt of the privileged.

While the scope of the revolt in the late 1960s remains open to various interpretations, it is obvious that prominent individuals played an important role in producing images of the era. Representatives of fine arts and the intelligentsia have often been exalted as pioneers in articulating the spirit of the times, the productions of the romantics and modernists remaining perhaps the most conspicuous examples of such tendencies. Regarding the 1960s, however, it is evident that the groups who conspicuously shaped the spirit of the times included not only artists and intellectuals but also those working in the fields of fashion, journalism and entertainment. Furthermore, as the division between "low" and "high" was increasingly challenged (as epitomized in the Swinging London phenomenon), categorizations of prominent individuals overlapped and popular culture celebrities—such as rock stars— were acknowledged, and even expected to act, as socially concerned artists and intellectuals. The increasing dialogue between entertainment culture and counterculture led celebrities to articulate hopes and expectations that were projected onto them. It is instructive that in some cases, established stars were more or less forced to participate in this dialogue and comment upon social issues in their songs, most notably Elvis Presley with his "In the Ghetto" and "If I Can Dream" and the Supremes with their "Love Child."

John Lennon's involvement in radical arts and politics undoubtedly was associated with the overturning of old conventions and the expectation of a new kind of artistry and intellectualism in popular music. Lennon not only reflected such impulses but also attempted to add substantially to their momentum. The extent to which he reinvented cultural traditions and symbolized revolutionary elements in popular music culture is a question that I shall discuss in more detail in the next two sections; what is apparent, however, is that he has come to symbolize revolutionary elements of the entire milieu. The imperative of social activism and the idea of a star as a person who can influence people and produce zeitgeist are keys to an understanding of Lennon's stardom in the late 1960s.

For Lennon, who at a more personal level desperately sought new ways to express himself and redefine his star identity, the methods of the avant-garde provided a way of connecting art and social mission. A central influence on Lennon's increasing enthusiasm for the avant-garde was undoubtedly his future wife, the Japanese-born artist Yoko Ono. It was after Lennon invited Ono to experiment with sound effects at his home in 1968 that they became closely involved with each other, and the couple began to be seen in public. Shortly afterward Lennon divorced his wife Cynthia and married Ono. It is well known that Ono had established herself as a prominent avant-garde artist before meeting Lennon. Ono was born in Japan in 1933 but moved to New York with her family in 1953. In the early 1960s she joined the loosely organized art group known as Fluxus,[1] which sought to demolish the boundaries between art and life, combining music, visual art, poetry and drama. Within Fluxus, Ono presented a variety of experimental activities involving music, film, poetry, painting and sculpture and, above all, organized several art events and performances, or "happenings," which at the time were increasingly becoming a trademark of avant-garde art. She soon came to be labeled as the "High Priestess of the Happening" (Hopkins 1987; Gaar 1993).

Because of his art school background, Lennon was to some extent familiar with the avant-garde, although he also remained skeptical about it. Until Ono's intervention, he frequently declared that "avant-garde is French for bullshit" (Evans 1987, 19). Prior to his collaboration with Ono, Lennon had nonetheless experimented with approaches similar to avant-garde art. His two collections of satirical verse and grotesque drawings, *In His Own Write* and *A Spaniard in the Works*, bore similarities to experimental literature, but it was his music that disclosed more explicitly his radical tendencies. Lennon had experimented with tapes in his home studio, and some of the ideas, including running the tape backward, variations in the tape speed, and echo effects, had made their way onto the Beatles' records, as in the early example, "Tomorrow Never Knows." Inspired by Ono, Lennon continued with sound experiments, although only one uncompromisingly avant-garde piece appeared in the Beatles catalog, the sound collage "Revolution 9" on *The Beatles* double album, informally known as the White Album.[2]

It was when Lennon began his relationship with Yoko Ono that his interest in avant-garde music and experimental art really flourished. Over a short period, the couple released three records, *Unfinished Music No. 1: Two Virgins* (1968), *Unfinished Music No. 2: Life with the Lions* (1969) and *Wedding Album* (1969), all of which challenged the traditional aesthetic of music and art. Furnished with tape loops, reversed recordings, filtered noises, random effects and vocal experiments, these records sounded more like modern musique concrète than late 1960s experimental rock. The main reason for Lennon and Ono to draw on musique concrète arguably was that there were preexisting models in the tradition of avant-garde music, while avant-rock was then still in its infancy. Nonetheless, the cultural atmosphere seemed propitious for the convergence of avant-garde music and rock in the late 1960s.

Avant-garde has been understood as a child of progress in a technologized society (Huyssen 1986, 4, 9). Similarly, despite its nostalgic strands late 1960s rock music developed a dynamic relationship with new technology and the idea of progress. Influenced by new studio technology, psychedelia and the dialogue between "high" and "low," which had so visibly emerged among the "popocracy" of Swinging London, pop musicians began to venture into musical experimentation. Groups like Cream, Pink Floyd and the Soft Machine experimented with pop psychedelia, blues rock, modern jazz and sound experimentations. In *Their Satanic Majesties Request* (1967), the Rolling Stones took the idea of collage one step further than the Beatles had with *Sgt. Pepper*. Mick Jagger composed the Moog synthesizer music for Kenneth Anger's film *Invocation of My Demon Brother* (1969), while George Harrison released two experimental albums, *Wonderwall* (1968) and *Electronic Sounds* (1969). In America, the Fugs brought obscenity-laden poetry and rock cabaret together, the Velvet Underground rejected hippie optimism, toying with dissonant rock sounds and the idea of musical incompetence in close association with Andy Warhol, and Frank Zappa relied on sophisticated craft techniques, sound experimentations and modern classical influences, lampooning trends and fashions of popular culture. Yet, avant-rock soon reached an impasse, Zappa remaining the only prominent figure of the genre. In spite of being studded with star performers, the convergence of rock and the avant-garde remained a minor strand in popular culture. Lennon, Ono and the majority of avant-garde artists did not achieve either popularity or critical acclaim with their modernist music.[3]

Working at the interface of various musical genres and cross-fertilization between different arts was perhaps too innovative for rock culture, but it could also be argued that avant-rock was, at least in Britain, a part-time hobby or merely a diverting novelty for most of the rock stars involved in it. For example, the Beatles' Zapple, an experimental record label from Apple, was intended as an ambitious outlet for a range of improvisational and spoken word recordings, but it ceased operation after only two releases (Rogan 1997). It is reasonable to conclude that avant-garde was for the Beatles just another passing experiment, like folk rock, Indian ragas, psychedelic rock and other trends they had helped popularize.

Another reason for the lack of success of avant-rock lies, of course, in the tradition of the avant-garde itself. The aim to challenge the popular with dissonance and radical aesthetics is a key to avant-garde experiment and can be traced back to early twentieth-century modernism. Regarding themselves as a group of pioneers or, as in the original French meaning of avant-garde, the "vanguard of an army," experimental artists and their works are often rejected by the masses as incomprehensible. It is also typical of the avant-garde that it despises categorization and challenges its own tradition. In a way, Yoko Ono exemplified this development in the 1960s.

The majority of experimental artists in the 1950s had created weighty, serious and permanent objects and worked in the traditional media of painting and music (Wiener 1985). By drawing on everyday or unconventional materials, or no materials at all, Ono created ideas and performances that were humorous and ephemeral. Ono's art, also known as concept art and instructional art, often placed emphasis on playful ideas and imagination rather than physical works. In *Wind Piece*, for example, the audience was asked to move chairs and make way for the imaginary wind (Ono 1970, pages not numbered). Nonetheless, the new avant-garde had its serious side. Ono and other avant-garde artists opposed any compromise of their experimental mission, and mounted a critique of bourgeois art and its ideology of autonomy. They thus followed the tradition expressed by the dada and surrealist movements half a century earlier. The new avant-garde, however, took its critique one step further. While in the 1950s avant-garde had largely left its audience to the detached contemplation of its work, the 1960s avant-garde drew its audience into the process of art more actively. One of the doctrines of the 1960s avant-garde was that the work of art was "unfinished" until the audience intervened. This idea was articulated in Ono's absurd book of poems, *Grapefruit*, first published in 1964, which was meant as a guide for people as to how to participate in happenings and to produce performances of their own. As epitomized in John Cage's famous piece of silence, "4'33"," the new avant-garde could even conceive of the audience as the main creator of the artwork. As a result, participation became a central theme of the 1960s avant-garde, patterned after the counterculture and its design for interaction and social gatherings such as the hippie movement's vogue for "be-ins" (Huyssen 1986; Frith & Horne 1987).

The hallmark of the avant-garde sensibility was the deliberate depersonalization of the work of art, in the sense of the elimination of craftsmanship and the artist, or at least a drastic reduction of the artist's role as an interpreter of experience. The avant-garde artist advocated a suspension or abolition of conscious control, "not in order to open himself to the promptings of his unconscious thoughts and desires but in order to extinguish every suggestion of his own personality" (Lasch 1984, 165). This impulse informed Lennon and Ono, to whom the reconfiguration of the relationship between the artist and the audience formed a guiding principle in the late 1960s.

While for Ono depersonalization of the artwork had already become familiar, for Lennon it was a radical area hitherto unexplored. Even though Lennon had been the focus of the media and fans since Beatlemania, he had become more estranged from his audiences after the Beatles' abandonment of the concert stage and withdrawal into the studio. At first "art for art's sake" seemed an appropriate ideology, but it soon conflicted with the late 1960s impulse toward social involvement. The new avant-garde seemed to provide a perfect key to the problem: It was interactive, it was demonstrative and it was still Art.

For Lennon at least, the avant-garde was a means of restoring the contact with his audience that he felt had been lost during the Beatles' studio period.

Lennon began to reconsider himself as an artist whose duty was to
communicate with and in society: "Just as journalists are responsible
for telling the news as it is, we are responsible for showing our pieces
as they are, and any artist who doesn't do that part is lazy, a lazy egoist"
(Watts 1971, 25; see also Smith 1969a; Cott 1982a; Yorke 1982b). But who
defined the standards of such communication? Although this subject
will be dealt with in more detail in the next two sections, it should be
noted that the converging methods of the avant-garde and the practices
of rock stardom provided a solution to the artist-audience dilemma.
The problem was that the avant-garde music of the 1960s was primarily
intended to be performed and experienced live, not to be captured and
immortalized in recording formats. No matter how Lennon and Ono
emphasized the "unfinishedness" of their experimental records, it
seems that the idea of participation through avant-garde music was for
them more a theoretical axiom than a practical method for calling people to interact in the creation of art.

Neither was the idea of interaction realized in Lennon and Ono's
four avant-garde rock concerts. For example, at Toronto's Rock 'n' Roll
Revival Festival, where Lennon appeared with his Plastic Ono Band in
September 1969, the result was, if possible, more confusing than his recorded experiments.[4] The hastily formed group first performed a number of rock 'n' roll standards and two new Lennon songs, which,
according to D. A. Pennebaker's documentary film *Sweet Toronto* and
the live album of the event, were relatively well received. The same did
not apply to the latter part of the concert, which developed into blues-
rock free jamming and feedback experimentations, Yoko Ono taking
the leading role with her wailing and screaming. The rock 'n' roll-ori-
ented audience was stunned into silence as the band left the stage.

What really was confusing about such expressions was the unsuccessful attempt to combine romantic visions and modernist methods.
The new avant-garde emphasized the idea of communication and community, which resembled the "folk argument" then current in rock music and counterculture. Its methods, however, drew on the tradition
that appreciated elitist experimentation, irony and shock elements, all
of which were foreign to folk romanticism's emphasis on sincerity, di-

rectness and naturalness. It is thus hardly surprising that avant-garde music did not establish living dialogue between the artist and the audience. It only provided imaginary communication, a fantasy of interaction. The other paradox was that while 1960s avant-garde art embraced interaction between the artist and the audience and put the emphasis on the artist's role as the mediator, it could not escape, especially in its musical forms, the ideologies of art itself. Through their experimental music as well as minimalist films,[5] Lennon and Ono still appeared as self-conscious artists, controlling what sounds to include in their records and what to shoot for their films. It should also be remembered that Lennon's attempt to demystify art and the cult of the artist failed because he had already achieved such a high and individualized profile in popular culture. Now, by producing such idiosyncratic music, Lennon in fact emphasized his position as a clearly differentiated ego, an eccentric visionary, and contributed to the modernist belief that the authentic artist must constantly reinvent herself/himself and cross artistic boundaries. Hence, the avant-garde did not demystify his status, but accentuated his authenticity as an auteur who seemed to be able to control his products and the process of stardom.

The limits of the avant-garde were perhaps realized by Lennon and Ono themselves since their interest in experimental music soon abated. They may have noticed that the doctrine of participation applied much more effectively to popular music performances—as demonstrated by "Give Peace a Chance," a song that was recorded in a freewheeling hotel-room session during the Montreal bed-in and that became Lennon's most famous musical contribution to the peace campaign. The couple certainly realized that the ideals of the new avant-garde could be cultivated in nonmusical situations such as bed-ins and other events for peace. Not only music, film or other forms of art, but also the entire celebrity lifestyle could become material for the avant-garde and send serious social messages. This also meant that Lennon's stardom became more pluralized, dispersed and controversial.

Conflicting Expectations: Forms of Messianic Intensities

Stoned on the Jesus thing!
—T-shirt in the late 1960s

It was reported on December 4, 1969 (*The Times*) that Tim Rice and Andrew Lloyd Webber had asked John Lennon to play Christ in their rock opera *Jesus Christ Superstar*. The offer interested Lennon, but he did not have the opportunity to pursue it since the writers of the opera changed their minds, announcing that a celebrity "like Lennon would imprint his own personality to such an extent that people would read the star's character into the character of the part" (*The Times*, December 5, 1969). The writers specified that rather than an established star, they would prefer an unknown to play Christ. Notwithstanding this assertion, Rice and Webber then attempted to sign Robert Plant, the lead singer of Led Zeppelin, to sing the role. When this failed, they found Ian Gillan, who had just joined another famous hard rock group, Deep Purple (Wale 1972). It thus seems that the explanation "people would read the star's character into the character of the part" referred most particularly to John Lennon's stardom, that is, his reputation not only as an eminent rock artist and Beatle but his visibility as a messenger of peace and love. In a way, Lennon had already been playing Christ.

John Lennon's enthusiasm for and identification with Jesus Christ was widely publicized at the time (see Harry 2000). Although Lennon did not announce a religious awakening, as Little Richard and Cliff Richard had done so conspicuously some years earlier, he referred to the topic with warmth. Moreover, Jesus' mission provided a significant model for Lennon in the peace events that he conducted with Yoko Ono. Lennon's optimistic faith drew strength from the power and ubiquity of modern media, which seemed to provide great possibilities in making, as he said in a press conference in Amsterdam, "Christ's message contemporary" (quoted in Coleman 1988, 317). Lennon even began to adopt visual imagery traditionally associated with Christ. He let his beard grow, parted his long and straight hair and often dressed himself in a simple white suit. This visual change prompted a journalist of *New Musical Express* to suggest that "John's long hair and beard gives him an intellectual, almost holy appearance which his Beatle cut didn't" (Nesbit 1969, 4). Lennon's interest in the message of Christ was clearly related to the promotion of world peace, which became a major mission for him and Yoko Ono in the late 1960s. It is arguable that this shift was perhaps a reflection of guilt at being a wealthy and famous rock star attempting to negotiate countercultural demands of social liberation and the ethos of utopianism. My intention, however, is not to conjecture regarding Lennon's psyche and motivations, but to explore religious dimensions of Lennon's stardom in the late 1960s and to investigate the dialogue between Lennon and those who mediated and reconstructed his image. What was the relationship between Lennon's interest in Christianity and expectations that were imposed upon him as a star?

It should be recalled that Western popular culture was at the time pervaded by spiritual and religious impulses. Steve Turner (1995) suggests in his study of rock music and religion that the 1960s lurch into gnosticism, paganism and pantheism was generated by the young who complained about the deadening materialism of older generations. Countercultural leaders and rock stars played an important role in this development. The experimentalism and the drug experience of many rock musicians "suggested messages from the initiated": "Like the first-century gnostics who believed that there were those who had received 'gnosis' (knowledge) and those who hadn't, the 'acid heads' assumed superiority over the 'straights' who'd not turned on" (56). What makes this development interesting in terms of stardom is that eminent rock stars came to be regarded not so much as music industry commodities, but as figures who embodied certain (countercultural) ideals of behavior and sentiment. While stars still were dependent on the institutions of a capitalist economy to promote their products and mobilize audiences for profit, they now were understood as operators of powerful images and types within cultural codes and processes.

Late 1960s "rock gnostics" were in many ways regarded as semi-spiritual mentors of the new rock and counterculture generation. They represented the potential not only for social transformation or collapse but also for individual change. The private spheres of rock stars, their pursuits of gnosis, took many forms and were conspicuously made public in the late 1960s. Stars like the Beatles, Mick Jagger, Keith Richards, Brian Jones, Pete Townshend, Eric Burdon and Donovan (as well as American stars) expressed their enthusiasm for Eastern philosophies, attended courses in meditation and discussed the spiritual immaturity of modern Western societies. Through their mentor roles, rock stars arguably contributed to the spirituality and the quest for "truth" that in the late 1960s became a fashion and an industry in itself, "with everything from pagan magic to Zen Buddhism on the market" (Turner 1995, 50–51).

Gnosis was more sought than found among rock celebrities, most of whom abandoned their spiritual journeys within a few months of initiation to the subject. In retrospect, it was hardly surprising. The thought of the celebrity retiring in reclusive meditation conflicted with the "limelight doctrine" of stardom and also appeared unfashionable when countercultural voices began to demand that rock stars should express their commitment to revolutionary events.[6] As a result, it became crucial for rock culture to combine the pursuit of gnosis and the compulsion of participation. Attempts to articulate this balance were conspicuous among some American rock writers, who reinvented the term *Dionysian* to describe the rock star phenomenon on one hand as a site of the artist's inner visions, and on the other hand as a site of countercultural commitment. The term derived from Friedrich Nietzsche's theory of aesthetics and his argument that the development of art is bound up with the duality of the Apollonian and the Dionysian, invoking two art deities in Greek mythology. For Nietzsche (1967, 33–38), the Apollonian form of art was characterized by the beautiful and "joyous necessity of the dream experience," meaning that artistic energies burst forth from nature and in the image world of dreams. The Dionysian form, on the other hand, was perceived as "intoxication," whether meaning "the influence of the narcotic draught" or the ecstasy of the "potent coming of spring." Many rock journalists who sought to define and legitimate rock experience in terms of the philosophical vocabulary of "high" culture were themselves intoxicated by Nietzsche's words about the Dionysian artist feeling "himself a god" and becoming "a work of art." Walter Breen wrote in *Crawdaddy*: "The ecstasy of Dionysus is that of being overwhelmed with the sheer glory of motion of what is beyond, being taken over by it, becoming no longer merely human but an instrument of the godhead, a part of the cosmic dance, a tongue of flame in the Sun" (1970, 17–18; see also Meltzer 1970). For Breen, rock was primarily Dionysian since it presented religious manifestations, ecstasies and experiences that threatened the Establishment. The rock star, especially the male rock star, could most effectively embody such ideals. Mick Jagger and Jim Morrison in particular became the epitomes of the excess of Dionysian rock, representing the intense, extreme, ecstatic, wild, dangerous, divine, demonic and sexual sides of popular music culture.

Because of its semireligious connotations of transcendence, Dionysian rock can be comprehended as a subcategory of a broader ethos prevailing in the late 1960s culture and celebrity phenomenon: messianism. That "messianism" became one of the catchphrases of late 1960s rock stardom was not only a result of the combination of excess and innocence—it was also a result of rock stars' new, quasi-religious mentor status and reflected a more general change in the relationship between popular culture and Christianity. The shift was epitomized in the hippie movement which, according to journalist Tom Wolfe (1993, 282), was "religious and yet incontrovertibly hip at the same time" and indeed "made religion look hip." What followed was the late 1960s' and early 1970s' "Jesus boom," which in America took forms traditionally associated with the commercialization of entertainment and mass culture rather than religion. Variations of hippie and psychedelic jargon ("Getting high on Jesus," "Jesus tripping") were printed on T-shirts, buttons, stickers, shorts and bikinis (Jasper 1975, 95). This particular reconfiguration of the relationship between Christianity and rock music was also manifested in the ways that evangelical writers, some of whom (like Billy Graham) had earlier considered rock music to be a form of mass hypnosis and satanic inclinations, now began to see popular music in a more positive light and attempted to establish rock as a conduit through which young people might open their hearts to the Son of God. In Britain, Christian communities produced several pop-folk musicals in the early 1970s, including *Alive, Rock* and *Lonesome Stone*, all of which, however, received adverse critical receptions (Jasper 1975).

Music theater is a good example of how rock not only appealed to Christianity, but how the idea of a Messiah was exploited by secular writers. The rock musical *Hair*, which had its premiere in 1967 and soon became a popular-culture milestone of the era, combined hippie sentiments and semireligious elements. Another example of the development was *Tommy* (1969), which was written by Pete Townshend, of the Who, and which the Who recorded as well as performed live. Often cited as the world's first rock opera, *Tommy*, which was later staged and filmed, presented the metamorphosis of a young man from "holy fool to Rock & Roll Messiah" (Schaffner 1982, 127). It was, however, the aforementioned rock opera *Jesus Christ Superstar*, first shown on Broadway in New York in 1971, that epitomized rock messianism. It became a huge success, begetting a variety of side products, the soundtrack album of the play alone selling more than 3 million units worldwide (Jasper 1975). The "God rock" boom continued with *Godspell* (1971), a musical that made David Essex, the singer cast as Jesus, a pop star.

All these productions reflected the growing interest in understanding modern music stardom as "a mad, messianic intensity" (Savage 1988a, 124). Stardom was perceived as a state of salvation, sacrifice and presence. It was typical of these plays to present enigmatic, solitary and suffering stars at the epicenter of a media hurricane and at the mercy of audiences, who carefully monitored their heroes for signs of hubris. This star-versus-the-world scenario was also presented in rock journalism, which began to apply messianic standards to some stars, especially Bob Dylan, who had already been compared to a Messiah during his groundbreaking British tour in 1965 (Marcus 1997). The pattern continued during Dylan's two-year seclusion from 1966 to 1968. The "second coming" of the hero was loaded with prophetic gravity that was to some extent vindicated, as Dylan, now transformed from a witty folk rocker to a serious-minded mystic, returned with new songs (and a new "Jesus-look") embroidered with religious allusions. Dylan's status as a modern pop Messiah remained unquestioned for years. Interwoven with the discourse of Dylan's messianism was the accusation of being a "fraud," a star who had betrayed his pied piper image because of his wealth, reclusiveness and loss of musical inspiration (Anderson 1981).

John Lennon had already toyed with the idea of messianism before the late 1960s. In 1963 he announced that, together with Paul McCartney, he would write a play about Jesus Christ, who has returned to earth and lives in the urban slums disguised as a man called Pilchard (Smith 1963c, 10). The project, apparently a casual joke, never materialized. In his works Lennon occasionally dealt with religion, mainly in the form of ironic remarks on Christian life.[7] He also discussed the subject with journalists, most famously in the furor-raising *Evening Standard* interview (Cleave 1966), in which he suggested that pop stars had begun to provoke the kind of receptions that signaled messianic expectations. This itself was no news, since a certain religious fervor, especially in the behavior of fans, had already been associated with stardom before the Beatles. What distinguished Beatlemania from earlier star phenomena was the scale of such fervor. The air of divinity seemed to surround the Beatles wherever they traveled. A fan called David Jacobs recalls that when the Beatles returned to Liverpool in 1964, they were received as if "four messiahs" had arrived to save their hometown (Burn & Tennant 1983, 20). The Beatles' press agent Derek Taylor described how in Australia "sick people rushed up to the car as if a touch from one of the boys would make them well again" and how the Beatles were greeted "as if some Saviour had arrived and people were happy and relieved as if things somehow were going to be better now" (Aronowitz 1969, 192).

The thought that stars had the power to heal and save took strange and even troubling forms during the Beatles' tours. Not only young female fans but handicapped adolescents, brought by their mothers and nurses, were desperate to reach the group, as though in hope of the healing touch from the pop saviors. For Lennon, facing "spastics" in his travels was confusing: "Listen, in the States, they lined 'em up and you got the impression the Beatles were being treated as bloody faith healers" (Coleman 1965d, 11). He later recalled that mothers and nurses would push handicapped children at him "like you were Christ or something, as if there were some aura about you which will rub off on them" (Wenner 1980, 14–18).

In relation to the messianic aura of the Beatles' stardom, late 1960s rock gnosticism, the Jesus boom, and Lennon's personal interest in religion and the peace movement, it is hardly surprising that Lennon's identification with Jesus Christ became so conspicuous in the late 1960s. It was, however, not an untroubled development for him. Negative responses to the Beatles and Lennon had been sporadic up to this point, but as Lennon began to appropriate elements of the modern rock Messiah, criticism sharpened. It took many forms, emerging simultaneously from different areas of Lennon's starnet.

Before exploring more closely the maelstrom of Lennon's stardom in the late 1960s, it is useful to recall that at that time the role of the rock star generally began to entail more complex and conflicting expectations. This was articulated by the stars themselves. James T. Coffman (1972) observed at the time how references to audience expectations, the music industry and the performer infiltrated the lyrics of the music, as in "Under Assistant West Coast Promo Man" by the Rolling Stones, "Drug Store Truck Drivin' Man" and "So You Want to Be a Rock 'n' Roll Star" by the Byrds, "A Song for All Seasons" by Jefferson Airplane, "Me and My Destiny" by Doug Sahm and the Sir Douglas Quintet and "Won't Get Fooled Again" by the Who. For Coffman, the increasing number of songs by rock stars about rock stars reflected the conflict between the counterculture and the music industry, each of which promoted competing definitions of social reality as well as ideological and generational conflict. As a member of both groups, the rock musician was subject to these conflicting expectations and standards. On the one hand, the music industry had expectations to which performers as employees were required to respond; on the other hand, countercultural audiences, and the underground media as their representative, attempted to influence performers to incorporate themes, values and ideas that were felt important in their products. In addition to these conflicting expectations, the performers had their own role expectations that were increasingly pervaded by auteurship thinking. In Coffman's words, the performer "desires to control his music and its content, and struggles to extend this control to the recording and performance sectors of his role" (265).[8]

Although Coffman understood the media merely as a mouthpiece of the countercultural audience and thus disregarded the role of the mass media, his suggestion about conflicting expectations is a useful starting point for an examination of the character and scale of Lennon's messianism in the late 1960s. As the following cases suggest, expectations of the music industry, the media and the audience conflicted with Lennon's own expectations about his works and his role as a celebrity.

The first major sign of the change between Lennon and his record company EMI was the release of Lennon and Ono's avant-garde album *Unfinished Music No. 1: Two Virgins*, in 1968. EMI was reluctant to release the album, mainly because of two photographs of naked Lennon and Ono on the cover. Although it was decided that the album would be issued on the Beatles' new Apple label, objections continued since EMI maintained the catalog numbers and handled the distribution for the label. After some heated discussions, the company agreed to press the album, but demanded that it be wrapped in a protective brown paper bag. EMI still refused to distribute the album, and the task was undertaken by Track, the label partly run by the Who. In the United States the distribution was handled by the small independent company Tetra-grammaton (Rogan 1997).

It is evident that John Lennon's artistic ambitions as expressed through *Two Virgins* did not meet the expectations of EMI, which in a number of ways attempted to control the release and distribution of the album. It seems that for an established recording company such as EMI, the dream of "Youth Culture" was still too powerful in the late 1960s. Nudity and "naturalness" were familiar themes in the arts (as in the musical *Hair* and the play *Dionysus '69*) and the hippie movement in the late 1960s, and they soon became prominent in many of Lennon's non-musical activities.[9] The major companies of the music industry, however, did not view such ideas and images as appropriate. A significant part of the controversy of *Two Virgins* was that the album brought the nude element into the field of pop stardom, prompting EMI's concern about the impact the cover might have on the Beatles and its own reputation as a record company. To EMI's mind as well as for the majority of the audience, *Two Virgins* remained a creation of a pop star despite the fact that the album was a result of a collaboration and had the aesthetic of the avant-garde. For many, John had gone beyond the limit of decency, as the American folk singer Rainbo (a.k.a. actress Sissy Spacek) complained in her single "John, You Went Too Far This Time."

Other cases demonstrate that not only EMI but the British media, especially the mainstream press and the underground media, became increasingly concerned about and even hostile toward Lennon in the late 1960s. Whereas radio and television took a rather conciliatory attitude toward Lennon and Ono, the British tabloid press seized upon their promotion of world peace, particularly the first "bed-in," which became one of the most widely reported stories about the couple. For seven days the newlyweds welcomed reporters and photographers into their bedroom (the presidential suite of the Amsterdam Hilton) to give interviews about peace and pose for pictures, lying in bed together in white pajamas. British papers were amused, yet also outraged by the event (Wiener 1985; Coleman 1988). Hostility increased six months later when Lennon returned his MBE, the medal he had received from the Queen in 1965, as a protest against Britain's support of wars in Biafra and Vietnam. A *Daily Mirror* journalist wrote ironically that because "everything depressed Beatle John Lennon when he woke up yesterday," the star "decided that a protest was called for" (Wilson 1969). In an article titled "Go Back to Bed Mr. Lennon!" Vincent Mulchrone of the *Daily Mail* analyzed Lennon's explanations for returning the medal, concluding that Lennon's "MBE is the irrelevancy of the decade."

The British press clearly was confused by Lennon's shift from pop stardom and rock artistry to flamboyant promotions of world peace. It could be suggested that this confusion was also a result of the transitional phase of the media themselves. Largely because of the impact of television, the popular press, such as the *Daily Mail*, the *Daily Mirror*, *The People* and the *Sun* (earlier the *Daily Herald*), as well as more esteemed papers like *The Times* and *The Observer*, began to concentrate increasingly on scandals, celebrities, trends and fashions and provided the idea that the printed media alone "could tell the public what was really going on" (Levin 1989, 340–41; see also Sampson 1982).[10] In this context, Lennon and Ono were as much a scandal as scandalized. It could also be suggested that their stagings of avant-garde events and attempts to use the media in order to convey their message to the audience disturbed the press. Lennon's role as a messianic peace advocate was criticized because in such a media-sensitive situation it exceeded certain boundaries of how the pop celebrity was supposed to act.

Whereas the British mainstream press criticized Lennon on the grounds that he had gone too far for his audience, the alternative press, which was the most crucial medium and network of the underground movement (Fountain 1988), took the opposite view. The growing opinion among journalists and artists who were in favor of New Left politics was that although rock stars did not possess institutional power, they nonetheless were influential, and their influence should be cultivated and harnessed to serve social(ist) purposes. In an interview given to British underground paper *IT*, French film director Jean-Luc Godard accused wealthy pop stars such as the Beatles of being socially passive people who do not utilize their influence, their "minds," in the service of radical social reform (Demoraine 1968, 4).

The most critical voices of the underground press were aggrieved, believing that the Beatles and Lennon had begun to appear as opponents of the Left and were failing to apply their influence to the remedy of social inequities and oppression. Some leftist writers (Beckett 1968; Merton 1968) alleged that unlike the Rolling Stones, who expressed their revolutionary rhetoric through the single "Street Fighting Man," the Beatles and Lennon were less critical and thus pro-Establishment.

As evidence, the critics cited the Beatles' single "Revolution," which insisted that revolutionaries should repudiate their destructive tendencies. In his "Open Letter to John Lennon," published in the leftist alternative paper *Black Dwarf*, John Hoyland (1968, pages not numbered) argued that Lennon should abandon such antileftism and join the ranks of revolutionaries on the grounds that the ruling class "still hates you." This led to a public exchange of correspondence (which then was distributed internationally through the global underground press) between Lennon and the editors of the paper. Lennon (1969) rejected the accusation that he was bourgeois and declared that not only was he against the Establishment but he also opposed violent social revolution. He wanted to distance himself from the underground movement because it attempted to "smash" the world while he wanted to "build around it." The paper's rejoinder, attributed to Hoyland (1969), claimed that changing the way people think was not enough "when all around you you see people's individuality being stunted by the system." The writers appealed to Lennon to join the movement, and argued that as an influential person who already had raised social consciousness among people such as the editors of the paper themselves, he was in a position to initiate more concrete activities.

Levin (1989) argues in his overview of the 1960s that the countercultural movement in Britain had little mass backing and lacked any visible figurehead. It was perhaps because of this that expectations about rock stars like Lennon became a sensitive and controversial issue. Behind the argument that socially concerned rock stars should engage in the struggle for social change lay a hope that stars like Lennon would attract more people to the movement, or at least unite divided elements of the revolutionary forces. It was clearly a disappointment for the British underground that Lennon rejected the mantle of the countercultural leadership and began to preach a more abstract idealism of peace. In the early 1970s Lennon eventually became warmer to New Left ideology, but at that stage the protest movement in Britain was already dispersing and Lennon himself was about to move to the United States with Ono.

The liberal rock press took more diverse positions in the debate. Several articles and interviews backed Lennon, stating, as in *New Musical Express*, that "The Establishment must not drive the Beatles out" (Gray 1969, 3) and "John and Yoko's peace gimmicks do make sense"

(Coxhill 1969, 4). Ritchie Yorke, a journalist writing for *Rolling Stone*, even became a semiofficial envoy of Lennon and Ono and traveled to several countries to promote their peace campaigns (Harry 2000). Nevertheless, critical voices were raised. Alan Walsh, for example, wrote in *Melody Maker* that "handing nuts to world leaders" or spending "a week in bed in a plush hotel" was not only ridiculous but also insulting and spoke disparagingly about Lennon's "lack of communication" (1969, 7).

In addition to EMI and most of the media, the audience became more reserved toward Lennon. After the release of *Two Virgins* and the staging of the Amsterdam bed-in, critical letters from readers poured into editorial offices (see, e.g., *Melody Maker*, April 12, 1969). Even though many people still supported Lennon's activities, the number of nonsupporters was notably higher compared to earlier phases. The fan mail also became more critical (Coleman 1988). A significant pattern in the responses was that most of the negative comments were not primarily directed toward Lennon himself, but to his new partner, Yoko Ono, who appeared as a "homewrecker" for many. Ono's visible presence clearly was a catalyst for growing criticism toward Lennon. After the couple's wedding, Ono announced that she would refuse to play the role of the traditional wife (*The Times*, March 22, 1969). It was, however, not only Ono's demand for marital equality but her background that set critical tongues wagging. Ono was a Japanese-born woman and an eccentric artist who did not match the stereotype of a servile Asian female. This released racist and sexist comments among the media and the audience. Fans swarming outside the Apple office called Ono "Nip," "Jap," "Chink" and other insulting names, insisting that she should get back to her own country (Hopkins 1987, 89). There apparently was a fear among the audience and the fans that Lennon would be snatched away from his original followers. An instructive example is that the couple's wedding was described as an event during which Ono "took Beatle-John" (*Daily Mail*, March 21, 1969). The extraordinariness of Lennon's new marriage clearly confronted conventional practices of pop stardom, that is, the idea that the marital life of the star should be as invisible as possible. By appearing by the side of the woman who refused to stay in the background, who assumed equal status with him, who was eccentric, foreign and also older than he, Lennon violated the pattern of "free masculinity" that had been characteristic of his stardom during Beatlemania.

It was not only the music industry, the media, and the audience that began to see Lennon in a more controversial light. In October 1968 the police raided Lennon and Ono and arrested them for possessing marijuana. In the court, Lennon pleaded guilty and was fined. That the Establishment began to scrutinize more seriously Lennon and other rock stars—Mick Jagger, Keith Richards and George Harrison were also raided—symbolized a shift in music stardom: Rock stars no longer represented privileged "popocracy" in Britain.

When former darlings of the nation were vigorously criticized and harassed even by official authorities, Lennon, who regarded himself as an innocent messenger of peace and love, felt that he was becoming a victim. Since the ideal of direct self-expression had increasingly permeated Lennon's musical activities, it was natural for him to deal with feelings of affliction in his songs. Two songs in particular can be seen to represent a sense of heroic victimization or martyrdom: "The Ballad of John and Yoko" and "Working Class Hero."

Even though "The Ballad of John and Yoko" was released as a Beatles single in May 1969, its title leaves no room for doubt about its autobiographical content. The song mainly chronicles Lennon and Ono's marriage and honeymoon, complaining of the media's derision and discrimination. In the chorus, the idea of martyrdom is introduced as Lennon sings how he might be crucified.[11] Some writers (Goldman 1988; Turner 1996; Harry 2000) have noted that in the lyrics of this song, the tendency to emphasize Lennon's role as victim has distorted autobiographical facts. In the first verse Lennon sings that he and Ono were not allowed to board the Channel ferry. Yet, he does not explain that this was so because they had forgotten their passports. When the couple finally managed to make "the plane into Paris," it was not a regular charter flight but a hastily organized private plane. Although Lennon did not exactly lie in his lyrics, he gave an impression of having been cruelly treated and thus romanticized himself as a victim of some undefined Establishment.

"The Ballad of John and Yoko" has been described as an attack against the media, which ignore their dependence on the celebrities they invest in, help perpetuate and then demolish (Elliott 1999, 16). Yet, the song has also been criticized as a piece of egocentrism and paranoia

(Walsh 1969, 7; MacDonald 1995, 277). Either way, "The Ballad of John and Yoko" stands as a typical example of a song whose "message" is publicly defined by its lyrics. It was the lyric of the song that attracted attention in the first place;[12] it is the lyric that underpinned later interpretations of the song as Lennon's self-referential lament for being a mistreated celebrity. More detailed musicological analysis could, however, open new interpretations. The way the song is presented (fast rock 'n' roll shuffle) and its mode (a "joyful" major key) are in a juxtaposition with a balladlike narrative, and together these tend to contest the interpretation of a self-pitying Lennon. The musical arrangement of the song gives an impression of a jaunty songwriter who is perhaps not so uncritically wallowing in martyrdom and who wishes to nuance the image with irony. In fact, the last verse, which chronicles how Lennon and Ono face a warm welcome when returning to England from their honeymoon, has a very positive tone. The "message" of "The Ballad of John and Yoko" thus remains ambivalent.

"Working Class Hero," released eighteen months after "The Ballad of John and Yoko" on the *John Lennon/Plastic Ono Band* album, appears less ambiguous. Although the song lacks the explicit self-referentiality of "The Ballad of John and Yoko," critics have seen it as a reflection of Lennon's growing pessimism. The song has been described as a sarcastic and cynical attempt to cast the hero's identity as both psychic profile and social role, and as a warning regarding the way the media and the Establishment still control people's lives and suppress discussion of freedom and the classless society (Wiener 1985, 7–8; Du Noyer 1997, 30; Elliott 1999, 41). Thus, the song has been understood both as a confessional statement and a social protest. Lennon sings of how clever ones are hated and the fool despised and how religion and television keep people "doped." Each of five stanzas ends in Lennon's ambivalent remark of how a working-class hero is "something to be." Yet, it is only after the final stanza that the first-person narrator is presented, as Lennon, arguably with an ironic undertone, calls potential heroes to "follow me."

At the time, Lennon himself described "Working Class Hero" as a "revolutionary song" written "for workers" (Wenner 1980, 110). In his detailed analysis of the lyrics of the song, Harker (1980) argues that it basically functions as a rich rock star's public confession of guilt rather than as a call for social change. The persuasiveness of Harker's argument is compromised, I think, because, like so many other commentators, he concentrates solely on the lyrics. However, his argument could be fortified by the proposition that the musical delivery of "Working Class Hero" does not invoke "collectivity." By keeping his voice in the lower register and relying on sparse acoustic strumming, Lennon, albeit creating a folk and protest song pastiche, provided an atmosphere of painful confession and introverted intimacy, rather than a rallying call for social mobilization. "Working Class Hero" is perhaps a "guilt song," as Harker argues, but considering the musical arrangement as well as the lyrical scenario (the narrator surrounded by oppressive forces), it is also a "victim song." This interpretation is also strengthened by the context of the album, especially songs like "Isolation" and "I Found Out," which arguably are based upon the same model.

It could be concluded that because of conflicting expectations that were disclosed in his starnet, Lennon began to see himself as a victim. Moreover, because of his identification with Christ, this self-image also bore the marks of martyrdom. In this sense, there was a connection between Lennon's star image and the Dionysian rock culture, an intensity that built the profile of martyrdom out of various rock deaths (most notably Jimi Hendrix, Brian Jones, Janis Joplin and Jim Morrison) in the late 1960s and early 1970s. Yet Lennon's status as victim incorporated elements that distinguished him from the pattern. He did not seriously equate martyrdom with death, nor, apart from the standard metaphor in his lyric (as above), did he use visual "shock effects" like crucifixion postures, which would later be established in pop/rock star iconography. Second, messianism for Lennon meant a semievangelical mission for peace, an Apollonian dream about a peaceful future as epitomized in 1971 in his most famous solo recording, "Imagine." This understated meditative utopianism was foreign to the "live now" spirit of Dionysian rock.

The third reason relates to the fact that the concert and the display of the physical presence, the body of the star, were keys to Dionysian rock; at this time they had ceased to play any role in Lennon's stardom. Even though Lennon gave concerts and appeared nude, his body was not sexualized in the way that Jimi Hendrix's, Mick Jagger's or Jim Morrison's bodies were, primarily because Lennon did not flirt with the idea of free male sexuality but posed together with his wife, with the emphasis on an unglamorous and even domestic naturalness.

For Lennon, the late 1960s meant not only a gradual disengagement from the Beatles but from rock culture in general. He neither valued the happy-go-lucky "pop" culture nor committed himself to countercultural "rock." Rather, he became an eccentric all-around celebrity and artist who rejected the expectations of the music industry, the media, the audience, the Establishment and rock culture. If this seemed a radical abrogation of the role that had been created for him during Beatlemania and subsequently during the *Sgt. Pepper* period, there nevertheless was, as will be argued in the next section, a less pietistic side to Lennon's messianic stardom.

Fool of the Year 1969

Let no man deceive himself. If any man among you seemeth to be wise in this world, let him become a fool, that he may be wise.
—*St. Paul*

In pop memory 1969 has remained the year when John Lennon not only identified himself with Christ but also seemed to go mad, or at least to be acting feeble-mindedly. "His motives are admirable, but his means are childish," George Melly wrote in 1970 (228), referring to Lennon's "clapped-out avant-garde." Donald Zec, one of the first British journalists to contribute to the Beatles' success six years earlier, had difficulties in accepting Lennon's semievangelical manifestos, "the most sustained twaddle and tosh since Zsa Zsa gave way to Cassius Clay" (1969).

Lennon himself considered his and Yoko Ono's behavior playful rather than trivial: "Our opposition, whoever they may be, in all their manifest forms, don't know how to handle humor. And we are humorous" (quoted in Wiener 1985, 91). It is arguable that the humor of John Lennon in the late 1960s derived both from his own background as a witty joker and from the doctrines of new avant-garde art. "I didn't have to sort of have much knowledge about avant-garde or underground art, but the humour got me straight away," he explained (Wenner 1980, 172). Lennon told his childhood friend Pete Shotton that his media events with Ono were presented to the audience as avant-garde art when in fact they simply were adult versions of those "practical jokes" he and Shotton used to indulge in at school (Shotton & Schaffner

1983, 187). Thus, methods of the avant-garde provided a model for the revival of a characteristic of the young Lennon and a conspicuous aspect of his star image during Beatlemania.

The humor of experimental art also provided an instrument for Lennon to reinvent his artistic identity. It appears that in 1969 he consciously adopted the role of the fool. He recognized that his highly publicized and extravagant peace campaign was considered childish and understood that many saw him as behaving stupidly. Yet, he persisted with this activity for nearly two years. As indicated in the previous section, Lennon's personality, behavior and way of thinking in the late 1960s seemed to be fundamentally different from the accustomed patterns of Beatles celebrity as well as from rock stardom in general. Being childish was an extension of this rejection of star expectations. Avid followers of the Beatles, peace activists and the rock press may have supported Lennon's campaign, but they were outnumbered by those who saw his conduct as oddly amusing, trivial and naive. The ridicule and criticism were perhaps best exemplified in March 1969 when British newspapers published a number of cartoons caricaturing the Amsterdam bed-in. After this particular event, Lennon was widely called a fool.[13]

By deliberately inviting people to laugh at him, Lennon represented a particular comic model, the fool. We can identify specific techniques associated with the traditional fool and which typified Lennon's conduct at this time. The repertoire of the fool involves, for example, outward appearance, including extraordinary clothing and accessories, or no clothing at all; verbal games, including wordplay, stream-of-consciousness "gobbledygook" and the license to say whatever comes to mind without being held accountable. Professional fools also are usually capable of singing and playing instruments. Scholars have identified these features as formal markers of folly, especially in Renaissance England, which is regarded as a historical apex of the phenomenon (Welsford 1968; Willeford 1969, Korhonen 1999). Such traditional features also characterize a nonconformist like Lennon. His songs "Come Together" and "Sun King," on the Beatles' *Abbey Road* album (1969), incorporated gobbledygook, including nonexistent Mediterranean-sounding words. These techniques, however, could be regarded in general as elements of a wide range of comic styles, and it is necessary to construct a more precise model by which to explore the relationship between the tradition of folly and Lennon's stardom. In her unpublished study of Renaissance England folly, Finnish historian Anu Korhonen has classified fools into two groups. The first type is the "natural fool," a person who is truly, and without choice, a simpleton; the second type is the "artificial fool," the wise person who has assumed the role of a fool (1999, 13). As a man who had already shown artistic talent and intelligence, Lennon undoubtedly represented the second type. Nevertheless, Lennon's foolery also contained strands that were more or less "natural" or at least naturalized.

First, Lennon was a "fool in love." As a newly married man who was visibly distracted with happiness, Lennon was almost a caricature of the besotted newlywed, incoherent in his intimate "love talk," but which in his case often became public. As Levin writes in his account of the 1960s, the intimate conversation of the newly married is not usually expected to be filmed, recorded and made public to the extent that Lennon's and Ono's was (1989, 37). An hour-long film, *Honeymoon*, which premiered in 1969, documented highlights of their Amsterdam bed-in, while the audio verité equivalent, *Wedding Album*, celebrated the couple's wedding and invited the audience to join in their happiness. The album contained a long musical piece involving two hearts beating and the couple continuously intoning each other's names. The boxed set of the album also featured a copy of the marriage certificate, a photograph of a slice of wedding cake and other marital memorabilia. By making their romance a shameless media spectacle, Lennon and Ono distinguished themselves from the majority of other "fools in love." In relation to the tradition of popular music celebrity, such frank self-promotion also radically violated one of the guiding principles of 1960s star machinery, the balancing and regulation between the star's private and public personae.

Lennon also manifested his rejection of the conventional star role in other musical activities. While the "fool in love" theme, of course, is ubiquitous in popular songs (see Cooper 1997), it is not usual that performers explicitly identify themselves when they sing about fools who are mad about love and often blind to predictable consequences of their behavior and their manipulation by others. Although the lyrics sung by the performer frequently use the first-person singular in their narrations, it is conjectural to equate the narrator with the fool figure. What distinguished Lennon from this tradition was that he made his musical narratives of folly explicitly self-referential, and thus a part of his public image. Not only did he sing about love and romance in general terms, but he was not ashamed to declare that it was he, John Lennon, who was in love with his wife, Yoko Ono. From 1969 onward, the intimacy between "John" and "Yoko" was frequently celebrated in his songs, most notably in "Oh Yoko!" on the *Imagine* album.

The second strand of Lennon's "natural" foolery was related to what is often identified as a conspicuous national type, that of the eccentric. As with his romance, this was a trait that Lennon himself emphasized: "The English are famous eccentrics. I'm just another one from a long line of eccentrics" (Watts 1971, 25). John Lennon posing with his expensive and exotic possessions in 1966 or with his psychedelic Rolls-Royce arguably were manifestations of the eccentric and its subspecies, in these two cases the "aristocratic collector" and the "dandy." Such posturings, of course, were common manifestations of a form of eccentricity in British pop music culture, reflecting a long-standing tradition that became more prominent during the Swinging London phenomenon and has continued ever since.

Lennon's peacenik phase, however, cannot be comprehended simply as an extension of eccentricity. Lennon's rapid transformation from a high-spirited Beatle to a high-profile peace advocate discloses more about his mercurial temperament than can be made intelligible by reference to the routinized model of "classic" British eccentricity. Furthermore, one component of that model has been a lack of inclination to invite other people to participate in the eccentric's nonconformity (Sitwell 1971, 250). By being a highly visible celebrity with a major mission who evangelized on behalf of his way of life, Lennon clearly did not conform to this "outsider" element of eccentricity. Furthermore, even though eccentricity has been tolerated and even cherished in Britain, the hostility toward Lennon and Ono suggests that certain boundaries of acceptance were exceeded. It is arguable that because of his marriage to a woman who was foreign and equally "crazy" as her spouse and who thus challenged the traditional masculine complexion of eccentricity, Lennon was not seen as a harmless and authentic eccentric. The idea of eccentricity arguably provided a vehicle to which Lennon could naturalize and harness his foolishness, but in public he was not considered an acceptable example of the traditional English eccentric.

That Lennon's foolery was "artificial" is confirmed by the fact that the role of the fool proved to be a transitory strategy that was replaced by interests in primal scream psychotherapy and serious-minded revolution politics in the early 1970s. The brevity of this phase and the suddenness of the transition out of it suggest something of the "festival fool," the carnivalesque temporary assumption of the role of the fool, "without devoting their whole life to it or being branded fools themselves" (Korhonen 1999, 59). However, this model is not consistent with what seems to have been the sincerity of Lennon's commitment to the peace ideal. Can we then consider him as an example simply of the stage fool or clown, the amusing character type with whom Lennon identified himself on several occasions? In Lennon's case the comic element of amusement was subordinate to a serious social message, so it is difficult to categorize Lennon unproblematically as a stage fool, simply out for laughs. While the comedy of clowns has sometimes been perceived as providing indirect yet profound truths about the human condition, proselytizing is not normally part of the clown stereotype (Willeford 1969). It seems that the most appropriate way of categorizing Lennon's activities in 1969 is not the festival fool or the stage fool, but the intellectual fool. More specifically, mainly because of Lennon's semievangelical mission and his identification with Christ's way of life, we may think of him as a 1960s version of the holy fool.

The role of holy fool is rarely recognized in Lennon historiography. Karl Dallas wrote in 1971 in his account of pop music stars that the "torment of the modern superstar is that he is a god in a new time of myth, whether he likes it or not," and that the star either has to "come down from Olympus or be crucified" (19). Dallas does not inquire into the reasons for this martyrdom, which he reserves for male rock stars only. His attention was evidently taken by the growing interest in rock messianism and the ambiguous demands of stardom. This at least is suggested in a chapter on Lennon. Dallas writes that all those "crazy things" that Lennon produced were the way to prevent the audience from "taking him so seriously that they nail him up" (87).[14] Dallas thus interpreted Lennon's foolery as a defense mechanism against the demands of stardom. Whether Lennon's humor in the late 1960s was a calculated or intuitive survival technique need not be traced here. What is relevant is the way the role of holy fool established a connection between the "crazy things" and the serious, and thus gave a particular coloration to Lennon's messianism.

John Lennon was not literally a holy fool, particularly in the Christian tradition of such a figure. He clearly did not devote himself to God or become a "fool for God's sake," a scholarly Christian humbly submissive to a supreme power. Nevertheless, by being almost a dogmatic peace evangelist who voluntarily subjected himself to ridicule, Lennon's public conduct suggests a Christlike folly. Like Christ, who "had to become a fool in order to be truly clothed in humanness" (Taylor 1985, 78), Lennon was not concerned about being called mad but continued to hold peace meetings together with his wife. "Bed-ins are something that everybody can do and they're so simple. We're willing to be the world clowns to make people realize it," he preached (Yorke 1982a, 57).

Innocence was a key to such preaching. Like Christ, who in Erasmus' ironic words taught apostles "to shun wisdom, and made his appeal through the example of children, lilies, mustard-seed and humble sparrows, all foolish, senseless things" (1980, 199), Lennon encouraged people to become innocent and childlike fools before entering the Age of Peace. The first event to mark this was *Two Virgins*. The title of the album, the creation of a rippling soundscape and, most notably, the nude shots of Lennon and Ono suggested a return to paradisal innocence. Five verses from the *Book of Genesis* were printed on the cover to legitimize the naturalness of the modern-day Adam and Eve. The last verse was typographically emphasized: "And they were both naked, the man and his wife, and were not ashamed." The advertisement designed by Apple invoked the Edenic concept: "It isn't a trend or a trick—it's just two of God's children singing and looking much as they were when they were born, only a little older" (cited in Hopkins 1987, 88). The paradox was that although innocence was crucial to Lennon's foolery, the role of innocent fool was strategic, a result of premeditation. This, in fact, connected Lennon and his wife to the long tradition of holy folly, those fools who "were never fools from birth, as natural fools were supposed to be" but had chosen to become fools of their own volitions (Korhonen 1999, 90).

The emphasis on innocence in holy folly does not necessarily provide exemption from pain and suffering. If the foolery exceeds certain boundaries, then the fool may modulate into another symbolic image, the scapegoat (Boyd 1988). Thus with Lennon: Although there is no evidence that he suffered physical pain (apart from whatever discomfort might be produced by staying in bed for seven days), or that he suffered serious mental problems because of his foolery, he did become the victim of verbal attacks, as exemplified above. While humor might provide a new way of playing the publicity game and a way of surviving stardom, for Lennon's critics it reprehensibly trivialized his message.

It is this combination of foolery and potential martyrdom that perhaps best explains the ambivalence of "The Ballad of John and Yoko." On the one hand, Lennon used crucifixion as a theatrical metaphor of his victimization; on the other hand, the positive mood of the song indicates that the performance was also in part a way of playing the fool. In some of his interviews, Lennon seemed to feel that his clowning would protect him from figurative martyrdom. Although he said that he "wouldn't mind dying as the world's clown" (Coxhill 1969, 4), he certainly did not seek such a fate. Rather, he stated that he and Ono "don't intend to be dead saints" but rather "living freaks" and the "living Romeo and Juliet" of their time (Smith 1969b, 3). Thus, being a scapegoat or martyr was simply a theoretical option for Lennon in 1969, when neither he nor the public could have foreseen his tragic death in 1980.

Lennon attempted to justify his foolery on grounds of temperament—his natural sense of humor, of romance, his eccentricity and innocence. Nonetheless, it was obvious that his behavior was intellectualized rather than unself-conscious, though his foolery seemed to be relatively straightforward in 1969. He was willing to play the fool to get his message across. One significant result of Lennon's foolery was that it displaced him from what had been his primary role, that of the serious rock star. Assuming extravagant postures was by no means exceptional in late 1960s rock stardom, but in Lennon's case it took exceptional forms. Even though rock stardom conspicuously dwelt upon messianic intensities and even though the image of the clown was effectively used by some performers (Ian Anderson of Jethro Tull, Frank Zappa and early David Bowie, for example), rock stars were not in favor of mixing messianism and clowning. Thus, if Lennon had, during Beatlemania as well as during psychedelia, embodied the current lineaments of popular music stardom, this was no longer so. His sphere of celebrity had already in the early 1960s gone beyond the boundaries of purely musical activities, but now extended over terrains that had been unimaginable a few years earlier.

The articulation of unique visions and the breaking of new ground of course reinforced Lennon's auteur status, giving him the aura of an artist of limitless possibilities, who cannot be controlled by the industry. For the media and the public, however, he had become too much of an uncategorizable hybrid to comprehend. Lennon may have been one of the world's most visible persons in 1969, but compared to other celebrities and particularly to other rock stars, he was a lone soul, sui generis, almost an anachronism in all his Apollonian dreams and holy folly.

7 Relocating a Star Identity in the 1970s

Street Politics: Lennon, New York and Radicalism

Be a realist: Demand the impossible.
— *Yippie slogan*

"Will the Beatles ever get back together?" "Why do you want to stay in America?" From 1971 to 1975, after which John Lennon went into a period of seclusion that would last five years, these were the two most popular questions in his interviews. They reflected two important watersheds in his career. First, the Beatles ceased to exist as a recording group in 1970 and were formally ended next year in the High Court in London. Disagreements between the members of the group still continued, not ending until 1975 when the Beatles as a business enterprise were finally dissolved. Second, in September 1971 Lennon and Ono flew from London to New York, where they then decided to stay. The couple soon plunged into radical politics and began a four-year battle against Lennon's deportation order. While I shall concentrate on the meaning of the Beatles in Lennon's rock stardom in the next chapter, here my focus is on Lennon's transition from one geographical context to another and different expectations that were imposed upon him during the process. In what ways did Lennon attempt to relocate himself? How were his efforts understood?

That an eminent rock star like John Lennon expatriated himself to America was, of course, news, but it was by no means exceptional. Apart from the cases in earlier popular music, the pop star exchange between America and Britain had been under way since the 1960s when several American pop and rock performers, including P. J. Proby, the Walker Brothers and Jimi Hendrix, found Britain a convenient stepping-stone for their star careers. In the 1970s the stream of migration reversed, as David Bowie, Rod Stewart, Elton John, Fleetwood Mac, Ian Hunter and other British pop and rock performers began to systematically develop their transatlantic careers. Some stars not only committed themselves to touring or recording music in America but also decided to stay there, especially in Los Angeles. Some journalists (e.g., Fudger 1975) claimed that British musicians were primarily in flight from the high tax rates of their native country. This might also have been an extra impulse for Lennon's emigration, but being an artist who had since the mid-1960s disparaged the question of money, he denied that this was an issue (Coleman 1974). Lennon's emigration was undoubtedly prompted more by Yoko Ono and her desire to return to the city that had formerly been her artistic base. What is also evident is that Lennon's problems with visas and gaining full resident status in the United States fortified his decision; having once made the move, he was worried that if he left America he would not be readmitted.

Whatever the reasons behind his emigration and residency, Lennon clearly considered America more congenial than Britain. He explained enthusiastically that while in his home country he was merely regarded as "somebody who won the pools," in America he was respected and treated as a serious artist (Watts 1971, 24). Although Lennon remained ambivalent about Britain, he did not repudiate his English connections: "I get letters from England saying, 'don't forget us'. Well, there's no way I can forget them and I don't want to" (Horide 1975, 17).

Indeed, it would have been impossible for Lennon to ignore his national background as long as he continued to give interviews to British journalists, many of whom articulated their anxieties about losing their homegrown star to America. In a way, these concerns were a continuation of the debate over the ownership of the Beatles in the 1960s. In the early 1960s fans in Liverpool had feared losing their heroes to London; in the mid-1960s, British fans had complained that the Beatles' frequent touring abroad kept their pop idols away from them. Now, in the 1970s, as the Beatles dispersed and one of them even deserted his native soil, the community defined through Beatles fandom in Britain was being dismantled. It is hardly a surprise that in his interviews Lennon was continually forced to define his position in relation to the issues of the nation-state and nationality. In spite of all the criticism that had been directed toward him, he still was a national treasure, a pop star who had played an important role in bringing Britain back to international focus.

As I discussed in chapter 2, section 2, "Northern Stars: From Local Heroes to National Obsession," geographical backgrounds and localities may play important roles in popular music stardom. In the early

1960s "northernness" and "Liverpoolness" were essential to the images of the Beatles and John Lennon, at least in Britain, where the impact of the group was to a large extent due to their being "outsiders" in popular culture. Until about 1966 the Beatles were regarded more as Liverpudlian lads than Londoners, and while northernness then gradually diminished in their image for English fans, it was not replaced by other geographical identities and characterizations. Although Lennon became involved in Swinging London's "popocracy," made friends in the city's art scene, used local studios and other music infrastructure, and lived for eight years in London (or the surrounding area), he was not specifically identified as a Londoner.

As a result, in the late 1960s there was no fixed geographical reference point connecting Lennon to his audience. Lennon was neither a Liverpudlian rocker nor a London pop performer. He was an English rock star, but the notion of Englishness did not pervade his image as explicitly as before. Although Lennon emphasized the "English eccentric" side of his image, he did not unproblematically fall into the stereotype. His promotion of world peace suggested that a national spirit, which had been a vital part of Beatlemania, was replaced with an internationalist and therefore largely placeless idealism.

In terms of spatiality and stardom, New York meant a change for Lennon. He not only became the most famous British rock expatriate of the era but one who openly attempted to overlay his star identity onto a particular place, a city that, according to the author Jerome Charyn (1986, 17), is "the most American of any city in the world." While London was an implicit and therefore invisible reference point for British rock musicians, New York was "other" to the national construction of British popular culture and its localities. For a British rock star, New York represented an exotic and mythologized metropolis, and in his interviews Lennon was extremely articulate on the subject (see Badman 2001, passim).

Lennon's positive attitude toward New York interestingly echoed the way the Beatles had expressed their pride in being Liverpudlians in the early 1960s. The difference of course was that whereas Liverpool worked as a background and source of identity, a place where the star came from, New York formed a promised land for Lennon, an unexplored resource for redefining and relocating the down-to-earth star identity. Apart from interviews, Lennon expressed this potential in his

diary-like song "New York City," which was released on the double album *Some Time in New York City* in 1972. Whereas Liverpool was never
explicitly mentioned in the Beatles' lyrics and barely remarked upon in
Lennon's solo output—only in "The Luck of the Irish," on *Some Time in
New York City* and "You Are Here," on *Mind Games* (1973)—and whereas the culture and geography of London were almost completely ignored, his new home city was explicitly identified and celebrated as a
locus of political and artistic freedom.

New York appealed to Lennon as a cradle of tolerance and an urban
paradise but this was in many ways a romanticized and imaginary construction. In the early 1970s New York was heading for a deep economic recession that in mid-decade led to a dramatic contraction in urban
services. The city was increasingly losing its "promised land" mythos
and earning a reputation of "the regional basket case" (Charyn 1986,
17–18). The promise of tolerance and freedom was questionable also in
terms of music and cultural policy. Paul Chevigny demonstrates in his
study *Gigs* (1991) that local government in New York systematically
sought to regulate and constrain live music. According to Chevigny,
the licensing regulations that had been introduced during Prohibition
to designate suitable and unsuitable sites for public performances were
still in force in the 1970s in spite of legislative reforms of the preceding
decade. Music continued to be confined to particular districts of the
city, and it was not until the late 1980s that this zoning finally ceased to
exist. It is reasonable to assume that Lennon confused—whether inten-
tionally or not—the whole entity of New York with the particular area
of the city, Greenwich Village, where he and Ono lived from 1971 to
1973.

Mainly because of the area's sociohistorical background, music and
other artistic forms were not regulated to the same extent in Greenwich
Village that they were in many other parts of the city. Greenwich Village's reputation as a site of alternative lifestyles had been recognized
during the massive immigration in the early twentieth century, but it
was after World War II that it became a notable center of alternative arts
and leftist activities, attracting artists, musicians, students and other bohemians from all over the country. Greenwich Village also became a
center of the national folk music revival, and during the 1960s a new
generation of musicians, including Bob Dylan, Paul Simon, John Sebas-
tian (of Lovin' Spoonful), Stephen Stills (of Buffalo Springfield) and

John Phillips (of the Mamas and the Papas) found the area a valuable springboard for their folk-rock careers (Shelton 1986; Cantwell 1996).

Even though in the 1970s Greenwich Village's national status was diminishing, it still enjoyed a reputation as a hub of alternative life-styles and cultural interaction. Lennon and Ono, who clearly were fascinated by the bohemian atmosphere and radical tendencies of the area, embraced this mentality and invited radicals, New Left leaders, feminists, underground poets, musicians and other artists to their two-room apartment on Bank Street (Wiener 1985). The idea of a vibrant community and communication came to pervade Lennon's star image in ways that seemed to represent a development of the avant-gardism that had increasingly interested him and Ono since the late 1960s. While their peace events and other experimental performances had attracted considerable interest, they were not based on a live interaction between the artist and the audience. What impressed Lennon in New York was that it was possible for him to communicate not only with those similarly disposed but with other people as well. He could talk with anyone in the street and no one would "bug," "hustle" or "shove" him, as he suggested in the above-mentioned "New York City." Lennon expressed relief that in New York he was able to stroll in streets without being disturbed by "star-chasers" as he had been in London where he "couldn't go through the front door" (Horide 1975, 17).

This street mythos had been a vital part of Lennon's working-class image in Liverpool but disappeared almost totally during Beatlemania. It was now revitalized. "The fact that he was really on the streets—that really turned me on," recalled musician David Peel, remembering an afternoon when he, Lennon, Ono and dozens of other people walked down the street strumming guitars and singing (Wiener 1985, 179). Being back "on the streets," that is, experiencing urban everyday life and being one of the people, fueled Lennon's new star credibility. It is instructive that Lennon's new backing group, Elephant's Memory, was hired on the grounds that it was a band "from the streets" (Harry 2000, 222). This "street" trope converged perfectly with the romanticized and mythologized image of urban popular music. As Goodwin notes, the idea that the musician comes from the "street" has been an important myth of rock music and is often promoted in rock marketing to authenticate the star (1993, 115–16). This street experience, or street credibility, has been so essential to rock and other popular music narratives that stars have often been forced to define and redefine their relationship to it, rap star Eminem's star vehicle film *8 Mile* (2002) being a telling example of the continuous articulation of this mythos.

Lennon's street period can thus be seen as a response to the issue of authenticity in rock music. Since the "street" in Lennon's case mainly referred to a particular area of New York that, apart from music activity, was also known as a center of radical energy and represented a long tradition of American "street socialism" (Eyerman 1994, 129–31), it also had a political dimension. In Lennon's case, the "street" as an experience and trope not only referred to the search for an audience and for rock authenticity, but also to the local radical community and its activities. A concrete example of this was Lennon's and Ono's participation in political campaigns that literally took place in streets, including demonstrations against Britain's policy in Northern Ireland, the war in Vietnam and the oppression of Native Americans. Their attendance at these events was, as Lennon said, "to show we care and that we don't just live in ivory towers in Hollywood watching movies about ourselves" (quoted in Wiener 1985, 199).

Because of his intense involvement in radical politics and identification with the "street," the John Lennon of 1971–73 has been characterized as a guerrilla minstrel (Hampton 1986), an agitprop singer (Du Noyer 1997), the balladeer of barricades (Robertson 1990), a protest singer (Rogan 1997) and a movement songwriter (Wiener 1985). To pursue a changing connection between politics and rock stardom, we must recall that there is a long tradition of linkage between popular music and social protest movements. Yet, the particular idea that rock stardom could function as an instrument of political and social change did not emerge until the ideology of folk entered into mainstream popular music and dissolved the distinction between "folk" and "rock." This marked the emergence of rock artists' continuing tendency to use their music and status as platforms for political statements on a variety of issues, including peace, racism, class, gender, sexuality, poverty, the environment and, generally, injustice.

Despite the robust history of political rock, the connection between rock stardom and politics has proved to be somewhat problematic. One explanation for this is that there is disagreement as to the cultural significance of the union between popular music and politics. Many academics have emphasized that it is very difficult to develop a general account of the political nature of popular music simply because we cannot locate the exact political meaning of music in any sound text. Popular songs may have political potential in terms of content, and they may be used in particular contexts of struggles, but since popular music generally is transitory by nature, songs can be connected to different political agendas in quite specific circumstances (Longhurst 1995; Rowe 1995; Balliger 1999). Nevertheless, there also are case studies that suggest that many listeners have had their ideological horizons both confirmed and extended through political rock (Shuker 2001).

Rather than studying the vexed question of the impact of music, two other lines of inquiry are useful in examining Lennon's political rock. The first is based on the fact that celebrities are often seen as powerful instruments for raising consciousness as well as acquiring support and capital for social mobilization (Lahusen 1996). Since celebrities in general are visible points of focus for collectively social types, values and myths, they are considered influential. That rock stars' public statements are significant is generally recognized. Popular music stardom provides a platform for ideas of broader social relevance, and these ideas may have real impact. Second, there are different forms of commitment associated with political rock, ranging from social philanthropy to radical subversion. John Street (1997) notes that the field of politics includes a range of causes and conduct, some of which fit more easily than others within the conventions of popular culture. It is, for example, more typical to use popular culture to fuel compassion for individuals rather than for general political causes and for "innocent victims" like children, who are frequently beneficiaries of popular culture's campaigns (31).

Because of this broad spectrum, a homogeneous understanding of political rock is misleading, and it may be more instructive to take up Shuker's concept of "conscience rock" to designate the "political potential of popular music to raise consciousness and money for social interventions" (2001, 236).[1] During his Greenwich Village period, Lennon clearly was such a "conscience rock" star. He used his music and star status to raise consciousness and funds for various causes. The political potential of popular music was crucial to his live performances. In the 1970s Lennon performed in only three scheduled live events—all of which, however, were benefit concerts.[2] What should be noted is that Lennon's "conscience rock" seemed to cover a spectrum of causes, ranging from a philanthropic campaign for handicapped children to more radical gestures.

Lennon's attempt to bring rock into convergence with explicitly political aims was perhaps most distinctively manifested in the rhetoric of *Some Time in New York City*. Whereas in his previous solo work Lennon had mainly written songs about himself or at least favored the first-person singular in his lyrics, *Some Time in New York City* invoked "the people," as in the songs "Attica State" and "Sunday Bloody Sunday," and through the solidarity of the first-person plural, "we," as in "Attica State," "John Sinclair" and "Angela."[3] Although this communalization had been foreshadowed in Lennon's singles "Give Peace a Chance" (1969) and "Power to the People" (1971), it now became increasingly pervasive and explicit in his songs. Such collectivist sloganeering, set to fiery rock 'n' roll arrangements on most of the songs of the album, implies that Lennon considered himself the mouthpiece of a larger community. This raises a question of the constituency of Lennon's audience. Who defined the "people" and "us"?

The identification of a single speaker with "the people" is part of the perennial populist rhetoric of political activists. Street notes that cultural populism "allows broadcasters, artists, cultural analysts and others to derive their claim that popular culture expresses the wishes and desires of the people" (1997, 17). The point is that "the people" are as much a rhetorical as a political fact. The people do not have a voice; they are given one by various interest groups who attempt to derive their authority from the people. These interest groups link their audience to a vision that in turn legitimizes their particular courses of action. "The people" do not just exist but are "created through the ways in which they are represented and spoken for" (18). Similarly, "we" is a concept that in politics signifies an uneasy combination of collectivism and demagoguery. Political and opinion leaders often consider themselves authorized to speak for "us" and tell what "we" think. Thus, such rhetoric serves to legitimize the leaders' status and conduct. In political rock, "we" may refer to different segments, ranging from the rock concert audience to the global village (as imagined later in the Live Aid vision of "We Are the World"). What is clear is that "we" as well as "the people," whether invoked by politicians, apolitical rock stars or political rock stars, are instruments to construct the spirit of community and "to create a following, to put together a 'people' (to create an identity) and to give them a focus for their passion" (13).

It could be argued that since in Lennon's case "the people" and "we" were emphasized by leftist intonations, his rock stardom came to be used as a forum for political propaganda. An essential part of the political rock phenomenon is that politicians and activists campaigning for social change have often tried to associate themselves with popular music and utilize the communicative power of its celebrities. Radical politicians in America recognized this potential and tried to appropriate Lennon as a campaign tactic. While British radicals had only partial success in attracting Lennon to their causes, Americans managed to co-opt him to a greater extent. The radical Yippie movement and its two most prominent leaders, Abbie Hoffman and Jerry Rubin, in particular became close to Lennon. Unlike revolutionaries and radical politicians in Britain, the Yippies in America were not interested in conventional politics, sustained and systematic strategies for the revolution or Marxist theories, but relied on absurd and outrageous media pranks, such as disrupting the Democratic National Convention in Chicago in 1968 by presenting a pig as their own U.S. presidential candidate (Gitlin 1987). The Yippies' humorous media spectacles obviously attracted Lennon, who had used similar methods and consciously played the fool with his own stardom. It is instructive that whereas Hoffman and Rubin saw Lennon and Ono as great politicians, Lennon and Ono regarded Hoffman and Rubin as great artists. As a result, Jerry Rubin became a "political adviser" for Lennon and Ono, and Lennon started to support the Yippies (Werbin 1982, 127). Hence, it could be suggested that "the people" and "we" were defined for Lennon by the local radical community of Greenwich Village. Critics have argued that as a newly arrived member of the local community and of American society, Lennon chose to comment on events he basically knew little about (Denselow 1989; Robertson 1990).

That Yippies succeeded in selling their political program to Lennon while other rock and folk musicians waved farewell to the radical Left has obviously had an effect on the consensus that *Some Time in New York City* is Lennon's worst album. At the time, the album was denounced by critics and ignored by the audience. Lennon himself was accused of being naive and simplistic, especially in his political lyrics (Wiener 1985; Rogan 1997). Whether the songs of the album were musically and aesthetically up to Lennon's compositional standards is a subjective matter; what is clear, however, is that they disconcertingly drew on a particular—and very long—tradition of folk songs and minstrels: topicality.

Half of the new songs in *Some Time in New York City* were topical, dealing with prison riots, Britain's foreign policy, the imprisonment of American radicals, and women's liberation. "We're like newspaper men, only we sing about what's going on instead of writing about it," Lennon explained on *The David Frost Show* (quoted in Wiener 1985, 199). What was confusing was their anachronicity: By the 1970s the topical songs genre had become passé in popular music. In the 1960s folk musicians such as Bob Dylan and especially Phil Ochs had written songs about contemporary events, but by 1972 topical songs were unfashionable even in folk music, let alone rock. Although the singer-songwriter movement, which became a major trend in early 1970s U.S. popular music, was a successor to the folk revival, it rejected topical issues, concentrating instead on intimate memories and the nostalgic evocation of a pastoral past. Singer-songwriters such as Jackson Browne, Harry Chapin, Jim Croce, Joni Mitchell, James Taylor and, to some extent, John Denver, Bob Dylan, Carole King, Don McLean, Bruce Springsteen and Neil Young introspectively explored the self rather than summoning people to sing-along hootenannies and political rallies. "We" and "the people" and "telling like it is" (that is, the idea of collective power and public social comment) were replaced by "me" and "saying how it feels" (that is, more inward and subjective meditations).

John Lennon clearly was not a sensitive and introverted folk musician in 1972. He also seemed to be isolated from the subgenres that characterized early 1970s white Anglo-American rock, for example, glam rock, heavy metal and progressive rock. More specifically, although Lennon considered himself a rock musician living in New York, his "street image" differed from those artists and groups who were associated with the city's rock scene in the early 1970s. The New York Dolls and Lou Reed, for example, rejected Greenwich Village's wholesome, folksy ethos and dwelt upon the image of the urban "wild side," and flirted with the ambiguity of glamor, androgyny and decadence.

As with his messianic "foolery" in the late 1960s, John Lennon's agitprop did not gain a foothold in popular music. Given that political rock became more prominent in the late 1970s with the emergence of the punk movement in Britain and various social causes supported by rock performers, most notably Rock Against Racism in Britain (1978) and No Nukes in America (1979), it could be suggested that John Lennon was ahead of his times rather than behind them. This is, of course, arguable, and I would suggest that, rather than contributing to the phenomenon of political rock, Lennon's period as a socially conscious songwriter stands as an early example of an increasing sensitivity in the relationship between politics and rock stardom. As I have discussed, the alliance between politics and rock stardom produces dissonant responses. While political interest groups usually enthusiastically welcome any support from the star, such commitment is often greeted with suspicion by journalists, fans and other stars. Lahusen (1996) notes in his study of political mobilization and celebrity endorsement in the 1980s and 1990s that those pop and rock celebrities who attempt to influence people are often criticized as being pretentious because such behavior is felt to contaminate or compromise the individual listeners' autonomy and freedom. Most celebrities respect the ideal of autonomous agency in popular music and systematically downplay their power to influence public discussion and individual choices. They prefer to see themselves as a medium through which individuals may articulate their own needs and actions (140–41). Thus, stars who speak with authority and independence about public issues, like John Lennon in the early 1970s or Sting and Bono in the late 1980s, are in danger of appearing too didactic and arrogant.

A further characteristic of the phenomenon of political rock is that celebrities' involvements in politics and charity often generate debates over credibility, motivation and sincerity. Live Aid, for example, raised a host of questions about stars' roles (Denselow 1989). The brevity of Lennon's radical phase suggests that his dedication to radical politics was not very durable. According to some biographers (e.g., Wiener 1985; Elliott 1999), Lennon was forced to renounce radical politics in order to avoid a deportation order and to obtain permanent residency status. Lennon himself explained later that his short, albeit intense, involvement in radical politics was "phony" and came "out of guilt" at being a wealthy celebrity (Graustark 1980a, 55).

At the time, however, Lennon was evidently sincere about radical politics. Nevertheless, it cannot be denied that the effect of his Greenwich Village experience—the desire to live simply, to walk freely in the streets, to talk with "the people," to participate in campaigns and demonstrations, to perform in benefit concerts and to tell the "truth" about topical issues—had as much to do with relocating and reauthenticating stardom as with changing the world. It was an extreme rejection of the hedonistic and insulated image of the superstar. It reflected some desire to prove that the star need not be separated from everyday realities, living in an ivory tower or some ethereal nonspace of the media. In Lennon's case, the particular emphasis was that the star can descend from the stratosphere of superstardom, return to the streets, live in a socially and political active relationship with "the people," and be sincere and direct in his expression. Such strategies clearly reflect the romantic mode of rock authenticity. Whereas Lennon's avant-garde period in the late 1960s could be viewed as the climax of a modernist phase, Lennon's street politics period remains his most orthodox version of rock's romantic authenticity.

The vigorous criticism that Lennon attracted in the early 1970s indicates that the restoration of his star status was not complete. Lennon's version of the "truth" was disapproved of partly because it was populist and carried Yippie associations, but also because he still was first and foremost regarded as a popular music celebrity rather than a politician or intellectual. Lennon's Greenwich Village period, which ended when Lennon and Ono moved to an apartment in the Dakota building on Manhattan's Upper West Side, was about the authenticity of rock stardom, but at the same time it proved that the combination of politics and rock stardom was more problematic than might be expected. Although Lennon was able to exercise control over the production process and release political rock music, he had no monopoly over the construction of his stardom.

"You Don't Get Me Twice": The Ethos of Survival

A balding or greying Beatle is unthinkable.
—Phillippa Dean, Beatles fan, 1966

My argument is that the ethos of survival was one of the most significant determinants of John Lennon's career from the early 1970s until his death in 1980. What I mean by "ethos" is that survival was not just a sporadic sentiment but a distinguishing attitude for Lennon in the 1970s, a view of life that was regularly addressed in his interviews as well as embedded in some of his songs. The redefinition of his star status through the idea of survival was not articulated without support. Apart from his own insistence on dealing with the subject, Lennon's survival mythos was visibly created, mediated and negotiated by other participants in his starnet, especially rock journalists.

Certainly, there were significant difficulties and struggles in Lennon's life in the early 1970s. Drugs, alcohol and marital problems affected his career and were widely discussed at the time. One of his most publicized struggles and one that attracted widespread sympathy was his four-year battle against deportation from the United States. The case reportedly included surveillance by the Federal Bureau of Investigation (FBI) and concluded when the U.S. Court of Appeals overturned the deportation order in 1975; permanent resident alien status, the "green card," was granted to Lennon eight months later. Since the case has been well documented, especially by Wiener (1985; 2000), I shall not focus on it. Instead I want to concentrate on three themes that were central to the ethos of survival in relation to Lennon: "the Sixties," Beatles stardom, and growing up. What is common to these is that they all touch on the question of the past, a fact that is hardly surprising since the idea of the survivor implies a history, that is, survival from something that has earlier happened in a person's life. My argument is that John Lennon's star image during the 1970s was not only characterized by his engagement with contemporary social and political issues but also by the past, which was increasingly important for the (re)identification of the star. This applied not only to John Lennon but to other established rock stars as well.

In many senses, *survival* was the catchword of the 1970s, especially in America. Christopher Lasch, the late historian and social critic, explored the significance of the term in two volumes, *The Culture of Narcissism* and particularly *The Minimalistic Self*, both of which seek to convey the instabilities of modern life and the obsessive self-concern that so conspicuously emerged during the 1970s, "the Me Decade," as journalist Tom Wolfe dubbed it in 1976. Lasch argues that in the 1970s the preoccupation with survival took protean forms and entered so deeply into popular culture and political debate that every issue, however fleeting or unimportant, presented "itself as a matter of life and death" (1984, 60–64). For example, a list of books on survival published at the time included books on ecology, nuclear war, Holocaust, technology and automation. Survivalism was the focus of a flood of "future studies," apocalyptic science fiction, psychiatric literature on "coping" and sociological literature on "victims." It included books setting forth "survival strategies for oppressed minorities," "survival in the executive jungle" and "survival in marriage." According to Lasch, a characteristic of the survival mentality was that it turned away from the major public questions of survival such as energy policy and the nuclear arms race, and concerned itself with individual matters and crises of everyday life. The abundant propaganda of disaster, the infiltration of everyday life by the rhetoric of survival, trivialized the idea of crisis.

Such a mentality was expressed in popular culture, especially, as Lasch briefly notes, in disaster movies and in fantasies of space travel, reflecting that people "no longer dream of overcoming difficulties but merely of surviving them" (1991, 49). Lasch did not discuss forms of popular culture in detail and, in fact, ignored the close relationship between 1970s survivalism and popular music. This connection has been noticed elsewhere, however. At least two writers, rock historians Greil Marcus (1994) and Jim Curtis (1987), have emphasized how the concept of survival was manifested in 1970s popular music. They also note that survival was widely used to characterize human experiences and describe the social and cultural atmosphere in the 1970s, especially in the United States. Marcus, writing in 1979 on rock deaths, suggests that it was about 1975 that the term *survivor* became a byword of the decade. Marcus remarks more cuttingly than Lasch that in the 1970s the term, which was earlier used to denote a person who had lived through a concrete threat to life and undergone conditions so harrowing that the experience had irrevocably marked the individual's personality, began to apply to anyone who had persevered or continued "any form of activity, including breathing, for almost any amount of time" (58). Inspired by Bruno Bettelheim's critique (and perhaps by Lasch's *The Culture of Narcissism,* which was first published in 1979) of survival as a modern self-justification, Marcus alleged that the 1970s version of the concept implied praise of something rather than a statement of fact and, as a term used particularly by the white middle class, trivialized and mocked real struggles.

Marcus suggests that in popular music the new application of the word *survival* appeared everywhere "as a justification for empty song-protagonists, washed-up careers, third-rate LPs, burnt-out brainpans," speaking for "everything empty, tawdry, and stupid about the seventies, to stand for every cheat, for every failure of nerve" (59). There were songs about survival (the Rolling Stones' "Soul Survivor," Gloria Gaynor's "I Will Survive"), album titles that invoked the idea (Adam Faith's *I Survive,* Georgie Fame's *Survival,* Grand Funk Railroad's *Survival,* Bob Marley and the Wailers' *Survival,* Eric Burdon's *Survivor,* Barry Mann's *Survivor,* Lynyrd Skynyrd's *Street Survivors*), and even the band Survivor. Although Marcus did not articulate reasons for his grievance against aging musicians' tendencies to glorify themselves, his thought-provoking arguments were clearly fueled by the emergence of punk rock and the new wave which, at least for him, were more significant forces for cultural momentum.

Curtis provides a more positive yet less detailed view of the subject of survival. He alleges that 1970s popular music celebrated the fact that people had survived a set of serious social crises. The genre in which this was most conspicuously articulated was disco, which not only represented a democratization of narcissism but also the antidote to feelings created by the Cold War, the oil crisis, the Vietnam War and, particularly, Watergate. To Curtis, it was not coincidental that "Staying Alive," the first song in the film *Saturday Night Fever* (1977), was a survival song, or that Gloria Gaynor's "I Will Survive" became such a success since disco, as Curtis boldly argues, "celebrated the fact that we had survived Nixon" (1987, 300).[4]

I feel that it is not very fruitful to retrace the route taken by Marcus and Curtis, measuring qualifications of survival or tracing how popular music reflects social crises. Nor is it my task to explore the general linkage between psychic survival and modern society, already elaborately studied by Lasch. Rather, I am interested in tracing the forms survival took, the ways it was promoted and the nature of cultural investments in such an image. My central question is not so much what constituted a 1970s rock survivor but how musicians and stars—in this case John Lennon—who were assigned the status of survivors functioned within the popular music industry and stardom. It is, however, important to recognize the historical circumstances that generated the theme of survival in popular music and in John Lennon's career in particular. Thus, before exploring more specifically the forms and functions of rock survival, I wish to argue that the ethos of survival in the 1970s was to a large extent related to "the Sixties," the era that, according to some historians (Hewison 1986; Gitlin 1987), psychically came to an end sometime between 1973 and 1975 and thus coincided with the beginning of the period of survival.

Both Marcus and Curtis suggest that *survivor* was perhaps first appropriated as a reference to those who had participated in the countercultural adventures of the 1960s. In this sense, the idea of survival in American culture in the 1970s was a result of the dissipation of radical impulses of 1960s counterculture and the pessimism reinforced by the economic and political crises. Thus, the determination to live on in the wake of the supposed defeat of more or less leftist dreams contributed to the ethos of survival. Among all the rock stars, such an interpretation is perhaps most deeply rooted in the post-1960s image of John Lennon. The significance of the 1960s dominated his career in the 1970s, pervaded the reception of his death and has become a continuous thread in his posthumous career. One manifestation of its durability is that in the 1970s Lennon was constantly asked about the "dreams" of the 1960s. From his first recollections, Lennon, a rock star who had been both a commentator on and participant in social and political issues during the 1960s, joined the ranks of embittered critics. For Lennon, nothing really had changed "except that there is a lot of middle-class kids with long hair walking around London in trendy clothes" and what had happened was only that "we all dressed up" (Wenner 1980, 11–12).[5] In his later interviews, Lennon appeared less cynical and more conciliatory about the dreams of that decade. In a *Rolling Stone* interview in 1980, he emphasized the idea of continuity and placed himself among those people of a generation who had been able to sustain some sense of past sentiment. Lennon concluded: "It's been fun seeing everyone we used to know and doing it all again—we've all survived" (Cott 1982b, 185).

Survival appeared to be a key word for Lennon as he recalled the 1960s. In an RKO Radio Network interview in 1980, he saw himself as an artist having surmounted the tumultuous decade and, more importantly, the hangover following it:

> We all survived Vietnam and Watergate and the tremendous upheaval of the world. We were the hip ones in the sixties, but the world is not like the sixties.

The whole world's changed and we're going into an unknown future, but we're still all here. (Quoted in Wiener 1985, 302)

Bob Edmands, originally writing for the *Rock File* book series in 1975, suggested that even though Lennon appeared to be on the slide commercially, and to some extent, artistically, he was still one of the survivors. Lennon was one of the remaining few seeking to invest rock music with a sense of moral responsibility, "despite the odium created by all those industry hustlers who turned radicalism into a fashion accessory to wear round the office" (1996, 134–35). To Edmands' mind, Lennon had not succumbed to the dangers of the 1970s and rock millionaire status—he had maintained an authentic commitment to 1960s idealism, which despite being now regarded as a naive attempt to connect music with political revolution still enjoyed respect among rock writers (see, e.g., Stokes 1977). In fact, it was particularly in popular music that attempts to establish the 1960s as a golden era took place. By the mid-1970s, something of a rock canon had formed, with the Beatles at the forefront of it (Cloonan 2000).

As I have indicated in the previous chapters, the dialogue with the past is characteristic of popular music in all times. Although Lasch (1984; 1991) emphasizes that a denial of the immediate past and the fear of nostalgia characterized 1970s America, it is evident that in popular music the past was not forgotten. On the contrary, behind the obsession with novelty, which arguably is characteristic of popular music irrespective of time and place, 1970s pop staged an audible dialogue particularly with the 1950s and 1960s. While the former was usually an exercise in romantic nostalgia, as epitomized in various attempts to revive styles, genres and stars of the era, the latter became a more complex issue. It became so primarily because it was assigned great importance in the early attempts to establish the autonomy of "rock." Accounts of rock music (e.g., London 1985; Szatmary 1991) have often emphasized how there was a feeling that the optimistic rock ambience of the 1960s had been delivered a fatal blow by the dissolution of the Beatles, a number of rock star deaths, and violence at post-Woodstock rock festivals. This has been followed by a period in which pop was more socially acquiescent, and any coherent social mission it might have earlier appeared to possess was occluded by a pluralization of pop styles, with teenyboppers, camp superstars, middle-of-the-road pop and exploitative record companies crowding the field.[6] In his survey on artists-and-repertoire (A&R) men, originally published in 1976, Frith (1996b) concluded that far more fascinating than top-selling music was the diversification of the record industry. The development of popular music in the 1970s also seemed to correspond to broader tendencies toward fragmentation in Western societies. They derived from the emergence of sociocultural configurations and were articulated around questions of class, gender, sexuality, race, ethnicity and, more diffusely, ecological issues.

Whether popular music was "better" aesthetically or socially more relevant in the 1960s than in the 1970s or subsequent decades is a debate that need not be engaged with here. What is evident, however, is that the field of popular music came to be regarded as more heterogeneous in the 1970s. It had, of course, very much to do with the fact that rock music had reached the age of excess, a point at which it was no longer possible for any single genre to dominate the field. One corollary of this was that it became difficult to relocate those stars who had once been "Sixties heroes" and who now were reappearing with various degrees of respectability. This is where the "survivor" cult arose. Brian Wilson, the leader of the Beach Boys, returned to public view in 1976, after years of mental problems, and was acclaimed as a "survivor." In the sardonic view of Marcus (1994), the rock press was not really examining what Wilson, who had survived his own life, had returned with. What mattered was witnessing the event itself, the return of a man who had written and produced masterpieces in the 1960s and had finally triumphed over the ravages that accompanied such a monumental achievement. If Brian Wilson in the 1970s was eclipsed by his own history, much the same applied to John Lennon and his public persona. Elliott notes that "in his post-Beatles solo work Lennon was constantly staging some kind of ongoing dialogue with his celebrity as a state of mind and lifestyle" (1999, 175–76). Since the 1960s appeared to be inseparable from Lennon not only in terms of social and political issues but also in terms of music and celebrity, the weight of the past was a significant part of this dialogue. It led to the formation of a bipartite star history: John Lennon's 1960s had been a narrative of both triumph and humiliation.

John Lennon had been a member of the most famous pop group in the world and one that epitomized the 1960s: the Beatles. He himself remained ambivalent toward this period throughout the last decade of his life. His history as a Beatle was constantly discussed in the media, particularly in the rock press. In fact, it is difficult to find any 1970s Lennon interviews in which the subject was not raised. If the search for the "next Beatles" became a key issue for the music industry, it was closely accompanied by the media's fascination regarding whether the original lineup would return one day and revive the "spirit of the Sixties" (see Badman 2001, passim). Moreover, the usual strategy for rock journalists interviewing Lennon was first to ask about his latest activities and then carefully approach the memories of the ex-Beatle. The media's need to discover the "true" history of the Beatles, such as what happened behind the scenes or who wrote which songs, constantly shadowed his later career.

After the dissolution of the group, each of the former Beatles explicitly attempted to break away from his past and the 1960s and to reinvent himself as an artist: John Lennon as a political activist, Paul McCartney as a down-to-earth band leader (of Wings), George Harrison as an Eastern-influenced musician and Ringo Starr as an actor. For a short period this seemed possible, with a rush of solo album releases, some critically acclaimed (most notably Lennon's *Imagine* and Harrison's *All Things Must Pass*). It soon became apparent, however, that the post-Beatles projects did not fulfill expectations imposed upon the members of the group. The past eclipsed the present. It is illustrative that during the 1970s the number of Beatles fanzines increased, indicating that while the Beatles had ceased to exist as an actual entity, they survived as the embodiment of an important and living memory. The continual presence of the Beatles meant that the activities of each of the Beatles would be compared with past achievements, as well as with the activities of the other members. "If I took up ballet dancing, my ballet dancing would be compared with Paul's bowling," Lennon stated sardonically (Hamill 1982, 155).

That John Lennon was primarily perceived and constructed as a living Beatle—a star eclipsed by his own history—for the rest of his life played an important role in his survival rhetoric. One strategy for him was to deny the glory of the Beatles and to stress the more negative aspects of the past. Such a view was first articulated in Jann Wenner's long interview, originally published in *Rolling Stone* and then as a book, *Lennon Remembers*. The most extensive document of Lennon's ideas in the early 1970s, the interview epitomizes the embittered and angry rock hero demeaning his erstwhile colleagues and reevaluating the 1960s as well as his own history. It was the Beatles' humiliating celebrity in particular that was vigorously attacked: "I remember what it's all about now, you fuckers—fuck you! That's what I'm saying, you don't get me twice" (Wenner 1980, 20).

Interestingly, in saying "You don't get me twice" Lennon was not referring to the Beatles' studio years but to the teenage-oriented star cult and pop celebrity of Beatlemania. It was this version of the Beatles' stardom, the period that Lennon considered unreal and uncontrollable, that had to be reevaluated. He equated survival with a humiliating disempowerment.[7]

With Lennon, the reassessment of pop stardom seemed to reach a new level of vituperative debate, resulting in a questioning and repudiation of stardom. Some sense of this had emerged in the mid-1960s in relation to the search for popular music authenticity and the split between "pop" and "rock," but it was during the 1970s that Lennon devoted himself to such reconfiguration more visibly and systematically. Yet, Lennon still was a star, a widely recognized individual who had acquired symbolic status in popular music and culture. What is interesting in this instance is that Lennon was a major contributor to an attitude that later became an inseparable element of rock hero mythology and star narratives, the late Kurt Cobain of Nirvana being the most conspicuous example of the development. In order to be an "authentic" celebrity in popular music, one strategy is the rejection of the "inauthenticity" of fame. The star machinery can be criticized and rejected—whether by the star herself/himself or by various components of the starnet. The paradox of such a strategy is, of course, that the publicity machinery that originally created star status is now deployed in an apparent attempt to demolish it.

As the years of supposed humiliation receded, the tone of Lennon's critique of Beatles stardom changed from bitterness to resignation. "I'm going to be an ex-Beatle for the rest of my life so I might as well enjoy it, and I'm just getting round to being able to stand back and see what happened," Lennon explained and admitted being into collecting Beatles memorabilia (Coleman 1974, 14). The theme of survival also entered into his song lyrics. In "Intuition" (in *Mind Games*, 1973) Lennon sang how he has learned to use his instincts "in order to survive." "Scared" (in *Walls and Bridges*, 1974), even though interpreted as a confession of

Lennon's private terror (Robertson 1990; Du Noyer 1997), includes rather maudlin words about surviving and staying alive. Also, "Whatever Gets You thru the Night" (1974), Lennon's first solo number-one hit in the United States, could be interpreted as a survival song, as Lennon apparently took the title from a line he had heard on a TV program about alcoholism (Du Noyer 1997).

If considered to be autobiographical statements, these songs imply that Lennon has experienced some tribulations, albeit unspecified. There is no evidence that the lyrics refer to the 1960s, nor do they mention the Beatles. What they seem to assert is that the narrator is no longer young but has reached a point from which he is able to survey past difficulties, reconsider life and persist. In other words, the narrator has grown up.

This leads us to John Lennon's third survival theme, the question of aging in popular music, which I suggest is a key to understanding one distinct strand of 1970s rock stardom. In the 1960s it was typical for stars, including Lennon, to proclaim that it would be impossible for them to continue as pop performers into their thirties. As summarized by John Maus of Walker Brothers, "you can't do a big rock and roll act if you're balding" (*Melody Maker*, December 3, 1966, 3). This was a logical position to take in relation to the values of the time. Pop music was widely seen as a phenomenon of the adolescent sensibility. Frith (1978) recalls that there was a feeling that when young people grow up they abandon activities relating to pop music and become interested in more serious matters such as education, work and family. When he went to university in the 1960s, Frith assumed that he had reached the end of his "teenage bopping days," and he did not even take his records with him (9). Such an attitude was challenged in the 1970s. Well-established stars, many of whom were approaching their forties, declined either to retire or to enter new careers, as Tommy Steele and other 1950s rock celebrities had previously done. Partly as a result, the age profile of rock performers expanded in the 1970s. The problem was that at first there was no model for aging performers or for their audiences to negotiate the shift. This situation changed as the music industry began to recognize the market potential of adult-oriented rock music, and the idea of "staying alive" was incorporated into a new construction of star identities.

John Lennon's protracted "lost weekend" in 1973–74, and especially the retrospective accounts, exemplify this new survival discourse.
During this period Lennon and his wife Yoko Ono lived separately,
Lennon mainly spending his days in Los Angeles with his mistress May
Pang. Even though the period coincided with the beginning of Lennon's "staying alive" narratives, as exemplified in the above-mentioned songs, his activities at the time were not so much characterized
by the appearance of maturity as by a bachelor rock lifestyle and rejection of "adult responsibility." Barney Hoskyns, the historian of Los Angeles' popular music, suggests that Lennon was almost an "archetypal
seventies Brit-in-LA," "shaking off the grime of England" and joining
the city's party life (1996, 251). To Hoskyns, Lennon's "lost weekend"
reflected the self-destructive hedonism prevalent in Los Angeles between 1973 and 1975[8].

In interviews following the "lost weekend," such as the one given
to *Disc*, Lennon said that he was a "bit fed up" with his period in Los
Angeles, especially the fact that he would "go out for a night" and the
next day he would "read about it in the papers" (Horide 1975, 17). If
Lennon's adventures in Los Angeles reflected the decadence of the city,
then his penitential declarations that he had grown out of such experiences also coincided with the ethos of survival in American popular
music and culture. In this connection, it is possible to perceive Lennon's
"lost weekend" as a typical representation of the masculine quest for
self-definition and male validation, a rite of passage in search of the
right road. Yet, this period could also be interpreted as a trip of an aging
rock star to the bachelor rock life and back, a theme that has dominated
several subsequent narrations of male rock stars, among them Aero-
smith and the Red Hot Chili Peppers. In any event, this was the view
that Lennon himself promoted. In 1980 he confessed that "he could
have died" from "consuming at least a bottle of vodka a day, and a half
a bottle or more of brandy," "jumping out of cars" and having "a crazy
kind of teen-age game" (Hilburn 1980). The transforming moment had
already taken place in 1975, however. Soon after sobering up, Lennon
told *Rolling Stone* that "I feel like I've been on Sinbad's voyage, you
know, and I've battled all those monsters and I've got back" (Hamill
1982, 146–47). The interview presented John Lennon as the mature survivor: "I've decided I want to live. I'd decided I wanted to live *before*,
but I didn't know what it meant, really" (154). In another interview giv-

en at the time, Lennon emphasized that he had grown up and paid his dues and that he is now trying to "live out all the things" he has learned "in thirty-four years, to apply every day" (quoted in Giuliano & Giuliano 1995, 126).

The survivor model was developed further with Lennon's subsequent rejection of the links between death and rock music, which seemed to have reached a new level of mythologization in the 1970s: "Making Sid Vicious a hero. Jim Morrison—it's garbage to me. I worship the people who survive" (Sheff 1981, 101). The toll that the so-called rock 'n' roll lifestyle had so visibly taken since the late 1960s in fact gave the "rock survivor's" special status some validation in the 1970s. When many other musicians had fallen, to persist and to possess "staying power" were significant accomplishments in rock culture.

Some critics and journalists explicitly collaborated with Lennon's narrative and started to accord the ex-Beatle the status of veteran rock hero who had endured and survived major crises. In his otherwise critical biography *One Day at the Time*, first released in 1976, art critic Anthony Fawcett described 1975 as Lennon's "year of survival" (1980, 145). In his introduction to the above-mentioned *Rolling Stone* interview, Pete Hamill wrote that an era was now irrevocably past and the most famous embodiment of that epoch—John Lennon—was moving, as a human being and an artist, toward "full maturity" (142–43). These contours would later become an essential part of Lennon historiography.

It thus seems that in one particular area of 1970s popular music stardom, the aging of the rock performer was made valid through the ethos of survival. Growth, development and self-actualization became new key ideas in rock stardom, occasionally presenting survival almost as a spiritual progress. The accumulated "rock wisdom," which could be handed on to future rock generations, provided a legitimation for aging rock stars. By presenting his past as a burden and by discussing the benefits of growing up, Lennon, the former Sixties hero and Beatle, not only intensified the 1970s milieu as a decade of survival but also promoted this rock survivor image. In fact, it is arguable that his greatest contribution to rock stardom in the 1970s was his position as a prime mover in authenticating rock maturity, a concept that previously had been relatively mute in youth-oriented rock music. The growth of this idea would not have been possible, however, without the complicity of the rock press. Reinforced by journalists, other musical mediation and musicians themselves, stories of musicians who had "paid their dues" and were on this basis deserving of recognition, entered into rock star narratives in the 1970s and gradually became one of the most mythologized elements of popular music. Current rock magazines aimed at readers over thirty (*Mojo* and *Rolling Stone* are the best examples) disclose the entrenched durability in rock writing of the binary that positions those who have survived against those who have not.

What must be remembered, however, is that not everyone was gratified by the maturing of John Lennon, and it generated controversies, particularly during Lennon's years of fatherhood and isolation, from late 1975 to 1980. The Beatles' short retirement, from 1966 to 1967, had attracted tentative speculation about the role of pop stars, which intensified through Lennon's last years. He was still a star, and being a star in popular music still meant appearing in the media limelight.

Present Father, Absent Star

> *The word home takes on a coloring in Manhattan, a particular shape, a philosophical density that it has nowhere else on the planet.*
> —*Jerome Charyn, author*

Since the 1980s, it has become common for many major popular music stars to absent themselves for periods of time from activities associated with the music business and the phenomenon of celebrity. Depending on the level of control a star has over her or his relationship with the music industry, the media and the audience, the time between releasing music products may last several years. Such a strategy was extraordinary in the 1960s. The Beatles' retreat into isolation in 1966 lasted barely nine months, but it provoked speculation about the fate of the group. Pop stars were not supposed to hide away from the public eye. Although in the 1970s pop and rock performers were able to regulate their public appearances more flexibly than before, the convention still persisted that obliged stars to respond to expectations and needs generated by the music industry, the media and the audience. John Lennon's 1975–80 seclusion clearly challenged this practice.

Two basic features of Lennon's withdrawal were notable: its duration and its totality. During this time Lennon neither made nor released records. He gave no personal interviews. There were, however, a few interruptions. Lennon held two press conferences, first in New York in 1976 to celebrate his newly granted permanent resident status, and second in Tokyo in 1977 to explain, together with Ono, the reasons for their retirement. The couple also published an advertisement in major newspapers in 1979, titled "A Love Letter from John and Yoko to People Who Ask Us What, When, and Why." In the letter they enigmatically discussed "The Spring Cleaning" of their minds and the need for "quiet space." Referring arguably to criticism of their seclusion, Lennon and Ono declared that their "silence is a silence of love and not of indifference." There is disagreement as to whether Lennon's silence really was a "silence of love." When he returned to public life in 1980 to promote his and Yoko Ono's collaborative *Double Fantasy* album, he repeatedly recalled that he had spent five years as a househusband. He described how he had reared his son Sean, who was born in 1975, and how he left his guitar hanging on the wall while Ono took care of business matters. Many biographers have questioned these statements and suggested that Lennon was far from happy during his seclusion. Albert Goldman (1988; see also Rosen 2000; Giuliano 2001) argues that Lennon divided his seclusion between drink and drugs, had sexual relationships with women other than Ono and was an emotional and physical wreck for much of the time. This cannot absolutely be verified. Publication of Lennon's own journals — contrary to his earlier habit, Lennon kept written accounts of his life during his final years — might clarify the question of the househusband period, but to this day his diaries have remained something of a mystery, raising rumors of their intriguing contents.[9]

It is important to distinguish these retrospective reconstructions of the mystery of Lennon's seclusion from the interpretations that were articulated during Lennon's lifetime. While later historiography of John Lennon has concentrated on tracing the complex man behind the mask of domestic bliss, contemporary attempts to plumb the psyche of a star were not as conspicuous. Lennon's rejection of public life was discussed, of course, but instead of revealing the personal dimensions of his seclusion, journalists were more interested in contrasting Lennon's withdrawal with his history as a rock star and with masculinized rock

culture in general. Rather than tracing a particular profile of the alien-
ated celebrity, it is here more important to examine the supposed obligations and responsibilities of the rock star. Second, what was the role
of gender politics in relation to Lennon's seclusion?

The specific enabling factor for Lennon to have a vacation from
public life and stardom was that in the late 1970s he was not officially
committed to recording. Lennon did not renew his EMI/Capitol recording contract, which expired in January 1976. Nor did he respond to any
of the tempting offers he received from other major recording companies. For the first time since 1961, when Lennon and other Beatles had
signed a contract with manager Brian Epstein, he was a free agent in the
music business. Since Lennon had been one of the most famous rock
stars in the world, and since the presence and availability of the star,
whether physically or as mediated images and products, is central to
the star phenomenon, Lennon's decision not to renew his contract but
to retreat into isolation aroused skepticism. Confusion was compound-
ed because—as with the Beatles' withdrawal in 1966—there was no official announcement about Lennon's retirement. It was not until 1980
that Lennon and Ono signed a contract with newly created Geffen
Records.

For Lennon, the decision to leave EMI and refuse other offers for
five years was justified through his survival tactics. After his return in
1980, he explained that his seclusion had been a haven from the demands of the music industry and stardom. "My whole security and
identity was wrapped up in being John Lennon, the pop star," he
claimed (Hilburn 1980). He described his recording contract as "the
physical manifestation of being in prison," and it took "constant rein-
forcement" to reject "the image of what the artist is supposed to do"
(Sheff 1981, 76).

The rejection of contractual obligations may have been a significant
impetus for Lennon to retire, but at the time it was not the main issue
in the discussion of his seclusion. There was something else that made
Lennon's withdrawal intriguing. In his account of the celebrity phenomenon in America, Jib Fowles writes that it is not unusual that, "having tasted the fruits of stardom, stars often retreat to the normalities of
everyday American life" (1992, 206). The desire to live like ordinary
people is a theme that has frequently arisen in modern star narratives.
This, however, is often subordinate to the convention that stars must

maintain their public profile, at least to some extent. This Lennon did not do. His seclusion was almost total. On the other hand, total withdrawal is not entirely unexceptional in the star phenomenon. Throughout the history of modern celebrity, loneliness and alienation have been regular themes in accounts of stars' lives. In rock music culture in particular, alienation has played an important role not only as a subject of songs but also as an image of how behind the excess and glamor of stardom there may lurk feelings of suffering and despair. The dark side of fame is a theme that is inseparable from rock narratives, as typified, for example, in Alan Parker's fictitious film portrait of a rock star, *Pink Floyd: The Wall* (1982). At the time of Lennon's seclusion, signs of personal tragedy were, however, not apparent in his life. Nor did Lennon himself attempt to publicize any such signs. Thus, his retreat into domestic isolation did not conform to the theatricalized alienation of the self-destructive rock artist and celebrity.

Lennon's withdrawal was difficult to comprehend also because it conflicted with his history as a socially active rock star. The imperative of "change" had been central to Lennon's career, but this time his shift from a street politician and survivor to a nonactivist recluse gave a particular impetus for criticism. Perhaps the most notorious example was Laurence Shames' "John Lennon, Where Are You?" which was published in the November 1980 issue of *Esquire* and which thus coincided with Lennon's return to public life. In the beginning of his ten-page piece of investigative journalism, Shames portrayed a star "who had always shot his mouth off, who had offended everyone without having to try," and "whose pained, goofy, earnest, and paranoid visage was the emblem and conscience of an age." The Lennon he found—not literally but through interviewing Lennon's employees and investigating the star's estate—was not the hero he went looking for but "a forty-year-old businessman who watches a lot of television" and "who's got $150 million." "Is it true, John? Have you really given up?" Shames asked. (32)

Shames thus implied that Lennon had betrayed his own ideals and at the same time those dreams of the Sixties generation he had helped to create. Not only had Lennon "licked the old order" but "he'd joined it" (38). Hence, what was relatively acceptable for multimillionaire Howard Hughes, another famous recluse of the time, or the Beach Boys' mastermind Brian Wilson, who because of his problems with drugs and mental health had led a life of the hermit at his Bel-Air mansion for almost a decade, was not appropriate for "Lennon the Fierce, Lennon the Snide" (32). To Shames' mind, there was no justifiable explanation for Lennon's seclusion.

Although Shames did not articulate the particular mode of celebrity that Lennon had rejected, it is easy to see that his writing reflected 1960s countercultural rock ideology and the idea that stars are continuously at risk of becoming corrupted. Some other writers commenting on Lennon's seclusion were more forthcoming in prescribing this mode, which continued to be dominant in writings and theories about popular music stardom until the postmodern reconfiguration of "pop" in the 1980s. Stopping short of explicitly accusing Lennon of being a fraud, journalist Neil Spencer nonetheless was saddened to see the former Beatle absent from current rock music culture. In an article published in *New Musical Express* in 1978, Spencer expected more than silence from Lennon because "the ideas and principles he'd so fervently espoused a few years back were being put into rude practice by a new generation— or at least a new wave—of rockers intent of dragging the music and everything that accompanies it back to the roots." According to Spencer, Lennon's indifference to these events was "disheartening and miserable" (22).

In his long analysis of Lennon's first solo record, *John Lennon/Plastic Ono Band*, Spencer alleged that the album's raw intensity and the burning of illusions of superstardom (especially in the song "God") had foreshadowed punks who "show a refreshing unwillingness to be the recipients of the kind of Messiah projection that so many of the '60s stars welcomed and invited." Finally, Spencer addressed Lennon directly, asserting that punks "started the revolution without you, mate, but then you started it without waiting for anyone else," and "that's no reason for you to opt out now" (23). Spencer thus saw the former Beatle as a mentor, inspiring his descendants, punk rockers and new wavers. This generalization about the proper role of a star was predicated very selectively on one particular phase of Lennon's career. In order to give substance to his accusation that Lennon had in some way betrayed his obligations as a rock star, Spencer was forced to base his sense of those obligations on only one aspect of Lennon's multifaceted career that seemed to correspond to sentiments of punk and new wave rock. In this scheme, celebrity types such as Lennon the teenybop star, Lennon the psychedelic visionary, Lennon the avant-gardist, Lennon the fool and Lennon the dreamer were ignored, while Lennon the revolutionary who once had been disillusioned with rock superstardom was emphasized. The paradox was that although Spencer hailed Lennon's past repudiation of stardom, he at the same time wanted him to be more publicly involved in the musical revolution that was taking place at the time of the writing. Thus, Lennon's denial of stardom in the late 1970s was the wrong kind of denial.

Lennon's enduring image as a major representative of "conscience rock" was also addressed in an editorial of *The New York Post* (September 25, 1979). The writer took a stand on Lennon's jeopardizing of the proposed Beatles concert for refugees of Vietnam and Cambodia, the "boat people." Since Lennon had "probably written more of compassion and the need to help the less fortunate than any other lyricist," he was accountable for more than just "wishing and praying" in seclusion. Such an attitude, the editorial concluded, "will not help the Boat People."[10]

These three examples indicate that Lennon's earlier profile conflicted with his new position. This situation seemed to reproduce the pattern I have discussed above, noting that Lennon's status as a star in the 1970s was to a large extent defined by his past achievements. Lennon's history as a Sixties rock hero was a reference point that eclipsed his present activities and which now conflicted with his inactivity and seclusion. Disappointed because Lennon could not meet the expectations of stardom he himself had created, critics, especially Shames, came to the conclusion that in terms of countercultural rock, he had "sold out" or "copped out." When Lennon returned to public life in 1980, he was forced to respond to such allegations. A major thrust of his response was the denial of countercultural versions of stardom and the declaration of a new kind of celebrity. This rehabilitation of stardom invoked issues of gender in rock music culture.

Asked about his absence from the public eye, Lennon explained enthusiastically and at great length that he had "been baking bread and looking after the baby" which, "as every housewife knows, is a full-time job" (Sheff 1981, 76). This vindication was also promoted in some of his new songs, particularly "Cleanup Time" and "Beautiful Boy (Darling Boy)." Whether baking bread and rearing a child really was a full-time job for Lennon was highly questionable, since during his househusband period there were at any given time approximately a dozen full-time servants on Lennon and Ono's payroll, including a nanny. Although Lennon mentioned to the journalists of *Newsweek* and *Playboy* that he is a "rich housewife" with a number of servants (Graustark 1980b, 119; Sheff 1982, 124), he did not expound upon the subject. Lennon's public identification with housewives and the pressing responsibilities of homecraft is arguably disingenuous, since, as a millionaire, he was easily able to grant himself a five-year paternity leave. Nevertheless, the fact that he propagated this image of domestic life, promoted child care and openly celebrated the joys of fatherhood was in many ways exceptional.

Fundamental to the criticism that Lennon attracted in the late 1970s was the presumption that he was assuming a role that conformed neither to the ideals of traditional masculinity nor to the masculinized image of the rock star. Lennon's new role as a househusband was ridiculed in cartoons and television sketches in which he was typically positioned as a henpecked husband wearing an apron while his wife was caricatured as a businessman with a tie (Howlett & Lewisohn 1992). The comic force of such representations, of course, relies on the implied norm of gender relations, of which the John and Yoko model was an inversion. In relation to conventions of masculinity, Lennon's role as a househusband was at least confusing and at worst threatening because it did not correspond to a certain kind of patriarchy dominant in American culture.

Historians of masculinity have argued that while the demand for sexual equality has been a prominent issue in Western societies since the nineteenth century, the issue of men's responsibilities—or rights—for homecrafting and child rearing is very new (Pleck 1987; Cohen 1990; Roper & Tosh 1991; Hearn 1992). The lack of campaigning on behalf of fatherhood is arguably related to the effects of industrialization and modernization and the view that masculinity is constructed in the public rather than the private sphere, that is, home, which has traditionally been identified as a female realm. The ideal father, as evolved during the nineteenth and early twentieth centuries, focused on breadwinning rather than child care. It could be suggested that during the 1970s the model of the distant father-breadwinner came under reassessment in Western societies. Pleck argues in his writing on the history of fathering in America that while the father-breadwinner model unquestionably was still dominant in the 1970s, the image of "the new father," the man who is present at the birth of his children, who is involved with his children as infants, and who participates in everyday work of child care and other domestic responsibilities, was slowly gaining ground. For example, the husband's proportion of the total housework and child care in America rose from 20 percent to 30 percent between 1965 and 1981 (1987, 95).

In the early 1960s Lennon appeared as a father who maintained his family but delegated the responsibility for childrearing to his wife. He clearly represented the father-breadwinner model that was dominant in the 1960s. Lennon's role in the late 1970s can be seen as a manifestation of the new expectation that men should take a more active role in domestic matters. It could be argued that by being a visible celebrity — albeit in seclusion — Lennon not only reflected such ideas but was involved in creating them. Marshall argues that celebrities "are intense sites for determining the meaning and significance of the private sphere and its implications for the public sphere," representing fundamentally "the disintegration of the distinction between the private and the public" (1997, 247). In relation to this argument, it could be suggested that Lennon operated as a powerful sign within changing cultural codes and images of masculinity. Although he shamelessly placed on display the everyday reality of his private sphere, in the context of masculinity and celebrity his reversing of gender roles, his declaration of househusbandism and the creation of the image of a caring father paved the way for the "new father" image that gained prominence in the 1980s.

As long as Lennon was predominantly considered a rock star, his construction of the private sphere took a particular coloring. Lennon's absence from public life was not attributed to drugs, alcohol, mental problems, alienation or other destructive symptoms associated with the rock lifestyle, but related to a sphere that had traditionally been considered problematic in rock. Even though in the history of popular music we can find a considerable number of artists whose star images have incorporated marriage and family ties, these have usually been associated with music genres other than rock, which has more typically proclaimed family ties in terms of colleagues or "mates."[11] I have earlier discussed how in rock mythology "home" has been considered a threat to free masculinity and how in the case of the Beatles there were even explicit attempts to exclude this trope from their images. In relation to Lennon's seclusion, the idea of home as a constraint on stardom persisted in the 1970s. Spencer found it depressing that "Lennon couldn't take the role of rock star into dignified and meaningful getting-on-for-middle-age" as, for example, "Bob Dylan, for whom a kid for five didn't necessarily spell artistic stagnation" (1978, 22). The most strident criticism came from Mick Jagger, who asserted that Lennon was using his domestic responsibilities as an excuse to abandon rock while he could have easily had both the family and rock music (Howlett & Lewisohn 1992).

What should be remembered, however, is that in the context of Lennon's star history the accentuation of domesticity in the 1970s was a logical development of some of Lennon's earlier practices. By having made his marriage with Yoko Ono a public spectacle in 1969, Lennon, the "fool in love," had already refused to conceal the private sphere of domestic life. The visibility of his marriage challenged conventional practices of pop stardom. More specifically, it eroded the image of the Beatles as a single large family of four "brothers." Lennon introduced Ono to the Beatles' community and allowed her to stay and even participate in the Beatles' recording sessions, which until then had conspicuously been nonfemale events. As a consequence, the Beatles' masculinized group activity was challenged. Usually, women who wish to be part of the male-dominated group must accept norms of "male bonding" and must be able to decode male behavior patterns, such as "engaging in coarse joking, teasing and sharing the informal work values of men" (Fine 1987, 131–32). Ono refused to act like "one of the boys," and it was partly because of this that she was criticized in the late 1960s. As the Beatles attempted unsuccessfully to revise their hitherto effective working arrangements, she later carried the blame for the dissolution of the group.

Ono's refusal of the masculinist rules reflected in part her commitment to artistic integrity, but it also drew on her interest in the women's movement. Ono became an active feminist in the 1970s, writing several feminist songs as well as producing articles about women's position in society. In an article printed on her *Approximately Infinite Universe* album cover (1973), she claimed that "the whole society is geared to living up to a Hollywood cum Madison Avenue image of men and women." Child care did not fit in "such an image-driven culture" as it represented "a direct threat to our very false existence."[12]

The feminist movement in America, the second wave of which emerged during the 1970s, and its criticism of paternal gender-role modeling, provided some of the most important impetus to the new father image (Pleck 1987). In his interviews in 1980 (Graustark 1980b; Peebles 1981; Sheff 1982), John Lennon stated that the women's movement had also influenced him. This interest had first been disclosed in the song "Woman Is the Nigger of the World," which was released in 1972. Lennon also said that he had read feminist books like Elizabeth G. Davis' *The First Sex* and that living with a feminist had taught him feminist thinking. Interviewers were given to understand that his seclusion was not only a consequence of his weariness with rock stardom but also drew on a commitment to the politics of the women's movement. This politics, he seemed to assert, had helped him to abandon the music business in favor of a long paternity leave.

It should be emphasized that Lennon was not particularly well read in gender politics or feminist theories. His thoughts on feminism were expressed in rather schematic sloganeering, with a simplistic focus on women as victims of oppression; likewise, his critique of masculinism concentrated on the violence of traditional masculinity, or what he called the "macho ethic" (quoted in Wiener 1985, 305). Nevertheless, it was relatively uncommon in the 1970s for a male rock star to show concern with such issues. Male rockers might have played with androgynous images and thus challenged traditional gender roles superficially, but apart from a few popular songs, such as Donovan's "Liberation Rag" (1976) or the Tom Robinson Band's "Right on Sister" (1978), engagement with feminism and the women's movement was sparse. In America, it was not until grunge rock in the early 1990s that such interest emerged.

Given that "the personal is political" was a guiding slogan for the 1970s feminist movement, it could be suggested that Lennon's househusbandism was not only a personal choice but a political statement, or that he at least attempted to make it political in 1980. In a sense, Lennon's seclusion and his subsequent manifestations of househusbandism can thus be understood as an extension of the social activism that had characterized his career since the late 1960s. This was not recognized at the time, simply because political rock, or "conscience rock," largely excluded feminist thinking. It is reasonable to argue that by refusing to adopt more conventional political positions and by concentrating on "home" in the late 1970s, Lennon rebelled, yet not against those values and institutions that it was fashionable to deride among the counterculture and its rock music. Lennon's househusband period was a rejection of hegemonic masculinity and the countercultural version of rock stardom.

I suggest that as a pattern in Lennon's career in the 1970s, this gesture was far more radical than his street politics in Greenwich Village or his bachelor "lost weekend" in Los Angeles. This time it was not only the expectations of the music industry or the media that were resisted but also the ideology of rock. Lennon's gesture is not compromised by the fact that he was a privileged millionaire who was able to hire servants in great numbers. While biographers have later alleged that Lennon distorted the truth about his seclusion and househusbandism, at the time he was questioning masculinist myths of rock music culture.

Such questioning clearly was a part of Lennon's survival mythos, his attempt to validate aging in rock music culture. It was also about re-authenticating a star. Having returned to the public, Lennon took pains to establish his authenticity in media texts through signs and gestures of sincerity, uniqueness and other ideals associated with the authentic rock star. He emphasized self-directedness, responsibility and independence from public pressures and controls, and thus began to construct his private sphere as an ultimate site of "truth." Because of Lennon's murder this project remained unfinished. In fact, it was soon forgotten. While biographers, journalists and fans have often speculated as to what Lennon would have thought or done about a variety of issues and events had he not been killed, the question of whether he would have continued to celebrate his domestic life or abandoned it as a passing phase has scarcely received any attention. It may be that it appears as a trivial and unglamorous subject for discussion. It may also be that because of a violent event on a December evening in 1980, the househusband image of John Lennon was immediately eclipsed by the mythologization of heroic martyrdom.

8 Stardom and Death

Death of a Hero

If we came together for one reason, we could make it together!
—John Lennon in 1970 on the Toronto Peace Festival, which did not materialize

As the news of John Lennon's murder on the evening of December 8, 1980, started to spread, reactions of disbelief and shock emerged. For many, there was a need to share the grief. Within hours after the murder, fans and other people began to gather outside the Dakota apartment building, holding candles, crying and chanting. Spontaneous and emotional memorials took place in dozens of cities all over the world, and when a worldwide silent vigil for Lennon was held on December 14, crowds of mourners assembled. New York's Central Park, across the street from the Dakota, was the site of a vigil of 50,000 to 100,000 people, according to varying estimates, while in Liverpool approximately 25,000 attended a ceremony. Apart from these gatherings, in the aftermath of the tragic event fans made pilgrimages to places associated with Lennon's career (Garbarini & Cullman 1980; Badman 2001).

Lennon's death was also marked by grieving tributes in the media. Radio stations revised their playlists while television stations broadcast Lennon and Beatles retrospectives. Journalists produced Lennon obituaries and histories. Furthermore, record shops reported runs on Beatles and Lennon albums, responding to the public's "need to have something of John Lennon's right now," as one record store clerk explained (Garbarini & Cullman 1980, 22). Five gunshots had stolen John Lennon from his fans and the general public, but at the same time his history and memory emerged as a unifying force. In Lennon's career, Beatlemania, *Sgt. Pepper's Lonely Hearts Club Band* and the campaign for world peace had connected people, but it was, paradoxically, his death that most effectively brought people together. As a physical person, Lennon was irrevocably absent; as an image and memory, he was intensely present.

The moment of John Lennon's death produced a momentum that at the time was almost unprecedented in the history of modern celebrity.[1] I would like to suggest that the mourning was also defined by the sense of the past or, more precisely, a synthesis of recollections of the past and present experience. It is, of course, customary that when someone dies, friends, relatives and colleagues dwell upon the memory and the history of the deceased. Furthermore, when a celebrity dies, journalists and other commentators publish recollections of the star's career, identifying its most important moments. These mourning rituals tend to strengthen group solidarity, and Lennon's death was no exception. What is significant is the particular character and scope of the "history" that the memorializing assigned to Lennon. He was seen as inseparable from the Sixties and the so-called Sixties generation.

Fred Fogo's sociological study *I Read the News Today: The Social Drama of John Lennon's Death* (1994) is based on the proposition that Lennon's death was an important event in the social drama of contemporary life. Fogo's central assumption is that Lennon symbolically embodied various values and feelings associated with the 1960s and the generation that identified itself with that period. If anyone epitomized the 1960s, its social conflicts and its reforming utopianism, it was John Lennon. Fogo argues that while Lennon's death was broadly equated with the final demise of the dreams of the 1960s, the event also "opened a mass-mediated space where a generational segment talked to itself about its identity and 'place' in the social order through a ritual grieving process that implicitly strove for unity and consensus" (xi). Relying on a profusion of elegiac writings published in American newspapers and magazines, and using the sociologist Victor Turner's theory of social drama, Fogo classifies reactions to Lennon's death in order to explain the larger cultural crisis. He approaches this moment of identity exploration through themes of nostalgia, scapegoating, resignation, and acceptance. While nostalgic tributes to Lennon focused on him as the emblem of the countercultural ethos, *scapegoating* referred to attempts to explain the horrifically irrational act of Lennon's killer, Mark Chapman. Narratives of resignation accepted that the 1960s and its dreams were finished, though beyond that there emerged an attempt to imagine how the countercultural ideals could be incorporated into new realities. Fogo's underlying argument seems to be that Lennon's death coincided perfectly with a transitional dilemma then current among the generation which had lived its youth through the 1960s. Lennon's death became the means by which this generation could say farewell to the era to which they were both nostalgically attached, yet also traumatically growing out of as they sought a place in the conventional structures of society.

Lennon's death came to mean the nostalgic triumph of the memory of the 1960s. According to Fogo, two sorts of elegies emerged. First, Fogo analyzes elegies that engaged a sense of communitas. In this scheme, Lennon was presented as a symbol of mystical union and individualism which in the context of Sixties communitas was the very foundation of community or, rather, the imaginary and emotional sharing of countercultural communion (43–47). While much of the mourning for Lennon in 1980 invoked the sense of freedom and the sense of countercultural communitas among the Sixties generation, Fogo also considers elegies that expressed more personal nostalgia and suggested the "polysemic" nature of John Lennon as cultural symbol (52). Some of the writers blended personal memories with collective understandings of Lennon while some expressed personal nostalgia not connected to the 1960s communitas. Many writers recounted how Beatles music and Beatlemania had marked their childhood and adolescence, including, for example, first romances and growing hair longer. These memories often dwelt upon the pre-hippie era and recalled the early Beatles as symbols of innocence. Common to all elegies was the emphasis on the 1960s.

What I think is important, and what Fogo remarks upon only in passing in his otherwise thoughtful section about memorializing Lennon, is that many of these elegies stood as examples of a mass-mediated relationship with the star and that Lennon's murder was a significant catalyst for the subsequent remembrance of the Beatles and Lennon. Remembering Lennon typically includes memories by "insiders," people who concretely were associated with Lennon, and "outsiders," people who have happened to have a "piece" of him in one way or another (for example, attending concerts or collecting items touched by the Beatles), or people who never met Lennon in person but instead grew up with the mediated version of him. Although it is the insiders' biographies and memoirs that top the hierarchy of the memory industry of Lennon and the Beatles, attracting the greatest attention and being evaluated as the most authentic form of recollection, we are also constantly presented with secondary yet very personal narratives. Although these outside memories have their own hierarchies, the two most obvious ones being the above-mentioned physical witnessing versus mediated images, and the division between those who experienced the 1960s and those who did not, what these all share is that the mediated image of John Lennon remains the most significant site for recollecting.

Mediation, of course, does not diminish the importance of these stars and their involvements in people's lives and identity construc-tions. What must be emphasized, however, is that mediation incorpo-rates a range of cultural intermediaries and is a meaning-making process whereby the star comes to be circulated among different audi-ences. Although the circulation of images, songs or any other cultural products is usually accompanied by struggles over their meaning, in some cases mediation can result in the construction of an unambiguous profile. It is not unusual that in the immediate aftermath of the death of the star, her or his image is generally deified through such a process of consensual canonization.

Fogo assumes that almost all who mourned Lennon belonged to the "Sixties generation," which itself is part of the larger demographic phe-nomenon known as the baby boomers (3). Certainly, other people (in-cluding myself) than those of the Sixties generation grieved as well. It is more reasonable to argue that although mourning was not the privi-lege of a particular generation or any other distinct group of people, Lennon's demise assumed a distinctive character among those who had experienced the Sixties. Furthermore, it could be alleged that at least in the Anglo-American context it was the voice of the Sixties generation that dominated the mourning, eclipsing other voices and creating Len-non's death as to signify "the last nail in the coffin of the 60's," as one mourner expressed in *Newsweek* (December 22, 1980, 36).[2]

Although Lennon had a professional career of almost twenty years, writers mainly dwelt upon only the first ten, and identified the Sixties hero whom they had promoted and lauded. Lennon's death was not, for example, perceived as a sad end of survivalism, the ethos of which since the early 1970s had characterized American culture and Lennon's image (and which in fact disappeared from the cultural vocabulary in the 1980s); nor was Lennon's death imagined as a closure of the 1970s. Furthermore, Lennon's most recent period, as a househusband, did not receive the same recognition in elegiac writings as his public years in the 1960s. One possible explanation for this is that at least in the United States it was almost exclusively men who were involved, as Fogo notes, in the "priestly tasks of elegizing the fallen leader of the tribe," while women were most conspicuous in visual images as weeping mourners (103). Thus, it could be argued that Lennon's meaning and history were distorted because the production mechanism of knowledge itself was distorted. It could of course also be argued that, by whatever standards, the 1960s were more important in artistic, commercial and cultural terms in Lennon's career than the 1970s. But in any event it remains notable that hardly anyone challenged the elegiac and male-oriented understanding of Lennon as a Sixties hero. The death of John Lennon was the zenith of the career of John Lennon in the sense that he became a Sixties icon.

This raises a further question about Lennon's role as a hero. The celebrity category called hero carries meanings different from those associated with stardom. The film scholar James Monaco (1978, 8–9) articulates categories of public personalities, arguing that at the apex is the "hero," a famous person (for instance, an astronaut, a scientist, or an inventor) who has actually done something in what Monaco calls "an active sense." Below the hero is the "star," who works on playing the role of her- or himself, and below the star is the "quasar," which is the lowest category of celebrity and refers to a mediated individual who has no control over her or his image. Although this is an interesting set of categories, Marshall (1997) finds it underdeveloped in the sense that it does not take into consideration how celebrities are connected to the interests of the audiences and how contemporary media play an important role at all levels. Moreover, as these terms are used loosely and in a variety of situations (apart from quasar, which has not been established in the taxonomy of celebrity), it is evident that Monaco's schematic categorization does not provide an appropriate tool for general studies of modern heroism and stardom. It can be argued, however, that particular events and cases exist in which a clear line between these categories can be drawn. If nothing else, John Lennon's death clearly marked a shift from the imagery of stardom to that of heroism.

Wayne Hampton's study of American protest singers, *Guerrilla Minstrels* (1986), provides a rare attempt to understand Lennon's heroism. Hampton argues that it is only through a discussion of heroism that the puzzling power of Lennon's death, with its massive and relatively coherent public response, can be resolved. The image of Lennon clearly corresponded to those characteristics associated with heroism. Tributes and obituaries implied that he had some kind of magic power, charisma and the ability to comprehend the reality behind the facade, that his career had a messianic quality, that he suffered and that, in a sense, he was a martyr to his noble principles. Hampton's essential point is that the hero, like John Lennon, is not the individual behind the image but rather a collective and even imaginary idealization that is associated with that individual. The hero thus is a public personage and a mythos around whom social unity and action crystallize. This activity often takes the form of a cult that, especially after the death of the hero, first mythologizes the individual, embodying in the hero's image the ideals to which the collectivity aspires, and then attempts "to gloss over or ignore those aspects of the individual that do not fit neatly into the mold of the myth" (6). Hampton argues that heroism is basically centered on the notion of "totalization," the process that supports "the activities that maintain the sense and sensibility of community" (43).

Although I feel doubtful about the notion of totalization since it does not take into consideration how Lennon's stardom is multidimensional by nature, and although I find Hampton's closer analysis of Lennon's career rather old-fashioned and even confusing,[3] Lennon clearly was constructed into an appropriate icon. An instructive example of how the image of Lennon appeared as a totalizing agent was that some negative reviews of Lennon and Ono's just-released *Double Fantasy* album were withdrawn in the wake of the tragedy (Christgau 1987). In his analysis Hampton attempts to prove that Lennon's role as an active hero—a social missionary and peace politician—draws on Lennon's past deeds and reputation. While this is to some extent obvious, we should note that the canonization process also related to the cruel and unjust manner of Lennon's death.

On December 10, 1980, the front-page headline of the *Daily Mirror* screamed "Death of a Hero." It could be read either as a death of a particular hero or that a hero had died a hero's death. In conventional terms there was no heroic element involved in Lennon's fate. He was murdered, but the particular situation and the moment of the murder did not imply heroism. He was not demonstrating for peace or performing for human rights but coming home from his workplace, the recording studio, when Mark Chapman fired on him. On the evening of

December 8, Lennon appeared more as a rock musician having called it a day than an active hero. Yet, it was the act of violence, the murder of a star, that ultimately caused a relatively tranquil rock survivor to be identified as a hero.

Violence, killing and murder have been incorporated into the history of rock music, as in the imagery of rock songs (for example, the album *Murder Ballads* by Nick Cave and the Bad Seeds), theatrical star images (Alice Cooper, Marilyn Manson), particular genres (death metal, black metal), and in discussions of rock's potentially destructive effects on listeners (Did the Beatles' "Helter Skelter" inspire the mass murderer Charles Manson?). We can also find rock performers who have faced violent death. In his macabre account of rock deaths in the 1970s, Marcus (1994) lists 116 cases, of which more than half were caused by accidents, drugs or heart attacks. Twelve performers—none of whom, however, can really be considered "stars"—were murdered. Another curious catalog can be found on the Christian *Dial-the-Truth Ministries* (2001) web site. It lists 321 "premature deaths of rock stars" up to 1997 and lists heart attacks, drug overdoses and "miscellaneous medical" as the three most common causes of death. Although the figures appear reliable, there is some overstatement, in the sense that most of the names included cannot be classified as "rock stars" but rather as performers of a range of musical styles and different degrees of fame. This list counts eighteen murder victims to whom the term *star* could be applied: Sam Cooke, Marvin Gaye, John Lennon, Notorious B.I.G., Selena, Tupac Shakur and Peter Tosh. Thus, rock stars may occasionally die violently, but violent deaths are not particularly characteristic of rock stardom—nor are they necessarily peculiar to the phenomenon of celebrity in general. In Jib Fowles' (1992) early account of deaths of American celebrities, based on a sample of one hundred famous people and general information on American mortality in 1974, stars are more than twice as likely to expire in accidents and more than three times as likely to die by their own hand than is the general American population. Yet, homicide as a cause of death did not notably differ between stars (1.4 percent) and the general American population (1.1 percent).

Among these statistics, John Lennon stands as the best-known example among murdered popular music stars. While his death falls into the category of premature rock star deaths, the circumstances of his death distinguish him from many of his colleagues who simply died too young. His death was not caused by drugs, alcohol, suicidal tendencies or other causes traditionally associated with the "fast" lifestyles of male performers. He did not perish from "vulgar excesses — the speeding car or the prolonged party," which according to Pattison (1987, 123) are rock's version of romanticism's aestheticization of death as the ultimate form of excess. Nor was Lennon's death shrouded in mystery, which would have fed rumors of his second coming, as with Jim Morrison or Elvis Presley. Lennon did not waste away from a painful and lethal disease, as Freddie Mercury and George Harrison later did, nor did he perish, like Buddy Holly, in the flames of a crashing airplane while touring. In sum, his death did not correspond to the romanticized and mythologized death of the male rock star.

Just before his death, Lennon had criticized rock lifestyles and hegemonic masculinity, announcing that he had survived the hazards of the rock life. Lennon identified himself with oppressed housewives, emphasizing the sphere traditionally associated with femininity rather than masculine rock. His death, however, had no points of contact with a domestic lifestyle, nor was it parallel to those archetypical features of premature deaths of female stars. Robyn Archer and Diana Simmonds allege in their collection of biographical essays on female stars that if male stars have died of excess, women have perished in deprivation and frustration because of their powerlessness to control circumstances and events (1986, 5; see also the statistics in Fowles 1992). It does not require further analysis to conclude that Lennon's fate does not correspond to this mythologized category: He was not forgotten, not deprived of material comforts, and having made a successful comeback at least in commercial terms, his death did not occur in response to career paralysis.

Lennon's death was compared to those of past celebrities, but these were political and religious leaders rather than entertainers. Especially in America, John Lennon's death immediately evoked parallels with the political assassinations of the 1960s. In both the ABC and CBS television evening news for December 9, 1980, commentators compared Lennon's death to those of Martin Luther King, Jr. and John F. Kennedy (see Vanderbilt Television News Archive 1997). Likewise in Britain, Donald Zec, the journalist who had ridiculed Lennon's peace campaign in the late 1960s, now wrote: "Not since that mad day in Dallas perhaps, when a bullet ended John Kennedy's life, has there been such an immediate world-wide sense of shock" (see also Ball 1980; Leapman 1980; *Liverpool Echo*, December 10, 1980; Reynolds 1980). These analogies imply that John Lennon was considered not simply a pop star but a political figure and a hero who had in his lifetime actively done something and then faced a martyrlike death. Lennon's death was aligned with those of Christ, Gandhi, Martin Luther King, Jr., and other heroes who had died for their principles.[4] The choice of Lennon songs that were played on the radio and television tributes in December 1980 is a further reflection of this sentiment. Hampton writes that it struck him as very odd that the headlining songs were almost without exception "Imagine" and "Give Peace a Chance" rather than "Working Class Hero" or "Mind Games," which to him would have more accurately captured the essence of Lennon (1986, 6). The song selections, which at a time of confusion apparently were more intuitive than conscious, emphasized Lennon's role as a defender of noble principles and thus contributed to Lennon's iconic quality. Yet, Lennon's dreams about world community represented only one part of his career and activities, to say nothing of his song catalog, in which the theme of community certainly is outweighed by expressions of personal struggle. It also is worth remembering that Lennon had rejected countercultural agendas in the 1960s to experiment with different notions of community in the 1970s, those of the radical left and the family, which now were more or less ignored. In one of his last interviews, Lennon had strongly advised people not to follow leaders and create hero worship (Sheff 1981, 144). After his death, he himself became the subject of hero worship.

This hero worship, of course, worked as a means of articulating the grief and reflected the way Lennon and his music had been integral to forms of positive identification. Yet, Lennon's fate also signified the darker side of hero worship. What makes his death more tragic and exceptional among rock star deaths is not only that he was killed in cold blood but that he was killed by a fan. It is well known that Mark Chapman was one of the "Lennon people," and it is this circumstance that makes the murder of John Lennon one of the most notorious deaths in the history of modern fame. It reminded us that not all fans are harmless in their admiration and identification. In a sense, this one act problematized the idea of star worship for years, a demonstration for many that fandom is potentially pathological, deviant and dangerous.

Although addictive fandom is as old as stardom itself and has caused fans to stalk their idols, Mark Chapman advanced the model to the point of homicide for reasons that still are debated. In general, the motivations of stalkers are various, ranging from the sense of power or self-importance to psychopathological conditions and the frustration at being denied a relationship with the idol (Evans & Wilson 1999). Sometimes stalkers also seek to share the fame of their target, and this seems to have been the case with Mark Chapman, who after his act made no attempt to escape from the crime scene. This pattern was repeated in 1981, when John Hinckley tried to kill President Ronald Reagan in an attempt to be noticed by the world and to impress his object of love, actress Jodie Foster. The typical suggestion (see, for example, Lahr 1984) is that such distorted fame-seeking reflects the profound influence of media on modern societies and people's lives. In his psychoanalytic profile of Chapman, Anthony Elliott disagrees with this view and argues that attacks against celebrities are not merely a result of modern social conditions or "a design flaw in the entertainment industry" but reflect a "curious sort of violence intrinsic to fandom," meaning that the "relation of fan and celebrity is troubled because violence is built into it" (1999, 139). Elliott suggests that fandom is a common way of cultivating a sense of intimacy with distant others in contemporary culture and can enrich the emotional development of the self and contribute significantly to an individual's sense of the interpersonal world. The cultivation of this bond, transferring personal hopes and dreams onto the celebrity, usually appears in a positive light, but as it happened with Chapman, the identification can also destroy the self. The fan may feel disillusioned or swindled if he or she discovers human failings within the realm of celebrity and may come to despise the once-loved celebrity and to entertain fantasies of revenge. According to Elliott, Chapman was "caught in an emotional deadlock between narcissistic idealisation and abject hatred of Lennon" (138).

Elliott is not the only writer to suggest that the main motive for Chapman's disillusionment with Lennon was that his former idol had rejected his earlier star role and the prospects for social change, and was now interested only in his estate and family. Chapman himself explained later that Lennon had become "phony" (Jones 1994). Whatever Chapman's motives were, it remains undeniable that Lennon's murder was intertwined with ways in which stars are constructed and idealized in given cultural conditions. Violence may be built into the troubled relation between the fan and the celebrity, as Elliott alleges, but this relationship is troubled also because it is based on the convergence of personal fantasies and mediated images, and the expectations that are imposed upon the star. It should be emphasized that Chapman had no personal knowledge of Lennon. His disillusionment was largely a result of a mediation of Lennon as a star who for five years had rejected traditional obligations of rock stardom. It was the conflict between the image of a socially active rock hero and the image of a passive and irresponsible recluse that, in a sense, incited Chapman to pull the trigger.

Certainly, this is conjectural, and should be presented as such. I am not arguing that it was the countercultural rock ideology that created a killer, but it is nonetheless notable that it was the same ideal of John Lennon, the profile that Chapman felt had been betrayed, that was reconstructed in the aftermath of December 8. The same revolutionary Lennon who had been Chapman's prime object of admiration became reconstructed in the elegies. Whereas Chapman's act arguably was fueled by Lennon's abandonment of his heroic ideals, the grief-stricken memory network led by the rock press and the counterculture legacy refabricated these ideals, attempting to turn Lennon's death into a noble, worthy martyrdom.

John Lennon's life exemplifies the proposition that within the pattern of the starnet different interests and expectations often conflict. His death stands as a rebuttal of this generalization. I have argued that the media reception of Lennon's death was characterized by a consensus about Lennon's meaning as a cultural symbol. This consensus centered upon the issues of the past becoming present and the individual representing community. Lennon's death was accompanied by a canonization process in which Lennon was mythologized as a Sixties hero who dreamt of a better world and was sacrificed because of his commitment to peace and understanding. Furthermore, Lennon's brutal murder evoked parallels with 1960s political assassinations, rather than resembling the mythology of premature rock star deaths. Lennon was thus shifted from the realm of stardom to the realm of heroism, coming to serve as an exemplary and iconic model for a particular community, that of the Sixties generation. In a sense, the death of Lennon also was the zenith of his career.

Although a sense of consensus often emerges in the aftermath of celebrity deaths, in Lennon's case the media's reactions were almost unanimous. But as always with tragic fates of celebrities, this consensus gradually yielded to different interpretations, different Lennons. Controversies over John Lennon momentarily disappeared in December 1980, only to reemerge after the waves of grief had abated.

The Posthumous Debate on John Lennon

There is little information on the physical properties of (4147) Lennon. Even its diameter is uncertain—a range of 7 to 15 km is probable. You will need a telescope to see this minor planet as its maximum brightness is some 1/4108 of the brightness of the faintest objects that can be seen with the unaided eye.
—Minor Planet Circular on the planet Lennon, which was discovered in 1983

The last two decades have demonstrated that all those changing and diverse facets of John Lennon's stardom in the 1960s and the 1970s did not vanish with his death in 1980. In fact, Lennon's murder was the catalyst for a new phase that has now lasted longer than the period of his celebrity while he was alive. Whether understood as a living person operating in the 1960s and the 1970s or as a part of his continuing history, Lennon was and remains constantly constructed and reconstructed as a cultural phenomenon. Since we can find abundant historical examples of "great men" who have been reevaluated as well as debated after their deaths, this in itself is unremarkable. Such phenomena have, however, become more prominent during the age of mechanical and digital reproduction, when the image of a public person can continue to survive and develop without the celebrity being physically present. In some cases, star afterlife may surface as a significant cultural force. The profitable posthumous career of Elvis Presley, with countless impersonators and other recyclings of his star image, has arguably been as interesting and important as his actual career and a target for more or less serious study as well (e.g., Marcus 1992; Rodman 1996; Plasketes 1997). If stars die, but star images do not, it is therefore reasonable to suggest that we have not yet reached the end of John Lennon's story. New and old Lennon products are distributed and sold, he is consumed and experienced, and his meaning is still discussed.

Under scrutiny here is how Lennon's stardom has been understood, constructed and used since his murder. What is significant for this phase is the fact that Lennon himself can no longer participate in defining his position and is thus unable to act as a prime authorizer of his stardom. The absence of this authoritative point of reference has allowed a fuller range of controversies among the Lennon estate, promotional agencies, biographers, documentarians, journalists and the audience. As a public person who aroused much controversy even in his lifetime, Lennon continues to be a source of mixed feelings. He has been central to debates over who has the right to use the star and in what ways when the star is no longer there to authorize himself. I shall explore this debate and its two major strands, personal and cultural, which are closely linked. While I shall scrutinize the first strand through the biographical debate that took place in the 1980s, I will focus on those aspects of Lennon's posthumous career that deal with his artistic and cultural heritage. I shall concentrate primarily on the British context and explore three major issues that clarify contemporary discussions and cultural ideas of Lennon: attempts to utilize Lennon's musical products, efforts to locate him, and his idealization by fans.

In approaching the debate on Lennon's personality, such questions as "Who was he really?" "What were his aims?" and "What was the background for his psyche?" have been asked in various articles and biographies on him. This was especially so in the 1980s. Beginning with May Pang's (Lennon's mistress in the 1970s) *Loving John* and Steven Gaines and Peter Brown's (Brown was the Beatles' assistant) *The Love You Make*, both published in 1983, various memoirs and biographies have from time to time questioned Lennon's saintlike image and martyrdom. The most notorious attempt to reveal "the man behind the myth" has undoubtedly been Albert Goldman's mammoth *The Lives of John Lennon*, which provided scandalous stories about Lennon's violent behavior, (homo)sexual activities and drug use. The book, which was published in 1988 and immediately became an international bestseller, was, unsurprisingly, received with rage both by critics and fans. Philip Norman, the writer of the Beatles history *Shout!*, set the tone by confessing that Goldman was the only author whose works he had physically destroyed (Williams 1988). In the United States, *Rolling Stone* magazine in particular took up an active defense of Lennon and refutation of Goldman. Lennon's friends and colleagues urged a boycott of the book, and it was rumored that in Liverpool fans openly burnt copies of it (Fogo 1994; Elliott 1999).

John Lennon's widow, Yoko Ono, was disgusted by Goldman's book, believing it an effort to rob her former husband of dignity and pointing out the fact that "John isn't here to answer the things said about him" (Norman 1988). Goldman's response was that stars will do their utmost to ensure that biographical material more nearly resembles a press release than the "truth." If they are dead, they cannot, Goldman said (quoted in Sweeting 1988). Later he would claim that the rock star biography is becoming a more and more misleading genre because it gives the impression that the stars invent themselves when, instead, the real protagonist is always the public: "It's the audience's manias, the audience's images, the audience's cravings, yearnings, delusions, that's really decisive. The performers are the puppets of what the public wants" (quoted in Miles 2000). However, in his biography of Lennon, Goldman was not really writing for the benefit of the audience but rather attacking the myth of a creative and authentic rock hero. Goldman's decisive error was to ignore his own power in the process of (post)stardom and not to recognize himself as a part of the "real protagonist," the public. Furthermore, he arguably projected his own fantasies of the dark side of rock stardom onto Lennon and supposedly distorted the facts. Despite hundreds of interviews conducted for the book, it has been argued that Goldman's main sources were not reliable and that he had a tendency to give credence to the vilest gossip on Lennon (Fogo 1994; Hertsgaard 1995; Elliott 1999).

Whatever the truth, the fact remains that Goldman, whose earlier biographies on Lenny Bruce and Elvis Presley had provoked similar indignation, is still regarded as an iconoclast. Attempts to understand both Goldman's intentions and the rage over his work have appeared only recently (e.g., Fogo 1994; Elliott 1999; Miles 2000). Nevertheless, it is obvious that at least for Yoko Ono, and Lennon's fans, *The Lives of John Lennon* will stand as a "form of primitive attack," while Goldman, who died of a heart attack in 1994, will be remembered as an "assassin with a pen" (Ono 2000). The book's reputation was tellingly summed up by a fan called King of Marigold (1998) on an Internet review page: "The Lennon biography that fans love to hate—even if they haven't read one word of it."

Two months after the publication of Goldman's book, the biographical film *Imagine: John Lennon* (Solt 1988) premiered in New York City. According to Fogo (1994), who gives a thorough account about the biographical battle over the memory of John Lennon in 1988, the film seemed to be an official counterdocument to Goldman's book. It emphasized the positive aspects of Lennon and attracted more sympathetic reviews than *The Lives of John Lennon.* However, since the film was fully authorized by Yoko Ono and was heavily marketed, critics also noted its role as a public relations battle over Lennon's memory and were to some extent disappointed with what they saw as its sycophantic and superficial portraiture. Although Yoko Ono became an object of sympathy following Lennon's death, that sympathy, as Fogo notes, "apparently was short-lived" (132).[5]

Since Goldman's biography, there has been no major controversy regarding John Lennon's personality. Two subsequent biographies, Robert Rosen's *Nowhere Man* (2000) and Geoffrey Giuliano's *Lennon in America* (2001), have provided convergent portraits of Lennon. Both writers claim that their descriptions are more or less based on Lennon's personal diaries, which give a picture of an isolated, depressed and tormented star obsessed with astrology, numerology, drugs and Jesus Christ during his final years. It is instructive that these books did not provoke significant reaction. This suggests that the biographical debate here has followed the route typical of the posthumous careers of cultural heroes. The discussion starts with elegies, praise and idealization arising from the atmosphere of shared grief; it proceeds to a more distanced tone, criticism and even iconoclasm, and, finally, results in some sort of reconciliation of the two positions. We can find such a pattern in Elvis Presley's posthumous career, for instance. After the waves of grief abated, more controversial interpretations of Elvis appeared, culminating in Goldman's major biography (1981) on Elvis as a psychologically ill star. These revelations have subsequently been replaced by imaginative uses and celebrations of Elvis as a living legend. Likewise, in the case of John Lennon, a certain consensus now prevails. What is at issue now is not the personal secrets of Lennon but his musical, artistic and cultural heritage.

The cultural debate on John Lennon lies at the heart of the triangle of promotion, media and audience—that is, all those participants in the starnet who are actively involved in producing images of Lennon. The image of the individual star can be fluid and traversed by tension because of the temporal and spatial dimension of stardom. In relation to John Lennon, a good illustration of this is his famous song "Imagine," which has attracted some interest among scholars of popular music. Since its original publication in 1971, "Imagine" has been played, performed and recorded continually all over the world. It is undoubtedly Lennon's most popular post-Beatles track, but what kind of song is it and what kind of history has it had, especially after 1980?

First, there have been discussions of the true meaning of "Imagine," that is, the message of its lyrics. This interest has not been confined to journalists and Lennon biographers, but has also appeared in more or less scholarly writings. "Imagine" has on the one hand been described as an example of a "deeply apolitical and classically utopian impulse" (Martin 1981a) and on the other hand as a "political and musical success" (Street 1986) or "vision of peaceful global Communism" (Denselow 1989). Different interpretations of the song have prompted Jon Wiener, known for his study of Lennon's political activities and FBI files, to express his surprise at how critics have misunderstood the simplicity of the song and its utopian imagination as a leftist "key step toward social transformation" (1985, 160–61).

According to Keith Negus (1996, 194–96), these kinds of attempts to find the exact meaning of "Imagine" are based on a simplistic model of producing and communicating popular music, on the idea that a song has a straightforward message that is then transmitted, received and understood. Even though composers play an important part in determining how a song might be decoded, Negus is inclined to emphasize the way songs, especially songs like "Imagine" that have great ambiguity and enduring appeal, accumulate and connect with new meanings and beliefs as they pass through time and place. It is incontrovertible that "Imagine" has been subjected to a range of interpretations during its circulation. Negus recalls that in 1987 "Imagine" was collectively sung at a Conservative party conference at Wembley Stadium in London to greet Margaret Thatcher. Elsewhere it was chanted as a call for peaceful change in an attempt to mobilize people against a conservative agenda in communist countries of eastern Europe. During the 1991 Gulf War, the BBC categorized "Imagine" among those songs that might upset listeners and took action to prevent its being broadcast. On that occasion, the political dimension of "Imagine" was totally different from that of the Conservative party conference four years earlier.

Furthermore, even though "Imagine" has been considered to have an explicitly secular message and even though at the time of its publication many religious listeners apparently were disturbed by its imagery, it has later become a favorite tune at modern-minded religious events (Du Noyer 1997; Rogan 1997). To provide another example mentioned by Wiener (2000, 74–75), back in 1972 a high school class in Wisconsin attempted to designate "Imagine" as their class song, but the principal rejected their choice, claiming the song was "anti-religious and anti-American with communist overtones." Twenty years later, the ban was overturned and class members were free to sing "Imagine" at their reunion. It should also be recalled that after the terrorist attacks in the United States on September 11, 2001, "Imagine" was used in various ways and situations as a spiritual message of hope and courage.

These few examples illustrate how music as well as music stars can be consumed and used in different ways in time and place. Music historian Carl Dahlhaus (1985) argues that although the concept "work" is the cornerstone of music history, "work" is not confined to its moments of origin but it may subsequently accumulate. For example, Beethoven's Ninth Symphony is not only a historical event anchored in the conditions of its original production in the early nineteenth century, but has had a significant afterlife, with reevaluations and sets of mediations, including countless recordings and performances. The first posthumous *point de la perfection* of Beethoven's symphony, or, in Dahlhaus' words, the subsequent *kairos* of the symphony, occurred in the mid-nineteenth century when it inspired several composers and writers. Later, its time came more than once (156–58; see also Attali 1985). Likewise, "Imagine" has had several cultural apotheoses, one of them being in the wake of Lennon's death when the song was constantly played on radio stations around the world. In Britain, the song has been reissued twice since Lennon's murder: It topped the charts in 1981 and reached number three in 1999. One culminating moment occurred on the brink of the new millennium, when the BBC announced the results of a major poll to determine Britain's all-time favorite song lyrics. "Imagine" won the honor (Harry 2000).

The history of "Imagine" is characterized by the variety of uses and cultural appropriations, indicating that while its genesis is as the work of an artist, as a cultural text the song comes into existence in a process of negotiation and refuses to confine itself to any particular context. These kinds of cultural texts can be considered as "travelers" which, having been once transmitted, then connect with various contexts. The ability for these texts to migrate from one context to another challenges attempts to assign final meanings to them (Lehtonen 2000). With its re-appearances, "Imagine" is of course one example of the celebration of the past in current popular music and, in a sense, a song of constant kairos. This is not to say that the actual text of "Imagine" does not matter. On the contrary, it is arguable that partly because of its affinity with so many situations and its adaptability to manifold forms, "Imagine" has remained a classic pop song and been a source of inspiration and encouragement to many.

One interesting aspect of John Lennon's posthumous musical career is that it has coincided with the past becoming more of a presence in contemporary popular music culture. Although this could be attributed to the nostalgia of an aging rock generation (resulting, for example, in the legion of re-formed bands), it has as much been due to new expanding practices in music culture. In the 1980s, both music recordings and music videos established themselves as central to the marketing and selling of popular music and contributed to the increase in world sales of music recordings. Together with new music technology (such as samplers) and the expanding volume and new formats of the media (such as cable television and satellite television channels), this development promoted the boom in reissues as well as enabling the more effective exploitation of musicians' posthumous careers and the reconstruction of old materials in popular music. As with many deceased artists, through such practices John Lennon's past achievements became more present and commonplace. Even though Lennon's posthumous catalog does not represent the most exploited one in popular music, it is rich in variety.[6] An important question underlying this development has been whether Lennon himself would have endorsed this exploitation of his artistic remains. One particular case, the "reunion" of the Beatles, was specifically fueled by this kind of question.

The Beatles' reunion in 1995 was a project that incorporated a number of scheduled events under the title *The Beatles Anthology*, including the first-time release of three double CDs with rare recordings and outtakes and the production of an authorized television series on the

band's history. The centerpiece of the project, which would be completed five years later with the major release of the printed version of the
band's story, was the reunion of the three remaining Beatles—or, in
fact, the reunion of the four, since during the project Paul McCartney,
George Harrison and Ringo Starr finished two songs that Lennon had
recorded as home demos in the late 1970s. Thus, the artistic history of
the Beatles really did not end in 1970 but temporarily resumed a quarter of a century later.

In Britain, the rock press in its special editions on the Beatles was
primarily in favor of the reunion, perhaps because the Beatles' project
coincided with the climax of Britpop and its flirtation with national issues and references to the 1960s pop revolution. After all, the Beatles
embodied—and now concretely revived—the patriotic past of British
pop music better than any other band or artist. Other papers took a
more critical view. When rumors of the Beatles project surfaced, Caitlin
Moran (1994) of *The Times* predicted that it would "diffuse the memory
and cheapen the past," since to her mind pop music was primarily
meant to catch the moment rather than to dig among the graves of history. Later, Moran (1995) concluded that the remaining Beatles had
clubbed John Lennon "to death with video treatments and bank statements." Generally, the CD anthology and new songs were regarded as
less disappointing than the television series, which was declared to be
"uninformative," "pure Reader's Digest TV" and "terrifyingly bland,"
yet also enjoyable. The series'"authorized" status—it was produced by
the Beatles' own company, Apple—led some critics to complain that
the story had little controversial or new to say and appeared "more of
a corporate PR exercise than an objective study" (see the summary of
press reception in Davis 1996).

The physical absence of Lennon provoked speculations as to
whether he would have been in favor of the reunion and, particularly,
of the reconstruction of his home demos. His original comments on the
subject were rummaged through and his friends were interviewed,
while journalists and fans were given opportunities to represent their
viewpoints. For example, Tony Barrow (1996), former Beatles press officer, was convinced that while Lennon would have taken a less negative view of the anthology television series, he would not have been
agreeable to the release of the two songs which he had already rejected
years earlier. Discussing the merits of "Free as a Bird," Giles Coren

(1995) of *The Times* suggested that Lennon "would have been ashamed to think it would ever see the light of day." In *The Beatles Monthly Book* (February 1996) fans were divided between the "John would have hated it" school of thought and those who were openly delighted by new Beatles products.

To reconstruct posthumous tapes or mix new material into them was not a new practice in popular music. Buddy Holly was supposedly the first rock star to "get the Lazarus touch" when after his death in 1959 his solo demos were supplemented by a backing group, ensuring a steady flow of new Buddy Holly products. Later examples of similar, if more elaborate, practices have included cases such as the Doors' musical backing to a tape of Jim Morrison reciting his poetry for the album *American Prayer*, Natalie Cole's duet with her father, Nat King Cole, and Queen's additional accompaniment to unreleased Freddie Mercury vocals. When digital technology became commonplace in the 1980s, it contributed to "necropop," as journalist Patrick Humphries (1995) sarcastically calls it, becoming a popular music phenomenon. Even though dead music stars' virtual participation in new productions had by the mid-1990s become fashionable, and posthumous Lennon material had already been issued to some extent, the resurrection of the Beatles provoked an animated discussion—mainly because the possibility of a comeback of the most famous pop group in the world carried with it the hopes and expectations of a quarter of a century. More concretely, since Lennon had forbidden the publication of "Free as a Bird" and "Real Love" in the first place, the project lacked the ultimate blessing. This led to the collision of opinions within the communication network of Lennon's posthumous stardom.

Anthony Elliott suggests that the debate over Lennon's likely involvement in the reunion reflected "an inventive, though anxious, redemption of our personal investment in his art," entailing "a consideration of the complexity of our feelings about Lennon" and "the ways in which he is remembered" (1999, 164). Taking a positive viewpoint on the discussion, Elliott argues that as much as the reunion project and the overall 1990s surge in Beatles activity was about returning to the past, it was also about escaping from the drabness of contemporary musical standardization. The reunion, with its reconstructed music, was thus nostalgic but not in regressive terms: It was an attempt to return to the past for the purpose of dealing more constructively with the present and the future. According to Elliott (177), the nostalgia encountered here had a certain transformative quality, permitting the recovery of lost memories, thoughts and feelings as a medium for contemporary artistic experiences. Yet, since Lennon as an artist strove for authenticity and represented a star seeking to reconfigure utopianism and realism, politics and aesthetics, celebrity and genuineness, the reunion's rehabilitation of the past for the present raised thorny questions about the legitimacy of such a process.

In this connection Elliott does not really focus on the question of Lennon's image in the reunion process but discusses his past identity and, in the end, leaves him a mythical rock hero. For example, in his song analysis Elliott suggests rather conventionally that "Free as a Bird" and "Real Love" can be viewed as maps of the mental territory Lennon was charting in the late 1970s (178). But what kind of territory did they represent in the 1990s? To develop Elliott's conclusion, "Free as a Bird" and "Real Love" and the overall reunion project did not merely stand as an artistically autonomous interaction between the past, remembrance and nostalgia, but also represented the technological and industrial development of popular music in the 1990s, and were just another—if major—continuation in a tradition of attempts to reuse and relocate the Beatles and Lennon in contemporary culture. In fact, what the 1990s demonstrated in terms of John Lennon's stardom was the increasing attempts to place and locate him concretely.

To Elliott's mind, the Beatles reunion constructed Lennon as an identity transacted between the eternal and the evanescent, past and present, memory and image, materiality and metaphor (172). If this list of oppositions seems ambiguous, it nevertheless matches some characteristics of the phenomenon of stardom. In his notable cultural study on the posthumous career of Elvis Presley, Rodman (1996) argues that stardom is typically an ethereal, nonspatial phenomenon. It is difficult, if not impossible, to confine stars within any specific context, since stardom, after all, is a phenomenon entirely dependent on a strong infrastructure of interrelated media institutions. Stars are famous primarily because of their activities within the realm of this infrastructure. They may walk and talk and move about in the same world as "ordinary" people, but since their existence as public personae is dependent on the media, to the vast majority of the audience they primarily travel in the ethereal nonspaces of media texts and public imagination (99–101).

With deceased, "nonphysical" stars this is even more evident, because they enter various places and times as re-mediated public figures of a technological landscape. According to Rodman, the only real exception to this rule is Elvis and his home Graceland. From almost the first moment of his stardom, Elvis was associated with a very specific site on the map, a mansion in Memphis that he bought in 1957, "in a way that no other star ever was—or has been since—with the long-standing connection between these two icons working to transform the private, domestic space of Elvis' home into a publicly visible site of pilgrimage and congregation" (102). It is arguable that as a famous tourist attraction Graceland has no equivalent in contemporary popular music culture. A few hundred fans may go on a pilgrimage to Jim Morrison's grave in Paris every July to participate in rituals based on the cult of a rock hero, and the anniversary of John Lennon's death may be marked by a small informal gathering of fans outside the murder site, the Dakota apartment building in New York City, but these statistics come clearly second to 2,000 or more daily visits at Elvis' *locus sanctus*, his grave in Graceland.

What Rodman overlooks is that in popular music, attempts to identify and locate stars with particular places have not been rare and that there are places associated with particular stars and musical sounds. Stars may be dependent on a nonspatial media realm, but their star identity is still, in most cases, connected to more concrete determinators that usually partake of their national, ethnic and geographical backgrounds. In popular music studies, scholars (e.g., Cohen 1991; Straw 1991; Shank 1994; Negus 1996) have frequently emphasized how local cultures and "scenes" have played important roles in creating the imaginaries and authenticities of particular styles and stars.

Within the posthumous starnet of John Lennon, there have been several attempts to locate him. For various reasons, however, it has been difficult and has provoked some disagreement. Even though Liverpool and Liverpoolness certainly characterized Lennon's personal identity as well as his star image, in artistic terms his most celebrated phases occurred in London, where he stayed from 1964 to 1971, and in New York, where he lived the rest of his life (apart from his drunken "lost weekend," the fifteen-month period he spent in Los Angeles from 1973 to 1975). As a rock cosmopolitan, Lennon left his mark on the most famous cities of popular music, but not exclusively. A further reason why no particular *locus sanctus* has emerged is that there is no physical landmark indicating the place of rest of the deceased hero.[7] Finally, although in the late 1960s and the early 1970s Lennon appeared as an enlightened messenger of world peace and a political activist, he later repeatedly forbade people to consider him any kind of leader. In one of his last interviews, Lennon spoke against worship and the personality cult:

> Don't expect Jimmy Carter or Ronald Reagan or John Lennon or Yoko Ono or Bob Dylan or Jesus Christ to come and do it for you. You have to do it yourself. (…) I can't wake you up. You can wake you up. I can't cure you. You can cure you. (Sheff 1981, 144)

In spite of the series of "refusals," surprisingly frequent attempts to locate the heritage of Lennon or at least to confer various degrees of respectability on his name have surfaced. Recently, a John Lennon Museum was opened in Saitama, near Tokyo; in St. Petersburg there were in the late 1990s plans to build a John Lennon Rock 'n' Roll Temple, which would have operated as a center for various art and educational activities; in Prague one of the latest tourist attractions is the spontaneously developed "Lennon Wall" with its graffiti epitaphs and paintings of Lennon; in London similar writings and messages are to be found in the front wall of Abbey Road Studios, where the Beatles recorded most of their work in the 1960s. Apart from the studios, which were opened to the public in 1983, London has provided other Beatles-themed activities, like sightseeing and walks. In New York City, a special section in Central Park, created in memory of Lennon and conceived by Yoko Ono as an international garden of peace, was opened in 1985 and named Strawberry Fields after one of Lennon's songs—which, interestingly, originally had nothing to do with New York but referred to a now-famous Salvation Army orphanage in Liverpool.

Given the fact that Liverpool stands as the mythologized birthplace of John Lennon and that the Beatles were the first rock group to make their local identity and cultural background a fundamental part of their fame and image, it is hardly surprising that efforts to locate the heritage of Lennon and the Beatles have most conspicuously taken place there. Being a Londoner or a New Yorker never defined Lennon to the same extent as Liverpoolness. Furthermore, whereas Liverpool is famous for being the home of Lennon and the Beatles, metropolises like London and New York are too diverse to be identified with just one person or one pop group.

Liverpool's ad hoc efforts to harness Beatles tourism have gone through many phases (see Cohen 1997b). It was only in the mid-1980s that more concerted efforts took place, replacing previous attempts by dedicated fans and enthusiasts. Currently, there are three main players involved. The most influential of them, Cavern City Tours Ltd., organizes among other things the daily sightseeing Magical Mystery Tour and the Beatles Festival, to which tens of thousands of fans and dozens of tribute bands travel every August. Two other businesses are the Beatles Shop and the Beatles Story, a heavily merchandised Beatles exhibition at the Albert Dock area. While there are various tourist attractions scattered around the city, the center of activities is located in Mathew Street, which is lined by a number of cafés, pubs and specialty shops devoted to Beatles history, as well as a replica of the legendary Cavern Club.

Sara Cohen (1997a; 1997b) has noted that while rock music as a form of tourism plays an important role in Liverpool, the shift of thematic emphasis has changed from the "live" to the "past." Most of the rock tourists do not arrive to see new groups but to experience Beatles history. This has occasionally attracted criticism that strategies of urban regeneration are excessively based on Beatles tourism and nostalgia and that music as consumption and leisure has replaced aspects of production and creativity. In this connection the relationship between the Beatles and Liverpool appears as a "contested process" in which the Beatles are typically considered either a curse or blessing to the city (1997b, 102–3). Another issue is that questions of authenticity, a culture of replica and the overall re-creation of the past have led to debates as to who is allowed to define and canonize the Beatles' history in Liverpool (1997a). Is this privilege reserved for local authorities, politicians and tourist organizations, or do fan clubs, tourists, shopkeepers or their employees have anything to say in the matter? Who owns the Beatles?

One occasion that focused the relationship between John Lennon and Liverpool and the controversies of ownership was the John Lennon Tribute Concert in May 1990. The press release preceding the concert asserted that the charity event dedicated to the "genius of John Lennon could only be held in Liverpool, his birthplace and the city which had cradled his unique talent" and that "Liverpool's gain is New York and

Los Angeles's loss" (cited in Gray 1990). The concert, which was supported by Lennon's estate, faced heavy criticism not only because of its marketing rhetoric but for numerous other reasons as well: Many of Lennon's former colleagues as well as local prominent rock identities were excluded. The evening was organized more around televisual than live concert practices. The beneficiary of the charity was unclear. There was little advance notice that some "top international stars" who were billed would appear only on video. The event gave the national papers a chance to needle Liverpool about a supposed attempt to cover up the city's decline and deprivation. More important, however, was the conjecture that Lennon himself might not have approved the event. In a report to *The Guardian*, Robin Thornber (1990) concluded: "Lennon, the wayward iconoclast, the proto-Green in a stretch-limo, might have shrugged off his municipalisation. Let it be. But would he have appeared on the same bill as Kylie Minogue?" The last paragraph in *The Times'* review, written by David Gray (1990), carried a more cynical tone:

> If he had still been alive, I am perfectly certain that, like George Harrison, he would have had the instinct and taste to stay away. And if he had watched it on television and heard his songs sounding so bland and boring, he might have felt like killing himself.

In reply to Gray, Dave Edmunds (1990), the concert's musical director, attacked the gratuitous viciousness of the review. For him, standing on stage at the end of the evening with other artists, the seventy-piece orchestra behind them, and the 20,000 Liverpudlians singing "Imagine" in front, the moment was deeply moving and by no means any kind of musical disaster. Edmunds concluded his letter: "The world does not need Mr. Gray to tell it what John Lennon would or would not have liked."

In Lennon's case this kind of appeal has been rather common. The variety of Lennon's star afterlife demonstrates that his history or that of the Beatles is certainly not confined to the vaults of the past, but continues to unfold as a remarkable cultural narrative conducted by Lennon's estate, various heritage organizers and the media. As a further dimension to this narrative, fans also play a significant role in the starnet of John Lennon's posthumous career.

Compared, for example, to the Beatlemania of 1963 through 1966, when both John Lennon as a star and the fans as his most devoted audience were interdependent, the death of Lennon meant a new configuration of the pattern: The star was no longer present to react to fans' hopes, desires and demands. Central to Lennon fandom after 1980 has been, not the interaction between the star and the fan, but rather, the ways fans imagine and consume the star, how they communicate to each other and how fandom is established in the overall starnet.

Current fan activities related to the Beatles and Lennon are very vigorous and diverse, including conventions, fan clubs, fanzines, tribute bands and collecting memorabilia.[8]Instead of mapping and studying them—which in itself would be a valuable task for understanding the continuous fascination of the Beatles—I want to focus on one particular area of Lennon fandom which, I think, crystallizes his "star afterlife" as well as clarifying the current debate on him.

The Internet is a relatively new forum for fans to comment on Lennon's career and personality. Reflecting the larger debate on the Internet and modern communication technology, some Lennon fans have taken the web as a potential access to some kind of utopia. One Lennon fan stated on his web site:

> When you are using the internet tonight, think about how you can use it to make our world a better place. Remember John Lennon's song Imagine. Perhaps he really wasn't such a dreamer after all! (Homer, 1998)

On the other hand, the Internet has raised awkward questions of copyright. As one particular case demonstrates, they have also applied to John Lennon.

In December 1994 a fan called Sam Choukri (1997) launched the John Lennon Web Page, which included photographs, sound files, films, record covers and other Lennon-related material. It remained a very popular site until November 1996, when Choukri was informed that the owner of the web server, the University of Missouri, had turned it off because of "potential copyright infringement." The request was initially made by the estate of John Lennon, or through its lawyers, who then sent a letter to Choukri charging that "our client has not granted you the right to exploit the copyrighted artwork or our client's trademarks." Choukri tried to respond that he did not make any money off his site and he did not have anything there demeaning to Lennon's character, on the contrary, in his opinion, the site only helped increase the wealth of the Lennon estate. After some negotiations and proposals, Choukri received a rather aggressive letter repeating that he had no authority to use any copyrighted material owned by the estate. In the meantime, Choukri had launched another Lennon site, Bagism, this time with legal material, and finally he decided to tell the story to the rest of the world—or at least to other Lennon fans.

This case manifests in many ways the potential collision between fan activities and production companies. Henry Jenkins (1994), who has researched *Star Trek* fans, claims that fans' cultural activities can encounter problems if a clear border of ownership and copyrights is crossed. Jenkins writes that fans respect the original text, yet fear the measures that might be taken by production companies. The usual scenario is that the original creator, like *Star Trek*'s Gene Roddenberry, remains almost a holy figure, while the faceless industry becomes the villain (453, 464–65). In such a configuration, the audiences do not usually possess institutional power, but their role as consumers and meaning-makers may play an important part. As Negus has pointed out, while audiences have historically been physically separated or dislocated from most of the sites of musical production, they have not been separated or dislocated from the processes of musical production (1996, 35).

In Choukri's case the debate concerned a person no longer alive. If he existed as a "trademark," it was only through the mechanism of the estate. Reflecting this, Choukri wrote:

> I'm proud for what Bagism has become and I like the direction it's headed. It's been a challenge to create a compelling site without all the "eye candy" that I used freely on the former site. To me, that shows that John Lennon is not a "thing" that a lawyer can give you permission to use, but rather John Lennon was a person, a real person, who left an indelible imprint on a generation of people (and now, a second generation) that no lawyer can ever take away from us. The lawyers only represent John Lennon's money... his fans represent the man himself. (1997)

Choukri received a lot of support from other fans, some of whom had faced similar problems. The usual comment was that John Lennon was a believer in the freedom of speech and he would not have agreed to such activities (see What Do You Think? 1998). The question again returns: Would John have agreed? In this case, fans answered, no. He would not have agreed to the "business side" and its activities that worked against fan culture. Even though we do not know what Lennon really would have said about Choukri's case or other similar incidents,[9] it is obvious that people appeal to a certain image and authority of his for help. Lennon himself is outside the debate, but since he was known as a person who dreamt of "a better world," he is continually implicated as well as often idealized. It could be concluded that while the post-Lennon phase of fandom may lack institutional power, it nonetheless can contribute to maintain certain ideals of Lennon's stardom.

John Lennon's star afterlife seems to be closely connected to the question of whether he would have assented to various ways of treating his life, works and image. This question, which has perpetually been raised by critics and fans in particular, is entangled with that of the cultural ownership of Lennon's posthumous career. In this starnet pattern, Yoko Ono, the estate of John Lennon and tourist officers have their own ideas on the heritage of Lennon, opinions that may not satisfy critics and biographers seeking to respect or, as in some cases, sensationalize Lennon. Fans' idealization may oppose all the other elements of the starnet.

The significance of the question of cultural ownership sets Lennon apart from the majority of other dead music stars. Do we ever ask the same question with the same frequency and emphasis about Elvis Presley, Billie Holiday or Jimi Hendrix? One reason for the significance of the question in Lennon's case presumably rests in his auteur status, which derives from the change of the Beatles' career in the mid-1960s. Lennon's image and reputation as a conscious, self-defining, and authoritative rock artist perpetuates his star afterlife with a force that has no equivalent in popular music culture. If Elvis today is more ubiquitous than Lennon, it may partly be because he carries no such ideological controversies and is free—apart from legal restrictions—to appear everywhere. As Rodman notes, although Elvis' fans and critics have occasionally tried to put together a case for Elvis as a musical auteur of one sort or another, this dimension plays a rather insignificant role in his posthumous career (1996, 140–46).

Within the starnet of John Lennon, all controversies seem to come back to the personal qualifications of the deceased star and what he would have thought and what he would have agreed to today. Lennon is remembered as a man of opinion and as a man of voice, if not a spokesperson, of a generation. It is obvious that because of his auteur status and the tragic manner of his death, which carried connotations of the fates of political and religious leaders rather than rock stars, Lennon is not only considered a rock hero but an icon of social change and utopian impulses. Yet, there are many Lennons waiting to emerge. One paradox is that just before his death, Lennon was more willing to promote his survival from "rock life" and joys of fatherhood than world peace and political activism. These are not the qualifications Lennon is primarily remembered for now.

Different versions of John Lennon as a person may appear, but they will be eclipsed by questions of the legitimacy and ownership which characterize his star afterlife. Because of Lennon's auteur status and different expectations articulated by the participants in the starnet, his stardom remains a complex and contested texture. If John Lennon aroused controversy during his lifetime, it certainly persists in his posthumous career.

9 Conclusion: Imagine a Rock Star

John Lennon appeared—and, in a sense, still appears—as a chameleon-like figure. He was an innovative artist, developing and receptive to influences and ideas that at different periods seemed to emerge as significant. Yet, as a mass-mediated star he also was a creation of his time, a construction who was discussed and debated in public and given meanings by other people. From the point of view of stardom, the history of John Lennon appears to be a history of negotiations among different participants involved in the weblike structure of communication, or what I described as the starnet, in which several groups seek to construct the star as a public phenomenon. I identified four main components that have been crucial to Lennon's stardom. At the core there is the star himself with his public activities. The starnet is also made up of the music industry, the media and their comments and the audience's public response. Lennon's career demonstrates that within this starnet different interests, expectations and investments connect with each other, compete and collide, and that between these weavers of the discourse there are hierarchical relations that change in terms of time and place.

I argued that in the early 1960s modes and frequencies of Lennon's and the Beatles' star appearances were prescribed by conventions of the music industry, which were channeled through manager Brian Epstein, and audiences' demands. In the heyday of Beatlemania the roles of live performance and the widely reported presence of screaming masses of fans were more significant as a shaper of Beatles stardom than they were a few years later, when the band had finished touring. In the early 1960s these expectations were not considered a major problem in popular music stardom. What the Beatles demonstrated by abandoning the concert stage and concentrating on studio work—and this perhaps is the most significant and enduring aspect of their stardom—was that the obligations these mechanisms imposed upon music performers could be seriously challenged and that popular music stardom could, at least to some extent, be regulated by stars themselves. During this time the emphasis of the starnet communication moved to artistic self-determination and related media comments. It should be noted that this change, however, occurred only after the Beatles had established their star status and, at a more general level, after new youth movements and ideologies had begun to invade popular music culture.

Another telling illustration of changing power relations in Lennon's starnet is Lennon's role as a messenger of peace. In the late 1960s his attitudes conflicted with those of the music industry, the countercultural press, the mainstream press and the audience. This gave Lennon a particular messianic profile which was paradoxically completed after his death, as the same peace philosophy resurfaced as a pervasive theme in the mourning over the hero. What has followed is that the star himself is no longer available to authorize discussion of his stardom, which has passed to the music industry, the estate, the media, the fans and other keepers of the memory. I have covered the main arguments and sentiments underpinning this discussion, but since Lennon's posthumous career has been multifaceted and contested, the area certainly deserves further investigation.

Stardom is not only about conflicting interests but also about relationships and mediations that provide resources for the star. Lennon's career was characterized by fruitful interactions and exchanges of ideas between a number of artists, performers, other influential persons and groups, including the other Beatles, Liverpool's beat scene, Brian Epstein, George Martin, Bob Dylan, London's "popocracy," hippies, Yoko Ono and the Yippies. But it is also evident that EMI, with its distribution machinery, pop/rock journalists, who enthusiastically provided a public forum for a witty and articulate artist, and fans, with their love and support, all contributed to Lennon's stardom. It is notable that as early as 1964 the Beatles had conspicuously expanded from being a music group to a highly mediated and circulated product that incorporated a range of star modes and contributed to the development of various forms of fandom. The Beatles' early fame was underpinned not only by music, albeit it remained at the center of their celebrity, but by appearances in different media forms and situations, as in comic television shows and films. In fact, before rock music established itself as a serious cultural phenomenon, a major pattern in the entertainment industry was the encouragement of music stars to enter other networks of circulation or even to plan alternative careers. This was argued on the grounds that pop stardom in itself is not an adequate way to establish celebrity status.

It is often argued that in the late 1960s the Beatles widened the scope of pop stardom. While this is true in terms of ideology, the range of their star appearances was in fact wider in the early 1960s. Thus, when we discuss how marketing stars and circulating star images in various media forms have become conspicuous in current popular music culture, it should be remembered that similar mechanisms and forms of mediation already existed in the 1960s and even earlier.

Although the phenomenon called John Lennon appears to be a hybrid, a protean manifestation of the meaning of an artist, two major elements can be distinguished. First, Lennon's celebrity is inseparable from the notion of authenticity. Since the idea of authenticity has been central to the discourses of popular music, and often reduced to clichés, the conclusion that John Lennon is an ultimate embodiment of rock authenticity may seem unnoteworthy and self-evident. On the contrary, however, it should be noted that, first, the idea of authenticity has been and still is significant in our understanding of popular music and, second, in Lennon's case authenticity incorporates a number of complex and ambiguous features that, furthermore, have not previously been studied as systematically as I have attempted to do in this book.

In Lennon's case the most visible form of authenticity draws on the convergence of romantic and modernist rock authenticity and the particular idea of the rock auteur, a view that the performer possesses an "aura" of artistry and thus to a significant extent represents ideals of creativity, uniqueness, self-expression, independence and sincerity. My study has considered how Lennon not only reflected but also produced this ideology, for example, the distinctive idea of the rock survivor in the 1970s, and how this process was dependent on the given modes of star production and ideologies. I have also shown how there are authenticities that are distinct from the rock auteur theory and complicit in issues such as local/cultural identity, community, gender, and politics. Furthermore, since the history of John Lennon's rock stardom is characterized by different perspectives and negotiations among them, it is also evident that authenticity as a part of this constellation is not exclusively owned by the star. The history of Lennon demonstrates that just as the star is constructed, produced and circulated, so is authenticity. And it is a polysemous construction.

I have demonstrated that in Lennon's stardom the notion of authenticity has had two distinct temporal phases of interpretation. My main interest has been in the first phase, those views and interpretations that were articulated at the time of Lennon's actual career. Although the idea of authenticity became conspicuous in rock music only in the late 1960s, and although the term itself was not explicitly appropriated in popular music studies until the 1980s, related notions have implicitly defined the entire history of popular music stardom, including the early fame of Lennon and the Beatles. In the British context, the Beatles' cultural background, "Liverpoolness," conferred a distinctive aura upon their fame. Later, *Sgt. Pepper* clearly represented a triumph of the construction of authenticity, although without the notable use of the term. In the 1970s Lennon's embittered rejection of Beatlemania arguably became a model for "serious" rock artists attempting to "throw spanners in the works of stardom," that is, to subvert the idea of stardom and its publicity machinery, which is often considered formulaic and inauthentic.

The second phase, that of retrospectivity, is marked by the continuous (re)construction of authenticity. The posthumous career of Lennon may be a contested process in terms of ownership and legacy, but the view that Lennon per se is authentic is widely shared and evidently dates from the early 1980s and the canonization process that constructed the unambiguous profile of a "Sixties hero." In this scheme, interpretations often are biased toward the rock auteur. In fact, the idea of the rock auteur has become so established in retrospective thinking about Lennon that it has achieved a degree of hegemony, resulting in an obsessive search for the "real" Lennon and the fruitless objective of establishing the "true" reading of his works. Some particular cases, such as Lennon's songs "Help!" and "Imagine," produce questionable interpretations that invoke notions of the auteur and the autonomous artwork and ignore the social processes of meaning-making as well as subsequent histories of cultural products. Since in popular music it is easier to historicize persons and their products than institutions or ideologies, and since the fascination with stars in general draws on audiences' wish to locate the core of the individual, the "secret" of a personality behind the mass-mediated image, these attempts are of course understandable. Yet, such tendencies have occluded the polysemic nature of Lennon's stardom. It should be emphasized that although my own study clearly falls into the category of retrospective analysis, my main aim has not been to produce a reconstruction of Lennon as a person (though it cannot be entirely avoided) but to explore the discourses around Lennon, the fabric of his stardom.

These temporal dimensions of the debate about authenticity lead us to another major idea that characterizes the history of Lennon's stardom: the meaning of the past. John Lennon is often regarded as an innovator and pioneer who sought new artistic and cultural territories. My argument has been that rather than being a linear story of progress, Lennon's stardom is based on the polyphonic relationship between the past and present. It was not so much the exploration of new frontiers that defined Lennon's stardom, although in an overall dynamic of youth and pop culture it may have seemed so. Rather, Lennon's stardom was about deploying and challenging traditions.

John Lennon was a star whose image migrated across different domains of culture. As such, his stardom was an extension, albeit a notable extension, of those star mechanisms that were established in the early twentieth century. Of course, more specific traditions can be identified. To begin with, Lennon was not a "Sixties inventor" but rather an inheritor of the practices, possibilities and ideologies that were established in the 1950s. The Beatles emerged as an exciting cultural force situated, however, in existing mechanisms of popular music, particularly those of the English entertainment industry. On a more ideological level, Lennon's image as a teenybop idol stands as a major example of how stars may challenge particular traditions and at the same time support them. In terms of gender, Lennon represented "new" androgyny, yet as his links to domestic life were excluded from his public image, he also reflected "old" masculinity. This is only one illustration of how the dialogue between the past and the present characterized Lennon's stardom. Even in the late 1960s, which have often been regarded as the most innovative years for Lennon in particular as well as for popular music culture in general, this dialogue was audible at both levels. The ideal of the rock auteur drew on the convergence of British art school experience and American folk ideology, both of which already had a long history. The element of nostalgia that pervaded Lennon's image and his attempts to construct identity also characterized the phenomenon of English psychedelia. Lennon's experimental phase in the late 1960s was based on the tradition of the avant-garde. His short period as a fool was highly anachronistic, oddly referring to and revitalizing the centuries-old history of the holy fool.

There are, of course, cases when existing practices were regarded as constraining. In the history of popular music, new technologies have often challenged and reshaped old aesthetics, but in the Beatles' case it was old technologies that were decisive for their new aesthetics. Inadequate concert technology prompted the Beatles to abandon live performances. The making of *Sgt. Pepper* was later canonized as a process during which the Beatles successfully and creatively exploited the "primitive" state of recording technology.

Whether the past provided possibilities or constraints, the dialogue between temporalities remains fundamental to the 1960s cultural history of John Lennon's rock stardom. In the 1970s the meaning of the past in Lennon's stardom took more personal forms. Lennon's career, of course, continued a dialogue with traditions at a more general level, as, for example, through the idea of topicality, which had been a familiar motif among American protest singers in previous decades, but it was now the personal history of Lennon as a Beatle and Sixties star that emerged to define his celebrity. I have emphasized that this was not primarily an emanation from the star himself, but an issue produced by a media that was obsessed with the Beatles and the Sixties. Lennon was a Beatle in the 1960s and continued to be a Beatle in the 1970s when he was constantly asked to evaluate his past, to comment on the meaning of the Beatles and the Sixties, and whether the group might re-form one day and thus revive the spirit of a past era. Lennon attempted to break away from his history through the rhetoric of survivalism, which was reinforced by the general fashion for such rhetoric in popular culture and, more specifically, because rock culture needed the idea of survival to negotiate a shift from teen pop to adult rock. But the past was inescapable. As I have shown, the linkage between these specific temporalities of a star was then cemented through reactions to Lennon's murder in December 1980.

"Authenticity" and the meaning of the past are two major themes in a cultural history of John Lennon's stardom. Although the idea of authenticity has been questioned frequently, it remains a powerful ideology in popular music. It ebbs and flows. The aura of the rock performer was challenged during the so-called postmodern era and the celebration of "artificial pop" in the late 1980s, but it did not disappear. Currently, there are signs that growing criticism of globalization, particularly of entertainment conglomerates that subscribe to massive branding strategies, has revitalized notions of authenticity in rock music. Furthermore, hip-hop and techno, which in the late 1980s and 1990s emerged as a counterforce to rock, have created their own versions of authenticity and even aspired to an auteurship similar to that which was formerly criticized. John Lennon is a significant case study in the relationship between the history of popular music and the notion of authenticity. This is not only because he represented and contributed to different values and qualities that are ascribed to the notion of authenticity but also because he is historically constructed as the apotheosis of rock authenticity.

Authenticities persist in popular music stardom, and so does the past, because knowledge and experience of it are essential parts of popular music. Rock stardom may celebrate the present moment, but the past is built into the present. A corollary to this is that as rock music and rock musicians continue to age, the past will become even more powerful.

Although it has become evident that rock does not occupy the center of popular music to the same extent as it did in the 1960s and 1970s, there is every reason to think that John Lennon will remain a notable figure and model in the continuing development of pop/rock culture. In any event, Lennon remains important not only on the basis of his artistic innovations and achievements but also because his career conspicuously embraces themes that have defined the history of popular music and stardom. As further recollections and hitherto unpublished Lennon products appear, as Lennon continues to be consumed, debated and remembered, and as his stature has been almost irrevocably established, the narrative of his stardom will continue to unfold.

Indeed, considering the persistence of Lennon in contemporary culture, from regular rereleases of his music to forms of rock tourism, from appropriations of "Imagine" to tribute concerts, and from fan culture to protean media coverage, it can be said that we are simply living through another phase of the career of a star.

I have a feeling, I "Imagine," that the "true" history of Lennon—and the Beatles—is only just beginning. I believe that the meaning of John Lennon will continue to inhabit and be constructed by the popular imagination. Such is the power of stars that John Lennon will survive even after the last traces of the 1960s and 1970s have vanished from living memory. Primary recollections simply will be replaced by another kind of narrative, the reproduction and rearticulation of the memory of a star.

Notes

Chapter 1

1. It is partly because of the mediating effects of secondhand history that I have been reluctant to rely on new interviews rather than on earlier accounts and original sources, albeit critically, of course, since they can be highly unreliable as well. For example, Paul McCartney alleges that early interviews of the Beatles were sometimes made without the involvement of the group and even if they were available for journalists, the group "might have felt like joking that day" (Miles 1998, xii). Second, because of the wealth of existing Beatles/Lennon material, I have had no need to gather a new round of verbal accounts. On source criticism, memory and the Beatles, see Nurmesjärvi 2000; Mäkelä 2001.

2. It is perhaps justified to say that Mark Lewisohn and Bill Harry are the most authoritative experts on the subject. Lewisohn was for a long time the only researcher privileged to sift through the archives of EMI, which owns the recordings of the Beatles, and write books and compile new records based on this activity. It was not until 1993 that the first outside journalist, Mark Hertsgaard, gained access to the catalogue, resulting in an interesting survey of the Beatles' creative process which was otherwise unsurprising, *A Day in the Life*. Bill Harry published Liverpool's first pop magazine, *Mersey Beat*, in the early 1960s and had a close association with the Beatles. He has written several accounts of the subject.

3. Besides documentaries there is one major biopic, Sandor Stern's authorized *John and Yoko: A Love Story* (1985). There are also other fictionalized accounts of certain phases of Lennon's career, including his early years (Iain Softley's *Backbeat* in 1993 and David Carson's *In His Life: The John Lennon Story* in 2000) and the possible sexual liaison with manager Brian Epstein (Christopher Münch's *The Hours and Times* in 1991).

4. I sometimes use the terms *rock* and *pop* interchangeably. Although both can be regarded as subcategories of popular music, the term *pop music* was already in use before World War II, whereas *rock music* derives from the 1950s. The two terms became ideologically differentiated in the mid-1960s. Currently, it is difficult to draw the line between them, since both rock and pop are open and unfinished categories, existing in a highly complex relationship to each other as well as to other genres of music. The most accurate term here would arguably be *pop/rock*, but because of its clumsiness, I prefer mainly *rock* rather than *pop*, for historical reasons relating to both John Lennon and popular music in general. As a star Lennon certainly exemplified more clearly ideas associated with rock culture, although occasionally, and especially in his early career as a celebrated Beatle, he was referred to as a "pop" musician as well. I employ some latitude in the distinction,

but when the context requires stressing one or another term, I will use quotation marks to indicate the difference. See further discussion of *rock* and *pop* in chapters 4 and 5.

5. Since the 1980s, "grand narratives" in the history of rock music have gradually disappeared (at least in written forms), to be replaced by surveys with more elaborately nuanced outlines. New histories of popular music have had links to gender (for example, women and rock), genre (progressive rock) and nation/geography (the history of Finnish rock), to mention just a few directions. See further historical accounts of rock music, Belz 1969; Thornton 1990; Frith 1996b; Negus 1996; Kallioniemi 1998; Rodman 1999; Inglis 2000a.

6. In his famous and often cited article "On Popular Music," originally published in 1941, Adorno argued that the types of popular music are differentiated in production. It is on this basis that the listener knows, as Adorno shortly notes, that Benny Goodman is "swing" and Guy Lombardo "sweet" (1990, 309). The main argument in the article is that the listener to commercialized popular music (as opposed to "serious" music) is caught up in a standardized and routinized set of responses. Adorno's accounts have been carefully scrutinized, and a significant critique is that he sees popular music in terms that are far too narrow. Nevertheless, he provided a decisive point of departure for subsequent writers and established certain theoretical parameters which remain functional. See summary of Adorno's criticism, Longhurst 1995. Reconsidering Adorno's theses, see for example Gendron 1986; Goodwin 1992.

7. According to Marshall (1997), there have been three approaches to the star phenomenon in film studies: economic, psychoanalytical and sociological. The history of film stars as economic entities within corporations was taken up by Alexander Walker (1970), while the psychoanalytical study of the power and pleasure of the cinematic experience was first conducted by French film critics in the 1960s and, somewhat later, by Christian Metz (1982). The third level of study engaged in a sociological reading of the uses made of film stars by audiences and by culture at large. Two seminal works appeared. In his study *The Stars*, originally published in 1957, the French sociologist Edgar Morin examined the history of the star system by distinguishing such themes as heroism, industrial mechanisms, audiences and embourgeoisement. The Italian sociologist Francesco Alberoni provided in his article "The Powerless 'Elite': Theory and Sociological Research on the Phenomenon of the Stars" (first published in 1962) one of the first interpretations of stars as a considerable phenomenon emerging from the increased complexity and social fluidity of modern society.

Chapter 2

1. Notwithstanding his sarcasm, Cohn himself was one of the first British rock journalists/historians, along with Dave Laing (1969), Richard Mabey (1969) and George Melly (1970), to give at least some attention to the early British rock scene. Furthermore, some notable reassessments were conducted by later rock historians

(e.g., Frith 1978; Chambers 1985; Rogan 1988; Bradley 1992; Kallioniemi 1998). Generally speaking, however, the view that the early British rock scene exists solely as a background to the beat boom and the Beatles has tended to prevail.

2. In 1962 the station ventured into printed media with an annual publication, *Radio Luxembourg Book of Record Stars*, which imitated the happy-go-lucky mood of the actual programs. This thus added a new dimension to the company's musical mediation.

3. During the 1960s *Melody Maker* struck a balance between information for musicians and more frivolous teen news. Its rivals *New Musical Express, Disc* and *Record Mirror* focused more explicitly on pop stars. It was only after the fading of the first bloom of teen magazines and fanzines—peaking in the height of Beatlemania— and the "coming of age" of rock music in the late 1960s that the journals started to reorganize their strategies. This included retargeting their readership and hiring new, critical rock journalists, many of whom had already cut their teeth as editors and writers in the then flourishing underground press.

4. Jack Good, Oxford graduate and former theater buff, was the producer for *Six-Five Special* and *Oh Boy!*, among other shows. His role has been frequently celebrated. Cohn (1972) calls him "the first pop intellectual," Melly (1970) sees him as a "master of selling excitement," and for Whitcomb (1986) he stands as the "Svengali of rock."

5. It is often claimed that the Beatles were the first pop artists to write songs of their own. Before them, however, Billy Fury composed all the songs on his first album, partly under the pseudonym of Wilbur Wilberforce. Apart from him, Tommy Steele also had a hand in writing many of his biggest hits.

6. Peter Sellers, on one of his satirical LPs, included a track on which a journalist interviews a young pop idol under the eye of his owner, a ferocious whip-cracking colonel. Val Guest's pop film *Expresso Bongo* (1959), which was the first star vehicle film for Cliff Richard, introduced a hustling 10 percenter who bore a clear resemblance to Parnes. Furthermore, Julien Temple's film adaptation (1986) of Colin MacInnes' famous novel *Absolute Beginners* (1959) visualizes a Svengali called Harry Charms, who is conspicuously based on Parnes' image. See Melly 1970; Whitcomb 1983; Rogan 1988.

7. In the field of local amateur music-making practices, perhaps the most influential academic studies have been Ruth Finnegan's study of amateur musicians in Milton Keynes, Buckinghamshire (1989), Sara Cohen's ethnography of Liverpool rock bands (1991) and Barry Shank's account of Austin, Texas (1994).

8. It has been often claimed that *Mersey Beat* was the first local rock paper in England, but Alan Clayson (1996) awards this honor to Sheffield's *Top Star Special*. It is, however, obvious that it was the success of *Mersey Beat* that paved the way for the new rock press boom. According to Clayson, Britain already had nineteen local rock papers in 1963. Incidentally, for a short time *Mersey Beat* even had a local competitor called *Combo*. On the history of *Mersey Beat*, see Harry 1992.

9. The pattern did not change during the Merseybeat era. It was actually only after punk that London's control over popular music was for the first time seriously challenged. See Milestone 1996; Savage 1996c.
10. My thanks to Bruce Johnson for pointing this out in conversation with me.
11. This was particularly an English phenomenon. Carl Belz (1969, 125) claims that in America the Beatles' accent was not widely recognized as distinctively regional but rather as a generalized British accent. Since in America British vernacular had been considered a symbol of intelligence and sophistication, the Beatles' Scouse was thus marked by the "aura of dignity." See also Curtis 1987; Ehrenreich, Hess & Jacobs 1992.

Chapter 3

1. The term *Beatlemania* was first coined after the Beatles' appearance on the popular television show *Sunday Night at the London Palladium* on October 13, 1963.
2. The majority of songs composed and performed by the Beatles from late 1965 to 1970 were considerably slower than those they had recorded previously (McCarthy 2001).
3. Peter Sellers, who was Lennon's favorite Goon, connects with the Beatles through several minor episodes. The most famous one—and probably the funniest—was the performance on a Granada TV special *The Music of Lennon & McCartney*, in which Sellers, dressed as Richard III, recited a Shakespearian rendition of "A Hard Day's Night." A single of the number was released and became a minor hit in Britain, reaching number fourteen and encouraging Sellers to record other "accented" Beatles covers.
4. MacDonald (1995) mentions four Beatles songs which, he suggests, include notable Goon influences: the piano intro in "The Word" (1965), the fade-out in "Tomorrow Never Knows" (1966), shouts in "Yellow Submarine" (1966) and the novelty atmosphere of "You Know My Name (Look Up the Number)" in 1970. According to Spike Milligan (see Turner 1996), Lennon once informed him that *The Goon Show*'s dialogue inspired "Lucy in the Sky with Diamonds" (1967), among other songs.
5. Even though the film concept and other extended projects of the same type were not brought into use, there was a constant discussion in the media that they could possibly take place. Attempts to follow the path that *A Hard Day's Night* and *Help!* had created presumably included at least five plans: *A Talent for Loving* (a western satire based on Richard Condon's novel), *Three Musketeers* (with Brigitte Bardot), J. R. R. Tolkien's *Lord of the Rings* (possibly with Stanley Kubrick or Michelangelo Antonioni as director), *Shades of a Personality* (a tale of multiple personality, again possibly with Antonioni as director), and *Up against It* (Joe Orton's anarchistic screenplay). The main reason for the search for a new film was a three-picture deal that had been arranged with United Artists. The contract was eventually fulfilled by the documentary *Let It Be* (1970). Even though the Beatles did not venture into other feature films as a group, individually they appeared in various films.

Furthermore, they directed collaboratively *Magical Mystery Tour* (1967) for television and licensed their characters and songs to the animated *Yellow Submarine* (1968). See Harry 1992.

6. The satire boom was born around 1960 when a new generation of university comedians raised awareness with their live and media performances. A great deal of satirists' material was concerned with parodies of television shows and advertising, the clichés of journalism, the jargon of trendsetters and the new ambience of the glossy magazines. Attacks were also directed at representatives of the "Establishment," including politicians, the upper classes, the judiciary and even royalty. Social mockery was bread and butter for revues (Beyond the Fringe, Cambridge Circus), clubs (The Establishment), magazines (*Private Eye*), television shows (*That Was the Week That Was*) and even one classic film, Stanley Kubrick's *Dr. Strangelove: Or How I Learned to Stop Worrying and Love the Bomb* (1963). See further Wilmut 1980; Carpenter 2000.

7. Cohen's words reflect current views on masculinity and gender. Since the 1980s it has been argued, particularly in the field of cultural studies, that gender is at the same time constructed and always under construction. Instead of approaching gender in universalized or essentialist terms, scholars of cultural studies have insisted that it must be depicted in terms of social, economic and political relations that are geographically, historically and culturally specific.

8. Even though gender and sexuality have been key issues in recent popular music studies, the body of writing on masculinity has been rather limited. The seminal texts include Frith & McRobbie 1990 (originally 1978), Cohen 1991, and Walser 1993.

9. It should be noted that besides managers the structure of promoting personal appearances also included concert promoters and agencies. It was, however, managers who prepared pop talents and generally handled relations with record company executives, producers, agencies and lawyers. See further on the music industry in the 1960s, Chapple & Garofalo 1978.

10. As if to attest to their virtual invisibility, sexual relationships between women had never been covered by the law that was being repealed. Hence, it was the specific domain of male sexuality and masculinity that had been considered to be a problem requiring legal control.

11. The Beatles' famous hairstyle, which had such nicknames as "Pilzen Kopf" in Germany, "Hamlet" in Sweden and "Moptop" in the United States, was perhaps fluffier and more impressive compared to previous styles in pop music, but it was far from being totally new. For instance, a few years earlier British pop singer Adam Faith had already worn a similar hairstyle, or at least combed his hair forward. For a biographical debate on the birth of the Beatles' hairstyle see Clayson & Sutcliffe 1994; Lewisohn 1996; Harry 2000.

12. This construction of women is not a recent development growing out of a minority culture like the Beats. The irony is that the Beats, in the name of nonconformity and rebellion, very largely reproduced the misogynistic politics of mainstream Western society. That women have corrupted and enervated the potential of men

and have been associated with the evils of modernity has indeed been one of the themes of Western civilization. There is a lot of literature on this—see, for example, Beauvoir 1964; Lerner 1979; Huyssen 1986; Hearn 1992; Hester 1992; Offen 2000.

13. On attempts to maintain the available masculine image of the Beatles, see also *The Beatles Monthly Book* 71, June 1969; Barrow 1981; Coleman 1988; Goldman 1988.

14. There were, of course, preferences within the group. The two main composers, John Lennon and Paul McCartney, formed an independent unit, a collaboration recalling such famous songwriting teams as Rodgers-Hammerstein, Goffin-King and Leiber-Stoller, even though Lennon-McCartney differed from them in being also performers and stars. Such collaborations have often been regarded as seamless, including in the case of the Lennon-McCartney partnership in the 1960s. It was actually after the breakup of the band that journalists and scholars began to specify more carefully the particular composers of the Beatles' songs.

15. The former secretary of the Beatles fan club in America discovered that in 1964 the average Beatle fan was thirteen to seventeen years old, a girl, middle-class, white, Christian, a B-minus student, weighed 105 to 140 pounds, owned a transistor radio with an earplug attachment and had Beatle photographs plastered all over her room (Steinem 1987).

16. The Beatles fan club was by far the biggest one in popular music. According to Bob Dawbarn (1965b), the Rolling Stones had 13,000 registered fans, while Roy Orbison had 12,000 and Herman's Hermits 1,000 members in their fan clubs.

17. After the Beatles stopped touring, fans en masse disappeared, but the most dedicated fans, known as Apple Scruffs, took up virtually permanent posts for years outside the Beatles' homes, their recording studios and office buildings. In 1970 the group even launched its own magazine about Beatle activities, and it is reported that the Beatles' associates used to read it to stay abreast of the times. See Burn & Tennant 1983; Bedford 1984; Mitchell & Munn 1988; Harry 1992.

18. The distribution of Beatles singles was even more varied. For example, two of the first five Beatles singles released in Finland, "Twist and Shout" and "All My Loving," were not originally issued as singles in Britain. Different national versions of Beatlemania certainly deserve further studies.

19. The teenybop side of Beatles fandom also attracted scorn from certain other adolescents, including intellectuals such as descendants of the Beats and working-class males such as "rockers" and, to some extent, "mods." Hence, the line was not entirely generational, but also a matter of class and gender. See Frith & Horne 1987; Muncie 2000.

20. Such behavior is by no means extraordinary in fan culture, which often incorporates characters of fetishism and religious fervor. See Morin 1960; Vermorel & Vermorel 1985; Marcus 1992; Rodman 1996; Cavicchi 1998; Evans & Wilson 1999.

21. Interestingly, "From You to Us" inspired the Beatles to write "From Me to You," which became their second hit on the U.K. charts. See Smith 1963b.

Chapter 4

1. "Michelle" (1965) is a wonderful example of how these experiences were later recalled in the Beatles' songs. It has an origin in Paul McCartney's attempt to imitate "French tune" and thus appear "enigmatic" to girls at one of these parties (Miles 1998, 273).

2. Although it is difficult to reductively identify a basic philosophy of early nineteenth-century romanticism, scholars broadly agree that the primary emphasis of the romantic ethic was on the characteristic of creativity and a unique and personalized spirit, that of individual "genius" (Williams 1971; Sennett 1993). It has also been suggested that "Bohemia is the social embodiment of Romanticism, with Bohemianism the attempt to make life conform to Romantic principles" (Campbell 1987, 195). Central to this aestheticism and sensibility was the ideal of self-expression with the aim of realizing individuality through creativity, plus the abolition of all those "bourgeois" laws, conventions and rules that prevented this from occurring.

3. The importance of art schools in British pop music was already being recognized, although not analyzed, in the late 1960s. See Mabey 1969; Melly 1970; Booker 1992.

4. Prior to these studies and as exemplified in Walter Benjamin's study of the "aura" in his famous article "The Work of Art in the Age of Mechanical Reproduction," first published in 1935, authenticity had already emerged as a key concept in discourses about modern culture. It has been suggested that the philosophers loosely associated with existentialism, most notably Heidegger and Sartre, were significant popularizers of the term (Berman 1971). On the other hand, the concept of authenticity has been a significant value in Western culture for centuries. For example, in the eighteenth century the French Royal Academy of Music found it necessary to categorize authentic and inauthentic art music (Peterson 1997).

5. Auteur theory was originally developed by French film critics and directors in the 1950s, including André Bazin and Francois Truffaut. Their main objective was to locate the dominant personality, the author (auteur), in individual films, usually showing how various American directors had transcended the restrictions of the Hollywood studio system and created their own distinctive styles.

6. The folk argument was obviously bound up with rural romanticism and nostalgia, finding its habitat predominantly in the East Coast urban districts and middle-class students. Such a development had already been foreshadowed in the 1920s when authenticity, self-expression and "honesty" were pinpointed during the first wave of systematic collection and recording of folk music. Alan Lomax's *Folkways Anthology of American Folk Music* (1952) would later become the milestone in this collecting process. See further on the American folk revival Vassal 1976; Cantwell 1996.

7. It is interesting to note that 1965 was also the year when the leading female folk singer Joan Baez used electric guitar for the first time, on her album *Farewell,*

Angelina. It did not result in any notable controversy, indicating once more that the triangle of folk, rock and authenticity was constructed on a masculinized grid.

8. The British Invasion reached its peak in early May 1965 as nine British singles were simultaneously listed in the U.S. top ten. While this has often been regarded as a unique event in pop history, the figure was actually higher in 1983 when at one time over 60 percent of the U.S. top hundred were recorded by non-American artists, the majority being British.

9. Inglis has elsewhere (1995) argued the ability to articulate radical explanations, to undermine seemingly secure conventions and to depart from existing modes of behavior form criteria that are rarely fulfilled in popular culture. If accompanied by enduring success and widely recognized artistic merits (as is the case with the careers of the Beatles and Dylan), such behavior constitutes "the Innovator" in Inglis' star typology (67–71). This definition is actually similar to that of the rock auteur presented in the beginning of this section. Other character types in Inglis's model, which is based on qualifications of "ideology" and "duration" of a star's career, are the Idol, the Perennial, the Arriviste, the Eccentric and the Rebel.

Chapter 5

1. In fact, according to photographs taken between 1966 and 1973, Lennon had several pairs of spectacles that differed only slightly from each other. Prior to his *How I Won the War* film role, Lennon had worn similar glasses in a scene of *Help!*, masquerading as an old man in a wheelchair, and, as pictured on the back cover of the *Revolver* album, released in August 1966, he also had toyed with rectangular glasses. Lennon's flirtation with a variety of spectacles was later epitomized in the self-portrayal sleeve of his solo album *Walls and Bridges* (1974).

2. In *Melody Maker* and *New Musical Express* during Beatlemania, for example, I have found only one picture (in Roberts 1964a) showing Lennon with his glasses on.

3. Although nostalgia has often been criticized as pathological, regressive and delusional, it is on the other hand possible to see it as a search for continuity that enables new and productive ways of reading the past. Within the realm of nostalgia, previously overlooked historical materials and practices may be recuperated. See Tannock 1995.

4. In fact, the lyrics of "Strawberry Fields Forever" and "Penny Lane" themselves do not tell us that the songs are about actual places in Liverpool or about childhood experiences. For the majority of Beatles listeners, this was revealed through reviews and comments on the songs. The theme was also emphasized in promotional strategies. Whereas the back of the U.K. and the U.S. sleeve of the single presented four photographs of the Beatles as children, the newspaper advertisement (at least in Britain, see, e.g., *Melody Maker*, February 18, 1967) included the map of Liverpool with typographical markings of the actual Penny Lane and Strawberry Fields (which was a Salvation Army orphanage).

5. Memories and the feelings associated with them have of course been a main theme in the history of popular songs. The Beatles song "Yesterday," originally

written by McCartney, stands as a classic example, but the first Beatles song qualified as containing autobiographical memories is "In My Life," from *Rubber Soul* (1965). The paradox is that Lennon's and McCartney's own memories about the origin and credits of the song are contradictory, making it more obscure than any other song in the Beatles catalog. See Compton 1988; MacDonald 1995; Turner 1996.

6. Situated at the corner of Baker Street and Paddington Street in London and opened in December 1967, Apple Boutique became the first of the Beatles' Apple ventures. The shop was a financial disaster and lasted barely eight months. See Miles 1998.

7. Since wearing glasses is no longer unusual and since "grannies" became a fashionable model for young people to wear in the 1980s (at least in Europe and the United States), distinctive associations of intellectualism have diminished compared to the situation in the 1960s. The image, however, still persists, as exemplified in popular films and their convention of using glasses as a signifier of literary interests.

8. The most conspicuous exception to the rule was Buddy Holly, who perhaps because of his large-framed glasses is often thought of as the first pop intellectual. As indicated in the epigraph of this chapter, Holly's choice to use spectacles presumably was very conscious.

9. The identity of the artist behind the paintwork is one of those mysteries of Beatles history. Goldman writes that the idea of a fairground or carousel style was first suggested by Ringo Starr and then put into practice by a BBC scene designer (1988, 266). Harry suggests that the painting was executed by The Fool, a group of Beatles-associated avant-garde designers from the Netherlands (1992, 248). Although this has been the most frequent assumption, Clifford (1999) proves in his detailed article on the history of Lennon's Rolls-Royce that this was not the case and that the car was probably painted by a Romany artist or artists traveling with a fair then based near Lennon's home in Surrey. Cynthia Lennon possibly meant Romanies when recalling in her book that her husband employed a firm of "barge and caravan designers" to do the task (1980, 142). Davis gives this credit to sixty-two-year-old freelance designer Stephen Weaver (1998, 116).

10. After the beat boom, the geographical locus of pop music in Britain clearly moved from the North to the South. Whereas psychedelic pop was a London-based phenomenon, the folk and progressive rock scenes were permeated by pastoral "Little England" sentiments, representing a middle-class antithesis to northernness, provincialism and the working-class nature of the beat boom (Kallioniemi 1998).

11. Even though the Silver Shadow was called "revolutionary," it did not radically differ from other models. Hence, it was not the Rolls-Royce that changed but the people who drove it.

12. Two incidents are particularly instructive. When Brian Epstein was asked if he and the Beatles were millionaires, he staunchly refused to answer the question (see Coleman 1965b). Second, the Beatles' Apple company, launched in February 1968, was justified with explanations of artistic freedom within a business struc-

ture. The more concrete—and less publicized—reason was that the Beatles were forced to invest their astronomical wealth to offset taxes (Harry 2000).

13. Following Charles S. Peirce's semiotic categorization of "signs," Fiske proposes that Rolls-Royce is an index of wealth and a symbol of its owner's social status (1982, 116). Fiske does not go on to explain the third semiotic dimension of signs, that of icon, but it could be suggested that at this level Rolls-Royce represents success.

14. In this context, Lennon's Rolls-Royce, as well as his granny glasses, could be viewed as 1960s versions of *bricolage* in popular culture. According to French cultural anthropologist Claude Lévi-Strauss (1966, 16–22, 36), who first used the concept in relation to cultural semiotics, the logic of bricolage works like a kaleidoscope. When the person looking through the instrument turns it, sporadic fragments project models of intelligibility. By reorganizing the existing conjunction of contingent elements, the *bricoleur* thus produces a pattern that signifies a new situation, conveying a message different from the "old" discourse. The idea of the structured improvisation of bricolage was in the 1970s often used to explain how youth subcultures created meaning and relocated everyday objects as well as culturally loaded signs—as, for example, the swastika and its use in punk style— to construct new styles (see, e.g., Hebdige 1983). This kind of system of communication and construction was later criticized (e.g., Clarke 1990) as giving a too-comprehensive interpretation of subcultures, which in reality are usually organized more or less heterogeneously. Rather than studying a group of people, the concept of bricolage would arguably provide a more suitable tool for semiotic analysis of styles of individual stars and episodes relating to their careers.

15. By telling a surrealistic story about a coach trip in southern England and presenting a gallery of English types and traditions, *Magical Mystery Tour* and its sense of community not only referred to sentiments of hippie culture but also attempted to embrace a feeling of national identity. The concept of the film, however, was predominantly influenced by the author Ken Kesey and his Merry Pranksters, who toured California in a psychedelically painted bus, spreading the word about the joys of drugs, especially LSD. Kesey's group has received a lot of attention even though it was by no means unique. For example, the amateur musician and future mass murderer Charles Manson, now an archetype of hippie-gone-mad and the cultish embodiment of "rock notoriety," used to do similar "tours" with his group. In England, the bus theme was explored by the Who in their song "Magic Bus" (1968), which became one of their concert climaxes. See Curtis 1987; Taylor 1987; Miles 1998.

16. In fact, the Beatles occasionally faced an audience after 1966, as in some television shows and the famous Apple Corps rooftop show in 1969. These, however, cannot be classified as actual, advertised live concerts.

17. The historical meaning of the album has remained relatively stable. In various all-time top album rankings by critics, journalists and listeners, *Sgt. Pepper* has usually placed close to the top. Recently, however, its supremacy has been challenged by another Beatles album, *Revolver* (see, e.g., Larkin 1998). For more detailed

descriptions of *Sgt. Pepper*, see Harry 1992; Whiteley 1992; Hertsgaard 1995; Mac-Donald 1995; Lewisohn 1996; Negus 1996; Moore 1998.

18. In Sydney from the 1950s, for example, all the major international concerts were arranged in the huge Sydney Stadium, presenting performers with a range of acoustic problems. See Rogers & O'Brien 1975; Sturma 1991.

19. Glenn Gould, an extrovert Canadian pianist and Bach expert, had two years before the Beatles' seclusion refused to give any public performances on the basis of their "degrading nature" and decided to concentrate on recordings. His retirement was greeted with surprise. Bob Dylan's seclusion from the summer of 1966 to 1969 has parallels with the Beatles' situation, although his decision was originally due to injuries sustained in a motorcycle accident. Nonetheless, by prolonging his retirement Dylan created the same kind of mystery as the Beatles. After the commercial failure of Ike and Tina Turner's "River Deep, Mountain High" in 1966, producer Phil Spector announced his self-imposed exile and did not return until the end of the decade, when he was hired to finish the Beatles' last album, *Let It Be*. Perhaps the most famous act of reclusiveness in the history of pop music had taken place in the late 1950s, however, when Elvis Presley discontinued his star career and did a two-year stint in the U.S. Army. After returning from the army Presley refused to play live until 1968, but although he was not physically within reach of his fans, frequent releases of new Elvis records and films guaranteed the constant circulation of his star image.

20. It should be remembered that among 1950s English pop stars changing ordinary names to exciting fictitious names (Tommy Steele, Billy Fury, Marty Wilde, and so on) was more a rule than an exception. The idea of fiction in pop music was later developed by progressive rock bands, some of whom (such as Yes) ventured deep into fantasy worlds. Furthermore, many 1970s glam rockers, including David Bowie, Alice Cooper and KISS, promoted similar ideas and toyed with star alter egos.

21. George Martin's career exemplifies the shift among producers and sound mixers from the craft union and the entrepreneurial mode to the team-oriented art mode. In 1967 he was no longer "only" a technician or an engineer but a respected visionary and sound artist who worked intensively with the Beatles, displaced Brian Epstein (who died in August 1967) as a "fifth Beatle" and also had more opportunities to explain his role and studio technology in the media. See changing modes of record producers in Kealy 1990.

22. Paradoxically, the mastery over technology has sometimes been proclaimed by pop innovators who, after harnessing new inventions, turn back to more primitive technologies. Examples include Phil Spector's "back to mono" project in the time when stereo sound had already established itself as a cornerstone of hi-fi, or, more recently, hip-hop musicians' and lo-fi artists' interests in old sounds and retro-style music technology. Such antitechnological practices imply that for auteurs, primitive equipment constitutes a rejection of advanced technology in the interests of creativity and craft, and a guarantee of authenticity.

23. It should be added that *Sgt. Pepper* was the first Beatles album whose contents were not modified for the U.S. market.

Chapter 6

1. Even though Fluxus has remained one of the most significant art groups of the era, influencing 1960s and 1970s art movements as well as aesthetic practice in general and individual artists in particular, it did not gain significant popularity. As an eclectic movement, Flux art could not be institutionalized in the same way as happened with the more famous art movement of the time, pop art.

2. Partly on the basis of this single piece, Lennon has been regarded as the major experimentalist in the Beatles, even though it was Paul McCartney who was first more involved with the London countercultural avant-garde and was familiar with the modernity of Karlheinz Stockhausen, Edgar Varèse, Luciano Berio and John Cage, as well as with the free jazz of John Coltrane and Albert Ayler. When the Beatles recorded an experimental sound collage in January 1967 for the *Carnival of Light* event in London, McCartney took the leading role in the process (see Miles 1998). For some reason, his sound experiments never appeared on the Beatles' records, subsequently reinforcing his image as a less radical Beatle than Lennon.

3. See further on the reception of Lennon and Ono's avant-garde music, Hopkins 1987; Robertson 1990; Rogan 1997. Yoko Ono has later been given credit for pioneering women's rock and, more particularly, paving the way for the extraordinary singing of Lene Lovich, Nina Hagen, Kate Pierson of the B-52's, and John Lydon (Johnny Rotten). Interestingly, histories of postwar art, including histories of art music and avant-garde music, barely mention Ono, much less her experimental collaborations with Lennon. See further on Ono's rehabilitation in popular music, Gaar 1993.

4. The other three live performances took place at a University of Cambridge avant-garde concert (Lennon playing noisy electric guitar and Ono experimenting with her voice), in London at the UNICEF benefit concert (with the Plastic Ono Band and guests), and in New York at the Fillmore East (Lennon and Ono joining Frank Zappa and the Mothers of Invention).

5. From 1968 to 1971 Lennon and Ono produced a series of films of two basic categories. The first were the promotional short films for the songs "The Ballad of John and Yoko," "Give Peace a Chance," "Cold Turkey" and "Imagine." The second category included the "concept" films *Smile, Two Virgins, Rape, Self Portrait, Apotheosis, Apotheosis No. 2, Fly, Clock* and *Freedom,* most of which stylistically resembled the minimalism of Andy Warhol and Michael Snow. Lennon and Ono also documented their peace events on film. See Hoberman 1982.

6. Some stars, like Lennon, expressed their disappointment at "fake" gurus. Given his ever-changing moods, Lennon arguably also became impatient with a spiritual journey of long duration.

7. See, for example, "Victor Triumphs Again and Mrs. Weatherby Learns a Lesson" in *In His Own Write* and "I Believe, Boot..." in *A Spaniard in the Works*. Regarding songs, Lennon later insisted that "Girl," on the Beatles album *Rubber Soul*, criticized the Christian ethic of pain (Wenner 1980, 130).

8. As this view suggests, it was typical of critics to consider rock stardom purely as a site of masculine activity.

9. Lennon wrote a masturbation scene for Kenneth Tynan's play *Oh, Calcutta!* (1969), another notorious play with full frontal nudes, and appeared in his and Ono's avant-garde film *Self Portrait* (1969), which presented 15 minutes of slow-motion footage of his semierect penis. The sexual consummation of Lennon's marriage to Ono was documented in his *Bag One* lithographs which, when first exhibited in London, were confiscated by the police.

10. The rivalry among the papers was fueled by the entry of Robert Murdoch, who in the late 1960s bought *News of the World* and the *Sun*. He successfully relaunched them as tabloids about scandals, forcing other papers, especially the popular press, to follow the trend.

11. Interestingly, Lennon was worried that "the way things were going," it was only he, not he and Ono, who would be crucified.

12. The song was banned in the American South and Australia on the grounds that it was blasphemous.

13. See, for example, readers' letters in *Melody Maker*, April 12, 1969, 24; Smith 1969b, 3. Interestingly, Yoko Ono was only rarely called a fool. This suggests that she was not considered laughable in the same sense as Lennon, if at all, and that her actions were not seen as fool's play. It is arguable that because of her ethnic and artistic background, and perhaps even for reasons of gender, she was simply regarded as predictably irrational.

14. Another writer exploring Lennon's "holiness" is Rogan P. Taylor, who in his study on shamans and superstars perceives Lennon as a "classic Middleworlder," a rock 'n' roll shaman who "imported the dream world into our everyday" (1985, 200–206). To my mind, he mystifies stardom and romanticizes Lennon's star role.

Chapter 7

1. According to Shuker, the new phenomenon of political rock emerged in the mid-1980s, with popular musicians joining and reinforcing international concern at the grim effects of mass famine in Africa and taking up antinuclear, environmental, and other international causes. Although the huge charity rock festivals of the 1980s, of which Live Aid in 1985 was the major catalyst, clearly took conscience rock to a new level, the phenomenon itself was not new. Organizers, inspired by the long tradition of benefit concerts in folk music, put together several politically focused rock concerts in the late 1960s and the 1970s. For example, the Concert for Bangladesh, which was held in New York in 1971 and included top artists like George Harrison, Eric Clapton and Bob Dylan, was regarded not only as a major rock concert but a significant cultural event. Another celebrity-filled benefit con-

cert to relieve mass famine in Bangladesh took place in London later the same year.

2. These were Ten for Two in Ann Arbor, Michigan, a benefit concert for the jailed White Panther and manager of the MC5, John Sinclair; a performance at the Apollo Theater, in New York, to raise funds for the dependents of the victims of the Attica state prison riots; two performances in New York's Madison Square Garden in the One to One benefit concert for mentally handicapped children. Prior to these, Lennon had performed with Yoko Ono and the Plastic Ono Band at the UNICEF benefit in London in 1969.

3. Although critics and biographers have often considered *Some Time in New York City* as a part of Lennon's solo discography, it should be emphasized that the album, which comprised ten new songs and the *Live Jam* bonus disc, was in fact credited as a collaboration with Yoko Ono. Although "New York City" and "John Sinclair" were actually written by Lennon, five songs were credited to him and Yoko Ono and three to Ono.

4. Released in 1979, "I Will Survive," the epitome of 1970s pop survivalism and the semiofficial anthem of feminists and gays, became the swan song of the disco boom.

5. In Lennon historiography, the star's role as a major critic of the decade has led to some interesting song analyses. Take, for example, "God," the climactic moment on Lennon's first solo album, *John Lennon/Plastic Ono Band* (1970), and its key line "The dream is over." Even though, in the light of the rest of the lyrics, the line mainly refers to the Beatles and their dissolution, Lennon's statement has also been perceived as a death knell for an entire era. For Johnny Rogan (1997, 46; see also Robertson 1990; Du Noyer 1997), the myth of the Sixties "was washed away in four short words."

6. It is hardly surprising that the most vigorous critics of the 1970s and subsequent popular music are to be found among Beatles enthusiasts (e.g., MacDonald 1995; Elliott 1999).

7. John Lennon was of course neither the first nor the only star to rail against his supposedly specious and manufactured celebrity. During the heyday of the Monkees, Michael Nesmith, arguably the most talented musician of the group, called an unofficial news conference and told the press how they had been hyped as a group and never even allowed to play on Monkees records. This initiated a controversy over the manufacturing of groups and their exploitation in selling them to the teenage market (Barnard 1996). As presented in chapter 2, section 1, British pop manager Larry Parnes' maneuvers in the late 1950s and early 1960s raised similar debate.

8. According to Hoskyns (253–55), it was a paradox of the times that the "rest of the world jeered at Los Angeles as a pseudo-paradise of laid-back bliss, when the reality of the place was that people were running around with their nerves frayed by cocaine." Los Angeles in the early 1970s, when not only members of the British pop elite (Lennon, David Bowie, Peter Frampton, Keith Moon, Ringo Starr, Rod Stewart and Fleetwood Mac) but Hugh Hefner's *Playboy* imperium moved to the

city, was not about happiness but "Hefner heaven," permeated by degeneration and self-destruction. Hoskyns also notes that one of the key elements of Los Angeles noir was that there were surprisingly few bars. The image of sunny Los Angeles prevailed because all the "bad things happen behind closed doors (or electronic gates)." This also explains why Lennon's "rock 'n' roll lifestyle" did not at first attract attention in the media. It was only when Lennon started to cause trouble in public spaces, for example, by brawling in the Troubadour nightclub, that his lifestyle and marital problems became news.

9. The history of Lennon's personal diaries is characterized by several surprising turns. In 1981 Yoko Ono's assistant Fred Seaman stole Lennon's journals from the Dakota apartment. Seaman gave them to his partner in the joint venture, Robert Rosen, explaining that Lennon himself had earlier authorized him to take the diaries in case something exceptional should happen. Rosen immediately began to write a manuscript based on the journals. Seaman, whom Ono had now fired, then restole Lennon's diaries and Rosen's material for the book. Rosen rewrote the biography on the basis of his own memory of Lennon's diaries and approached several publishers, claiming he had a photographic memory, but he was ignored. According to Rosen himself, in 1982 he contacted Ono, who then used Rosen's personal diaries to have Seaman arrested. When this succeeded, Lennon's journals were returned, with the exception of the final 1980 diary. In 2000 Rosen finally managed to publish his manuscript, "a work of investigative journalism and imagination," in which he claims that Yoko Ono had not returned the diaries Rosen gave her in 1982. It has also been reported that some of Fred Seaman's personal diaries, which were a major source for Goldman's iconoclastic Lennon biography, were mysteriously found in a garbage dump in Harlem, after which they fell into the hands of Yoko Ono. In addition, Beatles historian Geoffrey Giuliano claims that he obtained a copy of Lennon's diaries in 1983. His biography *Lennon in America, 1971–1980* is based in part on these diaries. See further Hopkins 1987; Harry 2000; Rosen 2000; Giuliano 2001.

10. It should be noted that efforts to bring the Beatles back together in the late 1970s were often made in the name of benefit concerts.

11. Married couples who have worked in partnership include Ike and Tina Turner, Sonny and Cher, members of Abba, members of Fleetwood Mac, and Bruce Springsteen and Patti Scialfa, to mention but a few examples. Bands with mutual family ties have been common in black music (the Jacksons, the Isley Brothers, Sister Sledge, the Pointer Sisters, not to mention the web of family ties in the Motown company in the 1960s), in the teen pop genre (the Osmonds, Hanson) and "pop" (the Bee Gees, or "Brothers Gibb," Ace of Base). Interestingly, the closest point of comparison to Lennon and Ono in the 1970s was Paul and Linda McCartney. In both cases, wives were often seen to represent a negative influence on their husbands.

12. The article was also published in *The New York Times* and *Sundance*.

Chapter 8

1. In America, the premature deaths of Rudolph Valentino, Will Rogers, Babe Ruth and Elvis Presley had caused extravagant outpourings of grief, but apart from the case of Elvis they did not attract the same level of international attention. The most spectacular example of how deaths of mass-mediated celebrities can capture the public imagination is that of Diana, princess of Wales, in 1997.

2. The Sixties also dominated the mourning in British print media. The editorial in *The Daily Telegraph* (December 10) perceived Lennon as a child and troubadour of "the swinging sixties," while in *The Times* editorial (December 10) Lennon was credited as having been an essential figure in creating "the sound of the sixties." Some of the hastily published tribute magazines took an even more straightforward attitude, constructing Lennon as a "powerhouse of the swinging sixties" (*John Lennon. Give Peace a Chance* 1980, 3). Of four other British tribute magazines issued in 1980, the *Daily Mirror's* special issue *Tribute to John Lennon* (written by Patrick Doncaster) and *John Lennon: Working Class Hero* (written by authors closely associated with *New Musical Express*) had their emphasis almost exclusively on the 1960s, while *John Lennon: The Life & Legend* (produced by *The Sunday Times*) and *John Lennon: A Melody Maker Tribute* provided wider perspectives.

3. Hampton's analysis of Lennon is reduced to a rather standard biographical narrative of the hero's deeds and motives, except that he places Lennon in a tradition of American folk and protest song. We can undoubtedly find similar patterns of struggle and suffering in the careers of Joe Hill, Woody Guthrie and Bob Dylan, three other study cases in Hampton's monograph, but to concentrate on this strand means that in Lennon's case ideologies, mediations and constructions of modern rock stardom are ignored. Furthermore, although Hampton criticizes the counterculturized canonization process, he himself gets carried away by a similar ethos, the romanticized version of the rock star as a truth-seeker and radical mouthpiece of "folk." Like many social critics before him, from Thomas Carlyle and Ralph Waldo Emerson to Leo Löwenthal and Daniel Boorstin, Hampton is disillusioned with the "artificial" hero-worship and the debasement of "authentic" community.

4. It is instructive that the term *assassination*, which refers to violent and treacherous killing for political reasons, is often used in discussions about Lennon's death. Speculation about a conspiracy theory is another thread through this discourse. Tyler (1981), Michael (1981a; 1981b) and, particularly, Bresler (1989) have suggested that Mark Chapman was not a lone assassin but was controlled by a secret intelligence unit or the Central Intelligence Agency. These theories have not attracted serious interest.

5. Journalists have often angrily commented on Ono's authority as an executor of Lennon's estate and her role as a shaper of Lennon's star image. There is no doubt that Ono has made use of this power. Take, for example, the video arranged around "#9 Dream," released in *The John Lennon Video Collection* in 1992, which reiterates the images of the love story of John and Yoko; the song itself, however,

derives from Lennon's "lost weekend" in the mid-1970s, when he had an affair with his secretary May Pang. Ono has also upset Lennon's fans by allowing Lennon's music and trademark to be used for various commercial purposes. See further Harry 2000.

6. The prime case of posthumous exploitation is Jimi Hendrix: The four albums that he released during his lifetime have been supplemented by more than thirty official subsequent releases. With Lennon, by spring 2003 the official posthumous catalog included two greatest hits compilations (*The John Lennon Collection*, 1982, and *Lennon Legend*, 1997), one four-CD box set on Lennon's solo career (*Lennon*, 1990), another four-CD box of outtakes, home demos and live recordings (*The John Lennon Anthology*, 1998), two albums of demo songs (*Milk and Honey*, together with Yoko Ono, 1984, and *Menlove Avenue*, 1986), one interview album (*Heart Play: Unfinished Dialogue*, with Ono, 1983), two soundtracks (*Live in New York City*, also issued on video, 1986, and *Imagine: John Lennon*, 1988) and various singles as well as remastered releases of Lennon's solo albums with bonus tracks. Other Lennon products include posthumous collection of his writings (*Skywriting by Word of Mouth*, 1986) and *The John Lennon Video Collection* (1992).

7. In fact, there is even some uncertainty about the fate of Lennon's ashes after his cremation. It has been rumored that they were scattered in the sea, interred privately in England or transferred to some other secret place. According to Harry (2000, 510), they were scattered in New York's Central Park.

8. Since the first post-Beatles convention in Boston in 1974, events celebrating the Beatles have frequently been arranged around the world. In England fan conventions with flea markets, auctions, special guests, soundalike "tribute bands" and video shows are currently organized almost every month. One area in which the enthusiasm for the Beatles and Lennon seems to be constant is collecting memorabilia. After Lennon's death, items relating to him and the Beatles emerged as market leaders of pop memorabilia in the auction room, reaching a peak in the world record price of $ 2.3 million paid by a Canadian millionaire in 1985 for Lennon's psychedelically painted Rolls-Royce Phantom V. The Rolls was, at that time, the most expensive used car in the world. See Harry 1984; 1985; 1992; Clifford 1999.

9. It is, however, possible to ask help from a virtual Lennon. The John Lennon Artificial Intelligence Project web site (http://triumphpc.com/johnlennon/) re-creates the personality of a dead Beatle by programming an artificial intelligence engine with his words.

References

Primary Sources

Print

Adler, Bill (Ed.) (1964). *Love Letters to the Beatles*. London: Blond.

Aldridge, Alan (1969). Beatles not all that turned on (orig. 1967). In Jonathan Eisen (Ed.), *The Age of Rock: Sounds of American Cultural Revolution* (138–46). New York: Random House.

Aronowitz, Alfred G. (1969). A family album. In Jonathan Eisen (Ed.), *The Age of Rock: Sounds of American Cultural Revolution* (189–99). New York: Random House.

Ball, Ian (1980). Chapman tale of "Satanic voices". *The Daily Telegraph*, December 11.

Barrow, Tony (1981). The Beatles and the press. *The Beatles Appreciation Society Magazine Book*, 62, iii–vi.

———(1985). The humour of John. *The Beatles Monthly Book*, 110, 4–9.

———(1996). The reunion. Would John have agreed? *The Beatles Monthly Book*, 238, 5–11.

The Beatles Monthly Book, 71 (1969). When did you switch on? 9–12.

The Beatles Monthly Book, 238 (1996). Beatles Anthology: The debate continues, 12–16.

Beckett, Alan (1968). Stones. *New Left Review*, 47, 24–29.

Big "Beatles" controversy (1977, orig. 1963). In Bill Harry (Ed.), *Mersey Beat: The Beginnings of the Beatles* (58–59). Facsimile. London: Omnibus Press.

Birnbaum, Jesse & Porterfield, Christopher (1967). The messengers. *Time*, September 22, 56–58.

Blackburn, Robert & Ali, Tariq (1987). Power to the people: John Lennon and Yoko Ono talk to Robin Blackburn and Tariq Ali (orig. 1971). In Elizabeth Thomson & David Gutman (Eds.), *The Lennon Companion. Twenty-five Years of Comment* (165–80). Houndmills & London: Macmillan.

Boring, Edward (1967). John Lennon's yellow peril or how to make an £11,000 Rolls-Royce look like a four-wheel flower show. *Daily Mail*, May 26.

Breen, Walter (1970). Apollo and Dionysus. In Jonathan Eisen (Ed.), *The Age of Rock 2: Sights and Sounds of the American Cultural Revolution* (16–27). New York: Random House.

Cardwell, Dave (1965a). Britain's biggest—The Beatles. *Teenbeat Annual* (pages not numbered).

———(1965b). Fun-loving Freddie and the fabulous Dreamers. *Teenbeat Annual* (pages not numbered).

Christgau, Robert (1987). Symbolic comrades (orig. 1981). In Elizabeth Thomson & David Gutman (Eds.), *The Lennon Companion. Twenty-five Years of Comment* (226–31). Houndmills & London: Macmillan.

Cleave, Maureen (1963a). The year of the Beatles. Part I. As they make the Royal Show: A study of how they did it. *Evening Standard*, October 17.

———(1963b). The year of the Beatles. Part II. This is where the "O" level becomes Rock ... *Evening Standard*, October 18.

———(1963c). The year of the Beatles. Part III. It's like living it up with four Marx brothers. *Evening Standard*, October 19.

———(1966). How does a Beatle live? John Lennon lives like this. *Evening Standard*, March 4.

Coleman, Ray (1963). Is this ballyhoo really necessary, Mr. Parnes? *Melody Maker*, July 13, 8–9.

———(1964a). How long can they last? *Melody Maker*, March 14, 9.

———(1964b). Sometimes, I wonder how the hell we keep it up. *Melody Maker*, October 24, 8–9.

———(1965a). Beatles say—Dylan shows the way. *Melody Maker*, January 9, 3.

———(1965b). I give the Beatles two or three years more at the top ... but then they will become really established as film stars. *Melody Maker*, January 16, 3, 15.

———(1965c). What difference will this piece of paper make to the Beatles? *Melody Maker*, February 20, 8.

———(1965d). Life with the Lennons. *Melody Maker*, April 10, 11, 16.

———(1974). Lennon—a night in the life. *Melody Maker*, September 14, 14–15.

Coren, Giles (1995). The Beatles: All you need is hype. *The Times*, November 21.

Cott, Jonathan (1982a). The first Rolling Stone interview (orig. 1968). In Jonathan Cott & Christine Doudna (Eds.), *The Ballad of John and Yoko* (46–55). London: A Rolling Stone Press & Michael Joseph.

———(1982b). The last Rolling Stone interview (orig. 1980). In Jonathan Cott & Christine Doudna (Eds.), *The Ballad of John and Yoko* (185–193). London: A Rolling Stone Press & Michael Joseph.

Coward, Noel (1987). The diaries. In Elizabeth Thomson & David Gutman (Eds.), *The Lennon Companion. Twenty-five Years of Comment* (57–59). Houndmills & London: Macmillan.

Coxhill, Gordon (1969). John and Yoko's peace gimmicks do make sense. *New Musical Express*, April 12, 4.

Daily Mail (1969, March 21). Yoko gets her man in just 3 minutes.

Daily Mirror (1963, November 5). Beatlemania. Night of triumph for four young men at the Royal Variety Show.

Daily Mirror (1980, December 10). Death of a hero.

The Daily Telegraph (1980, December 10). Music and mortality [Editorial].

Davis, Andy (1996). Beatles '96. A diary of recent news and events. *The Beatles Monthly Book*, 238, 27–44.

Dawbarn, Bob (1965a). Ban the Americans say the Nashville Teens. *Melody Maker*, March 6, 13.

———(1965b). Fan clubs. *Melody Maker*, June 19, 8.

———(1966). What now for the Beatles? *Melody Maker*, November 19, 14–15.

Demoraine, Hermine (1968). Jean-Luc Godard talks to Hermine Demoraine. *IT*, September 6, 4.

Doncaster, Patrick (1980). *Tribute to John Lennon. Daily Mirror Special Issue.*

Edmunds, Dave (1990). The Lennon tribute. *The Times*, May 14.

Faulconbridge, Sue (1971). Together—just Yoko and John. *Liverpool Echo*, July 27.

Fudger, David (1975). Once bitten Ian 'Unter fights shy of tax man. *Disc*, June 14, 24.

Gilliatt, Penelope (1964). Beatles in their own right. *The Observer*, July 12.

Graustark, Barbara (1980a). The real John Lennon. *Newsweek*, September 29, 54–55.

————(1980b). Two virgins: The exclusive Newsweek interview. In Vic Garbarini & Brian Cullman (Eds.), *Strawberry Fields Forever: John Lennon Remembered* (95–134). New York: Bantam Books.

Gray, Andy (1964). Beatles great comics! *New Musical Express*, July 10, 3.

————(1969). The Establishment must not drive the Beatles out. *New Musical Express*, March 15, 3, 5.

Gray, Michael (1990). Instant bad karma by the Mersey. *The Times*, May 7.

Hamill, Pete (1982). Long night's journey into day (orig. 1975). In Jonathan Cott & Christine Doudna (Eds.), *The Ballad of John and Yoko* (142–55). London: A Rolling Stone Press & Michael Joseph.

Hilburn, Robert (1980). Lennon: He doesn't believe in magic or the Beatles. *Los Angeles Times*, November 16.

Horide, Rosemary (1975). Rock 'n' roll exile III. *Disc*, June 14, 16–17.

Hoyland, John (1968). An open letter to John Lennon. *Black Dwarf*, October 27, pages not numbered.

————(1969). John Hoyland replies. *Black Dwarf*, January 10, pages not numbered.

Humphries, Patrick (1995). Dead pop stars mean big bucks. *The Guardian*, August 18.

Hutchins, Chris (1963). Fans invade homes but boys love 'em! *New Musical Express*, June 21, 8.

————(1964a). Roy Orbison catches John Lennon in his bubble bath! *New Musical Express*, April 17, 14.

————(1964b). Let's hope they enjoy the holiday they have earned. *New Musical Express*, May 8, 3.

————(1965). Ringo as a married man—by John Lennon. *New Musical Express*, February 19, 2–3.

————(1966a). The Lennon interview. *New Musical Express*, March 11, 3.

————(1966b). Beatles goon it up again. *New Musical Express*, December 17, 2.

Hutton, Jack (1964). Fab! Fab! Four! *Melody Maker*, July 11, 11.

————(1967). Beatle listen-in. *Melody Maker*, May 27, 5.

John Lennon. Give Peace a Chance. A Memorial Tribute (1980).

John Lennon. The Life & Legend. The Sunday Times. A Special Tribute (1980).

John Lennon. A Melody Maker Tribute (1980).

John Lennon. Working Class Hero. The Life and Death of a Legend 1940–1980 (1980).

Johnson, Derek (1963). After all the talk about it, who is the man who says "There's no Liverpool sound!" It's George Martin, a-and-r manager of Gerry and the Pacemakers, Billy J. Kramer, the Beatles. *New Musical Express*, June 7, 3.

————(1965). Should smaller fry American popsters be banned from Britain? *New Musical Express*, April 30, 5.

Johnson, Paul (1987). The menace of Beatlism (orig. 1964). In Elizabeth Thomson & David Gutman (Eds.), *The Lennon Companion. Twenty-five Years of Comment* (39–42). Houndmills & London: Macmillan.

Kelly, Danny (Ed.) (1994). *The Q/Omnibus Press Rock 'n' Roll Reader*. Presented free with *Q*, 91.

Landau, Jon (1969). John Wesley Harding (orig. 1968). In Jonathan Eisen (Ed.), *The Age of Rock: Sounds of American Cultural Revolution* (214–29). New York: Random House.

Leapman, Michael (1980). Wave of grief over John Lennon's murder. *The Times*, December 10.

Leary, Timothy (1998). Thank God for the Beatles (orig. 1968). In Robert Cording, Shelli Jankowski-Smith & E. J. Miller Laino (Eds.), *In My Life: Encounters with the Beatles* (69–81). New York: Fromm.

Lennon, John (1967). *In His Own Write & A Spaniard in the Works* (orig. 1964 & 1965). New York: Signet.

———(1969). A very open letter to John Hoyland from John Lennon. *Black Dwarf,* January 10, pages not numbered.

———(1973). Review of *The Goon Show Scripts. The New York Times*, September 30.

———(1977). Being a short diversion on the dubious origins of Beatles (orig. 1961). In Bill Harry (Ed.), *Mersey Beat: The Beginnings of the Beatles* (17). Facsimile. London: Omnibus Press.

———(1986). *Skywriting by Word of Mouth. And Other Writings, Including The Ballad of John and Yoko*. London: Pan Books.

Lennon, John & Ono, Yoko (1979). A love letter from John and Yoko to people who ask us what, when and why. *The New York Times*, May 27.

Liverpool Echo (1967, June 26). No prize for the Lennon Rolls.

Liverpool Echo (1980, December 10). The plague of violence that hangs over us all.

Lydon, Michael (1970). Rock for sale (orig. 1969). In Jonathan Eisen (Ed.), *The Age of Rock 2: Sights and Sounds of the American Cultural Revolution* (51–62). New York: Random House.

MacInnes, Colin (1993). Pop songs and teenagers (orig. 1958). In Colin MacInnes, *England, Half English* (45–59). London: Chatto & Windus.

Mayer, Allan J. (1980). Death of a Beatle. *Newsweek*, December 22, 17–21.

Melly, George (1964). Inside a Beatle. *The Sunday Times*, March 22.

Melody Maker (1965, March 20). Merseysound? Ridiculous! 8.

Melody Maker (1966, December 3). Too old at 25? 3.

Melody Maker (1967, February 18). Penny Lane/Strawberry Fields Forever [advertisement], 10.

Melody Maker (1967, June 3). Sgt. Pepper's Lonely Hearts Club Band [advertisement], 8.

Melody Maker (1969, April 12). Mailbag: Who's kidding who? [readers' column] 24

Melody Maker (1969, December 6). John and Yoko: Part one, 20–21.

Merton, Richard (1968). Comment. *New Left Review*, 47, 29–31.

Michael, John (1981a). The Lennon murder 1. *New Musical Express*, June 27, 6–7.

———(1981b). The Lennon murder 2. *New Musical Express*, July 4, 6–8.

Moran, Caitlin (1994). Whisper words of wisdom: Let it be. *The Times*, June 24.

———(1995). Let me take you down, 'cause I'm going to. *The Times*, December 1.

Morris, James (1966). What America was told about the Beatles. *Liverpool Echo*, September 2.

Mulchrone, Vincent (1969). Go back to bed Mr. Lennon! *Daily Mail*, November 27.

Nesbit, Jan (1969). And a bird's eye-view. *New Musical Express*, April 12, 4.

New Musical Express (1963, February 15). Lifelines of the Beatles, 9.

New Musical Express (1964, December 25). Beatles' annual chat (translated from Scouse!), 3.

New Musical Express (1965, June 4). From you to us [readers' column], 8.

New Musical Express (1965, July 30). From you to us [readers' column], 8.

New Musical Express (1965, November 26). From you to us [readers' column], 12.

New Musical Express (1966, November 11). Dave Dee, Dozy, Beaky, Mick & Tich go mad at "I was Lord Kitchener's Valet", 14–15.

New Musical Express (1967, June 3). Sgt. Pepper's Lonely Hearts Club Band [advertisement], 1.

The New York Post (1979, September 25). Nowhere man [Editorial].

Norman, Philip (1988). My John. *The Sunday Times*, September 11.

Ono, Yoko (1970). *Grapefruit. A Book of Instructions* (orig. 1964). London: Peter Owen.

———(2000). "Assassin with a pen." Yoko Ono breaks her silence on Goldman. *Mojo Special Edition*, Winter, 103.

Peck, John (1963). London versus the 'Pool. *Melody Maker*, July 6 [readers' column], 16.

Peebles, Andy (1981). *The Lennon Tapes. John Lennon and Yoko Ono in Conversation with Andy Peebles 6 December 1980*. London: BBC Publications.

Peyser, Joan (1969). The music of sound or, the Beatles and the Beatless (orig. 1967). In Jonathan Eisen (Ed.), *The Age of Rock: Sounds of American Cultural Revolution* (126–37). New York: Random House.

Philpott, Trevor (1995). Bermondsey miracle (orig. 1957). In Hanif Kureishi & Jon Savage (Eds.), *The Faber Book of Pop* (63–67). London & Boston: Faber and Faber.

Poirier, Richard (1969). Learning from the Beatles (orig. 1967). In Jonathan Eisen (Ed.), *The Age of Rock: Sounds of American Cultural Revolution* (160–79). New York: Random House.

Reynolds, Stanley (1980). The cruel and uncompromising working class hero. *The Guardian*, December 10.

Roberts, Chris (1963a). Pop stars—and marriage. Do wedding bells spell death for the big names?, *Melody Maker*, July 13, 10.

———(1963b). Dead!—that's Liverpool's beat scene, says Gerry Marsden. *Melody Maker*, September 21, 5.

———(1964a). John Lennon. *Melody Maker*, April 4, 3–4.

———(1964b). What next for the Beatles? *Melody Maker*, August 15, 3.

Roylance, Brian, Quance, Julian, Craske, Oliver & Milisic, Roman (Eds.) (2000). *The Beatles Anthology*. San Francisco: Chronicle Books.

Savage, Jon (1995b). This charming man. *Mojo, 15*, 48–50.

Shames, Laurence (1980). John Lennon, where are you? *Esquire*, November, 31–42.

Sheff, David (1981). Playboy interview: John Lennon and Yoko Ono. *Playboy*, January, 75–114, 144.

———(1982). *The Playboy Interviews with John Lennon & Yoko Ono* (orig. 1981). Sevenoaks: New English Library.

Smith, Alan (1963a). Beatles almost threw "Please Please Me" away. *New Musical Express*, March 8, 10.

———(1963b). From You to Us inspired From Me to You. *New Musical Express*, May 10, 10.

———(1963c). Final close-up on a Beatle John Lennon. *New Musical Express*, August 30, 10.

———(1963d). Beatles on holiday. *New Musical Express*, October 11, 3.

———(1963e). Backstage with the Beatles. *New Musical Express*, December 13, 3, 5.

———(1969a). Beatles music straightforward on next album. *New Musical Express*, May 3, 3.

———(1969b). Bore, fool or saint? *New Musical Express*, December 20, 3.

———(1977). "Liverpool audiences are great"says Cliff (orig. 1962). In Bill Harry (Ed.),

Mersey Beat: The Beginnings of the Beatles (44). Facsimile. London: Omnibus Press.

Spencer, Neil (1978). Start the revolution without John Lennon. *New Musical Express,* January 14, 22–23.

Steinem, Gloria (1987). Beatle with a future (orig. 1964). In Elizabeth Thomson & David Gutman (Eds.), *The Lennon Companion. Twenty-five Years of Comment* (31–42). Houndmills & London: Macmillan.

The Sunday Times (1964, April 12). The age of the Scouse.

Sweeting, Adam (1988). A raker's progress. *The Guardian,* December 8.

Thornber, Robin (1990). Are they gonna crucify Lennon? *The Guardian,* May 3.

The Times (1964, February 11). Americans decide the Beatles are harmless.

The Times (1964, July 7). Off-beat film on Beatles.

The Times (1969, March 22). The Lennons applaud the married state.

The Times (1969, December 4). Lennon asked to play Christ.

The Times (1969, December 5). Lennon not to play Christ.

The Times (1980, December 10). The sound of the sixties [Editorial].

Tyler, Andrew (1981). Was Lennon shot to order? *New Musical Express,* January 10, 5–6.

Walsh, Alan (1969). Lack of communication, could that be the trouble? *Melody Maker,* June 14, 7.

Watts, Michael (1971). Lennon. *Melody Maker,* October 2, 24–25.

Wenner, Jann (1980). *Lennon Remembers. The Rolling Stone Interview* (orig. 1971). Harmondsworth: Penguin Books.

Werbin, Stuart (1982). Some time in New York City: Jerry & David & John & Leni & Yoko (orig. 1972). In Jonathan Cott & Christine Doudna (Eds.), *The Ballad of John and Yoko* (126–34). London: A Rolling Stone Press & Michael Joseph.

Williams, Richard (1988). With a little help from his friends? *The Times,* August 10.

Wilson, Cecil (1964). Merseybeat Marxes! *Daily Mail,* July 7.

Wilson, James (1969). John Lennon sends his MBE back to the Queen. *Daily Mirror,* November 26.

Wolfe, Tom (1976). The me decade and the third great awakening. *New York Magazine,* August 23, 26–40.

———(1987). A highbrow under all that hair? (orig. 1964). In Elizabeth Thomson & David Gutman (Eds.), *The Lennon Companion. Twenty-five Years of Comment* (44–47). Houndmills & London: Macmillan.

Wood, Michael (1987). John Lennon's schooldays (orig. 1968). In Elizabeth Thomson & David Gutman (Eds.), *The Lennon Companion. Twenty-five Years of Comment* (145–49). Houndmills & London: Macmillan.

Yorke, Ritchie (1982a). Boosting peace: John and Yoko in Canada (orig. 1969). In Jonathan Cott & Christine Doudna (Eds.), *The Ballad of John and Yoko* (56–58). London: A Rolling Stone Press & Michael Joseph.

———(1982b). John, Yoko and year one (orig. 1970). In Jonathan Cott & Christine Doudna (Eds.), *The Ballad of John and Yoko* (58–73). London: A Rolling Stone Press & Michael Joseph.

Zec, Donald (1963). The big beat craze! Four frenzied Little Lord Fauntleroys who are making £5,000 every week. The Beatles. *Daily Mirror,* September 10.

———(1969). Clown of the year. *Daily Mirror,* December 18.

———(1980). After the sound ... silence. *Daily Mirror,* December 10.

Sound Recordings

The Beatles (1963). *With the Beatles*. Parlophone. PMC 1206.

———(1967). *Sgt. Pepper's Lonely Hearts Club Band*. Parlophone. PCS 7027.

———(1994). *Live at the BBC*. Apple. 7243 8 31796 2 6.

———(1995). *Rare Photos & Interview CD, vol. 1*. MasterTone Multimedia. JG 001-2.

Lennon, John & Ono, Yoko (1968). *Unfinished Music No. 1: Two Virgins*. Apple. T-5001.

———(1969). *Wedding Album*. Apple. Sapcor 13.

Lennon, John & Plastic Ono Band & Elephant's Memory (1972). *Some Time in New York City*. Apple. PCSP 716.

Ono, Yoko (1973). *Approximately Infinite Universe*. Apple. SAPDO 1001.

The Plastic Ono Band (1969). *Live Peace in Toronto*. Apple Core 2001.

Audiovisual Material

Bryant, Gerard (Director) (1957). *The Tommy Steele Story* [film]. Produced by Insignia/ Herbert Smith.

Laszlo, Andrew (Director) (1965). The *Beatles at Shea Stadium* [television film]. Produced by Sullivan Productions, Inc./NEMS Enterprises Ltd./Subafilms Ltd./Bob Precht. First screened by the BBC, March 1, 1966.

Lester, Richard (Director) (1964). *A Hard Day's Night* [film]. Produced by Proscenium Films/Walter Shenson.

———(Director) (1965). *Help!* [film]. Produced by Walter Shenson.

———(Director & Producer) (1967). *How I Won the War* [film].

Morgan, Brian (Director) (1996, March 20). *The Car's the Star: Rolls-Royce Silver Cloud*. Produced by the BBC/Jon Bentley. Screened by BBC 2, March 20, 1996.

Ono, Yoko, Lennon, John, Meola, Gerard & Purcell, Steve (Directors) (1992). *The John Lennon Video Collection*. Produced by A Picture Music International/Martin R. Smith, Gerard Meola, Stanley Dorfmen.

Pennebaker, D. A. (Director) (1967). *Don't Look Back* [film]. Produced by John Court Leacock & Pennebaker, Inc./Albert Grossman.

———(Director) (1988). *Sweet Toronto* [film]. Filmed at Toronto Rock and Roll Revival 1969. Produced by Kenneth C. Walker & Thor Eaton.

Pugsley, Dennis (Director) (1994). *Behind the Beat. Vintage Footage of the Fab Four* [video film]. Produced by Ray Santilli & Dennis Pugsley. MER1 002.

Solt, Andrew (Director) (1988). *Imagine John Lennon. The Definitive Film Portrait* [film]. Produced by Warner Bros, Inc./David L. Wolper & Andrew Solt.

Wonfor, Geoff (Director). (1996a). *The Beatles Anthology 1* [video film]. Produced by Apple Corps Limited/Chips Chipperfield. MVN 4916263.

———(Director). (1996b). *The Beatles Anthology 2* [video film]. Produced by Apple Corps Limited/Chips Chipperfield. MVN 4916273.

———(Director). (1996c). *The Beatles Anthology 3* [video film]. Produced by Apple Corps Limited/Chips Chipperfield. MVN 4916283.

———(Director). (1996d). *The Beatles Anthology 5* [video film]. Produced by Apple Corps Limited/Chips Chipperfield. MVN 4916303.

Electronic Documents

Choukri, Sam (1997, March 30). *Cease & Desist*. Retrieved July 11, 1997, from http://www.bagism.com/library/cease-n-desist.html.

Dial-the-Truth Ministries. *Rock Music—Premature Death of Rock Stars* (2001). Retrieved November 1, 2001, from http://www.av1611.org/rockdead.html

Homer, Rob (1998). *Imagine*. Retrieved April 8, 1998, from http://mypage.direct.ca/r/rhomer/rob.html.

King of Marigold (1998, February 24). [Untitled review]. Retrieved April 8, 1998, from http://www.bagism.com/library/book-reviews.html.

Vanderbilt Television News Archive (1997). News for 1980. Retrieved November 18, 1997, from http://tvnews.vanderbilt.edu/1980a.html.

What Do You Think? (1998, February 26). Retrieved April 8, 1998, from http://cgi.dreamscape.com/southrup/page-closings.html.

Secondary Sources

Biographies, Memoirs, Literature on John Lennon and the Beatles and Other General Writings

Aitken, Jonathan (1967). *The Young Meteors*. London: Secker & Warburg.

Badman, Keith (2001). *The Beatles Diary. Volume 2: After the Break-Up, 1970–2001*. London: Omnibus Press.

Bedford, Carol (1984). *Waiting for the Beatles. An Apple Scruff's Story*. Poole: Blandford Press.

Belz, Carl (1969). *The Story of Rock*. New York: Oxford University Press.

Booker, Christopher (1992). *The Neophiliacs. The Revolution in English Life in the Fifties and Sixties* (orig. 1969). London: Pimlico.

Boone, Pat (1960). *Mellan tolv och tjugo*. Orig. *'Twixt Twelve and Twenty* (1958). Astrid Borger (Trans.). Stockholm: AB Lindqvist Förlag.

Braun, Michael (1995). *Love Me Do! The Beatles' Progress* (orig. 1964). London: Penguin Books.

Bresler, Fenton (1989). *Who Killed John Lennon?* New York: St. Martin's Press.

Brocken, Mike (2000). Coming out of the rhetoric of "Merseybeat": Conversation with Joe Flannery. In Ian Inglis (Ed.), *The Beatles, Popular Music and Society. A Thousand Voices* (23–34). Houndmills & London: Macmillan.

Brown, Peter & Gaines, Steven (1983). *The Love You Make. An Insider's Story of the Beatles*. London: Pan Books.

Burn, Gordon & Tennant, John (1983). The long and winding road. *The Sunday Times Magazine*, February 27, 11–27.

Christgau, Robert (1987). Symbolic comrades (orig. 1981). In Elizabeth Thomson & David Gutman (Eds.), *The Lennon Companion. Twenty-five Years of Comment* (226–31). Houndmills & London: Macmillan.

Christgau, Robert & Piccarella, John (1982). Portrait of the artist as a rock & roll star. In Jonathan Cott & Christine Doudna (Eds.), *The Ballad of John and Yoko* (240–60). London: A Rolling Stone Press & Michael Joseph.

Clayson, Alan & Sutcliffe, Pauline (1994). *Backbeat. Stuart Sutcliffe: The Lost Beatle.* London: Pan Books.

Clifford, Steve (1999). Chasing the shadow of John's (in)famous Rolls-Royce Phantom V. *Beatlology*, November/December, 5–14.

Cloonan, Martin (2000). You can't do that: The Beatles, artistic freedom and censorship. In Ian Inglis (Ed.), *The Beatles, Popular Music and Society. A Thousand Voices* (126–49). Houndmills & London: Macmillan.

Cohen, Sara (1997b). Liverpool and the Beatles: Exploring relations between music and place, text and context. In David Schwarz, Anahid Kassabian and Lawrence Siegel (Eds.), *Keeping Score. Music, Disciplinarity, Culture* (90–106). Charlottesville & London: University Press of Virginia.

Cohn, Nik (1972). *AWopBopALooBopALopBamBoom. Pop from the Beginning* (orig. 1969). London: Paladin.

Coleman, Ray (1988). *John Lennon* (orig. 1984). London & Sydney: Futura.

————(1989). *Brian Epstein. The Man Who Made the Beatles.* London: Viking.

Compton, Todd (1988). McCartney or Lennon?: Beatle myths and the composing of the Lennon-McCartney songs. *Journal of Popular Culture*, 22 (2), 99–131.

Dallas, Karl (1971). *Singers of an Empty Day. Last Sacraments for the Superstars.* Birkenhead: Kahn & Averill.

Davies, Hunter (1968). *The Beatles. The Authorised Biography.* London: Heinemann.

Davis, Andy (1998). *The Beatles Files.* Godalming: Bramley Books.

DiLello, Richard (1973). *The Longest Cocktail Party.* London: Charisma Books.

Draper, Alfred, Austin, John & Edgington, Harry (1976). *The Story of the Goons.* London: Severn House.

Du Noyer, Paul (1997). *We All Shine On. The Stories behind Every John Lennon Song 1970–80.* Dubai: Carlton Books.

Ehrenreich, Barbara, Hess, Elizabeth & Jacobs, Gloria (1992). Beatlemania: girls just want to have fun. In Lisa A. Lewis (Ed.), *The Adoring Audience. Fan Culture and Popular Media* (84–106). London & New York: Routledge.

Einbrodt, Ulrich D. (2001). The Beatles in the internet: An analysis of the presentation of the Beatles in the world wide web. In Yrjö Heinonen, Marcus Heuger, Sheila Whiteley, Terhi Nurmesjärvi & Jouni Koskimäki (Eds.), *Beatlestudies 3. Proceedings of the Beatles 2000 Conference* (57–68). Jyväskylä: University of Jyväskylä.

Elliott, Anthony (1999). *The Mourning of John Lennon.* Berkeley: University of California Press.

Epstein, Brian (1981). *A Cellarful of Noise* (orig. 1964). London: New English Library.

Evans, Mike (1987). The arty teddy boy. In Elizabeth Thomson & David Gutman (Eds.), *The Lennon Companion. Twenty-five Years of Comment* (14–20). Houndmills & London: Macmillan.

Fawcett, Anthony (1980). *One Day at the Time. A Personal Biography of the Seventies* (orig. 1976). London: New English Library.

Fogo, Fred (1994). *I Read the News Today. The Social Drama of John Lennon's Death.* London: Littlefield Adams Quality Paperbacks.

Garbarini, Vic & Cullman, Brian (1980). *Strawberry Fields Forever: John Lennon Remembered.* New York: Bantam Books.

Geller, Deborah (2000). *The Brian Epstein Story.* Anthony Wall (Ed.). London: Faber and Faber.

Giuliano, Geoffrey (2001). *Lennon in America. 1971–1980, Based in Part on the Lost Lennon Diaries*. London: Robson Books.

Giuliano, Geoffrey & Giuliano, Brenda (1995). *The Lost Beatles Interviews*. London: Virgin.

———(1998). *The Lost Lennon Interviews* (orig. 1996). London: Omnibus Press.

Goldman, Albert (1981). *Elvis*. New York: McGraw-Hill.

———(1988). *The Lives of John Lennon*. New York: William Morrow.

Guralnick, Peter (1994). *Last Train to Memphis: The Rise of Elvis Presley*. Boston: Back Bay Books.

Hampton, Wayne (1986). *Guerrilla Minstrels: John Lennon, Joe Hill, Woody Guthrie, and Bob Dylan*. Knoxville: University of Tennessee Press.

Harry, Bill (1984). *Paperback Writers. The History of the Beatles in Print*. London: Virgin.

———(1985). *Beatles for Sale. The Beatles Memorabilia Guide*. London: Virgin.

———(1992). *The Ultimate Beatles Encyclopedia*. London: Virgin.

———(2000). *The John Lennon Encyclopedia*. London: Virgin.

Hertsgaard, Mark (1995). *A Day in the Life. The Music and Artistry of the Beatles*. London: Macmillan.

Hoberman, J. (1982). The films of John and Yoko. In Jonathan Cott & Christine Doudna (Eds.), *The Ballad of John and Yoko* (261–71). London: A Rolling Stone Press & Michael Joseph.

Hopkins, Jerry (1987). *Yoko Ono*. London: Sidgwick & Jackson.

Howlett, Kevin (1996). *The Beatles at the BBC. The Radio Years 1962–1970*. London: BBC Books.

Howlett, Kevin & Lewisohn, Mark (1990). *In My Life. John Lennon Remembered*. London: BBC Books.

Hutchins, Chris & Thompson, Peter (1996). *Elvis vastaan Beatles*. Orig. *Elvis Meets the Beatles* (1994). Jukka Jääskeläinen (Trans.). Jyväskylä & Helsinki: Gummerus.

Huxley, Aldous (1973). *The Doors of Perception and Heaven and Hell*. Harmondsworth & Ringwood: Penguin Books.

Inglis, Ian (1995). Conformity, status and innovation: The accumulation and utilization of idiosyncrasy credits in the career of the Beatles. *Popular Music and Society, 19* (3), 41–74.

———(1996). Synergies and reciprocities: The dynamics of musical and professional interaction between the Beatles and Bob Dylan. *Popular Music and Society, 20* (4), 53–79.

———(2000a). Introduction: A thousand voices. In Ian Inglis (Ed.), *The Beatles, Popular Music and Society. A Thousand Voices* (xv–xxii). Houndmills & London: Macmillan.

———(2000b). Men of ideas? Popular music, anti-intellectualism and the Beatles. In Ian Inglis (Ed.), *The Beatles, Popular Music and Society. A Thousand Voices* (1–22). Houndmills & London: Macmillan.

Jones, Jack (1994). *Let Me Take You Down. Inside the Mind of Mark David Chapman, The Man Who Killed John Lennon* (orig. 1992). London: Virgin Books.

Koski, Markku (1986). *Beatles. Erään yhtyeen anatomia*. Helsinki: Love Kirjat.

Larkin, Colin (1998). *All-time Top 1000 Albums*. London: Virgin.

Leigh, Stephen (1984). *Let's Go Down the Cavern. The Story of Liverpool's Merseybeat*. London: Vermilion.

Lennon, Cynthia (1980). *A Twist of Lennon* (orig. 1978). London: A Star Book.

Leslie, Peter (1965). *Fab. The Anatomy of a Phenomenon*. London: MacGibbon & Kee.

Levin, Bernard (1989). *The Pendulum Years. Britain and the Sixties* (orig. 1970). Sevenoaks: Sceptre.
Lewisohn, Mark (1988). *The Complete Beatles Recording Sessions. The Official Story of the Abbey Road Years*. London: Hamlyn.
———(1996). *The Complete Beatles Chronicle* (orig. 1992). London: Chancellor Press.
Mabey, Richard (1969). *The Pop Process*. London: Hutchinson Educational.
MacDonald, Ian (1995). *Revolution in the Head. The Beatles' Records and the Sixties* (orig. 1994). London: Pimlico.
Maitland, Sara (1988). I believe in yesterday—an introduction. In Sara Maitland (Ed.), *Very Heaven. Looking Back at the 1960s* (1–13). London: Virago Press.
Mäkelä, Janne (1999). The outsider within. The Beatles and the re-evaluation of the North in the early 1960s. In Maarit Leskelä (Ed.), *Outsiders or Insiders? Constructing Identities in an Integrating Europe* (126–36). Turku: University of Turku.
———(2001). The greatest story of pop music? Challenges of writing the Beatles history. In Yrjö Heinonen, Marcus Heuger, Sheila Whiteley, Terhi Nurmesjärvi & Jouni Koskimäki (Eds.), *Beatlestudies 3. Proceedings of the Beatles 2000 Conference* (47–55). Jyväskylä: University of Jyväskylä.
Marshall, P. David (2000). The celebrity legacy of the Beatles. In Ian Inglis (Ed.), *The Beatles, Popular Music and Society. A Thousand Voices* (163–75). Houndmills & London: Macmillan.
Martin, Bernice (1981a). Not Marx but Lennon. *Encounter, 56,* 49–51.
Martin, George & Hornsby, Jeremy (1979). *All You Need Is Ears*. New York: St. Martin's Press.
Martin, George & Pearson, William (1995). *The Making of Sgt Pepper* (orig. 1994). London: Pan Books.
McCarthy, Len (2001). Slow down! How the Beatles changed the rhythmic paradigm of pop & rock. In Yrjö Heinonen, Marcus Heuger, Sheila Whiteley, Terhi Nurmesjärvi & Jouni Koskimäki (Eds.), *Beatlestudies 3. Proceedings of the Beatles 2000 Conference* (215–30). Jyväskylä: University of Jyväskylä.
McDevitt, Chas (1997). *Skiffle. The Definitive Inside Story*. London: Robson Books.
Melly, George (1970). *Revolt into Style. Pop Arts in Britain*. London: Allen Lane.
———(1977). *Owning-Up* (orig. 1965). Harmondsworth: Penguin Books.
Meltzer, Richard (1970). *The Aesthetics of Rock*. New York: Something Else Press.
Miles, Barry (1998). *Paul McCartney. Many Years from Now* (orig. 1997). London: Vintage.
———(2000). Nemesis! *Mojo Special Edition*, Winter, 100–103.
Milligan, Spike (1974). *More Goon Show Scripts* (orig. 1973). London: Sphere Books.
Mitchell, Carolyn Lee & Munn, Michael (1988). *All Our Loving. A Beatles Fan's Memoir*. London: Robson Books.
Moore, Allan F. (1998). *The Beatles: Sgt. Pepper's Lonely Hearts Club Band* (orig. 1997). Cambridge: Cambridge University Press.
Morris, Jan (1982). In Liverpool. In Jonathan Cott & Christine Doudna (Eds.), *The Ballad of John and Yoko* (2–13). London: A Rolling Stone Press & Michael Joseph.
Muncie, John (2000). The Beatles and the spectacle of youth. In Ian Inglis (Ed.), *The Beatles, Popular Music and Society. A Thousand Voices* (35–52). Houndmills & London: Macmillan.
Napier-Bell, Simon (1982). *You Don't Have to Say You Love Me*. Sevenoaks: New English Library.

Norman, Philip (1982). *Shout! The Beatles in Their Generation* (orig. 1981). New York: Warner Books.

Nurmesjärvi, Terhi (2000). Liverpudlian identity of the early Beatles (1957–62). In Yrjö Heinonen, Jouni Koskimäki, Seppo Niemi & Terhi Nurmesjärvi (Eds.), *Beatlestudies 2. History, Identity, Authenticity* (87–110). Jyväskylä: University of Jyväskylä.

Nuttall, Jeff (1968). *Bomb Culture*. London: MacGibbon & Kee.

Pang, May & Edwards, Henry (1983). *Loving John*. New York: Warner.

Reising, Russell (Ed.) (2002). *"Every Sound There Is." The Beatles' Revolver and the Transformation of Rock and Roll*. Aldershot & Burlington: Ashgate.

Riley, Tim (1988). *Tell Me Why: A Beatles Commentary*. London: The Bodley Head.

Robertson, John (1990). *The Art & Music of John Lennon*. London: Omnibus Press.

Rockwell, John (1982). Rock and avant-garde: John and Yoko's record collaborations. In Jonathan Cott & Christine Doudna (Eds.), *The Ballad of John and Yoko* (272–77). London: A Rolling Stone Press & Michael Joseph.

Rogan, Johnny (1991). *Timeless Flight. The Definitive Biography of the Byrds* (orig. 1990). Brentwood: Square One Books.

———(1997). *The Complete Guide to the Music of John Lennon*. London: Omnibus Press.

Rollins, Hillary (1998). He loves you (yeah, yeah, yeah). In Robert Cording, Shelli Jankowski-Smith & E. J. Miller Laino (Eds.), *In My Life. Encounters with the Beatles* (142–48). New York: Fromm.

Roos, Michael E. (1984). The walrus and the deacon: John Lennon's debt to Lewis Carroll. *Journal of Popular Culture, 18* (1), 19–29.

Rosen, Robert (2000). *Nowhere Man. The Final Days of John Lennon*. London: Fusion Press.

Schaffner, Nicholas (1978). *The Beatles Forever*. New York: McGraw–Hill.

———(1982). *The British Invasion: From the First Wave to the New Wave*. New York et al.: McGraw–Hill.

Shelton, Robert (1986). *No Direction Home: The Life and Music of Bob Dylan*. New York: Beech Tree Books.

Shotton, Pete & Schaffner, Nicholas (1983). *John Lennon in My Life*. New York: Stein & Day.

Sinyard, Neil (1987). The English army had just won the war. In Elizabeth Thomson & David Gutman (Eds.), *The Lennon Companion. Twenty-five Years of Comment* (126–37). Houndmills & London: Macmillan.

Southall, Brian, Vince, Peter & Rouse, Allan (1997). *Abbey Road. The Story of the World's Most Famous Recording Studios*. London: Omnibus Press.

Sullivan, Henry W. (1995). *The Beatles with Lacan: Rock & Roll as Requiem for the Modern Age*. New York: Peter Lang.

Taylor, Derek (1974). *As Time Goes By* (orig. 1973). London: Sphere Books.

———(1987). *It Was Twenty Years Ago Today*. New York: Bantam Books.

Turner, Steve (1996). *Kovan päivän kirja. Kaikkien Beatles-laulujen tarinat*. Orig. *A Hard Day's Write. The Stories behind Every Beatles' Song* (1994). Timo Kanerva (Trans.). Helsinki: Tammi.

Whitcomb, Ian (1983). *Rock Odyssey. A Musician's Chronicle of the Sixties*. New York: Dolphin Books.

Wiener, Jon (1985). *Come Together: John Lennon in His Time* (orig. 1984). London & Boston: Faber and Faber.

———(2000). *Gimme Some Truth. The John Lennon FBI Files*. Berkeley: University of California Press.

Willett, John (1967). *Art in a City*. London: Methuen & Co.
Williams, Alan & Marshall, William (1976). *The Man Who Gave the Beatles Away* (orig. 1975). Sevenoaks & London: Coronet Books.
Wilmut, Roger & Grafton, Jimmy (1976). *The Goon Show Companion*. London: Robson Books.

Research Literature

Adorno, Theodor W. (1990). On popular music (orig. 1941). In Simon Frith & Andrew Goodwin (Eds.), *On Record. Rock, Pop, and the Written Word* (301–14). London: Routledge.
Alberoni, Francesco (1972). The powerless "elite": Theory and sociological research on the phenomenon of the stars. Orig. L'Elite irresponsable; théorie et recherche sociologique sur le divismo (1962). In Denis McQuail (Ed. & Trans.), *Sociology of Mass Communications* (75–98). Harmondsworth: Penguin Books.
Anderson, Dennis (1981). *The Hollow Horn. Bob Dylan's Reception in the United States and Germany*. München: Hobo Press.
Archer, Robyn & Simmonds, Diana (1986). *A Star Is Torn*. London: Virago Press.
Attali, Jacques (1985). *Noise. The Political Economy of Music*. Orig. *Bruits: essai sur l'économie politique de la musique* (1977). Brian Massumi (Trans.). Manchester: Manchester University Press.
Bacon, Tony (1981). *Rock Hardware. Instruments, Equipment and Technology of Rock*. Poole: Blandford Press.
Badinter, Elisabeth (1995). *XY: On Masculine Identity*. Orig. *XY. De l'identitee masculine* (1992). Lydia Davis (Trans.). New York: Columbia University Press.
Balliger, Robin (1999). Politics. In Bruce Horner & Thomas Swiss (Eds.), *Key Terms in Popular Music and Culture* (57–70). Malden & Oxford: Blackwell.
Barnard, Stephen (1996). In a week, maybe two, we'll make you a star (orig. 1974). In Charlie Gillett & Simon Frith (Eds.), *The Beat Goes On. The Rock File Reader* (120–31). London & East Haven: Pluto Press.
Bayles, Martha (1994). *Hole in Our Soul. The Loss of Beauty and Meaning in American Popular Music*. New York: The Free Press.
Beauvoir, Simone de (1964). *The Second Sex*. Orig. *Le deuxième sexe* (1949). H. M. Parshley (Trans. & Ed.). New York: Bantam Books.
Benjamin, Walter (1970). *Illuminations. Essays & Reflections*. Orig. *Schriften* (1958). Hannah Arendt (Ed. & Introduction), Harry Zohn (Trans.). London: Jonathan Cape.
Berman, Marshall (1971). *The Politics of Authenticity. Radical Individualism and the Emergence of Modern Society*. London: George Allen & Unwin.
Boorstin, Daniel J. (1977). *The Image. A Guide to Pseudo-Events in America*. Orig. *The Image, or What Happened to the American Dream* (1961). New York: Atheneum.
Boyd, Tom W. (1988). Clowns, innocent outsiders in the sanctuary: A phenomenology of sacred folly. *Journal of Popular Culture*, 22 (3), 101–9.
Bradley, Dick (1992). *Understanding Rock 'n' Roll. Popular Music in Britain 1955–1964*. Buckingham & Philadelphia: Open University Press.
Braudy, Leo (1986). *The Frenzy of Renown: Fame and Its History*. New York & Oxford: Oxford University Press.
Burke, Peter (1997). *Varieties of Cultural History*. Cambridge: Polity Press.
Cable, Michael (1977). *The Pop Music Industry Inside Out*. London: W.H. Allen.

Campbell, Colin (1987). *The Romantic Ethic and the Spirit of Modern Consumerism*. Oxford & New York: Basil Blackwell.

Cantwell, Robert (1996). *When We Were Good: The Folk Revival*. Cambridge & London: Harvard University Press.

Carlyle, Thomas (1983). *On Heroes, Hero Worship, and the Heroic in History* (orig. 1840/ 1908). New York: Chelsea House.

Carpenter, Humphrey (2000). *That Was Satire That Was. The Satire Boom of the 1960s*. London: Victor Gollancz.

Carrigan, Tim, Connell, Bob & Lee, John (1985). Toward a new sociology of masculinity. *Theory and Society, 14* (5), 551–604.

Caughie, John, with Kevin Rockett (1996). *The Companion to the British and Irish Cinema*. London: Cassell and British Film Institute.

Cavicchi, Daniel (1998). *Tramps Like Us: Music and Meaning among Springsteen Fans*. New York & Oxford: Oxford University Press.

Chambers, Iain (1985). *Urban Rhythms. Pop Music and Popular Culture*. London: Macmillan.

———(1987). British pop: Some tracks from the other side of the record. In James Lull (Ed.), *Popular Music and Communication* (231–43). Newbury Park: Sage.

Chapple, Steve & Garofalo, Reebee (1978). *Rock 'n' Roll Is Here to Pay: The History and Politics of the Music Industry* (orig. 1977). Chicago: Nelson-Hall.

Charyn, Jerome (1986). *Metropolis: New York as Myth, Marketplace, and Magical Land*. New York: Avon Books.

Chevigny, Paul (1991). *Gigs: Jazz and the Cabaret Laws in New York City*. New York & London: Routledge.

Clarke, Gary (1990). Defending ski-jumpers: A critique of theories of youth subcultures (orig. 1981). In Simon Frith & Andrew Goodwin (Eds.), *On Record. Rock, Pop, and the Written Word* (81–96). London: Routledge.

Clayson, Alan (1996). *Beat Merchants. The Origins, History, Impact and Rock Legacy of the 1960s British Pop Groups*. London: Blandford.

Coates, Norma (1997). (R)evolution now? Rock and the political potential of gender. In Sheila Whiteley (Ed.), *Sexing the Groove: Popular Music and Gender* (50–64). London & New York: Routledge.

Coffman, James T. (1972). So you want to be a rock and roll star! In R. Serge Denisoff & Richard A. Peterson (Eds.), *The Sounds of Social Change: Studies in Popular Culture* (261–73). Chicago: Rand McNally & Company.

Cohen, David (1990). *Being a Man*. London: Routledge.

Cohen, Sara (1991). *Rock Culture in Liverpool. Popular Music in the Making*. Oxford: Clarendon Press.

———(1994). Identity, place and the "Liverpool sound". In Martin Stokes (Ed.), *Ethnicity, Identity and Music. The Musical Construction of Place* (117–34). Oxford & Providence: Berg.

———(1997a). From the street to the museum: Popular music ethnography in the city. Unpublished lecture paper. Rock as Research Field, Ph. D. course at Magleås, Denmark.

———(1997c). Men making a scene: Rock music and the production of gender. In Sheila Whiteley (Ed.), *Sexing the Groove: Popular Music and Gender* (17–36). London & New York: Routledge.

Connell, R. W. (1995). *Masculinities*. London: Polity Press.

Cooper, B. Lee (1997). Wise men never try: A discography of fool songs, 1945–1995. *Popular Music and Society, 21* (2), 115–31.

Copeland, Peter (1991). *Sound Recordings*. London: The British Library.

Corson, Richard (1967). *Fashions in Eyeglasses. From the 14th Century to the Present Day*. London: Peter Owen.

Craik, Jennifer (1994). *The Face of Fashion: Cultural Studies in Fashion*. London & New York: Routledge.

Crisell, Andrew (1994). *Understanding Radio*. London & New York: Routledge.

Cunningham, Mark (1999). *Live & Kicking. The Rock Concert Industry in the Nineties*. London: Sanctuary.

Curtis, Jim (1987). *Rock Eras: Interpretations of Music and Society, 1954–1984*. Bowling Green, Ohio: Bowling Green State University Popular Press.

Dahlhaus, Carl (1985). *Foundations of Music History*. Orig. *Grundlagen der Musikgeschichte* (1977). J. B. Robinson (Trans.). Cambridge et al.: Cambridge University Press.

deCordova, Richard (1990). *Picture Personalities: The Emergence of the Star System in America*. Urbana: University of Illinois Press.

Denselow, Robin (1989). *When the Music's Over: The Story of Political Pop*. London & Boston: Faber and Faber.

Dyer, Richard (1986). *Stars* (orig. 1979). London: British Film Institute.

Easthope, Antony (1992). *What a Man's Gotta Do: The Masculine Myth in Popular Culture* (orig. 1986). New York & London: Routledge.

Edmands, Bob (1996). Have pity for the rich (orig. 1975). In Charlie Gillett & Simon Frith (Eds.), *The Beat Goes on. The Rock File Reader* (132–40). London & East Haven: Pluto Press.

Ellis, John (1988). *Visible Fictions: Cinema: Television: Video* (orig. 1982). London & New York: Routledge.

Emerson, Ralph Waldo (1950). *The Complete Essays and Other Writings*. New York: Modern Library.

Erasmus of Rotterdam (1980). *Praise of Folly and Letter to Martin Dorp 1515*. Orig. *Moriae Encomium* (1509). Betty Radice (Trans., with an introduction), A. H. T. Levi (notes). Aylesbury: Penguin Books.

Evans, Andrew & Wilson, Glenn D. (1999). *Fame. The Psychology of Stardom*. London: Vision.

Everett, Peter (1986). *You'll Never Be 16 Again. An Illustrated History of the British Teenager*. London: BBC Publications.

Eyerman, Ron (1994). *Between Culture and Politics. Intellectuals in Modern Society*. Cambridge: Polity Press.

Fine, Gary Alan (1987). One of the boys: Women in male-dominated settings. In Michael S. Kimmel (Ed.), *Changing Men. New Directions in Research on Men and Masculinity* (131–47). Newbury Park: Sage.

Finnegan, Ruth (1989). *The Hidden Musicians. Music-Making in an English Town*. Cambridge: Cambridge University Press.

Fiske, John (1982). *Introduction to Communication Studies*. London: Methuen.

Fornäs, Johan (1995). The future of rock: Discourses that struggle to define a genre. *Popular Music, 14* (1), 111–25.

Foster, Mo (1997). *Seventeen Watts? The First 20 Years of British Rock Guitar, the Musicians and Their Stories*. London: Sanctuary.

Fountain, Nigel (1988). *Underground. The London Alternative Press 1966–74*. London &

New York: Routledge.

Fowles, Jib (1992). *Starstruck: Celebrity Performers and the American Public*. Washington & London: Smithsonian Institution Press.

Frith, Simon (1978). *The Sociology of Rock*. London: Constable.

———(1981). "The magic that can set you free": The ideology of folk and the myth of the rock community. In Richard Middleton & David Horn (Eds.), *Popular Music 1. Folk or Popular? Distinctions, Influences, Continuities* (159–68). Cambridge: Cambridge University Press.

———(1984). *Sound Effects. Youth, Leisure, and the Politics of Rock 'n' Roll* (orig. 1983). London: Constable.

———(1986). Art versus technology: The strange case of popular music. *Media, Culture and Society, 8* (3), 263–79.

———(1987). The making of the British record industry 1920–1964. In James Curran, Anthony Smith & Pauline Wingate (Eds.), *Impacts and Influences: Essays on Media Power in the Twentieth Century* (278–90). London: Methuen.

———(1988a). Oh boy! In Simon Frith, *Music for Pleasure. Essays in the Sociology of Pop* (169–70). Cambridge & Oxford: Polity Press.

———(1988b). Why do songs have words? In Simon Frith, *Music for Pleasure. Essays in the Sociology of Pop* (105–28). Cambridge & Oxford: Polity Press.

———(1988c). Video pop: Picking up the pieces. In Simon Frith (Ed.), *Facing the Music* (88–130). New York: Pantheon Books.

———(1996a). Introduction—backward and forward. In Charlie Gillett & Simon Frith (Eds.), *The Beat Goes On. The Rock File Reader* (1–8). London & East Haven: Pluto Press.

———(1996b). The A&R men. In Charlie Gillett & Simon Frith (Eds.), *The Beat Goes On. The Rock File Reader* (93–107). London & East Haven: Pluto Press.

———(2001). The popular music industry. In Simon Frith, Will Straw & John Street (Eds.), *The Cambridge Companion to Pop and Rock* (26–52). Cambridge: Cambridge University Press.

Frith, Simon & Horne, Howard (1987). *Art into Pop*. London & New York: Methuen.

Frith, Simon & McRobbie, Angela (1990). Rock and sexuality (orig. 1978). In Simon Frith & Andrew Goodwin (Eds.), *On Record. Rock, Pop, and the Written Word* (371–89). London: Routledge.

Gaar, Gillian G. (1993). *She's a Rebel. The History of Women in Rock & Roll*. London: Blandford.

Gendron, Bernard (1986). Theodor Adorno meets the Cadillacs. In Tania Modleski (Ed.), *Studies in Entertainment. Critical Approaches to Mass Culture* (272–308). Bloomington: Indiana University Press.

Gillett, Charlie (1973). *The Sound of the City. The Rise of Rock 'n' Roll* (orig. 1970). New York: Dell.

Gitlin, Todd (1987). *The Sixties: Years of Hope, Days of Rage*. New York: Bantam Books.

Gledhill, Christine (1991). Signs of melodrama. In Christine Gledhill (Ed.), *Stardom: Industry of Desire* (207–29). London & New York: Routledge.

Goodwin, Andrew (1990). Sample and hold: Pop music in the digital age of reproducing. In Simon Frith & Andrew Goodwin (Eds.), *On Record. Rock, Pop and the Written Word* (258–73). London: Routledge.

———(1992). Rationalization and democratization in the new technologies of popular music. In James Lull (Ed.), *Popular Music and Communication,* (2nd ed.) (75–100).

Newbury Park: Sage.

———(1993). *Dancing in the Distraction Factory*. London: Routledge.

Gronow, Pekka & Saunio, Ilpo (1998). *An International History of the Recording Industry*. Orig. *Äänilevyn historia* (1990). Christopher Moseley (Trans.). London & New York: Cassell.

Grossberg, Lawrence (1992a). Is there a fan in the house?: The affective sensibility of fandom. In Lisa A. Lewis (Ed.), *The Adoring Audience: Fan Culture and Popular Media* (50–65). London: Routledge.

———(1992b). *We Gotta Get out of This Place: Popular Conservatism and Postmodern Culture*. New York & London: Routledge.

———(1994). Is anybody listening? Does anybody care? On "the state of rock". In Andrew Ross & Tricia Rose (Eds.), *Microphone Fiends: Youth Music & Youth Culture* (41–58). New York & London: Routledge.

Grossberg, Lawrence, Wartella, Ellen & Whitney, D. Charles (1998). *MediaMaking: Mass Media in a Popular Culture*. Thousand Oaks, Calif.: Sage.

Grossman, Loyd (1976). *A Social History of Rock Music from the Greaser to Glitter Rock*. New York: David McKay.

Hall, Stuart & Whannel, Paddy (1990). The young audience (orig. 1964). In Simon Frith & Andrew Goodwin (Eds.), *On Record. Rock, Pop and the Written Word* (27–37). London: Routledge.

Harker, Dave (1980). *One for the Money. Politics and Popular Song*. London et al.: Hutchinson.

———(1992). Still crazy after all these years: What was popular music in the 1960s? In Bart Moore-Gilbert & John Seed (Eds.), *Cultural Revolution: The Challenge of the Arts in the 1960s* (236–54). London & New York: Routledge.

———(1994). Blood on the tracks: Popular music in the 1970s. In Bart Moore-Gilbert (Ed.), *The Arts in the 1970s: Cultural Closure?* (240–58). London & New York: Routledge.

Hearn, Jeff (1992). *Men in the Public Eye: The Construction and Deconstruction of Public Men and Public Patriarchies*. London & New York: Routledge.

Hebdige, Dick (1983). *Subculture: The Meaning of Style* (orig. 1979). London & New York: Methuen.

———(1988). *Hiding in the Light: On Images and Things*. London & New York: Routledge.

Hester, Marianne (1992). *Lewd Women & Wicked Witches: A Study of the Dynamics of Male Domination*. London & New York: Routledge.

Hewison, Robert (1981). *In Anger. Culture in the Cold War 1945–60*. London: Weidenfeld and Nicolson.

———(1986). *Too Much. Art and Society in the Sixties 1960–1975*. London: Methuen.

Hill, John (1991). Television and pop: The case of the 1950s. In John Corner (Ed.), *Popular Television in Britain. Studies in Cultural History* (90–107). London: British Film Institute.

Hobsbawm, Eric (1989). *The Jazz Scene*. Orig. by "Francis Newton" (1959). London: Weidenfeld and Nicolson.

———(1994). *The Age of Extremes: A History of the World, 1914–1991*. New York: Pantheon Books.

Holden, Len (1998). More than a marque. The car as symbol: Aspects of culture and ideology. In David Thoms, Len Holden & Tim Claydon (Eds.), *The Motor Car and Pop-*

ular Culture in the 20th Century (28–40). Aldershot: Ashgate.

Hoskyns, Barney (1996). *Waiting for the Sun. Strange Days, Weird Scenes, and the Sound of Los Angeles.* New York: St. Martin's Press.

Huyssen, Andreas (1986). *After the Great Divide: Modernism, Mass Culture, Postmodernism.* Bloomington: Indiana University Press.

Immonen, Kari (1996). *Historian läsnäolo.* Turku: University of Turku.

Jasper, Tony (1975). *Jesus in a Pop Culture.* Glasgow: Collins.

Jenkins, Henry (1994). Star Trek rerun, reread, rewritten: Fan writing as textual poaching. In Horace Newcomb (Ed.), *Television: The Critical View* (448–73). New York & Oxford: Oxford University Press.

Jenson, Joli (1992). Fandom as pathology: The consequences of characterization. In Lisa A. Lewis (Ed.), *The Adoring Audience: Fan Culture and Popular Media* (9–29). London & New York: Routledge.

Johnson, Bruce (2000). *The Inaudible Music. Jazz, Gender and Australian Modernity.* Sydney: Currency Press.

Kallioniemi, Kari (1998). *"Put the Needle on the Record and Think of England." Notions of Englishness in the Post-War Debate of British Pop Music.* Unpublished doctoral dissertation. Turku: University of Turku.

Kantorowicz, Ernst H. (1957). *The King's Two Bodies. A Study in Medieval Political Theology.* Princeton, N.J.: Princeton University Press.

Kealy, Edward R. (1990). From craft to art: The case of sound mixers and popular music. (orig. 1979). In Simon Frith & Andrew Goodwin (Eds.), *On Record. Rock, Pop, and the Written Word* (207–20). London: Routledge.

Keightley, Keir (2001). Reconsidering rock. In Simon Frith, Will Straw & John Street (Eds.), *The Cambridge Companion to Pop and Rock* (109–42). Cambridge: Cambridge University Press.

Korhonen, Anu (1999). *Fellows of Infinite Jest. The Fool in Renaissance England.* Unpublished doctoral dissertation. Turku: University of Turku.

Lahr, John (1984). *Automatic Vaudeville. Essays on Star Turns.* London: Heinemann.

Lahusen, Christian (1996). *The Rhetoric of Moral Protest: Public Campaigns, Celebrity Endorsement, and Political Mobilization.* Berlin & New York: Walter de Gruyter.

Laing, Dave (1969). *The Sound of Our Time.* London & Sydney: Sheed and Ward.

Laing, Stuart (1991). Banging in some reality: The original "Z Cars". In John Corner (Ed.), *Popular Television in Britain. Studies in Cultural History* (125–44). London: British Film Institute.

Lasch, Christopher (1984). *The Minimal Self: Psychic Survival in Troubled Times.* New York & London: W. W. Norton.

———(1991). *The Culture of Narcissism: American Life in an Age of Diminishing Expectations* (orig. 1979). New York & London: W. W. Norton.

Lehtonen, Mikko (2000). *The Cultural Analysis of Texts.* A-L. Ahonen & K. Clarke (Trans.). London: Sage.

Lerner, Gerda (1979). *The Minority Finds Its Past: Placing Women in History.* New York: Oxford University Press.

Lévi-Strauss, Claude (1966). *The Savage Mind.* Orig. *La pensée sauvage* (1962). Chicago: University of Chicago Press.

Lewis, Peter (1989). *The Fifties. Portrait of an Age* (orig. 1978). London: The Cupid Press.

Lindberg, Ulf (1997). "La la la la la-la-la la." Making sense of rock lyrics. In *Papers from the Lecturers* (1–22). Unpublished collection of papers. Rock as Research Field,

Ph.D. course at Magleås, Denmark.

London, Herbert I. (1985). *Closing the Circle. A Cultural History of the Rock Revolution* (orig. 1984). Chicago: Nelson-Hall.

Longhurst, Brian (1995). *Popular Music and Society*. Cambridge: Polity Press.

Marcus, Greil (1976). *Mystery Train: Images of America in Rock 'n' Roll Music*. New York: E. P. Dutton.

———(1989). *Lipstick Traces: A Secret History of the Twentieth Century*. Cambridge: Harvard University Press.

———(1992). *Dead Elvis: A Chronicle of a Cultural Obsession*. New York: Penguin Books.

———(1994). Rock death in the 1970s: A sweepstakes (orig. 1979). In Greil Marcus, *Ranters & Crowd Pleasers: Punk in Pop Music 1977–92* (57–78). New York: Anchor Books.

———(1997). *Invisible Republic. Bob Dylan's Basement Tapes*. London: Picador.

Marshall, P. David (1997). *Celebrity and Power: Fame in Contemporary Culture*. Minneapolis: University of Minnesota Press.

Martin, Bernice (1981b). *A Sociology of Contemporary Culture*. Oxford: Basil Blackwell.

McRobbie, Angela (1988). Second-hand dresses and the role of the ragmarket. In Angela McRobbie (Ed.), *Zoot Suits and Second-Hand Dresses: An Anthology of Fashion and Music* (23–49). Boston: Unwin Hyman.

Medhurst, Andy (1995). It sort of happened here: The strange, brief life of the British pop film. In Jonathan Romney & Adrian Wootton (Eds.), *Celluloid Jukebox. Popular Music and the Movies since the 50s* (60–70). London: British Film Institute.

Meisel, Perry (1999). *The Cowboy and the Dandy. Crossing over from Romanticism to Rock and Roll*. New York & Oxford: Oxford University Press.

Metz, Christian (1982). *Psychoanalysis and Cinema. The Imaginary Signifier*. London: Macmillan.

Milestone, Katie (1996). Regional variations: Northernness and new urban economies of hedonism. In Justin O'Connor & Derek Wynne (Eds.), *From the Margins to the Centre. Cultural Production and Consumption in the Post-Industrial City* (91–115). Aldershot: Arena.

Monaco, James (1978). Celebration. In James Monaco (Ed.), *Celebrity: Who Gets It, How They Use It, Why It Works* (3–14). New York: Delta Books.

Moore, Allan F. (1993). *Rock: The Primary Text: Developing a Musicology of Rock*. Buckingham & Philadelphia: Open University Press.

Morin, Edgar (1960). *The Stars. An Account of the Star-System in Motion Pictures*. Orig. Les Stars (1957). Richard Howard (Trans.). New York & London: Grove Press & John Calder.

Murphy, Robert (1992). *Sixties British Cinema*. London: British Film Institute.

Negus, Keith (1996). *Popular Music in Theory. An Introduction*. Cambridge & Oxford: Polity Press.

———(1997). Sinéad O'Connor—musical mother. In Sheila Whiteley (Ed.), *Sexing the Groove: Popular Music and Gender* (178–90). London & New York: Routledge.

Nietzsche, Friedrich (1967). *The Birth of Tragedy* and *The Case of Wagner*. Orig. *Die Geburt der Tragödie* (1872) & *Der Fall Wagner* (1888). Walter Kaufmann (Trans., with commentary). New York: Random House.

Offen, Karen (2000). *European Feminisms, 1700–1950: A Political History*. Stanford, Calif.: Stanford University Press.

Olson, Mark J. V. (1998). "Everybody loves our town": Scenes, spatiality, migrancy. In

Thomas Swiss, John Sloop & Andrew Herman (Eds.), *Mapping the Beat. Popular Music and Contemporary Theory* (269–89). Malden & Oxford: Blackwell.

Packard, Vance (1970). *The Status Seekers* (orig. 1959). New York: Pocket Books.

Palladino, Grace (1996). *Teenagers: An American History*. New York: Basic Books.

Palmer, Tony (1976). *All You Need Is Love. The Story of Popular Music*. Paul Medlicott (Ed.). London: Weidenfeld & Nicolson and Chappell.

Pattison, Robert (1987). *The Triumph of Vulgarity: Rock Music in the Mirror of Romanticism*. New York & Oxford: Oxford University Press.

Peterson, Richard A. (1990). Why 1955? *Popular Music, 9* (1), 97–116.

———(1997). *Creating Country Music: Fabricating Authenticity*. Chicago & London: University of Chicago Press.

Plasketes, George (1997). *Images of Elvis Presley in American Culture 1977–1997: The Mystery Terrain*. New York & London: Harrington Park Press.

Pleck, Joseph H. (1987). American fathering in historical perspectives. In Michael S. Kimmel (Ed.), *Changing Men. New Directions in Research on Men and Masculinity* (83–97). Newbury Park: Sage.

Redhead, Steve (1990). *The-End-of-the-Century Party. Youth and Pop Towards 2000*. Manchester & New York: Manchester University Press.

Reynolds, Simon & Press, Joy (1996). *The Sex Revolts: Gender, Rebellion and Rock 'n' Roll* (orig. 1995). Cambridge: Harvard University Press.

Rodman, Gilbert B. (1996). *Elvis after Elvis. The Posthumous Career of a Living Legend*. London & New York: Routledge.

———(1999). Histories. In Bruce Horner & Thomas Swiss (Eds.), *Key Terms in Popular Music and Culture* (35–45). Malden & Oxford: Blackwell.

Rogan, Johnny (1988). *Starmakers & Svengalis. The History of British Pop Management*. London: Queen Anne Press.

Rogers, Bob & O'Brien, Denis (1975). *Rock 'n' Roll Australia. The Australian Pop Scene 1954–1964*. Stanmore: Cassell Australia.

Roper, Michael & Tosh, John (1991). Historians and the politics of masculinity. In Michael Roper & John Tosh (Eds.), *Manful Assertions: Masculinities in Britain since 1800* (1–24). London & New York: Routledge.

Rowe, David (1995). *Popular Cultures. Rock Music, Sport and the Politics of Pleasure*. London: Sage.

Salmi, Hannu & Suominen, Jaakko (2000). Cultural history of technology. *Tekniikan Waiheita* 4/2000, 5–13.

Sampson, Anthony (1982). *The Changing Anatomy of Britain*. New York: Random House.

Samuel, Raphael (1994). *Theatres of Memory. Volume 1: Past and Present in Contemporary Culture*. London & New York: Verso.

Savage, Jon (1988a). "Do you know how to pony?": The messianic intensity of the sixties (orig. 1982). In Angela McRobbie (Ed.), *Zoot Suits and Second-Hand Dresses. An Anthology of Fashion and Music* (121–31). Boston: Unwin Hyman.

———(1988b). The enemy within: Sex, rock, and identity. In Simon Frith (Ed.), *Facing the Music* (131–72). New York: Pantheon Books.

———(1991). Tainted love: The influence of male homosexuality and sexual divergence on pop music and culture since the war. In Alan Tomlinson (Ed.), *Consumption, Identity, and Style: Marketing, Meanings, and the Packaging of Pleasure* (153–71). London & New York: Routledge.

———(1994). *Psychedelia. A Mojo Music Guide 1*. Presented free with *Mojo*, 6.

————(1995a). Move it! *Mojo, 15,* 36–55, 61–62.

————(1995c). The simple things you see are all complicated. In Hanif Kureishi & Jon Savage (Eds.), *The Faber Book of Pop* (xxi–xxxiii). London & Boston: Faber and Faber.

————(1996a). Delicious surrender: British psychedelia (orig. 1994). In Jon Savage, *Time Travel. From the Sex Pistols to Nirvana: Pop, Media and Sexuality, 1977–96* (349–51). London: Chatto & Windus.

————(1996b). Pulp! The history of fan magazines (orig. 1977). In Jon Savage, *Time Travel. From the Sex Pistols to Nirvana: Pop, Media and Sexuality, 1977–96* (20–24). London: Chatto & Windus.

————(1996c). Swimming pool season: The regeneration of Liverpool (orig. 1992). In Jon Savage, *Time Travel. From the Sex Pistols to Nirvana: Pop, Media and Sexuality, 1977–96* (297–301). London: Chatto & Windus.

Sennett, Richard (1993). *The Fall of Public Man* (orig. 1977). London & Boston: Faber and Faber.

Shank, Barry (1994). *Dissonant Identities. The Rock 'n' Roll Scene in Austin, Texas.* Hanover, N.H.: Wesleyan University Press.

Shields, Rob (1991). *Places on the Margin. Alternative Geographies of Modernity.* London: Routledge.

Shuker, Roy (1998). *Key Concepts in Popular Music.* London & New York: Routledge.

————(2001). *Understanding Popular Music.* (2nd ed.). London & New York: Routledge.

Simpson, Mark (1994). *Male Impersonators. Men Performing Masculinity.* London & New York: Cassell.

Sitwell, Edith (1971). *English Eccentrics. A Gallery of Weird and Wonderful Men and Women* (orig. 1933). London: Penguin Books.

Spencer, Colin (1995). *Homosexuality in History.* New York: Harcourt Brace & Company.

Steward, Sue & Garratt, Sheryl (1984). *Signed, Sealed and Delivered. True Life Stories of Women in Pop.* London & Sydney: Pluto Press.

Stokes, Geoffrey (1977). *Starmaking Machinery. Inside the Business of Rock and Roll.* New York: Vintage Books.

Stokes, Martin (1994). Introduction: Ethnicity, identity and music. In Martin Stokes (Ed.), *Ethnicity, Identity and Music. The Musical Construction of Place* (1–27). Oxford & Providence: Berg.

Straw, Will (1991). Systems of articulation, logics of change: Communities and scenes in popular music. *Cultural Studies, 5* (3), 368–88.

Street, John (1986). *Rebel Rock. The Politics of Popular Music.* London & New York: Basil Blackwell.

————(1997). *Politics and Popular Culture.* Cambridge: Polity Press.

Studlar, Gaylyn (1996). *This Mad Masquerade. Stardom and Masculinity in the Jazz Age.* New York: Columbia University Press.

Stump, Paul (1997). *The Music's All That Matters. A History of Progressive Rock.* London: Quartet Books.

Sturma, Michael (1991). *Australian Rock 'n' Roll. The First Wave.* Kenthurst: Kangaroo Press.

Szatmary, David P. (1991). *Rockin' in Time. A Social History of Rock-And-Roll* (orig. 1987). Englewood Cliffs, N.J.: Prentice Hall.

Tannock, Stuart (1995). Nostalgia critique. *Cultural Studies, 9* (3), 453–64.

Taylor, Rogan P. (1985). *The Death and Resurrection Show. From Shaman to Superstar.* London: Anthony Blond.

Taylor, Timothy D. (1997). *Global Pop. World Music, World Markets*. New York & London: Routledge.

Théberge, Paul (1997). *Any Sound You Can Imagine: Making Music/Consuming Technology*. Hanover & London: Wesleyan University Press.

———(2001). "Plugged in": Technology and popular music. In Simon Frith, Will Straw & John Street (Eds.), *The Cambridge Companion to Pop and Rock* (3–25). Cambridge: Cambridge University Press.

Thompson, John B. (1995). *The Media and Modernity. A Social Theory of the Media*. Cambridge: Polity Press.

Thornton, Sarah (1990). Strategies for reconstructing the popular past. *Popular Music, 9* (1), 87–95.

———(1995). *Club Cultures. Music, Media and Subcultural Capital*. Cambridge: Polity Press.

Thwaites, Tony, Davis, Lloyd & Mules, Warwick (1994). *Tools for Cultural Studies. An Introduction*. Melbourne: Macmillan.

Turner, Graeme, Bonner, Frances & Marshall, P. David (2000). *Fame Games. The Production of Celebrity in Australia*. Cambridge: Cambridge University Press.

Turner, Steve (1995). *Hungry for Heaven. Rock 'n' Roll and the Search for Redemption* (orig. 1988). London: Hodder & Stoughton.

Vassal, Jacques (1976). *Electric Children: Roots and Branches of Modern Folkrock*. Orig. *Folksong: Une histoire de la musique popularie aux Etats-Unis* (1971). Paul Barnett (Trans. and adapted). New York: Taplinger.

Vermorel, Fred & Vermorel, Judy (1985). *Starlust. The Secret Fantasies of Fans*. London: A Comet Book.

Virtanen, Keijo (1993). Kulttuurihistoria humanistisena tieteenä. In Marjo Kaartinen (Ed.), *Metodikirja. Näkökulmia kulttuurihistorian tutkimukseen* (9–18). Turku: University of Turku.

Vulliamy, Graham (1977). Music and the mass culture debate. In John Shepherd, Phil Virden, Graham Vulliamy & Trevor Wishart (Eds.), *Whose Music? A Sociology of Musical Languages* (177–200). London: Latimer New Dimensions.

Wale, Michael (1972). *Voxpop. Profiles of the Pop Process*. London: Harrap.

Walker, Alexander (1970). *Stardom. The Hollywood Phenomenon*. London: Michael Joseph.

Walker, John A. (1987). *Cross-overs. Art into Pop/Pop into Art*. London & New York: Comedia/Methuen.

Walser, Robert (1993). *Running with the Devil: Power, Gender, and Madness in Heavy Metal Music*. Hanover & London: Wesleyan University Press.

Webster's Universal College Dictionary (1997). New York: Gramercy Books.

Welsford, Enid (1968). *The Fool. His Social and Literary History* (orig. 1935). London: Faber and Faber.

Whitcomb, Ian (1986). *After the Ball: Pop Music from Rag to Rock* (orig. 1972). New York: Limelight Editions.

Whiteley, Sheila (1992). *The Space between the Notes: Rock and the Counter-culture*. New York & London: Routledge.

———(1997). Little red rooster v. the honky tonk women: Mick Jagger, sexuality, style and image. In Sheila Whiteley (Ed.), *Sexing the Groove: Popular Music and Gender* (67–99). London & New York: Routledge.

———(2000). *Women and Popular Music. Sexuality, Identity and Subjectivity*. London &

New York: Routledge.

Wiener, Martin J. (1981). *English Culture and the Decline of the Industrial Spirit, 1850–1980*. London: Cambridge University Press.

Willeford, William (1969). *The Fool and His Sceptre. A Study in Clowns and Jesters and Their Audience*. London: Edward Arnold.

Williams, Raymond (1971). *Culture and Society 1780–1950* (orig. 1958). Harmondsworth & Ringwood: Penguin.

Wilmut, Roger (1980). *From Fringe to Flying Circus. Celebrating a Unique Generation of Comedy 1960–1980*. London: Eyre Methuen.

Wilson, Elizabeth (1985). *Adorned in Dreams. Fashion and Modernity*. London: Virago Press.

Wise, Sue (1990). Sexing Elvis (orig. 1984). In Simon Frith & Andrew Goodwin (Eds.), *On Record. Rock, Pop, and the Written Word* (390–98). London: Routledge.

Index

M U S I C
(M E A N I N G S)

GENERAL EDITORS: STEVE JONES, JOLI JENSEN, & WILL STRAW

Popular music plays a prominent role in the cultural transformations that are constantly reshaping our world. More and more, music is at the center of contemporary debates about globalization, electronic commerce, space and locality, style and identity, subculture and community, and other key issues within cultural and media studies.

Music[Meanings] offers book-length studies examining the impact of popular music on individuals, cultures and societies. The series addresses popular music as a form of communication and culture from an interdisciplinary perspective, and targets readers from across the humanities and social sciences.

For additional information about this series or for the submission of manuscripts, please contact:

Acquisitions Department
Peter Lang Publishing
275 Seventh Avenue, 28th Floor
New York, NY 10001

To order other books in this series, please contact our Customer Service Department:

(800) 770-LANG (within the U.S.)
(212) 647-7706 (outside the U.S.)
(212) 647-7707 FAX

or browse online by series:

WWW.PETERLANGUSA.COM